From the Soviet Bloc to the European Union

The Soviet Union's dramatic collapse in 1991 was a pivotal moment in the complex history of Central and Eastern Europe, and Ivan Berend here offers a magisterial new account of the dramatic transformation that culminated in ten former Soviet bloc countries joining the European Union. Taking the OPEC oil crisis of 1973 as his starting point, he charts the gradual unraveling of state socialism in Central and Eastern Europe, its ultimate collapse in the revolutions of 1989, and the economic restructuring and lasting changes in income, employment, welfare, education, and social structure which followed. He pays particular attention to the crucial role of the European Union as well as the social and economic hurdles that continue to face former Soviet bloc nations as they try to catch up with their Western neighbors. This will be essential reading for scholars and students of European and economic history, European politics, and economics.

IVAN T. BEREND is Distinguished Professor of History at the University of California, Los Angeles.

From the Soviet Bloc to the European Union

The Economic and Social Transformation of Central and Eastern Europe since 1973

IVAN T. BEREND

 CAMBRIDGE UNIVERSITY PRESS

CAMBRIDGE UNIVERSITY PRESS

Cambridge, New York, Melbourne, Madrid, Cape Town, Singapore, São Paulo, Delhi

Cambridge University Press
The Edinburgh Building, Cambridge CB2 8RU, UK

Published in the United States of America by Cambridge University Press, New York

www.cambridge.org
Information on this title: www.cambridge.org/9780521493659

First published 2009

Printed in the United Kingdom at the University Press, Cambridge

A catalogue record for this publication is available from the British Library

Library of Congress Cataloguing in Publication data
Berend, Ivan T. (Tibor Ivan), 1930–
From the Soviet bloc to the European Union : the economic and social transformation of
Central and Eastern Europe since 1973 / Ivan T. Berend.
    p.   cm.
Includes bibliographical references and index.
ISBN 978-0-521-49365-9 (hardback)
1. Europe, Eastern – Economic conditions – 1989–   2. European Union – Europe,
Eastern.   3. Europe, Eastern – Economic conditions – 1945–1989.   I. Title.
HC244.B3882   2009
330.943 – dc22   2008039995

ISBN 978-0-521-49365-9 hardback
ISBN 978-0-521-72950-5 paperback

Contents

Figures

Tables

Boxes

Preface

Between 1990 and 2003, I worked on and published an informal trilogy on the complex history of Central and Eastern Europe during the nineteenth and twentieth centuries (I. Berend, 1996; 1998; 2003). Now I am going to present a volume on the exciting economic and social history of postcommunist transformation of these countries that led to their joining the European Union. The beginning of the story, however, goes back to 1973, the year when a gradually emerging, long-lasting, and fatal crisis became manifest, signaled a turning point, and undermined the state socialist regime, leading to its collapse in 1989. Without understanding that period and its main problems, one cannot understand the post-1989 transformation process and its difficulties.

Some readers might be familiar with my 1996 Cambridge University Press book, *Central and Eastern Europe 1944–1993: Detour from the Periphery to the Periphery.* The last two decades I discussed in that earlier book will be covered again in this volume. This reexamination is necessary because of the quarry of information I mined during the past decade and a half, the huge reservoir of new statistical and scholarly research, including my research on the most striking and controversial new development of the world economy, globalization (I. Berend, 2008).

The historical perspective on developments after the collapse of state socialism is equally important. It facilitates deeper research and a clearer historical picture of that period. Last but not least, the post-1973 Central and East European trends in this book are compared to the Western economic trends: the drying up of its special sources and the halt of postwar exceptional prosperity. The West, however, embarked on a new road and responded positively to the challenge of globalization. This comparison contributes to a better understanding. This work, consequently, presents a novel approach to the history of the last decades of the twentieth century and a more complex view than the one that I wrote more than a decade ago.

The sudden historical transformation of Central and Eastern Europe inspired a large amount of research and publications. Many of the works discussed either certain periods of that history, or certain countries, and even more often some elements of the complex story such as the process of privatization, the role of foreign investments, rising poverty, elite change, etc. The new feature of this volume is its complexity, covering the entire region of seventeen countries and the combined economic and social process of an uncharted historical road. Furthermore, I have put the region's transformation into the framework of Europe and of its East–West relations.

This history is yet unfinished. Writing about the unfinished present is like shooting at a moving target. Besides, contemporary history also poses another difficulty. Paradoxically enough this is the overwhelming richness of information. Millions of facts, figures, pieces of information, and highly diverse, contradictory, and controversial evaluations make the picture confusing and sometimes result in a lack of transparency. The puzzle here is how to put these millions of pieces together or, using another metaphor, how to build the mosaic picture, in which small pieces are positioned in such a way that they depict the complexity of the real world. It is a real challenge.

I feel, however, some special encouragement and advantage. The rise of state socialism, its crisis, the 1956 Hungarian Revolution, the attempt at reform, its partial success, strong limitations, deep crisis and final failure, the feeling of the *must* of change and the longing to join Europe were all part of my personal life. Furthermore, between 1973 and 1993, I was a minor actor in the story I am going to write about. I participated in the reform process, and in the late 1980s chaired a committee of economists and worked out the first transformation, marketization, and privatization plan for Hungary. I was a member of an international advisory committee on transformation for three more years, and in the years I was working on this book I have been member of a European Union-initiated internal advisory Economic and Social Council of Hungary.

Does it mean that I can write this history *wie es eigentlich gewesen*, as it really happened – as Leopold von Ranke defined the goal of history writing? Most contemporary historians harbor doubts about this possibility in general, and speak about serious limitations of cognizance and cognizability. Presenting the transformation's decade-and-a-half-long complex economic and social history, the emerging new order in *statu nascendi* may, however, help a better understanding of the present and also the future of the region. That is the goal of this work. My interpretation, my view on the events, may – I hope – contribute to a collective effort to discover the truth.

Every study is the result of a collective effort. I am grateful to all of my fellow economic historians, statisticians, and sociologists who published inspiring works over the past decade and a half on various aspects of the Central and East European transformation. Without their results I would have not been able to cope with the immense task of writing this complex and comparative history of economic and social changes.

As always in the past eighteen years, I received inspiration and assistance from the University of California Los Angeles, my working home, which helped my research with its intellectual atmosphere, frequent debates, and conferences. Teaching also gave major inspiration and a permanent incentive for further research. Last but not least I should like to mention the outstanding collection of UCLA's Young Research Library and the research grants of the Academic Senate that helped my work tremendously.

This book gained its final form with the contribution of my friend, David Summers, who made a superb job of copyediting the typescript. I am also highly grateful for the anonymous reviewers and the professional staff of Cambridge University Press for their essential advice and careful preparation of the publication.

My heartiest thanks go to Kati, my wife, whose love, friendship, and intellectual contribution have had an indescribable role in accomplishing this book.

Introduction

The year 1989 has become known as the *annus mirabilis*, or miraculous year. And, indeed, what happened that year was neither predicted nor believable. It surprised the world. State socialism, which had established its isolated bridgehead in Russia after the Bolshevik Revolution of 1917, spread and conquered Central and Eastern Europe after World War II. Besides the Soviet bloc in the eastern half of Europe, it gradually incorporated nearly one-third of the world by the 1980s. The Soviet Union emerged as a superpower with an enormous army and nuclear arsenal. In times of crisis that threatened the system in other countries, such as the 1953 Berlin revolt, the 1956 Hungarian Revolution, the Prague Spring in 1968, or the Afghan crisis in 1979, the Soviet military machine did not hesitate to intervene and "save" socialism. The international military balance of power during the Cold War decades kept the postwar world order intact and, as everybody believed, unchangeable. Moreover, in 1975, the Helsinki Agreement reaffirmed international acceptance and guarantee of the *status quo*.

By the late 1980s, however, historical changes had rendered impossible a brutal military solution to such crises. Not even hardliners risked open confrontation and the use of force. In situations where force seemed the *ultima ratio*, they refrained from using it and capitulated. And, in 1989, state socialism peacefully collapsed in Poland and Hungary over the course of a few months, and then throughout Central and Eastern Europe within six weeks. This process concluded with the collapse of the Soviet Union itself in 1991. The miracle of peaceful revolution destroyed state socialism because nobody was ready to defend the regime. The elite prepared to save its position by giving up power, or at least part of it, through major reforms and compromises.

The year 1989 thus became a historical landmark of twentieth-century Europe. In retrospect, the situation offered no alternatives, and the

1

transformation from the late 1980s, as Timothy Garton Ash noted, "proceeds at break-neck speed with a quiet democratic revolution" or, in his coinage from the words *revolution* and *reform*, "refolution" (Garton Ash, 1989).

What happened in Central and Eastern Europe in 1989 was, however, not only a break with the postwar socialist past. The countries of the region followed a different historical path from that of the advanced West in most parts of the twentieth century: economic nationalism, self-sufficiency from the 1920s, authoritarian dirigisme during the 1930s and early 1940s, and later a Soviet-type non-market system with central planning. From the early 1930s and then during the entire period of the 1950s to the 1980s, the countries of Central and Eastern Europe belonged to isolationist regional alliance systems led first by Nazi Germany and then by the Soviet Union.

The unsolvable crisis of the 1970s and 1980s dramatically strengthened opposition to the state socialist regime and contributed to its collapse. Moreover, 1989 marked the end of a long revolt, from both the Right and the Left, against the West. Instead the trend turned to adjustment and "Joining Europe!" This slogan of 1989 targeted the replacement of the failed system that was unable to cope with the challenge of globalization. The countries of the region longed to follow the successful West and introduce its integrationist open market system. They wanted to be part of the European Union.

At the same time, the European Union itself experienced slowdown and crisis beginning in the late 1960s and early 1970s. It sought to regain its vitality, to reestablish its competitiveness, and to cope with the challenge of globalization. Western Europe was the only major player in the rapidly globalizing world system without an economic "backyard." Latin America and large parts of Asia became part of the production networks of the United States and Japan, respectively, and assisted their economic performance.

After 1989, the European Union was immediately ready to integrate and incorporate Central and Eastern Europe in order to stabilize peace on the continent and to build its own nearby production network. To achieve that, the Union was ready to direct and assist the transformation of Central and Eastern Europe, and to accept ten ill-prepared, former communist countries as EU members in the near future. The enlargement of the Union and the preparation for further enlargement in the Western Balkans were important for the economic interests of the old member countries of the European Union. The enlargement strengthened the EU's production network and stabilized the continent. The metamorphosis of Central and Eastern Europe is, therefore, also a chapter of the history of the European Union. Both East and West became winners through integration.

Central and Eastern Europe's transformation was thus determined by the dual characteristics of the turn of the millennium in Europe: globalization and the European Union's response to its challenge.

The first chapter of the region's transformation was essentially complete by the time ten of its countries were accepted to the EU in the new *anni mirabiles* of 2004 and 2007. The countries adjusted to the requirements of the West, abolished their dictatorial regimes and their state-owned, non-market systems, and rushed to introduce parliamentary democracy and free market economies. They abandoned gradualism, took risks, and made serious mistakes on an uncharted road, but in a decade and a half successfully changed their situation. The social cost was dear, and social pain, increased poverty, and income disparity affected wide layers of their societies. Even demographic trends worsened. The social shock, caused partly by the change of systems, but even more by radically changed values and culture, is not yet over and characterizes both winners and losers alike in these societies. It renders the political situation fragile, and it opens the door to the sort of populist-nationalist fundamentalism which spread through the region in the early 1990s, especially in the Balkans, and then reemerged again in Poland, Slovakia, and Hungary as late as 2006 and 2007.

A significant contribution to the rapid transformation of the region was the European Union's insistence on compliance with its legal and institutional requirements (*acquis communautaire*), combined with more financial assistance than was received under the postwar Marshall Plan, and an even higher amount of direct investments. The EU offered its markets and modernized the telecommunications and banking systems of the transforming countries. Central and Eastern Europe adjusted to the requirements of the free market and became an important part of the production network of old EU countries. An old dream came true, although the countries of Central and East European region are not yet equal partners in the formerly exclusive European club, and the new members often consider themselves second-class citizens in Europe.

The Central and East European income level, as a consequence of its different historical past, is much lower – from one-half to one-quarter of that of the established members of the European Union – and the region's economy is highly dependent on the West and Western investments. The social patterns of the new and prospective Union member countries also carry the heavy burden of an unfortunate past. The region consequently has a subordinate position in globalization. Will they break through and in time become prosperous equals? Will they achieve European Union levels in terms of such basics as income level, labor productivity, infrastructure, consumption, and modern social-occupational structures and attitudes?

Successful transformation does not mean merely full adjustment to the market system and the requirements of the European Union. In a broader sense it also requires adjustment to modern Western values and behavioral patterns, and achievement of advanced income levels similar to those in the West. Catching up with the EU-15 in this broader sense is a long historical march that requires a competitive economy based on domestic innovation, appropriate social and educational institutions, advanced domestic banking and the availability of venture capital, and a wide array of small- and medium-sized companies. Only the very first steps have been taken to establish all of that, and only in a handful of countries.

The process, however, has already begun. If it succeeds, Central and Eastern Europe will organically incorporate into a larger entity: Europe. The caravan of Central and Eastern Europe is on the move. The possibility of catching up with the West, which has motivated these countries from the early nineteenth century, has become a realistic goal for the first time in history, though it will be neither a quick nor an easy one to achieve. A positive outcome will require generations and is not a given or even evident at this stage of development. The door is wide open. Some of the countries will enter. Others will not, or will cross the threshold only much later.

This book covers the area of Central and Eastern Europe. At this point, I need to clarify what I mean by that.[1] The eastern half of the European continent, often called Eastern Europe, Central Europe, or Central and Eastern Europe, has a huge variety of definitions. Without summarizing a century-long debate and the various interpretations of the region from Leopold von Ranke ([1824] 1909) to Jenő Szűcs (1983), I am going to discuss the region that in earlier centuries was located between the German, Russian, and Ottoman empires, and which interwar German authors called *Zwischen Europa*, or "in-between Europe." History in this zone began half a millennium later than in the Western Carolingian Empire; Christendom conquered most of it in the ninth and tenth centuries, but this zone remained the frontier of Christian-feudal Europe for centuries, open to "barbaric" attacks from the East (N. Berend, 2001;

---

[1] I use the terms Southern Europe and Mediterranean Europe interchangeably to mean Greece, Italy, Portugal, and Spain, while Western Europe means Austria, Belgium, Britain, Denmark, Finland, France, Germany, Ireland, Liechtenstein, Luxembourg, the Netherlands, Norway, Sweden, and Switzerland.

2007). Unlike the western half of the continent, the region remained agrarian until World War II. Nation building remained unfinished, and borders and state formations have changed right up to the present, as multiethnic states divide and split apart. Most of the countries of the region belonged to huge multiethnic empires for up to five centuries, and they remained ethnically mixed, politically authoritarian, and oppressive against minorities.

In many ways, however, and in spite of important similarities, this region is different from the "East *par excellence*," as Szűcs (1983) called Russia. It is difficult to generalize about the various countries because they belonged to three empires in the middle of the nineteenth century, formed ten states in the interwar decades, and comprise seventeen countries today. One can differentiate between two distinct subregions, Central Europe and the Balkans, which exhibit significant differences. They, nevertheless, were and are characterized by basic similarities. All of them lost independence between the late fourteenth and eighteenth centuries and became incorporated into huge neighboring empires and, after regaining independence, they all formed part of the Nazi German *Lebensraum* and then the Soviet bloc in the twentieth century. Nowadays, they are all equally countries "in transformation." The historical trajectories of Central and Eastern Europe thus differ significantly from the West and, in many senses, from neighboring Russia and Turkey, as well (I. Berend, 2005).

This is a region which has existed as a historical unit for a millennium, but it might begin to disappear as a distinguishable entity if the transformation successfully continues, and if the countries of the area prove able to rise to the level of the West in the space of one or two generations.

CHAPTER 1

The economic factors in the collapse of state socialism and the new international environment, 1973–1989

The collapse of a regime always has more than one cause. In my interpretation, however, among the various international and domestic factors that led to the collapse of state socialism in Central and Eastern Europe, basic economic facts were primary. Accordingly, we must first unravel, out of the numberless threads that make up the fabric of history, the dramatic changes in economic processes brought about by the shock to the world economy caused by the oil crisis of 1973.

The economic base of state socialism was visibly undermined from the 1970s on, accelerating its collapse. For a full understanding of this process, it is important to give a relatively detailed explanation of the international economic situation, the Western reaction to a changing economic world, and the Eastern inability to adjust to it. These developments are not only the main factors in the collapse of socialism, but also explain the requirements and trends of postcommunist transformation. This is, therefore, the proper point of departure for analyzing the two crucially important decades around the turn of the century.

The year 1973 was indeed the beginning of a new chapter of greater European economic history, which, in the case of Central and Eastern Europe, led to the collapse of their state socialist regimes. It should be noted, however, that this chronological division is also somewhat artificial. As I explain below, the slowdown in economic growth and productivity in the region and around the world had been unfolding gradually over a longer period of time. Moreover, major political and economic crises had hit the Soviet bloc countries quite a few times already before. Nevertheless, I still begin with the politically motivated oil crisis of 1973, which made dramatically manifest this development's gradually accumulating limitations and emerging predicament.

Economic crisis, slowdown, and technological transformation in the West and lack of adjustment and decline in the East after 1973

The West

In the fall of 1973, the seemingly "endless" postwar prosperity in Europe came to an abrupt halt. As many contemporaries speculated, the sudden change might have been accidental, generated by a political drama – namely, the October 1973 Yom Kippur War in the Near East – followed by the boycott decision of the Organization of Petroleum Exporting Countries (OPEC). Crude oil prices soared from $2.70 per barrel in 1973 to $9.76 by 1974. Another political drama, the Iranian Revolution of 1979, generated a second "oil crisis" in 1979–80, and, taken as a whole, oil prices increased tenfold. This new development eroded the hope and prospect of adjustment.

From that time, nothing worked as usual. Economic growth stopped, prices and unemployment sharply increased, and Keynesian demand-side economics – according to which additional demand, and strengthening the purchasing power of the population through job creation and state investments, could enable governments to cope with economic crisis – became unable to cure the stagnation and decline any longer. In fact, it generated even higher inflation. The Philips curve, the classic "law" describing the inverse relationship between inflation and unemployment, i.e., increasing inflation decreases unemployment and vice versa, also stopped working as inflation and unemployment rose together. What followed was a sudden slowing down and decline accompanied by high inflation and unemployment. This odd pairing of stagnation *and* inflation led to the introduction of a new economic term: *stagflation*.

Why did Keynesian economics, which worked for roughly forty years, fail? Why did all the usual economic trends suddenly change? Was it the mysterious long-term Kondratiev cycle that has its 20- to 25-year upturn and then 20- to 25-year downturn, one following the other since the late eighteenth century? Was it the cycle's downturn which had arrived like a German train, right on schedule, following the postwar quarter-century of high prosperity? We have several more exact explanations, including a role for an overheated, exceptional boom, which gradually compromised itself. As Andrea Boltho stated:

The year 1973 represented a watershed . . . a very sudden break with the past, but the trend towards a deteriorating performance had already set in earlier. In a way, the success of the 1950s and 1960s had laid the preconditions for at least some of the failures of the 1970s. (Boltho, 1982: 28)

Herman Van der Wee also underlines the close connection between the high prosperity and its end by noting that the gross capital stock per employee in France, Germany, the Netherlands, and Britain went from $78,440 to $208,211 between 1950 and 1973 (in 1990 values):

[T]remendous over-investment [took place] in the traditional industrial sectors of the modern consumption economy during the 1960s, causing massive over-capacity. This over-investment and overcapacity in the West was accentuated by the industrialization process in the Eastern bloc and the Third World, a process which was often concentrated in identical sectors . . . the enormous investment in the secondary and tertiary sectors held out the prospect of a shortage of foodstuff, raw materials and energy. The turning of the terms of trade in favour of primary producers from the beginning of the 1970s came as a result of this growing imbalance. (Van der Wee, 1986: 90)

The price of energy and raw materials increased significantly before the oil crisis, and by as much as 63% in 1972–73, while the rate of inflation in Germany reached 7% in that year. The economy became overheated and industrial output in the advanced West increased by 10% that year.

A quarter-century of excessive growth and skyrocketing consumption led to the saturation of consumer goods markets. As part of this trend, exports also became more difficult, and their growth slowed. Mass pro-duction, a key factor of prosperity, became less and less sustainable. Robert Brenner commented: "The advanced capitalist world entered into a crisis well before the end of 1973, experiencing falling profitability, especially in manufacturing and increased rate of inflation" (1998: 138). For example, between 1965 and 1973 the aggregate manufacturing profitability of the seven wealthiest countries of the world declined by 25 percent.

In reality, the change in 1973 was not abrupt, and it was assisted by non-economic factors, among them mistaken policy interventions, which confused the usual trends. Clouds began gathering during the boom years. From the late 1960s, labor markets changed and, especially around 1968, led to the end of corporative cooperation between employers and employ-ees, a major stabilizing factor in the postwar period. In Michael Piore and Charles Sabel's explanation, both the workers' environment and their atti-tudes changed. Virtually full employment, the need for a reserve which can enter and leave the market, and a shortage of labor that initiated immigration strengthened the position of employees. The transformation of the labor environment went hand in hand with a generation change: "a new generation matured in the postwar prosperity, without memories of the Great Depression . . . the freedom from such constraints encour-aged protest." Collective self-restraint, the authors continue, disappeared. In France, wages were indexed to cost of living. The Italian Statuto dei

Lavoratori and the German Arbeitsförderungsgesetz gradually made wage levels and purchasing power independent of the labor market (Piore and Sabel, 1984: 167). Social unrest and rising political turmoil in overheated economies led to wage explosions in Germany, France, Italy, and several other countries.

This was accompanied, however, by employer responses and price increases to compensate for wage increases; as a consequence, a wage–price spiral pushed prices up. Domestic political upheavals, a mini-revolution in France in 1968, social disturbances in Germany, and the "hot autumn" in Italy in 1969 led to rapid increases in wages and social expenditures. The 1969 Italian contract stipulated a 19 percent wage increase for industrial workers, and public spending grew from 30 to 50 percent of GDP. In France, wages rose more quickly than GDP every year between 1968 and 1973. Prices also soared and rigorous fiscal measures were introduced in June 1972 (OECD, 1987: 129). In Germany, the rate of wage increases doubled in 1969–70. In France, a gradual inflationary spiral had emerged during the period of high prosperity and full employment, and became strongly visible between 1968 and 1970:

As early as the mid-1960s, it was evident that a slowdown of growth did not bring about any appreciable slowdown in price rises... The rise in oil prices at the end of 1973 only hastened a phenomenon that was already emerging more and more clearly. (Caron, 1979: 322)

The international monetary system, as a consequence of mistaken policy intervention, was also shaken. The immediate cause of the change was the deterioration of the United States' competitive position in international markets, which generated a significant increase in its balance-of-payments deficit. The Johnson administration avoided increasing taxes to finance the Vietnam War. Inflation had jumped to 6 percent in 1970. The dollar was devalued, and then the Nixon administration practically ended dollar convertibility in August 1971. The Bretton Woods agreement at the end of World War II, which had created stable exchange rates for a quarter-century, collapsed. Since the dollar was the international reserve currency, Europe was strongly challenged, and the floating exchange rate "made the price of goods in international trade hostage to forces only distantly connected to national economic performance – and almost impossible to forecast and control" (Piore and Sabel, 1984: 173–74). The collapse of Bretton Woods had widespread negative consequences. Stability, on which mass production was based, dramatically weakened:

not just inflation but the business cycle grew increasingly volatile... With the commitment to par values removed, agents had no reason to regard an acceleration of inflation as temporary. When governments stimulated demand in the effort to offset a recession, this provoked compensating wage increases; aggregate demand policies therefore elicited inflation rather than stabilizing output. (Eichengreen, [1994] 1996: 61)

Finally, in the instable international economic situation another mistaken policy intervention made the crisis complete. Under inflationary pressure, the American Federal Reserve Board decided to increase interest rates: Federal Reserve discount rates increased from 5.5% in 1977 to 13.4% by 1981. Banks' prime rates jumped from 6.8% to 18.9%. The advanced industrial countries declined into a deep recession. Less developed, indebted countries, which had tried balancing their economies with foreign credits in the 1970s, had to refinance at steeply increased rates because of their repayment difficulties. Repayment often became impossible. The International Monetary Fund (IMF), because it lacked sufficient funding from the rich countries, was unable to maintain the liquidity of the international banking system. Severe austerity measures became unavoidable and the circle was closed: "the economic disorder began as a crisis of supply then turned into a crisis of demand" (Piore and Sabel, 1984: 183).

The entire 1970s and even the early 1980s became a period of high, often double-digit, inflation in the world economy. A quarter-century of exceptional boom, full employment, and stability was followed by a decade of instability, slower growth, and occasional setbacks. Between 1950–73 and 1973–83, consumer price increases in the leading Western economies more than doubled (from an annual average of 4.2% to 9.4%). In the Mediterranean region they more than quadrupled (from 4.0% to 18.4%). World price levels had also more than doubled, reaching 233% of 1973 levels by 1982. Unemployment, averaging 2% to 4% in Western and Mediterranean Europe between 1950 and 1973, jumped to 12% by 1984–93, and reached more than 7 million people in Europe (Maddison, 1995a: 84).

Based on ninety-four countries with 98 percent of the world's population, the average annual rate of growth, i.e., the increase of produced goods and services, dropped from 3.4% between 1950 and 1973 to –0.1% between 1973 and 1987. Economic growth in the sixteen most advanced countries of the world economy slowed significantly: after complete stagnation in the first three years after 1973, average GDP in these countries increased by only 20% in the first decade after 1973. The volume of imports had dropped by 7% by 1975, and then increased by 18% in the first decade after the oil shock. In the same period, the terms of trade, i.e., the relation between import and export prices, declined by 20% in the advanced countries (Maddison, 1985: 13).

The leading economic powers were no longer the engines of European economic prosperity. The old, declining sectors of the Belgian, British, and French economies sank into crisis: the combined coal output of the three countries decreased by 40 percent between 1980 and 1983. In the same period, the combined textile production in Belgium, Germany, France, Italy, the Netherlands, and Britain dropped to less than half of the production levels of the 1960s (Fischer, van Houtte, and Kellenbenz, 1987: 117, 135). At its lowest point, industrial output had declined by 13 percent from these levels.

Exports, previously one of the most important driving forces of economic growth, were hit hard. During the first post-1973 decade, exports slowed to between roughly one-third and one-half of the previous rates (Maddison, 1989: 139). During the 1970s, the average rate of return on fixed capital in some countries, especially Britain and Italy, dropped below the real interest rate. This had never happened before in modern industrial history. After decades of fluctuation-free growth, these developments were shocking. What at first glance appeared to be a temporary consequence of a political conflict, the oil crisis, soon turned out to be an organic part of the economic process with deep internal roots. Kondratiev and the cycle theories were rediscovered.

Despite the evidence, however, it was still difficult to realize that the period of high prosperity was over. It is worth quoting an OECD report from 1974:

There is little evidence of any general slowing down in the rate of growth . . . [It] is a strong presumption that the gross domestic product of the OECD area may again double in the next decade and a half. (OECD, 1974: 166)

Even in 1977, a special OECD study, the McCracken report, concluded that "the poor showing of recent years was likely to be only temporary and that a return to strong growth was possible" (OECD, 1987: 53). In reality, it was not. The *stagflation* of the mid to late seventies was thus not an accidental event generated by political turmoil, but rather a characteristic cyclical phenomenon, a consequence of overinvestment in an overheated economy accompanied by market saturation for new staple consumer goods. The market had shrunk dramatically. Gross annual investment, which had increased by 6.7% between 1960 and 1973, decreased to 0.7% between 1973 and 1982. Private final consumption, which had grown at a rate of 5.4% per year between 1960 and 1973, slowed after 1973 to an increase of 2.3% per year in the West.

The depression of the mid-1970s, nevertheless, besides being a period of stagnation and decline, was a structural crisis. Nikolai Kondratiev, the economist who called attention to long cyclical waves in modern economies, offered an "initial hypothesis" to explain similar phenomena:

the . . . long cycle is associated with the replacement and expansion of basic capital goods, and with the radical regrouping of, and changes in society's productive forces. (Kondratiev, [1922] 1984: 94–97)

Inspired by Kondratiev's theory, Joseph Schumpeter offered a more convincing interpretation of the long cycle, which, he explained, is connected with

an "industrial revolution" and the absorption of its effects . . . These revolutions periodically reshape the existing structure of industry by introducing new methods of production – the mechanized factory, the electrified factory, chemical synthesis and the like; new commodities, such as railroad service, motorcars, electric appliances; new forms of organization – the merger movement; new sources of supply . . . new trade routes and markets to sell in . . . While these things are being initiated we have brisk expenditure and "prosperity" predominates [alongside an avalanche of consumer goods, articles of mass consumption, and increased purchasing power] . . . and while those things are being completed . . . we have the elimination of antiquated elements of the industrial structure and "depression" predominates. Thus there are prolonged periods of rising and falling prices, interest rates, employment and so on, which phenomena constitute parts of the mechanism of this process of recurrent rejuvenation of the productive apparatus. (Schumpeter, 1976: 67–68)

In Schumpeter's interpretation, the "whole set of technological changes" or industrial revolutions generates pressure for adjustment. Those firms and groups representing the older technologies and methods that are unable to change will disappear in time. Readjustment is difficult and a relatively slow process, especially because demands for investments, credits, and new skills may not be immediately satisfied. This causes a period of economic turmoil and recession. The significant slowdown and destruction are nevertheless "creative," since they clear the way for new technologies and methods. The former leading sectors of the economy become obsolete and the new leading sectors, based on new technologies and organizational principles, emerge, and the whole process brings about a restructuring of the economy. Once most sectors of the economy have been transformed by the new elements, a new wave of prosperity follows.

This interpretation suggests that the long downswings are essentially "structural crises" or periods in which we see the decline of the old and the dawn of the new technological regimes, the decline of the old and the dawn of the new leading and export sectors. This entire economic fluctuation is inherent in the market system and in free market competition, which generates endless inspiration and drive to introduce more competitive methods and products to conquer larger markets and achieve greater profits. Extra-economic factors, such as wars and political upheavals, also contribute to this process. These fluctuations are thoroughly international and hit all countries except those that are entirely isolated from the world economy.

What happened in the 1970s clearly fits into this interpretational framework. Those branches of industry that had developed the fastest during the postwar prosperity now suffered the most. The coal, iron, and steel industries, shipbuilding, and other sectors were downsized substantially, and some, such as the Swedish shipbuilding industry, were briefly on the verge of closing altogether. The Belgian mining industry declined by half between 1970 and 1979, and construction fell by one-third. Between 1970 and 1980, the share contributed to the gross value added of total industry by traditional industries – construction and building materials, iron and steel, traditional engineering, wood, paper, textiles, and clothing – declined in Germany by 40%. Small wonder that investments, which increased by 6.4% annually between 1960 and 1973, dropped to 1.8% between 1975 and 1979. By 1979, the German manufacturing labor force, counted in work-hours, had dropped 20% below the 1970 levels.

The structural crisis of the world economy hit Western Europe especially hard because of its arrival at a turning point in its postwar development. Western Europe's postwar economic miracle had certain peculiar factors: during the early postwar years, and until these countries reached their potential levels of output in the early 1950s, their economies were characterized by high growth rates typical in reconstruction periods after major turmoil such as war or depression (Jánossy, 1971).

During the later 1950s and 1960s, the region profited highly from its extensive development model, based on an increase in the factors of production: "brute force" capital accumulation, restructuring the labor force by shifting from lower-productivity agriculture to higher-productivity industries, and increasing the labor force by an average 1 percent per annum. Additionally, using the existing stock of technological knowledge, mostly transferred from the United States, bolstered this trend.

Western Europe also profited from its inherited institutions including, among others, its advanced banking system. The postwar development was also embedded in newly created institutions after the war: partly in Bretton Woods, which fixed international exchange rates and created a stable financial environment, but mostly by building up corporative social partnerships (Sozialpartnerschaften), agreements between labor unions and employers, which made possible wage and price moderation. Keynesian regulated markets, state assistance, and integrating national markets also played an important role.

The sources of this extensive development and its institutional framework, however, dried up and became inappropriate by the early to mid-1970s. The impacts of the oil crisis, structural crisis, and the exhaustion of sources of extensive development combined and necessitated difficult adjustment. It required a set of new institutions, because "the same institutions of coordinated capitalism that had worked to Europe's advantage in the age of extensive growth now posed obstacles to successful economic performance" (Eichengreen, 2007: 6–7).

The heart of the adjustment was the creation of new leading sectors based on new technology to replace the declining old leading sectors. Mere technology transfer, using existing American technological knowledge, was no longer possible. Europe had to turn toward the so-called intensive growth model, based much less on production factor inputs, and much more on new technology created by innovation, i.e., research and development.

After the 1973 oil crisis and the beginning of marked decline, the dawn of a new technological era, a new Schumpeterian "set of technological changes," was also signaled. The invention and early distribution of the personal computer in 1974 symbolized the new wave of technological revolution. While the old sectors declined, some of the new ones experienced impressive increase. Electricity output, in contrast to coal production, continued to grow. Between 1973 and 1983 it increased 67 percent in Europe. As a consequence of a revolutionary mechanization, electricity consumption in European Union households grew 77 percent during the last quarter of the century to 1,637 kWh/person (B. Mueller, 1965: 179; Eurostat, 1971–80: 176; 1998–99: 422).

The changing energy infrastructure and technology were exhibited in the rapid increase of nuclear power capacity, which characterized Europe throughout the second half of the century. In the fifteen member countries of the European Union, nuclear energy production reached 28% of total energy output at the end of the century. In some of the countries, nuclear energy became the most important energy source: in France, more than 78% of primary energy production was nuclear, but several other countries also registered a 30% to 60% share of nuclear energy in total energy consumption (Eurostat, 1998–99: 412).

The telephone spread to nearly all households during the last quarter of the century (table 1.1); additionally, cellular phones were introduced and spread rapidly in the European market. In the mid-1990s, besides the nearly 265 million fixed telephone lines, more than 23 million cellular phones were also in operation, and in a few years the number of cell phones surpassed the number of fixed lines throughout Western Europe. A developed telephone network established the base for the spectacular

Table 1.1 The spread of the telephone in Europe (in thousands)

Year	Telephone lines in use	1950 = 100
1950	22,146	100
1973	116,886	528
1993	264,533	1,194

Source: Based on Mitchell, 1998: 765–79.

spread of personal computers during the last quarter of the century in Europe. By 1995, Western countries already used 200 to 300 computers per 1,000 inhabitants. In Italy, Greece, Spain, and Portugal, the rate did not reach even 100 per 1,000 people.

Several European countries embraced the Internet immediately after its invention: in 1995 in Finland, there were more than 42,000 Internet hosts per 1 million inhabitants; in Norway, Sweden, Switzerland, the Netherlands, and Denmark between 10,000 and 20,000 per million; and in most other Western countries between 3,000 and 7,000. The Internet grew ever more popular: in 1998, 12 people out of every 100 used the Internet in the OECD countries, but two years later the rate was 26 per 100.

The automobile revolution, already important in Europe after World War II, intensified during the 1970s–1980s. In the sixteen Western and Southern European countries, fewer than 78 million cars were in operation in 1973, but there were more than 151 million by 1993. By that time nearly every second person had a passenger car (447 per 1,000 inhabitants, which was in sharp contrast with the 1950 figure of 22 per 1,000). The European car market became saturated (B. Mueller, 1965: 211; Eurostat, 1998–99: 200).

These last decades were a period of extensive freeway construction as well: by the mid-1970s, the freeway network linking seventeen West European countries stretched 22,000 kilometers; by 1987 it had expanded to 37,000 kilometers (Hoffman, 1990: 173). At the end of the century, it reached nearly 50,000 kilometers.

Civil aviation had become a major form of mass transportation in postwar Europe, but in the last quarter of the century it grew again by three to four times. In 1974, more than 100,000 million passenger-kilometers were flown by national airlines and, by 1990, roughly 300,000 passenger-kilometers. In the mid-1990s, on average 415 million air passengers traveled in the European Union countries annually, and 1,618 million freight-tons per kilometers were transported (more than 1,200 times more than in 1950) (Mitchell, 1998: 724–27; Eurostat, 1977:103; 1998–99: 205).

New technology radically transformed the old sectors as well. Although electrification and dieselization had already begun, the steam engine preserved its leading role in the European railroads until the early 1960s. By the end of the century, however, steam locomotives had virtually disappeared, replaced mostly by diesel locomotives, but also by electric trains. In Germany this transformation was accomplished by the end of the 1980s: 41 percent of the railroads were electrified, and all other lines used diesel engines.

The spread of personal computers partly signaled the mechanization of offices, since, in the first stages of their use, that is where computers were first implemented. Another invention which appeared first in offices was the fax machine. By 1995, nearly 8 million fax machines were in use in Europe, more than 95 percent of them in the West. In Denmark, Austria, France, Britain, the Netherlands, Norway, Sweden, Finland, and Switzerland, roughly 30 machines per 1,000 inhabitants signaled widespread use.

Taken as a whole, the new products based on new technology became the driving force of rising consumerism in the late twentieth century. On the other hand, differentiating between old and new industries grew increasingly difficult because of the renewal and revitalization – or "hybridization" – that took place in several old sectors through the introduction of new technologies. Certain sectors of engineering, for example, became closely connected with electronics. This revolutionized and renewed the car industry. Innovations resulted from further intersectoral technological links between mechanical engineering, precision engineering, electrical engineering, and electronics and communications. The merging of these four fields became known as "mechatronics."

Structural adjustment, building up new leading sectors in high-tech industries and downsizing old ones in mining, textile, clothing, and iron and steel, was the most important trend in Western Europe from the late 1970s onward. It was accompanied by a managerial and organizational revolution. This was the time when American organization and management techniques were broadly applied in Europe. This provided an incentive to develop further division of labor, especially by separating and professionalizing various kinds of services from production.

Services gained momentum: while the number of employees in manufacturing declined by 10 percent in Germany between 1970 and 1980, the number of people working in the service sector increased by nearly 23 percent (Bernini Carri, 1995: 238). In the fifteen countries which soon came to form the European Union, more than 52% of gainfully employed people worked in industry, agriculture, and construction, with less than

48% working in various services in 1973. Signaling the service revolution that followed, by 2000, less than 33% of the population worked in industry, agriculture, and construction, and more than 67% were engaged in services (United Nations, 1975; 2002).

Nevertheless, intensive growth based on innovation lagged behind that in the United States, where 3% to 4% of GDP was invested in research and development (R&D). Britain reached only half of the American investment level in R&D, and the other European countries had an even lower share. In the crucially important computer industry, the United States spent five times more on R&D than all the West European countries combined (Eichengreen, 2007: 257). As a consequence, Europe's international position in R&D-intensive sectors worsened after 1973 (OECD, 1987). Europe lost ground to international competition – mostly to the Americans and Japanese – in technology-intensive products. European companies held only a 9% share of the world market in computer and data-processing products, 10% in software, 13% in satellites and launchers, and 29% in data transmission services (ibid.: 213). In terms of world trade of products in R&D-intensive branches of industry, the combined share of France, Germany, and Britain decreased from 36% to 31% between 1965 and 1984 (Duchene and Shepherd, 1987: 36). In the mid-1980s, American and Japanese output of information technology was valued at $250 billion, while the joint output of the seven leading European countries was valued at only $66 billion.

Although Europe lost ground in the manufacture of high-tech products, and while the European Economic Community dropped from 88% to 75% of the average output of the advanced OECD countries in this area between 1970 and 1985, the Community did gain ground in low R&D-intensive branches of industry. Its level of production in this area increased from 98% to 115% of the OECD average (OECD, 1987: 214, 254).

Although it trailed the United States, research became a big industry in Western Europe. The French, German, and Italian research systems were based not only in universities, but also in big state-run research institutions: the Max Planck Society in Germany had sixty institutes, built around internationally known scientists. This network was 90 percent financed by the federal state, one-third of which was earmarked for basic research. The French Centre National de la Recherche Scientifique was organized into seven scientific departments and two national institutes, run by a National Science Research Council organized into forty-five disciplinary panels. Its laboratories were located on university campuses, employed 10,000 researchers, and received half of the budget for basic research (OECD, 1987: 106, 108).

A significant part of gross domestic product was spent on R&D throughout Europe. In the West, it was financed partly by governments and partly by private companies. Government expenditures were connected with the rapidly developing university training and research, but above all with military preparation. At the height of the Cold War, for example, worldwide annual defense expenditure topped two-thirds of a trillion dollars. Major scientific efforts were directed toward defensive and destructive weapons. Governments employed and financed armies of scientists and engineers who worked on developing radar, jet aircraft, rockets, computers, and the atomic and hydrogen bombs, and in the space programs. Government laboratories as well as contracted institutions and private companies worked on military projects. During the 1960s, the American military R&D budget varied between $7 billion and $8.5 billion per year. In the 1960s–70s, roughly half of the American budget was spent on military expenditures. This share was essentially the same in Britain, while France spent one-third and Germany between one-fifth and one-tenth of its budget for defense R&D.

Government-financed R&D represented about half of the R&D expenditures in market economies, while private companies financed the other half. Giants such as IBM and ITT built up the Watson and Bell laboratories, respectively. The computer, aerospace, drug, and semiconductor industries spent 5% to 7% of their sales, and 80% to 90% and more of their profits, on R&D in the early 1980s. These expenditures reached $3,000 to $4,000 per employee. Multinational empires such as General Motors, Ford, IBM, and General Electric had an R&D budget of $0.8 to $2.2 billion per year. In the late 1970s, roughly 600,000 scientists and engineers were employed in R&D in the United States, and about 300,000 in France, Britain, and Germany combined.

The countries of the European Community, however, on average spent the equivalent of one-sixth of their own industrial R&D funds on joint research, which internationalized technological development (OECD, 1987: 113). Industrialized research gave a tremendous boost to technological development, and brought to maturity the greatest results in technology. At the Lisbon meeting of the European Council in 2000, the European Union set the goal of transforming Europe into the world's most competitive science-based economy by 2010. At the halfway mark, the implementation of that program was behind schedule.

Rapidly rising labor productivity, measured in terms of production value per worker-hour, clearly expressed the gradual adjustment to the new technological revolution in the West. In the world's six leading economies, including four European countries, labor and capital productivity increased annually by 1.74% and 0.46%, respectively, between 1913 and 1950. This relatively moderate productivity increase, however, was followed by a 4.84% and 0.73% annual increase between 1950 and 1973. Industrial productivity improved only 1% to 2% per year before 1950, but by 5% to 6% during the following quarter of a century in France, Germany, and the Netherlands. On average, a West European worker produced between $2 and $4 (1990 value) GDP per hour in 1913; this increased to $16 in 1973 and $25–$28 GDP in 1992.

In 1950, the advanced European countries' productivity level was 40% to 60% of that of the United States, the technology leader; it rose to 70% by 1973, and 87% in the early 1990s. After another decade, labor productivity of Europe reached 95% of the American level, with countries such as France, Germany, the Netherlands, Ireland, Norway, Belgium, and Luxembourg surpassing the American level (Eichengreen 2007: 379).

This impressive development was accompanied and significantly assisted by the integration of Western Europe. First, the foundation of the European Coal and Steel Community in 1951, and then of the European Economic Community – later renamed the European Union – in 1957, played a decisive role in restructuring the West European economies. Within a decade of its foundation, the Community created a customs union, and gradually moved toward a single market and free flow of labor and capital, with a common central bank and currency, the euro:

The formation of the Single Market led to the rationalization and consolidation of industries previously fragmented along national lines. It made it attractive for extra-European producers . . . The EU attracted 21 percent of Japanese FDI [foreign direct investment] outflows in the late 1980s . . . The proportion of US FDI destined for Europe rose from 39 to 45 percent, while intra-European Union FDI as a share of total EU FDI outflows rose from 31 to 51 percent. (Eichengreen, 2007: 346)

The integration process was initiated by six countries in the 1950s, but the community became permanently enlarged after 1973. In that year, three countries – Britain, Ireland, and Denmark – joined the founding six, and during the 1980s, after the collapse of authoritarian dictatorships in Southern Europe, Greece, Portugal, and Spain were accepted. By the mid-1990s, Sweden, Finland, and Austria had joined, bringing European Union membership to fifteen.

The European Union launched a deliberate cohesion policy to assist the less-developed regions, which received significant contributions to help them draw level with the others. A massive catching-up process emerged in the Mediterranean countries and Ireland. As regards technology and structural renewal, an average worker in Ireland and Mediterranean Europe produced $2.89 of value per hour in 1950, and roughly $10 by 1973, reaching the Japanese level, and nearing the West European one, in the early 1990s. By 1992, an average worker in Spain and Ireland produced $20 in value and, together with Greece and Portugal, an average $18 of value per hour (Maddison, 1995a: 70; 1995b: 247). In the early twenty-first century, Ireland was among the most productive countries in Europe and had nearly reached the American productivity level.

During the final quarter of the twentieth century, an integrating Western Europe entered the age of globalization and began regaining its strength by adjusting to the challenge of a rapidly globalizing world economy. The European Union's role in the process, however, was strongly connected to the Eastern half of the continent. Before I return to this major change, in a later part of this chapter on the new international environment, let me juxtapose the post-1973 Western trends with those in Central and Eastern Europe.

The East

The impact of the oil crisis and the structural crisis which emerged hit the entire world economy. Following the pattern of the 1870s–'80s as well as the 1930s, the peripheries were most affected. The unique phenomenon of the 1930s, when the Great Depression failed to influence the isolated Soviet Union, was not repeated during the 1970s and 1980s. The Soviet bloc countries were no longer isolated from the world. Half or more of the foreign trade of Poland, Romania, Hungary, and Czechoslovakia was trade with free market economies. State socialist Yugoslavia, which did not belong to the Soviet bloc, was even more tightly integrated into the world economy. The relatively small or medium-sized countries were strongly dependent on foreign trade. In the mid-1970s, exports made up nearly half of the Hungarian GDP, and from one-fifth to one-quarter of the Polish, Yugoslav, and Romanian GDPs. The international decline of the old leading sectors, as elsewhere in the world, rendered some export products unmarketable, and brought sharply reduced prices for most of the others.

The effect on Central and Eastern Europe was exaggerated because of the structural policy of the industrialization drive of the 1950s and '60s. The command economies built up traditional coal, iron, steel, and heavy engineering branches as their leading sectors, based on technology that was obsolete even then. During the 1960s, they added basic, heavy chemical industries but not the corresponding processing branches. With a delay of one hundred years, Central and Eastern Europe built its own Manchesters and "Black Countries" in Katowice and Dunaujváros, in the infamous

"Black Triangle" spanning the borders of East Germany, Czechoslovakia, and Poland. Their industries were heavily energy-intensive because of obsolete technology: in 1980, energy intensity in the region, i.e., the amount of energy used to produce one unit of product, was nearly eight times that of the European Union.

As a consequence, pollution was seven times higher. The Soviet Union, calculated to the same output unit, had 2.5 times' higher pollution than the United States during the 1970s. Czechoslovakia – "the most environmentally devastated country in the whole of Europe" – and Bulgaria were ranked among the top ten in sulfur dioxide emissions (Turnock, 2002: 66, 96; Carter and Kantowicz, 2002: 187, 190; Pavlínek, 2002: 119). In relation to income level, sulfur and nitrogen dioxide emissions were nine times higher in Hungary than in the European Union. Poland was the sixth highest air-polluting country in Europe. In Polish Silesia, the concentration of respirable dust surpassed the OECD levels by nearly six times, and the concentration of benzopyrene in the air was ten times higher (Dingsdale et al., 2002: 161, 167, 172; Hertzman and Kelly, 1996: 73–74, 77).

The old-fashioned technology and economic structure made the negative consequences of the structural crisis much more serious in Central and Eastern Europe than in the West. The structural crisis in this region was also much more bound up with the crisis of the extensive growth policy than was the case in postwar Western Europe. Socialist economic policy was strictly based on forced capital accumulation, i.e., accumulating a great part of the GDP by suppressed wages and consumption. This was the base of high rate of investment that was combined with huge labor input, with the application of existing, somewhat obsolete (mostly Soviet, East German, and Czechoslovak) technology. Capital formation from the 1950s to the early 1970s jumped from the prewar 6% to 25–30%. For quite a while, unlimited labor resources in the agricultural countries of the region, and the mobilization of female labor, allowed a 6 percent annual increase in the labor force. Imported technology from the Soviet Union and the more industrialized bloc countries such as Czechoslovakia and East Germany also made possible the use of existing technological stocks to generate rapid growth. The institutional system of centrally planned economies, with maximal state intervention behind the shield of dictatorial political regimes, helped keep wages and consumption low and labor unrest virtually impossible. The institutional system thus promoted an extensive forced growth policy; one commentator noted that:

The centrally planned economies of Eastern Europe were able, initially at least, to perform tolerably well. The institutions of the command economy had several limitations . . . but they were best suited to the circumstances of catch-up growth. (Eichengreen, 2007: 5)

This situation changed, however: the sources of extensive growth policy were exhausted in the better-developed Central European countries during the 1960s–'70s. Forced capital formation based on suppressed wage levels and living standards, the exploitation of agriculture via the compulsory delivery system, and huge labor input were no longer possible at the same level. A political factor increased the limitations: after the riots and revolutions in the '50s and '60s, the regimes had to pacify their populations. The best way to achieve that was to increase consumption and revitalize agriculture through higher prices for food products. Capital formation had already dramatically declined in the mid-1950s: from 25% to 13% in Czechoslovakia and from 25% to 15% in Hungary. Later it recuperated and remained relatively high, but at significantly lower levels than before.

Restructuring labor by collectivization and industrial job creation dried up labor resources from the 1960s–'70s onward. The agricultural population reached 40% and 53% of the active population in 1950, but dropped to 18% and 24% by 1973 in Czechoslovakia and Hungary, respectively. The industrial labor force of the time grew to 35% to 50% of the active population in the Soviet bloc countries.

Extensive growth policy no longer worked. This was clearly demonstrated by the stagnation and decline in Czechoslovakia between 1961 and 1963, and by the severe imbalance in the Hungarian economy in the early 1960s. By that time, both countries' governments recognized the need for reforms and replacement of the extensive growth model. Yugoslavia, after the split with the Soviet Union in 1948, gradually turned toward building an independent model of socialism and also began changing the Soviet type of centrally planned economy. Yugoslavia, Czechoslovakia, and Hungary introduced reforms in 1965, 1967, and 1968, respectively. Compulsory plan indicators were abolished, market prices were introduced in certain areas of the economy, and companies were motivated by profit and markets. The introduction of market influences targeted higher efficiency and better adjustment to the world economy.

This reorientation, despite some positive results in Yugoslavia and Hungary, basically failed. In Czechoslovakia, the Soviet-led Warsaw Pact military invasion in the summer of 1968 eliminated the reform orientation, including the reformed economic system just introduced. Hungary, under strict Soviet control and helped by conservative domestic opposition, temporarily halted reforms in 1972–73. In Tito-led Yugoslavia, internal limitations resulted in barriers on the road to introducing intensive growth strategies. Other countries of the Soviet bloc did not even initiate a new orientation in their economic strategy.

The crisis after 1973 made the failure of the economy manifest in most of the countries. The conservative regimes, however, continued the traditional ideologically determined Soviet policy. Hungary was almost alone in its open recognition of the need for a change of model during the late 1970s. Let me quote from my own lecture at the May 1977 General Assembly meeting of the Hungarian Academy of Sciences:

the resources of extensive industrialization and economic development are exhausted... The only way for further development is the mobilization of the intensive sources of economic growth, the technological-organizational and productivity factors. (I. Berend, 1978: 200–01)

The Hungarian government's declaration of a new long-term economic strategy at the end of 1978 was the first acknowledgement in postwar history of the need to replace import-substituting industrialization policy with export-oriented growth. High productivity, technological innovation, and competitiveness were included in the core of the new strategy. The reform orientation of Hungary and Poland was also clearly expressed when they joined international institutions such as GATT (the General Agreement on Tariffs and Trade; 1973 and 1967, respectively) and the IMF (1982 and 1986, respectively). However, in spite of the radicalization of the Hungarian and Polish reforms in the 1980s, the possibility for profound change remained limited.

Some experts of the Soviet-type economic regime, such as János Kornai, maintained that the system was not reformable. He argued that:

[S]o long as the classical system can be sustained... it has a degree of stability and robustness, whereas the system undergoing the contortions of reform is inherently unstable... The reform destroys the coherence of the classical system and proves incapable of establishing a new order in its place... [N]owhere has it been able to survive lastingly. (Kornai, 1992: 571, 573)

Regardless of whether reforms and "market socialism" were feasible, in Central and Eastern Europe sufficient reform and replacement of the extensive, import-substituting growth model with the intensive, export-oriented model did not happen. As a consequence, neither the Soviet Union nor its satellites were able to adjust to the new technological requirements of the communications and service revolution after 1973. Under strict Soviet control, and led by orthodox communist ideological principles, the region was unable to follow the rapidly changing international economic conditions.

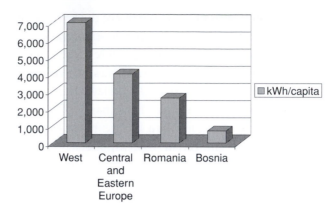

Figure 1.1 Consumption of electricity, 1990

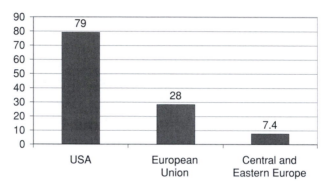

Figure 1.2 Telephone lines/100 inhabitants, 1980

One way to measure how much technological backwardness was preserved in Central and Eastern Europe is to compare annual per capita electricity consumption. At the end of the century, European countries fell into three groups. The Nordic countries reached the highest level (Sweden and Finland 14,000–17,000 kWh). The advanced West European countries, such as France, Germany, Britain, Austria, Belgium, and Switzerland, consumed 6,000 to 8,000 kWh per capita, while the less-developed countries of Central and Eastern Europe consumed 3,000 to 5,000 kWh. Some Balkan countries lagged further behind: Romania's 2,621 and Bosnia-Herzegovina's 675 kWh per capita consumption, respectively, reflected an era long disappeared from the rest of Europe (figure 1.1).

Another index measuring technological development was the spread of the telephone, which gained extraordinary importance in an age of communications and computer revolution. In 1980, when the United States had 79 telephone lines per 100 inhabitants, and the Nordic countries and the European Union had 45 and 28, respectively, Central and Eastern Europe, on average, had only 7.4 lines (figure 1.2). In addition, the lines were often out of order and it took hours to get a dial tone (Ehrlich and Révész, 1991: 83). As late as 1987, Moscow could not receive more than six long-distance calls simultaneously, while long-distance calls to other parts of the country had to go through Moscow (Mastanduno, 1992: 1).

The computer age, heralded in 1974 with the appearance of the personal computer, did not arrive in Central and Eastern Europe. The ratio of personal computers, between 5 and 50 per 1,000 people, reached only about 5% to 20% of the Western level. The number of fax machines in the early 1990s reached only 1 to 8 per 1,000 inhabitants, and only 5 percent of the fax machines used in Europe were in Central and Eastern Europe.

The service revolution, which dramatically increased the division of labor and labor productivity, also stopped at the borders of the region. While service employment increased to roughly 60 percent of the active population in the West by 1980, in Central and Eastern Europe two-thirds of the population were blue-collar workers and farmers.

Why did technological and structural renewal lag in the region? To answer this question, one must first consider the causes and prime movers of the permanent renewal of technology. Technological changes, explains Schumpeter, are inherent in a capitalist market economy and competitive market environment. In his interpretation, innovations are

new combinations of existing factors of production, embodied in . . . new firms producing either new commodities, or . . . [an as] yet untried method, or for a new market . . . [Innovation is] not any more embodied typically in new firms, but goes on, within the [existing] big units . . . It is not the knowledge that matters, but the successful solution of the task *sui generis* of putting an untried method into [hitherto untried] practice. (Schumpeter, 1928: 31, 34, 40)

The central figure in this process, the hero who must overcome the difficulties of changing practice, is the entrepreneur. Innovation is a genuine characteristic of competitive capitalism, which "not only never is but never can be stationary";

The fundamental impulse that sets and keeps the capitalist engine in motion comes from the new consumers' goods, the new methods of production or transportation, the new markets, the forms of industrial organization that capitalist enterprise creates. [The new combination] revolutionizes the economic structure from within, incessantly destroying the old one, incessantly creating a new one. This process of Creative Destruction is the essential fact about capitalism. (Schumpeter, 1976: 82–83)

Market and entrepreneurial interests, the engines of innovation and technological progress, were lacking in state socialism. Innovation and technological development are also dependent on modern managerial and organizational development. The modern economy has been characterized by permanent managerial and organizational revolution since multifunctional companies and Fordist production organization were introduced in the early twentieth century.

The Soviet economic model imposed in the Soviet bloc countries after World War II resulted in a rather different and static managerial and organizational system than in the West. All the previously existing multidivisional companies were abolished and each division was separated or merged horizontally with similar divisions. All industrial firms were detached from marketing. The central planning offices and the numerous branch economic ministries and their subordinated agencies acted as central offices. They dictated the performance of the companies by compulsory plan indicators and monitored their fulfillment. Alec Nove compared the ministers and deputy ministers of the branch economic ministries to "senior business executives" in the West. A few dozen ministers and deputy ministers, however, were not able to run huge industrial branches as real top managers since they were responsible for several giant companies. Bureaucratic management was unavoidable (Nove, 1966: 64–5). The company manager was responsible only for the execution of central decisions, and had nothing to do with strategic, long-term decisions.

During the 1960s, company reorganizations created exceptionally large firm units in Eastern Europe; it was the period of a socialist "merger mania," with the explicit goal of creating a single nationwide company in each branch of industry or trade: one company with thousands of branches for car repair, one company with thousands of gas stations, another one for any kind of electric repair and maintenance, a nationwide company for the production of beer, silk, oil, etc. The pattern was the same in the retail trade – a single company for paper goods, shoes, supermarket retailing, etc. Firm concentration grew extreme with the absolute domination of giant companies (Ehrlich, 1993; I. Berend, 1979).

Nevertheless, state socialism was unable to create modern managerial firms according to the development trend of the twentieth century, but instead operated with a managerial bureaucracy strictly subordinated to politics and party decisions. Real top managerial activity was thus replaced with highly bureaucratic government activity totally separated from market influences (Yudanov, 1997: 404, 410). In sum, market-driven innovations directed by independent entrepreneurs, crucially important to the Western market economy, were missing in the state socialist non-market system.

As noted above, there is another important factor that should also be mentioned: in the twentieth century, innovation itself was industrialized in market economies, and research became a big industry, mostly monopolized by multinational companies, which financed 70% to 80% of the R&D expenses of the advanced world.

The Soviet Union and the state socialist countries also built up huge basic research networks of their academies. Even in relatively small countries, such as Czechoslovakia, Hungary, and Bulgaria, basic research networks employed 7,000 to 15,000 researchers and staff in 30–40 research institutes. Academic basic research, however, was only loosely connected with research in application and development, which was ten times more expensive, on average, than basic research. Although the Soviet Union had a very advanced military R&D program, it was hermetically separated from the civilian economy and had very little impact on it, unlike in the West, where consumers benefited from the products of military R&D, such as lasers and Teflon. The region was thus, as always before, dependent on technology transfer.

The absence of opportunities for technology transfer

The less-developed or medium-level Central and East European economies, like all other countries of the world in this category, were never technology leaders. In their entire modern history they have been follower countries, which adopted new technology mostly by technology transfer.

Technology imports took on various forms. New technology was imported as a "complex bundle of knowledge which surrounds a level and type of technology." On this basis, David Charles and Jeremy Howells speak about the transfer of "embodied" knowledge (in physical products, plant, and equipment), and of "disembodied" knowledge of know-how, information, patents, technological services by engineers from abroad, and learning (Charles and Howells, 1992: 3–5).

Technology transfer has important commercial and non-commercial forms. As an example of the latter, the transfer of public health knowledge and instruments are widespread. In the second half of the century the World Health Organization (WHO) became an important agent of this transfer. The same is true in agricultural technology, where the United Nations Food and Agricultural Organization (FAO) plays a similar role. "Free knowledge" is spread via scientific journals, publications, scholarly meetings, and conferences. Technological and scientific capacities are also built up by education abroad. As in the eighteenth and nineteenth centuries, when American students studied at European universities, so in the second half of the twentieth century 300,000 foreign students studied at American universities annually, half of them in science and technology. On-the-job-training abroad and site visits also facilitate technology transfer.

Commercial transfer of technology is more important and direct. One of its effective forms is the construction of fully functioning firms in a foreign country, equipped with the newest technology and assisted by the donor's experts. Subsidiaries, established by multinational companies throughout the globe, represent this form and receive the latest technology transfers. This kind of transfer is sometimes realized by cost-sharing joint ventures. It is often combined with training of local workers. One should also not forget technological transfer by "reverse engineering," in which a product is taken apart and copied. Finally, technology is transferred by industrial espionage.

Belonging to the group of importers of new technology has its own advantages and disadvantages. The technological leader has all the advantage of the first comers in worldwide competition. The followers, however, can save a great deal of the cost of research and development and are able to adapt the most modern technology and inventions. Technology transfer is often responsible for faster growth in less-developed countries and may be a major factor of the catching-up process. It would nevertheless be mistaken to consider technological transfer a given. Robert Solow calls attention to the difficulties encountered in the spread of new technology. The financial requirements are evident,

but simply to have the resources available for investment is not a guarantee of development. Resources must be matched by the opportunity to use them . . . the social capacity to assimilate advanced technology. (Solow, 1966: 480)

Among the main prerequisites, he lists the competence of local scientists and science-trained engineers, an army of skilled craftsmen, the problem-solving competence and information-producing apparatus, the adaptation to prevailing forms of social and economic organization, and, last but not least, appropriate political conditions and modern, aggressive entrepreneurship in the receiving country. Moses Abramowitz (1971) speaks about the "social capability" of adopting technology and management. The weakness of these prerequisites blocked the road of technology transfer and created a greater disparity among countries.

Were these forms of technology transfer possible in state socialist Central and Eastern Europe? Some of the above-mentioned basic prerequisites, especially the well-trained and educated labor force, were present, but some significant others were missing, such as problem-solving, aggressive entrepreneurship and management. Nevertheless, and with certain limits, the area would be able to receive and adopt modern technology. The main obstacles for technology transfer were not internal, but external factors, such as the American-initiated and -controlled ban on the export of modern technology to Soviet bloc countries.

The policy of banning exports to the Soviet bloc was instituted with the beginning of the Cold War. The United States had introduced mandatory licensing of exports already in 1947. In September 1948 negotiations began with Britain and France, and in 1949 the Organisation for European Economic Co-operation took over coordination of export control. In November of that year the Coordinating Committee for Multilateral Export Controls (CoCom) was established. Operations began on January 1, 1950, and all NATO member countries, plus West Germany, Canada, and later Portugal, Japan, Greece, and Turkey, became part of it. CoCom had weekly meetings with the participation of middle-level officials. The US State Department and US Department of Defense were always represented, while the other countries sent representatives from their ministries of commerce. The basis of control and banning was established by the United States Export Control Act (1949) and then the Battle Act (1951), which empowered the president to block exports of "any articles, materials, or supplies, including technical data." CoCom operations and information were classified during the first period and decisions never made public. In 1952, the CoCom list contained 400 major categories, and later on about 150,000–200,000 items were on the list, which was periodically reviewed and updated.

During the 1970s and 1980s, all telecommunications technology, biotechnology, computer technology including software, and cutting-edge new technology was on the list, and their sales were banned. In 1982, President Reagan's Executive Order 12356 prohibited foreign researchers and graduate students from certain areas of research and training and sought to "classify the product and dissemination of on-campus scientific work." The Department of Defense required several scientific conference organizers to withdraw papers on sensitive subjects and to exclude non-US citizens from certain presentations (McDaniel, 1993: 112–13).

The CoCom policy, the first export ban during peacetime in history, despite periods of relaxation during the 1960s and part of the 1970s, successfully prevented technology transfer to the Soviet bloc. In July 1974, a few months after the oil shock, a task force was established under the chairmanship of J. Fred Bucy, the executive vice-president of Texas Instruments, and it presented its final report, the Bucy Report, in February 1976. It became a guideline for further export control and significantly strengthened restrictions in the face of a new technological-communications revolution. It included technology with a potential "dual use" – civilian and military – which made it possible to block most modern technology exports, since "virtually every material, product, or technology can be defined as having a dual use." Moreover, the report stressed the importance of hindering infrastructural development because "a highly capable infrastructure prepares a country to be a receptive host for subsequent revolutionary advances it may acquire." It recommended preventing the development of "cultural preparedness" on the part of the Soviet bloc countries to exploit advanced technology: "the widespread use of the computer, even in commercial application," it maintained, "enhances the cultural preparedness of the Soviets to exploit advanced technology" (Mastanduno, 1992: 193–94).

The report was accepted by the US Department of Defense in August 1977. It shifted controls from products to technology. The "critical technology list," created by the Department of Defense, contained fifteen groups, which incorporated computer technology, automated real-time control technology, guidance and control technology, microwave and sensor technology, and virtually the entire "contemporary techniques, including videodisk recording [and] polymeric materials" (Mastanduno, 1992: 215). From 1981, the definition of "defense priority industries" was so broad that machine tools, truck production, microelectronics, and metallurgy, as well as technical data, management and organization skills, and scholarly communication among scientists were equally banned (McDaniel, 1993: 11).

The CoCom policy was thus not only a strategic embargo prohibiting the trade of products of direct military importance. From the later 1970s on, the United States-led policy launched explicit economic warfare against the state socialist countries, aiming to weaken their entire economies. This control, although sometimes less strict and sometimes ignored by the Western allies, basically worked. The reluctant allies, even neutral countries who opposed the concept of economic warfare and disliked the American diktat, were practically forced to go along with the United States. During the 1950s, cooperation was a prerequisite for access to American aid. Later on, firms and countries which did not comply were blacklisted. The US Department of Commerce composed a blacklist as early as 1949. Sweden, not even a member of the CoCom agreement, was also forced to cooperate by the threat of restrictions on access to American technology and components. The American administration vetoed the German Standard Electric Lorenz's sale of a digital exchange system for the Hungarian telephone network in the 1980s in a similar way. The embargoes on telecoms and computer networking systems were still in force in the spring of 1991, even after the collapse of the communist regimes, when the

European allies argued that trade in these technologies was badly needed for the modernization of the transforming economies of the former socialist countries.

Lacking their own industrial R&D capacity and thwarted in their attempts at achieving technology transfer, Central and East European countries were cornered and unable to restructure their economies. The obsolete economic branches and export sectors were preserved. As a clear indicator of technological stagnation, labor productivity also stagnated during the post-1973 decades. Labor productivity in the region was traditionally low. In 1950, it only just reached the pre-World War I Western level. Between 1950 and 1973, labor productivity doubled, and even trebled, in some of these countries, but one worker-hour still produced only $5–6 of GDP, which hardly changed until the 1980s. In the Soviet Union, the productivity level declined by 14 percent and dropped to roughly one-fifth of the Western level, which by that time had already reached $25–28. Moreover, Spain, Portugal, and Greece, with a productivity level similar to that of Central and Eastern Europe in 1950, and about $10 in 1973, also increased their productivity level to $20/hour by the early 1990s. Stagnating labor productivity in the East was contrasted by rapidly rising productivity in the West and South of Europe.

Lenin's prophecy was turned upside down. After the Bolshevik revolution, he declared in his *Immediate Task of the Soviet Government* (1918) that "the fundamental task of creating a social system superior to capitalism . . . [is] raising the productivity of labour" (Lenin, 1974: 415). Capitalism proved to be superior and defeated state socialism in the labor productivity race.

Productivity was not even a main concern in state socialist Central and Eastern Europe, since it formed a self-sufficient economic bloc. Most export items of countries in the region were sold in the isolated market of the Council of Mutual Economic Aid (CMEA, or Comecon), established in 1949. This market was safe and had been highly protected since the 1950s. The non-competitive market, characterized by permanent shortages and fixed state-managed trade agreements, served to defend the economy of the Soviet bloc and had nothing to do with real markets and market demand. Until the early 1970s, Comecon trade comprised two-thirds to three-quarters of trade conducted by member countries. Trade with free market countries was marginal.

However, as the troubled Comecon market became less able to offer the required goods, more socialist countries had to look to the Western free markets. In turn, they had also to sell on the competitive markets. From the late 1970s and during the 1980s, with two or three exceptions, most of these countries had about a 50–50 split in Comecon versus free market trade. Their non-competitive economy was challenged. It proved unable to adjust, with tragic consequences.

Although it was not immediately evident what kinds of changes were transforming the world economy, the bureaucratic and centralized management system was itself an additional obstacle to adjustment. Lack of market influence and entrepreneurial interest played a crucial role in the extremely slow reaction of the socialist governments to the changing international economic environment. Even the government of reform-oriented Hungary stated

that the crisis disrupting the capitalist world economy would leave Hungary and other socialist countries unaffected – that it could be halted at the frontier. Quite a long time passed before it was realized that the factors behind the crisis were not temporary or rooted in political sanctions. (I. Berend, 1990: 232–33)

Most of the countries simply waited, without taking any action, and lost at least five years before they understood the need for a response. The Polish reaction was more detrimental than no action at all. The administration of Edward Gierek after 1970 attempted to overcome economic troubles through a policy of accelerated economic growth via hyperinvestments. During the first half of the 1970s, investments increased by 133%, and in 1975 Polish GNP increased by 29%. However, this took place without structural changes or technological renewal. In other words, Poland further expanded the obsolete, outdated industrial sectors of its overheated economy. The country, formerly an energy exporter, became an energy importer by the end of the 1970s (I. Berend, 1996: 229).

The effect of delayed and often mistaken reactions was exacerbated due in part to the erosion of Comecon trade. Lack of adjustment led to a rapid deterioration in the terms of trade, the countries' ratio of export to import prices. During the first five years after 1973, the Central and East European countries suffered growing trade deficits because of a 10% to 20% decline in the terms of trade. By 1985, countries which were heavily dependent on imported energy suffered a 26% to 32% decline in terms of trade. In other words, these countries had to boost exports by at least one-fifth, and sometimes one-third, in exchange for the same amount of imports (United Nations, 1990). One should also not forget that a decline in terms of trade, a growing gap between rising import prices and lagging export prices, already characterized the entire state socialist period: Hungary, for example, had a 50 percent terms-of-trade loss between 1938 and 1989.

Since Comecon member countries followed the traditional/ideological extensive fast-growth policy, they were trapped by ever-increasing trade deficits. State socialism was sucked into a whirlpool which pulled it deeper and deeper below. The process seemed to be unstoppable. It required a quick fix, which had seemed easy during the 1970s. The financial market was flooded with cheap "oil dollars," as a large portion of the tremendous extra income of the oil-exporting countries was exported as credits. It was cheap and easy to borrow at that time, and the governments of the region did not hesitate to bridge the trade deficit gap with loans. They also sought to use the credits for investment to rejuvenate their economies.

Most of all, however, they tried to fill the widening gap between decreasing income and unchanged or even increased expenditures. Political leadership, except in Romania, made every attempt to keep full employment, wages, living standards, and social benefits unchanged. All of these goals were too ambitious, and eventually proved impossible to fulfill. Nevertheless, all of these countries gave up the previously adopted policy of self-sufficiency and economic independence from the West, and turned to the international credit market. As a result, almost all fell into a trap of indebtedness. Between 1970 and 1989, the net amount of debt in the region increased from $6 billion to $110 billion.

The $20 billion debt that Hungary owed was approximately two times greater than the value of the country's hard currency export income, but Poland's $42 billion debt was five times greater. Debt service consumed 40% to 75% of the hard currency income of these countries combined. Meanwhile cheap credits disappeared and interest rates rose to 14–16 percent. New credits, however, were needed to repay the old ones. The credits were mostly consumed to keep the "achievements" intact, and only a small fragment of them was invested. From the $20 billion in debt that Hungary incurred, only $4–5 billion had been invested.

The crisis grew deeper: Poland, Yugoslavia, and Bulgaria became insolvent and requested a rescheduling of their debt payments. Romania tried to escape from the indebtedness trap as Nicolae Ceauşescu, the paranoid dictator, ordered repayment by cutting domestic consumption drastically. By 1985, electricity consumption had dropped to 20 percent of 1979 levels. The stores were empty, and cities and homes darkened and not heated in the winter. Romania, a broken and destroyed country, managed to repay its debts by 1989, a few weeks before a bloody uprising erupted, and the dictator was executed (I. Berend, 1996: 230–32).

The crisis in Central and Eastern Europe, similar to several other peripheral regions such as Latin America, was extremely severe. Growth policy had to be changed and the economy slowed significantly – from an annual 3.9% increase of the GDP between 1950 and 1973 to 1.2% between 1973 and 1989 (Maddison, 1995b: 97). Between 1978 and 1983, Polish GDP

Table 1.2 Per capita GDP of Central and East Europe as
a percentage of West European GDP

Country	1973	1989
Central and Eastern Europe*	**49**	**37**
Bulgaria	42	36
Czechoslovakia	57	51
Hungary	45	40
Poland	43	33
Romania	28	23
Soviet Union	49	42
Yugoslavia	34	35

*   Un-weighted average.
Source: Maddison, 1995a: 201.

declined by more than 10%. During the second half of the 1980s, Romania
experienced an annual growth rate of 0.7%; the economy of Yugoslavia
stagnated at an annual rate of 0.5%.

Several Central and East European countries which had fixed prices
under state socialism began to lose control over inflation. Hungarian consumer prices increased by 5.3%, 8.7%, 15.7%, and 17.1% annually between
1986 and 1989. In 1989, the rate of inflation in Poland reached 251%.
Yugoslavia fell into a period of hyperinflation measuring 1,269% (EBRD,
2001: 61).

Central and Eastern Europe and the successor states of the Soviet Union
could not follow the Western and Mediterranean trend of structural
change, with gradual transformation from an extensive to an intensive
growth model. The slow but permanent recuperation and growth of Western Europe from the mid-1980s that followed the crisis of the second half
of the 1970s did not happen in the East. During the first decade after the oil
crisis, Hungary suffered a loss equal to the severe destruction the country
suffered during the six months when it became a battlefield in World War
II. Hungary was not alone. The downward spiral became unstoppable.
Stagnation or decline became dominant.

The income level of the Central and East European countries, as table 1.2
shows, significantly declined from nearly one-half to slightly more than
one-third of Western Europe's between 1973 and 1989. The discrepancy
is even more obvious if one compares the quarter-century after the war
to the two decades after 1973, including the first years after the collapse
of state socialism, since the continued decline was, at least partly, still the
consequence of the previously mistaken development trend (figure 1.3).

Table 1.3 Comparative GDP growth rates/capita

Region	1950–73	1973–92
Central and Eastern Europe	3.79	−0.7
Soviet Union and successor states	3.36	−1.4
Western and Mediterranean Europe	4.8	2.0

Source: Maddison, 2001: 186.

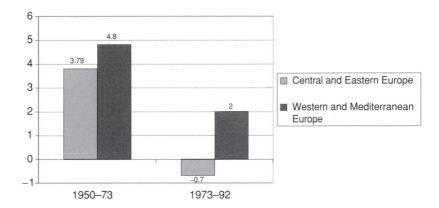

Figure 1.3 GDP growth rates compared, 1950–1973 and 1973–1992

While the West slowed down after 1973 to less than half of its previous growth rates, the rapid growth of the East, as table 1.3 reflects, was replaced by sharp decline.

What makes the Central and East European performance even worse is a comparison with that of Mediterranean Europe, since the latter was more or less on the same level as Central and Eastern Europe in 1950, and was hardly much better in 1973, but still achieved rapid growth, faster than Western Europe, and achieved a nearly 150 percent increase in its per capita income, thus making impressive progress in catching up and becoming an integrated part of the West. Central and Eastern Europe was unable to recreate the South European pattern of development and lagged further behind (figure 1.4, table 1.4).

The gap between Central and Eastern Europe and the West yawned wider. In 1950, according to Angus Maddison's calculations, Central and Eastern Europe's $2,120 GDP per capita stood at 46 percent of the West European level. By 1973, the per capita income had increased to $4,985, but it still represented only 43 percent of the Western level. By 1989, the $5,902 income of the region declined to 37 percent of the Western level (based on Maddison, 2001) (figure 1.5 and table 1.5).

Table 1.4 The growth of GDP/capita compared (1973 = 100)

Year	Western Europe[a]	Southern Europe[b]	Eastern Europe[c]
1973	100	100	100
1990	139	147	111

Source: Maddison, 1995a; 2001: 185.
Note: a: 12 countries.
    b: 4 countries.
    c: 8 countries.

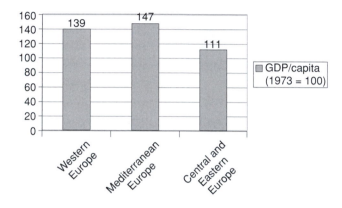

Figure 1.4 GDP growth rates between 1973 and 1990

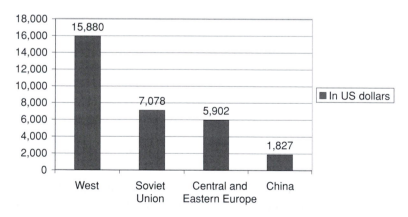

Figure 1.5 Regional disparities, GDP/capita, 1989

The year 1989 closed the postwar chapter of the history of Central and Eastern Europe. Triumphant state socialism, which incorporated nearly one-third of the world, and the Soviet superpower with its enormous army and nuclear arsenal, peacefully collapsed in 1991. The bulk of the peoples of Central and Eastern Europe considered state socialism an alien

Table 1.5 Regional disparity, GDP/capita (regions as a percentage of the West), 1950–1998

Year	Western Europe[a] $GDP/capita	%	Central and Eastern Europe $GDP/capita	%	Soviet Union $GDP/capita	%
1950	4,594	100	2,120	46	2,834	61
1973	11,534	100	4,985	43	6,058	52
1989	15,880	100	5,902	37	7,078	44

Note: a: 12 countries.

system, imposed on the area by dictatorial methods. The Poles revolted against it almost regularly, as the 1956, 1968, 1976, and 1980 uprisings, and the formation of strong opposition movements, testify. The Czechs accommodated themselves to the regime and, in a typical "Svejkian" way, obediently collaborated while passively resisting. The Hungarians, after their heroic revolution, attained a somewhat more acceptable compromise, and a more independent and livable version of the system. They looked over their shoulders to the north and east, and felt satisfaction with their "achievements." The Baltic peoples enjoyed a somewhat privileged situation within the Soviet Union. In the Balkans, people seemingly welcomed the modernization promised by the regime, which in a certain way was realized. The Yugoslavs were proud of their independent "national communism," and the international respect that went with it.

The huge majority of these societies were traditionally poor. It was relatively easy for paternalistic governments to satisfy their humble dreams. Through the 1960s and 1970s, people in Central and Eastern Europe appreciated the newly established socialist welfare institutions and the modest consumer orientation of the regime. At the same time, the same people were also dissatisfied with the shortage of practically everything. Petty corruption was part of everyday life. People also suffered from the lack of freedom. They had to mind what they said in company and what they wrote in letters. They knew that newspapers printed propaganda, and learned how to read between the lines. People felt that they were being watched. Plain-clothed secret policemen visited them and asked for "information" about others. People were tense, nervous, and often rude to each other.

In most of the countries of this region, except Yugoslavia, Poland, and Hungary, people were not allowed to travel to the West. Nevertheless, East and West were not separated by a Chinese wall. The prosperity of the West became known and envied. The comparison was humiliating, and it seemed to be out of reach. The people did not believe in the possibility of a change in the postwar world order. All of a sudden, however, the regime peacefully collapsed, in most cases without any resistance. It was an emerging revolutionary situation in which virtually nobody was ready to defend the regime. In retrospect, no alternatives were offered by the situation, and the collapse of the *status quo* was definitive.

The new international environment: end of the Cold War and the "new world order"

The Central and East European transformation began in an entirely new international situation. The Cold War was the "functional equivalent of World War III": a major empire disintegrated, political boundaries and political regimes changed (J. Mueller, 1992: 39–40). It was evident that a new world order was in the making. What emerged was not the New World Order hurriedly announced by the president of the only remaining superpower, the United States. President George H. W. Bush at the United Nations General Assembly meeting on October 1, 1990, spoke about a "whole world, whole and free," where, instead of confrontation, a new order of "partnership based on consultation, cooperation and collective action" would emerge. He spoke on several occasions about "shared commitment among nations, large and small, shared responsibility for freedom and justice" (Clark, 2001: 181).

In his speech to Congress on March 6, 1991, President Bush stated:

Twice before in this century, an entire world was convulsed by war. Twice this century, out of the horrors of war hope emerged for enduring peace. Twice before, those hopes proved to be a distant dream, beyond the grasp of man . . . Now we can see a new world coming into view. A world in which there is the real prospect of a new world order. (Bush library website, public papers)

In the post-Cold War world system, multilateralism was to govern through "institutionalized patterns of cooperation among Western democracies." "What we need to do now," said Lawrence Eagleburger on behalf of the American administration in November 1991, "is to widen this circle to include many new members of the democratic family" (quoted by Clark, 2001: 182). Several calculations were made about the prospective "peace dividend," thousands of billions of dollars worth of saved military expenditures after the Cold War arms race ended.

In reality, the high-minded term "New World Order" was soon ridiculed as "New World Disorder." Henry Kissinger once maintained that "the success of war is victory; the success of peace is stability." Stability, however, was the first victim of the post-Cold War "peace settlement." State borders, sacrosanct for half a century, suddenly became subject to debate and in several cases they changed. People became able to change them by peaceful agreement in Germany, the Baltic countries, the Soviet Union, and Czechoslovakia, or by military action in the Balkans.

Outside Central and Eastern Europe, pressure to change borders in the Middle East came from several sides. Bloody Kurdish efforts attempted to establish an independent Kurdistan provoked even bloodier Turkish and Iraqi responses. In this chaotic situation, Saddam Hussein miscalculated in his bid to change Iraq's artificial colonial borders by incorporating Kuwait by force.

Instead of multilateralism and cooperation, a Western hegemonic position, or American-centered arrangement, characterized the new global political order, supported by military posturing and pseudo-multilateralism. One of the first actions of the Bush administration after the fall of the Berlin Wall was to invade Panama, and the National Security Strategy Report to the Congress in March 1990 stressed the need for military power targeting primarily the Middle East where American interests were threatened. It also argued for strengthening the defense industrial base.

A group of neoconservative strategists led by Paul Wolfowitz, Lewis Libby, and others soon worked out a program for American rearrangement of the Middle East. It was only a decade after President Bush announced the new principle of multilateralism that his son openly replaced it with the principle of American unilateralism. The world did not become a "whole democratic family," and history, in spite of the prophecy of Francis Fukuyama in 1992, has not "ended" by melting into a uniform liberal world system. Soon the "clash of civilizations" predicted by Samuel Huntington frightened the globe.

Geopolitical rivalry had not ended either. What happened was the replacement of East–West rivalry with an Atlantic rivalry, and Asian–Western and Islamic–Western rivalries which gradually became manifest over the decade after the end of the Cold War.

The most striking feature of the new world order was the triumph of globalization. It emerged as the outcome of a combined process: the rise of global, multinational companies based on revolutionary technology, with subsidiaries all over the world and a deliberate policy to eliminate trade barriers and strengthen competitiveness by outsourcing workplaces and establishing a new division of labor. Multinational companies operating in two or more countries had already appeared by the end of the nineteenth century. Their number reached about 7,000 in 1973, but jumped to 66,000 during the following three decades, when they became dominant in the world economy. The dramatic expansion of their activities was connected with the foundation of hundreds of thousands of subsidiaries investing throughout the globe. Foreign direct investment increased by four times in the last two decades of the century. The multinationals monopolized 75 percent of world trade in manufactured goods.

The globalized world economy was characterized by steeply increased world trade and financial transactions. World trade increased by leaps and bounds as a consequence of international agreements, especially the Tokyo Round in 1979 and the Uruguay Round in 1986 that led to the foundation of the World Trade Organization (WTO). The value of international trade was $1.7 trillion in 1973. It jumped to $5.8 trillion, three-and-a-half times higher, in the last quarter of the century.

Instead of the traditional division of labor between industrial countries and those producing agricultural goods and raw materials, the West European countries invested in each other's economies. Intra-West European trade, comprising 30% of the trade of the countries of the region by the 1960s, increased to more than 60%. More characteristically, intra-industrial trade increased from 44% to 66% of total industrial trade in Germany, and from 46% to 76% in Britain; both France and Belgium reached the British share of intra-industrial trade in the last two decades of the twentieth century.

Crossborder transactions of bonds and equities that reached only 10% of the aggregate GDP of the most advanced G-7 countries in 1980 rose to 140% of GDP by the end of the century. Financial transactions per day stood at $15 billion in 1973 but increased to $1.3 trillion by 1995. This amount was fifty times higher than the value of world trade. The world economy entered a new era (Maddison, 2001: 127, 362; OECD, 1987: 273; I. Berend, 2008, forthcoming).

In a mostly globalized world market, the free flow of goods and capital led to new heights of productivity. The European Union's labor productivity level, i.e., the value produced per hour worked, increased much faster than it did in the United States, which was still in the lead. According to International Labor Organization (ILO) statistics, between 1980 and 2005 American productivity increased by 1.7% per year, but the British increase was 2.4%, the French 2.2%, and the German 1.8%. West European productivity was only half that of the United States in 1950. The gap was practically closed by the end of the century (*New York Times*, September 4, 2007).

Globalization allowed rich, highly developed countries to outsource labor-intensive and polluting sectors, along with the production of old goods in a declining lifecycle, to less developed countries. Outsourcing advanced countries were then able to concentrate on service and high-tech industries, as well as research and development. Globalization, in other words, was the way out of crisis and into a new paradigm of economic development for Western Europe.

On the other hand, globalization marked the end of the road for the state socialist economic system and played an important role in the collapse of the isolated, self-sufficient regime, which was excluded, and excluded itself, from the global economic system. History proved that globalization had its winners and losers, but those who remained outside the global transformation lost the most. The collapse of the Soviet bloc, however, resulted in a political environment favorable to further globalization, opening large new markets in a globalizing laissez-faire system.

This became the new driving force of European integration. The post-World War II integration process was driven by rising Cold War and East–West rivalry, which inspired both Winston Churchill (in 1946) and Alan Dulles (in 1948) to urge the foundation of a "United States of Europe." The Marshall Plan became an important vehicle for West European integration, the establishment of cooperation among victors and vanquished, and the foundation of the European Coal and Steel Community, and then the European Economic Community, during the 1950s.

The end of the Cold War eliminated the main impetus for Western integration against a Soviet threat. European integration, however, gained a stronger rationale. From the late 1970s through the 1980s, globalization became the new and strongest stimulus to further West European integration. As the Cold War environment dissipated, the European Community introduced the first major revision of the Treaty of Rome (1957) with the Single European Act implemented thirty years later, in the summer of 1987. Instead of a united Europe as an alternative to war, the act declared that the Community as a single entity protects the common interest of its member countries. The integration process moved into high gear: in December 1991, the Maastricht Treaty led to the establishment within the next decade of the European Union, served by a common currency and central bank. With the goal of "ever closer union," development toward a common foreign policy, citizenship, and a European constitution sped the integration process during the 1990s. In this environment, even before the total collapse of the Soviet bloc, Jacques Delors, the president of the Commission of the Community, declared in a speech in Bruges in October 1989:

The Twelve [member countries] cannot control history but they are now in a position to influence it once again. They did not want Europe to be cut in two at

Yalta and made a hostage in the Cold War. They did not, nor do they, close the door to other European countries ... The present upheavals in Eastern Europe are changing the nature of our problems. It is now merely a matter of when and how all the countries of Europe will benefit from ... the advantages of a single market. (Delors, [1989] 1998: 59)

In this international environment the window of opportunity was opened for the former Soviet bloc countries to join the new world system of a "liberal peace settlement." It helped the countries' democratic transformation, stabilization, modern marketization, and economic growth, but also strongly influenced the path they had to follow.

The "Washington consensus"

If one can speak about an international pattern which influenced Central and East European transformation, it was the so-called Washington consensus. This economic program, named by its author, economist John Williamson, was originally conceived in various Washington institutions to revitalize crisis-ridden Latin American economies. In the mid-1980s, the World Bank's Bela Balassa and a few Latin American economists, inspired by the contrast between Chilean prosperity and the general Latin American crisis, worked out a policy proposal advocating openness and macroeconomic discipline. In this decade a kind of "intellectual convergence" emerged among several American and American-trained economists and Washington-based institutions, such as the IMF, the World Bank, the US Treasury, and the Inter-American Development Bank, about the policy measures required to generate prosperity in Latin America.

The Carter administration advocated deregulation, while the Thatcher and Reagan governments initiated privatization. The latter was placed on the international agenda by the Reagan administration in the form of Treasury Secretary James Baker's speech to the annual meeting of the World Bank–IMF in 1985.

Williamson summarized the thinking on Latin American adjustment and progress at a November 1989 conference organized by the Washington Institute for International Economics, concluding

that the key to rapid economic development lay not in a country's natural resources or even in its physical or human capital but, rather, in the set of economic policies that it pursued ... [It was] geographically and historically specific, a lowest common denominator of the reforms that I judged "Washington" could agree were needed in Latin America as of 1989. (Williamson, 2000: 254)

The recommended policy measures contained ten main elements: fiscal discipline with a deficit not greater than 2 percent of GDP; public expenditures to be redirected from politically sensitive areas to fields with high economic returns; tax reform, broadening the tax base and cutting marginal tax rates; financial liberalization with market-determined interest rates; unified, "competitive" exchange rates; trade liberalization with restrictions eliminated, and low tariffs (of about 10 percent); elimination of barriers to foreign direct investment; privatization of state enterprises; deregulation to free the economy; and secure property rights (Williamson, 1997: 60–61).

"The suggested measures," as interpreted in 2001, "were a natural outgrowth of the neo-liberal policy framework that already held sway in the developed world" (Fine, Lapavitsas, and Pincus, 2001: x). Indeed, the transformation of the world economy ignited a neoliberal policy offensive in the West to parallel the Western human rights offensive. The prophets of this new *Zeitgeist*, Friedrich Hayek, Milton Friedman, and other members of the neoliberal school in the mid-1970s, launched an ideological war advocating deregulation, privatization, and free markets as the only solutions in the cutthroat global competition of a free society.

In Hayek's argumentation, freedom of the individual and freedom of the market are inseparable prerequisites for each other. He maintained that state interventionism is *The Road to Serfdom*, as the title of his 1944 book proclaimed, and that the only role of governments was to protect individual freedom and the freedom of market competition (Hayek, 1944; 1960).

Friedman became a stalwart of this ideology, attacking state intervention as the real cause of economic troubles, because, he claimed, it disturbed market automatism and undermined freedom. Friedman characterized the New Deal policy of the 1930s and the American road "that has been going on for the past forty or fifty years [as a road that leads] away from a free society." Privatization of various governmental functions lowers costs and increases efficiency, he argued, and a self-regulated market is able to provide healthcare, pensions, and various kinds of insurance. He characterized welfare institutions as a brutal intervention upon personal freedom, akin to "sending a policeman to take the money from somebody's pocket." Instead, he recommended a radical tax cut and the introduction of flat rate of around 16 percent; reducing government expenditure drastically by privatizing nearly everything; and making families and individuals responsible for their schooling, healthcare and pension plans (Friedman, 1959; 1963; 1969; 1978: 1–3, 7, 75, 79, 91). Both Hayek (in 1974) and Friedman (in 1976) were awarded with the Nobel prize signaling the victory of their ideas.

Market fundamentalism, as it was later called, was effectively preached to influence politics and public opinion. Prime Minister Margaret Thatcher and President Ronald Reagan fully accepted these ideas and based their policies on it. It became successful because of the failure of Keynesian economics in the 1970s. Rather than generating additional demand, Keynesian state interventionist measures pushed prices upward and contributed to the new phenomenon of stagflation. Besides Keynesian economics, both development and *dependencia* ideologies, which rejected the free market system and advocated isolation from the world market and the West, as well as the state socialist economic system, which realized most of those ideals, failed. All these ideologies – based on, to varying degrees, import substitution, planning, state ownership, and state interventionism – came into disrepute because of the economic failure of the countries which adopted them in Latin America, India, Eastern Europe, and elsewhere.

On the other hand, the advanced and rich core countries, especially the United States, which had turned to laissez-faire policies, adjusted relatively quickly to the new technological and communications revolution, and managed to cope with the structural crisis to generate a new prosperity from the mid-1980s onward.

Those institutions which represented and pushed this policy believed "that we know and agree on what is the best path." The success of the Washington consensus was guaranteed by prescribed conditionalities of the IMF, the World Bank, American loans and aid, and loan rescheduling by the London Group (of private creditors) and the Paris Group (of public creditors). The developing countries' debt burden left them no room for maneuver, which enabled Washington to impose its policy. If a government adopted an alternative policy package, as Frances Steward noted, it became an "international pariah," and could not secure international loans, investments, or debt rescheduling (Steward, 1997: 63).

After state socialism crumbled – the Berlin Wall collapsed in the same month the Washington conference drafted the "consensus" – the entire package of policy recommendations was "offered" to Central and Eastern Europe as well. The policy, which was intended to be "geographically and historically specific," suddenly became "one-size-fits-all." "When I asked Professor Jeffrey Sachs," recalled Károly Kiss in 1993, "whether there were any significant differences between his advice given to the Latin American countries and Poland and Russia, his answer was a flat 'no'" (Kiss, 1993: 85).

The former communist countries, burdened by severe indebtedness and rampant inflation, looked for debt rescheduling, aid, and loans from the international financial institutions and the G-7 governments. They had no alternative but to accept the conditions and Western advice. As often stated, alongside IMF and other financial institutions, Western advisers – such as Jeffrey Sachs in Poland, Anders Åslund in Russia, and Sylvia Ostry and most of the Western members of the Blue Ribbon Commission advising the Hungarian government – also advocated the neoliberal Washington package to the transforming countries. The Washington consensus created a globalized economic policy concept for the transforming countries to follow and, in its contradictory way, assisted European globalization.

Transformation was an unbeaten path. Did other kind of experiences, analyses, and recommendations exist besides the Washington consensus? In the very early 1990s, various transformation concepts were worked out and recommended. A whole set of policy concepts was offered by various groups of experts, as Kiss summarized in his *Western Prescriptions for Eastern Transition*, comparing the concepts of various economic schools (Kiss, 1993). The following paragraphs are based on that comparative analysis.

The Viennese Agenda Group held a series of seminars and published *The Market Shock* in 1992. Jan Kregel, Egon Matzner, Amit Bhaduri, Kazimierz Laski, and others offered a Keynesian approach. They condemned the transformation and the adoption of the Western market system from one day to the next – dubbed the "Big Bang" strategy – and they suggested "piecemeal privatization," since a complex set of market relations had to accompany the rise of market-oriented enterprises. Meanwhile, they maintained, governments had to improve the functioning of the existing state sector by giving managers appropriate rights and incentives. Government intervention, as well as economic and industrial policies along the lines of postwar Japan and the newly industrialized Asian countries, was strongly recommended (Kregel, Matzner, and Grabher, 1992).

This strategy coincided in several regards with that of the institutionalists, including Christopher Clauge, Joseph Stiglitz, and Mancur Olson, who stressed that "the privatization issue deserves somewhat less – and the institutional requirements of a market economy much more – priority." As Mancur Olson noted in the preface of *The Emergence of Market Economies in Eastern Europe*, "A thriving market economy is not . . . simply a result of letting capitalism happen . . . It requires a special set of institutional arrangements . . . " (Clauge and Rausser, 1992: 73).

The Research Institute of the Ministry of International Trade and Industry of Japan called attention to postwar Japanese experiences in 1992 in *Japan's Postwar Experience: Its Meaning and Implication for the Economic*

Transformation of the Former Soviet Republics. The Japanese recommended a cautious, gradualist approach. They pointed out that, in Japan, state regulations, strict price controls, and subsidies for increased output were all in force during the postwar years. The government selected branches of the economy for priority investment, and trade liberalization was partial and gradual. A unified exchange rate was introduced after four years, but import quotas and the control of international capital movements were in force even afterwards. Real liberalization of foreign trade and foreign exchange began only in 1960 when the competitiveness of Japanese industry had been achieved. It took twenty years before the Western level of economic freedom was achieved during the mid-1960s (Japan Ministry of Trade, 1992).

In these early debates, even the first successes of the Chinese economic reforms were noted. Inderjit Singh, in his 1991 "China and Central and Eastern Europe: Is There a Professional Schizophrenia on Socialist Reform?" called attention to the opposite starting point of Chinese reforms, *viz.*, strengthening the domestic market (starting with agriculture), instead of export-oriented growth. China's experience, to which I will return at its more mature stage, offered an alternative road to privatization: opening the gates for establishing private enterprises before privatizing the state-owned sector. The government, launching an active industrial policy, began restructuring state-owned companies. Trade and price reforms were also piecemeal, and foreign exchange controls and various exchange rate policies remained in force (Singh, 1991).

János Kornai, Peter Murell, and Yijiang Wang suggested a dualistic pattern: a market-based regime in the newly emerging private sector and an administrative one for the state sector. Murell and Wang spoke about the possibility of a long coexistence of the old state with the new private sectors (Kornai, 1989; Murell and Wang, 1993).

All of these strategies, however, were rejected. Oddly enough, while they were ignored in the case of the Washington consensus, historical differences and East European peculiarities were stressed to dismiss other models. Keynesian policy was disqualified during the 1980s–'90s. Regarding the Japanese industrial policy approach, Sachs warned, it might be counterproductive in Eastern Europe because of lack of competition: instead of stimulating the development of modern branches it would protect obsolete sectors. He also criticized the Chinese industrial policy as "disastrous without perspective," and declared the Chinese transformation policy of an agrarian country inappropriate in industrialized Eastern Europe.

John Flemming, then chief economist of the newly formed European Bank for Reconstruction and Development (EBRD), which was responsible for assisting the transformation of Central and Eastern Europe, recalled that policy measures of the transforming countries were the

reflection of local, not imported, thinking... We were acutely conscious that we could not say "You must... choose our model economy." Indeed, we and others said, "Stop. Think. What about the Asian example?" The reply was, we are Europeans and want the EC/EU model. (Flemming, 1997: 350)

These answers, however, reflected the *Zeitgeist*. They were the outcome of the noisy Western applause for "shock therapy" measures, opening countries from one day to the next, and fast, all-round "voucher privatization," which was later proven fraudulent. Those who advocated and realized these measures, such as Leszek Balcerowicz in Poland and Václav Klaus in the Czech Republic, believed that a painful but fast operation was the best way to cope with the towering problems of regime change. As Bronislaw Geremek, the legendary Polish dissident-turned-politician stated, "I was aware that we must move very quickly... because Europe had frankly no intention of waiting for us" (cited in Kowalik, 1994: 122).

The common wisdom, as Ralf Dahrendorf expressed it, was broadly accepted: "things get worse before they get better." Many leaders were convinced, as Michael Mandelbaum phrased it, that these countries "will emerge at the other end... of the valley of tears, into the sunlight of western freedom and prosperity" (cited in Islam and Mandelbaum, 1993: 15). It seemed convincing that the best way to pass through this valley of tears was as fast as possible. Those politicians who represented this idea and tried to realize it became celebrities overnight in the West. Most Central and East European scholars and politicians were eager to stress their "Europeanness" and mindful to be politically correct. To mention the importance of the role of the state in the transformation was more than outdated: it became politically incorrect at the time when an almighty state had withered away.

It took a few years and some dramatic failures before there was a new recognition that change was needed and a "new agenda" of post-Washington consensus emerged. The 1993 report of the World Bank, *The East Asian Miracle*, while recognizing the importance of strategic industrial policy to correct market failures, still concluded that one could not "draw a causal link between selective interventions and industrial performance" (Deraniyagala, 2001: 88). Recognition emerged slowly:

The major advance of the 1990s stemmed from recognition that the central task of the transition from communist to market-based economies involved building the institutional infrastructure of a market economy. This realization was complemented by a growing recognition that bad institutions can sabotage good policies. (Williamson, 2000: 261)

Stiglitz, former chief economist of the World Bank, became one of the pioneers of the new thinking. He recognized that markets of less-developed countries were not functioning well, and that development strategies should be based on that understanding. He stressed that speed was not an important factor: it is more important to do privatization correctly than to do it quickly. He argued that transformation is a complex process which includes income distribution and several social factors, and that the state has a major role in transformation, including education, industrial policy, competition policy, and technology transfer (Stiglitz, 1998; 1999). It was years before the executive secretary of the United Nations Economic Commission for Europe argued that the coincidence of the collapse of communism and the triumph of supply-side economics in the West was

unfortunate [and] led to a series of errors . . . the need for the state itself to manage the transition process was underestimated . . . the state has to provide . . . stable institutions and [a] policymaking framework . . . [and] some form of medium-term planning should be reestablished. (Berthelot, 1997: 229)

Yves Berthelot also praised the gradualism of the Chinese transformation, in which privatization of state-owned companies was not a key element, but new companies were started "from scratch," including foreign investments in special economic zones. Chinese reform meanwhile improved management and transformed the state sector as well. It took years for outstanding economists such as Lawrence Klein to confront the results of the uniform Washington consensus policy with the East Asian model, especially the industrial policy of the latter, the "real actions to promote the buildup of specific industries . . . picking [and promoting] winners." Klein also praised the gradualism of the Asian policy and the relative economic equality which resulted (1997: 100–01).

In short, instead of a better-tailored policy for less-developed transforming countries, the model of the most-developed Western countries was virtually forced upon Central and Eastern Europe, even as it was partly deliberately chosen by the target countries. It would be a mistake to argue that the Japanese, or Chinese, or any other model would be adequate for transforming Central and Eastern Europe. Nevertheless, several elements of the Asian experiments – the institutional considerations, the warnings about cautious and gradual liberalization, and the role of the state to guide and assist transformation – would have served as a much more appropriate transformation policy in the region. This did not happen, and the countries had to pay a high price for it.

A few years later, the dangers and failures became everyday knowledge: "Privatization across the Commonwealth of Independent States and much of the Balkans," argued Ilya Prizel, had a rather negative consequence, since it "created de facto a group of kleptocratic governments engaged in uncontrolled capital flight" (Prizel, 1999: 10). Charles King pessimistically stated as late as 2000: the "laggards in fact constitute the majority . . . The countries of the northern tier . . . are the exception not the norm in post-communist politics" (King, 2000: 152). Nevertheless, in this international and ideological environment, the Central and East European transformation and adjustment to the global economy and the European Union began.

CHAPTER 2

Radical transformation and policy mistakes: dramatic economic decline in the early 1990s

Deregulation and macroeconomic stabilization

The countries of Central and Eastern Europe began in the 1990s to transform economically as well, based on – and in parallel with – their political transformation from one-party, non-parliamentary regimes to multiparty, parliamentary democracies. The former state socialist countries hurried to eliminate the failed economic system based on state ownership, planning, strict central regulations, and in most cases collectivized agriculture. Changes were patterned on the Washington consensus guidelines, and the newly elected governments rushed to build a capitalist market system overnight. Other concepts and recommendations for transformation were not seriously considered and were almost universally rejected. The new elite believed that speedily copying the West would open the door to joining Europe almost immediately.

The Poles thought that the West bore a "moral responsibility" to reward them for their role in eliminating the Soviet danger. The Czechs believed they genuinely belonged to the West, and Václav Klaus often pointed to the map, noting that, geographically, Prague is more Western than Vienna. The Baltic peoples rediscovered their Nordic–Scandinavian connections. The Yugoslavs were convinced that their international recognition and historical advantage in reform would pave the way for an easy transformation.

Socialist economic planning, state control, and regulations were rapidly abolished. New laws brought about deregulation. The constitutions were either amended or new ones enacted by the new, freely elected parliaments. Private ownership was reestablished, and the road was opened for private business. State interference was significantly decreased. Subsidies and budgetary redistribution, which distorted the price system and competitiveness, were significantly cut: in Hungary, subsidies fell from 13%

to 7%, while state redistribution fell from 64% to 50%. The latter, which remained relatively high, approached the West European level of 35–40%. In Poland, subsidies of basic food items, housing, and energy, which totaled more than 30% of the state budget, were cut to 15%; they were mostly abolished for industrial and agriculture products, and substantially decreased for services. Elimination of agricultural subsidies became counterproductive since both the European Union and United States maintained subsidies valued at roughly 40 percent of total production.

Those countries which separated from larger federal units and became independent in the first years of transformation faced the additional task of establishing their countries as independent economic units. That major task burdened the three Baltic republics, Estonia, Latvia, and Lithuania, which departed from the Soviet Union; the successor states of Yugoslavia, such as Slovenia, Serbia-Montenegro, Croatia, Bosnia-Herzegovina, Macedonia, Montenegro (when it later separated from Serbia), and Kosovo, which, under United Nations control, became virtually independent; and the Czech Republic and Slovakia which replaced the Czechoslovak federal state. In addition to introducing their own new currency, most of them wanted to cut economic ties with their old natural partners in the previous multinational state, whether it was the Soviet Union, Yugoslavia, or Czechoslovakia.

The Baltic countries faced extraordinary difficulties: before 1991, 95 percent of their outside trade connected them to the Soviet Union. The shock was tremendous, and the three countries' GDP immediately declined by 40 percent. They also had to introduce their own currency: Estonia issued the kroon in August 1992, Lithuania the talonas in October 1992 (which, in 1993, became the litas), and Latvia used the Latvian ruble for a year, and then changed it to the lats in March 1993.

Deregulation went hand in hand with macroeconomic stabilization, marketization, and privatization. For one reason or another, that became the only road leading from a dead end and a prerequisite for integration with Europe. That was the way to answer the challenge of globalization. These measures characterized the early 1990s, and the countries of the region, though not in unison, emerged into a different economic system.

One of the most urgent tasks was macroeconomic stabilization. The transforming countries had to halt galloping, and in some cases hyper-, inflation. It was an enormous task: they had simultaneously to cope with the legacy of a shortage economy, to stabilize the state budget, to halt the ever-increasing debt crisis, and to reach equilibrium in the balance of payments. The stabilization project was part of the Washington consensus program, and it required fast action. Shock treatment, though controversial and doubtful as a general transformation policy, was more than appropriate for stabilization. The countries of the region were not left alone to do this difficult job.

The IMF, although its conditions were questionable, played a positive role in assisting the stabilization process. Some of the countries of the region such as Romania (1972), Hungary (1982), and Poland (1986) had already joined the IMF before the collapse of their respective regimes. Bulgaria and Czechoslovakia followed in 1990, and soon all the transforming countries had joined. Macrofiscal stabilization and monetary stability were helped partly by strict IMF rules, such as a wage control policy to keep pay raises to a minimum to avoid a wage–price spiral, and budgetary restrictions for state-owned companies to eliminate subsidies.

Although some independent decision-making and various technical solutions were allowed, all of the transforming countries had to establish an exchange rate system to reduce inflation, either fixed, pegged, crawling pegged, or managed floating. Pre-accession countries were advised by the European Commission to follow flexible exchange rate policies pegging their currencies to the euro within a broad band. However, while Poland opted for a free-floating exchange rate, the Baltic countries introduced a different policy, a fixed exchange rate regime (Piech, 2003: 85, 95).

Most of the countries of the region had to repay huge amount of debt as well. The Baltic countries did not have this burden since Russia adopted all foreign assets and liabilities of the Soviet Union. Czechoslovakia had accumulated only a small amount, and Romania had repaid the debt before the collapse of the regime in 1989. Slovenia also had a better legacy and a lower debt burden. The Polish, Hungarian, Bulgarian, and other countries' repayment was facilitated by capital inflow, partly from the IMF itself. Credits from the IMF served to create sufficient hard currency reserves to ease debt servicing. The very first arrangements for this purpose were ten- to twelve-month standby arrangements disbursed to Hungary as early as June 1989. This system was then somewhat changed and longer-term credits were given to Poland ($1.7 billion) and Hungary ($1.5 billion) in the early 1990s. These kinds of loans were followed by three- to five-year loans to offset export earning losses. Between the summer of 1989 and October 1991, a further $2.2 billion was transferred. Croatia signed its first stand-by agreement with the IMF in 1994 and an extended agreement in 1997. With the exception of Slovenia, there was no transformation country which did not receive IMF credits during the 1990s. By 1997, the amount of IMF credits to the area reached $27 billion. In 1997, a new form of special assistance was made available, a reserve loan in case of exceptional balance-of-payment difficulties (Jochimsen, 1999: 40–41, 43, 45–46).

Stabilization was a prerequisite for economic transformation and progress. The major previous faults and consequences of the state socialist regime, as well as the inflationary impact of price liberalization, had to be eliminated. The stabilization process turned out to be very successful. Inflation soon declined to single-digit figures, although, as I will discuss later, this required a longer period of time in some countries where inflation returned in later years.

Marketization

Except in Yugoslavia and Hungary, which were previously reform-oriented, and in Poland since the 1980s, the countries of the region had a strict non-market economic system. To introduce a market economy, they eliminated fixed prices and strict price controls: free market prices were introduced. Price liberalization formed one of the first milestones of systemic change. Hungary preceded the other countries of the region in this regard, accepting a three-year transformation plan in 1988, even before the regime collapsed, and within two years it had accomplished price liberalization – fortified by the results of the country's unique economic reform process, sometimes called "creeping transformation," which had been underway since the mid-1960s. Poland introduced market prices on January 1, 1990, and most of the prices in Czechoslovakia were also liberalized in 1990. Price liberalization followed in Bulgaria (except for energy prices) and Latvia in 1991, and in Lithuania and Estonia by the fall and winter of 1992, respectively. Romania implemented a price liberalization program over two years and completed the process by 1992. Slovenia liberalized most prices by the end of 1993, but rump Yugoslavia (i.e., Serbia and Montenegro) kept controls on about 60 percent of prices and heavily subsidized utility prices, abolishing price controls only in 2000. According to the report of the European Bank for Reconstruction and Development, price liberalization was accomplished and free market prices were introduced in the entire region around the turn of the century.

Closed borders were also opened, and not only for people but also for the free flow of goods and capital. Most of the countries of the region liberalized foreign trade either in a single year, or in a span of two to three years. State trading monopolies and other restrictions on trade were quickly lifted in most of the countries, and even in slow-to-reform Romania in the spring of 1992. Most of the countries of the region, except Slovenia and Romania, sought to demonstrate their commitment to laissez-faire capitalism, and went further in liberalization than established Western capitalist countries. They eliminated tariffs and other restrictions, while Western countries used these weapons when their interests were endangered.

Reform-oriented Hungary, which joined GATT in 1973, had already decreased its tariff level from the original 32% to 16% during the 1970s and 1980s. In 1991, tariffs were reduced to 13%, and to 8% after the Uruguay Round. In 1989, only 15% of domestic production was exposed to import competition, which increased to 33% in 1990. Nevertheless, trade liberalization continued as part of the country's three-year transformation plan, initiated before the collapse of the regime (I. Berend, 1989), and it was completed on schedule in 1991, when 86% of imports were liberalized. In the mid-1990s, 60% of Hungarian exports went to liberalized markets. This share was not far behind the West European proportion of about 75%.

What happened gradually in Hungary was effected in some other countries at once: Poland and Czechoslovakia turned instantly to free trade, Lithuania did so by the summer of 1993, and Estonia abolished all non-tariff restrictions in January 1994. In 1990, computers, telecommunications products, pharmaceuticals, farm products, and chemicals became duty-free in Poland. An extremely low 15% tariff rate was introduced for 70% of imports, while other products used 20% to 30% tariffs, with an average tariff rate of 14%.

However, regional experts soon realized that such overliberalization – fast and unilateral – was a mistake, and countries such as Poland and Slovakia reintroduced certain restrictions later. In Poland, after 1991, tariffs for some products, which had become duty-free in 1990, such as computers, farm products, pharmaceuticals, and chemicals, were increased to 20%. Czechoslovakia made a similar move: in 1990, an average 5.3% tariff level was introduced, but in 1992 a 20% import tariff was reestablished for 1,700 products. In 1993, both countries adjusted their tariffs to GATT norms. The import protection of the Czech and Slovak Republics and Poland became "lower and more uniform than in most OECD countries" (*Financial Times*, September 30, 1993). Slovakia, for its part, introduced import surcharges in 1999. The West also initiated wide-ranging measures. For example, the economic organization of the advanced countries, OECD, on average applied a 2.9 percent tariff to Hungarian products. However, they also defended themselves with various non-tariff barriers in the case of almost 60 percent of Hungarian export items.

The previously isolated and closed state socialist economic system became open to competition, and the former Soviet bloc countries began successfully integrating into the European and world economy. Before the collapse, the Baltic republics were integral parts of the Soviet economy, and some of the countries, such as Bulgaria and Czechoslovakia, had directed nearly three-quarters of their foreign trade to other member countries of the economic integration organization of the Soviet bloc, Comecon, while others, such as Poland, Hungary, and Romania, did so for 40% to 50% of their foreign trade. This organization, however, collapsed along with the regimes in 1990, and it was officially dissolved in 1991. The countries of the region no longer offered each other large markets, and the Soviet Union became unable to pay for imports. From the isolated regional agreement system, all of the countries were forced into the competitive world market. All foreign trade had to be reoriented. Moreover, as a consequence of the effort to open the countries for globalization, their own state territories also became part of the open world market. They had to compete with foreign companies which immediately penetrated their boundaries.

As an important part of trade liberalization, all of these countries introduced convertible currency. In the state socialist economy, one of the main factors behind economic isolation was the non-convertible currency, which used different exchange rates for private citizens, for trade and financial transactions, for hard and soft currencies, and for different economic fields. In certain periods, a complicated exchange regime existed, involving dozens and even hundreds of exchange rates. As a first step, exchange rates were unified. This happened long before the collapse of the regime in Hungary (1981) and Poland (1982), but in contrast only in January 1991 in Czechoslovakia; Latvia unified its rates before independence, in November 1990, while Romania waited until the spring of 1997 to do the same.

Full current account convertibility followed, with Poland leading the transforming countries in January 1990. In other countries this happened gradually: the Hungarian forint became *de facto* convertible for imports of goods and services in 1989 and 1993, respectively. In Czechoslovakia, the koruna became convertible for companies in 1991, and for the general population, in limited amounts, in 1991 and 1994. Convertibility was introduced in Estonia in the summer of 1994, in Croatia and the Czech Republic in the spring and fall of 1995, respectively, and in Bulgaria in September 1998. Although currencies became virtually convertible by 1995–96, certain restrictions remained intact during that entire decade. Trade was fully liberalized and currencies made convertible by the end of the century, and in the Czech Republic, Slovakia, and Hungary in 2001. In Serbia and Montenegro high tariffs and multiple exchange rates prevailed until the elections of 2000 (EBRD, 2003: 16; Palánkai, 2004: 274–77).

Marketization, in addition to deregulation and liberalization, required a whole new set of institutions and laws. Institution-building became a significant part of transformation. All of the countries of Central and Eastern Europe introduced Western-type progressive taxation. Some, such as Estonia and Slovakia, outpaced the Western countries and turned to flat rate income taxation. Value-added corporate taxation was also introduced: in 1985 in Hungary, in July 1993 in Poland and Romania, in January and May 1994 in Estonia and Lithuania, respectively, and in December 1998 in Slovenia.

Western-type national banks were also established, mostly by transforming the former state socialist central banks. In most cases, the new or amended constitutions regulated their status and guaranteed their independence from the government. Building democracy required the separation of powers and the creation of national banks independent from the government and from direct political influence. Although this practice was the consequence of a century-long process in the West, it was immediately institutionalized in the East. It became a requirement of European monetary union, which demanded strict monetary policy. Independent national banks proved easier to implement *de jure* than *de facto*. Both the Polish and Hungarian governments tried to control their national banks, and they attacked the first bank presidents who resisted, Grzegorz Wojtowicz, who was removed, and the independent-minded György Surányi:

Though the East European central banks are legally independent from government instructions, they nevertheless remain, in practice, vulnerable to government pressure . . . they have emerged in situations where the rule of law is still fragile. (Semler, 1994: 51–52)

A great variety of commercial banks was also opened. Stock exchanges opened in 1992 in Bulgaria, in 1993 in the Czech Republic and Latvia, in 1994 in Croatia, in 1995 in Romania, and in 1996 in Estonia and Albania.

Alongside deregulation, however, new regulations were also needed. The free market system required competition laws, bankruptcy laws, banking laws, mortgage banking laws, venture capital laws, property rights laws, commercial codes, and several other laws and regulations to establish the strict rules of the game and to secure the smooth functioning of the market. All of these laws were enacted in the transformation countries during the 1990s. Some countries lagged behind: in Serbia-Montenegro no bankruptcy law was enacted, and competition law was not applied. In this respect, "state desertion in the post-communist transformation" did not happen (Csaba, 2005: 103).

In some cases, the transformation philosophy neglected institution-building and concentrated on speedy transformation. The legal environment, e.g., public laws on administrative and judiciary areas, was created afterwards, in many cases in the early 2000s, after a delay of a decade. In the Czech Republic, the introduction of creditor protection and appropriate bankruptcy management required a long period of time. A new and adequate bankruptcy law was enacted at last in 2000. In several cases, legislation that was up to the European standard was enacted only around the turn of the century, in connection with European Union accession. In Slovakia, for example, a European legal environment was created only in 2001–02, with the adoption of a new accountancy law, an auditor act, a trademark law, and a patent law, and the amending of the commercial code. However, in countries weakened by corruption and missing appropriate legal knowledge, lax law enforcement resulted in a certain discrepancy between law and reality. At the end of the decade, despite the remaining weaknesses, the European Union reported that full-fledged market systems were in operation in the region.

Privatization

Along with marketization, privatization of the predominantly state-owned economy also began immediately. Privatization policy and practice in the various countries of Central and Eastern Europe exhibited some basic similarities, although important differences also characterized the transformation. Differences surfaced mostly in three major areas.

One group of differences concerned the goal and pace of privatization. In some countries, such as rump Yugoslavia, Croatia, Slovenia, and Romania, governments did not aim for rapid and complete privatization. In Yugoslavia, a genuinely reform-oriented country, the early departure from the Stalinist economic regime had led to the introduction of workers' self-management. This system was envied by reformers in other state socialist countries, and became an ideal for the Polish Solidarity movement. During the transformation period, however, it became a burden, an obstacle to privatization. In January 1989, the federal government of Yugoslavia targeted a "new socialism," which would combine self-management with a proper market environment. Unlike in Hungary at that time, or in Poland a few months later, privatization was not a goal. In December of that year, however, the government prepared a more radical program for a new economic and political system. Nationalist upheaval washed away all these plans. The civil war stopped the process before it got started, and privatization returned to the agenda only after 1995, but was implemented mostly following the end of the century. The so-called Yugoslav type of social ownership remained dominant in industry in the successor states. About 80 percent of banks were in the hands of socially owned companies until the end of the century.

In Romania, the first governments looked for a "third way" by privatizing only 53 percent of state assets, namely, the so-called *societati comerciale* or commercial companies, and keeping the other 47 percent – in particular, the so-called *regii autonome* or strategic branches, such as mining, energy, communications, transportation, and armaments – in state ownership. Moreover, even the privatized companies remained partly employee-owned (25%), or voucher-privatized (14%); in these cases, only 60% (and in some cases only 49%) of the shares were offered for sale. The 1,727 privatized "commercial" companies thus remained mostly state-owned, and only one-sixth of them had private majority ownership. Only 13 percent of privatized companies were bought by outside investors, and by the end of 1998 only half of these had acquired majority ownership. In other words, three-quarters of the companies remained in the hands of the state (Earle and Telegdy, 2002). Rump Yugoslavia, Croatia, Slovenia, and Romania were slow in privatization.

In some cases, the shortcomings of transformation and the lack of appropriate economic growth were explained by this Yugoslav-type insider privatization, in which the managers and workers became owners. Foreign participation in privatization was very limited in these cases. Balkan privatization was slow and did not generate major capital infusion and reorganization. As economist Lucian Cernat noted, Romania remained far behind the Central European countries in privatization: by 1995, only 20% of state-owned companies had become private. In Bulgaria, this share was even smaller, at 15%. By the time Hungary and Poland had privatized 60–65% of the industrial firms (measured in percentage of industrial output), the corresponding figures in Romania and Bulgaria were only 12% and 7%, respectively. Of the 2,471 privatization contracts that were concluded in Romania by 1996, only eleven involved foreign participation. The situation hardly changed afterwards: between 1996 and 2000, only 263 privatizations led to foreign ownership. Romanian capitalism emerged in the first period of transformation as a "state corporatist" regime (Cernat, 2006: 50, 55, 65).

Employee privatization, in most cases, did not promote renewal of the economy. Ivan Teodorović and his coeditors singled out insider privatization as the main obstacle to Croat economic success during the 1990s (Teodorović *et al.*, 2005). Christos Papazoglou explains the slow economic progress of the Balkans in terms of the slow progress of privatization:

The increase of the private sector share of GDP was much faster in the region of CE [Central Europe] since it had reached more than 70 percent of GDP by 1999, while the corresponding share for SEE [South Eastern Europe] was still below

60 percent during the same year and only marginally above that in 2003 ... The lagging of SEE relative to CE can be interpreted as a ... clear reflection of the overall slow progress of the region. (Papazoglou, 2005: 93)

However, equating privatization with modern economic transformation and restructuring is an oversimplification of the complexity of transformation. Slovenia, for example, followed a neocorporatist road, and it was only as a consequence of the accession process around the end of the twentieth century that it "was pressed [by the European Union] to speed up its sluggish privatization process and let foreign capital take over its strategic sectors" (Bohle and Greskovits, 2007: 12). The now independent country, carrying the same burden of previous Yugoslav reforms, undertook a gradualist approach to restructuring state-owned companies, arguing that they ought to be made profitable before being sold. At the end of the first decade of transformation, only half of the economy was privatized, a much lower proportion than in Central Europe overall. Slovenia was one of the least market-radicals among the transforming countries; the size of its privatized economic sector was no larger than in several of the Balkan countries, and it stood at exactly the same level as Croat privatization. Nevertheless, given its much better legacy as the most advanced part of Yugoslavia, having produced about one-third of the entire exports of the reform-oriented former federal republic, Slovenia became one of the most successful transforming countries in Central and Eastern Europe.

The Chinese example, to which I will return in chapter 5, is even more telling about many factors of economic success other than privatization alone. In the Slovene case, the state used its position to modernize the industrial sector, while in Romania the populist government's 48/1997 Ordinance imposed clear restrictions on restructuring the labor force (Cernat, 2006: 66). Labor productivity increased significantly in Slovenia, as in Central Europe generally, though in the Balkan countries it remained below 1989 levels.

Nevertheless, privatization gained momentum in several Balkan countries after the Kosovo war. The advanced process of accession led to the acceptance of the European Union's laws, and foreign capital inflow and the privatization drive considerably increased. Since that time,

significant proportions of large state-owned enterprises [have been] privatized in all countries. Bulgaria and Romania, the two [EU] accession countries, in addition to Croatia have made the most progress. (Papazoglou, 2005: 95)

Kosovo, *de facto* independent under the government of the United Nations Mission and the Provisional Institutions of Self-Government, also initiated a very late privatization process: in 2005, 130 of the 500 so-called socially-owned enterprises were privatized, and this process began coming to a close only in 2006 (Mildner, 2006: 52).

The second area where differences mattered, and which played a bigger role than the scope of privatization itself, was the method of privatizing: selling the companies piece by piece, or using a voucher privatization scheme, as it was called. The former method was based on transforming state companies into joint-stock companies for subsequent sale to private bidders. Hungary and several other countries followed this road. Other countries – in particular, Czechoslovakia, though it was later joined, at least partially, by Poland, Romania, Bulgaria, Albania, and Croatia – distributed vouchers among the adult population of the country, so that every citizen could receive stocks of state-owned firms. In this case, which will be discussed later, a large part of the shares remained in the hands of the state.

The third difference was the use of reprivatization, i.e., giving back nationalized companies to their original owners. Some of the countries, such as Hungary, rejected this system, except in the case of forcibly collectivized land, former church buildings, and other non-land church assets. Others, such as Czechoslovakia, Bulgaria, and Estonia, broadly used reprivatization. In Czechoslovakia, everything expropriated between 1955 and 1961, altogether about 70,000 properties, was returned to its former owners. These were mostly small and medium-sized firms, since the nationalization of major companies occurred before 1955.

In Bulgaria, the restitution law guaranteed the return of residential, industrial, commercial, and landed properties that were nationalized or confiscated after 1947. This uniquely radical restitution law became the most important feature of Bulgarian privatization, insofar as 85 percent of eligible land, 3,600 shops, 2,600 houses and apartments, 130 restaurants, and 600 industrial sites were given back to the original owners or their heirs. Estonia used a combination of reprivatization and voucher privatization. According to the new privatization law of June 1993, restitution of property lost in or after 1940 was mostly arranged by compensation vouchers. In addition, "work contribution" vouchers (based on years worked in Estonia between 1945 and 1991) were also distributed. The assets transferred per adult citizen averaged $1,000. A minority of shares in formerly state-owned companies were exchanged for vouchers. The majority, however, was sold to strategic investors for cash (Jeffries, 2004: 166–67).

In spite of all of these important differences, which left the Balkans only partially privatized, the basic process of privatization was rather similar throughout the region. In each country, it occurred in three different areas or levels: (a) *grass-roots privatization*, i.e., the foundation of new, mostly small and medium-scale private firms, which was an immediate consequence of deregulation after the regime change; (b) *small privatization*, which meant selling small state-owned firms, mostly single units of state-owned trade chains and service companies; and (c) *big privatization*, or the selling of the large, mostly monopolistic state-owned industrial, banking, and utility companies. As a consequence, private ownership largely replaced state ownership in the entire economy by the end of the first decade of transformation or, in several Balkan countries, in the early twenty-first century.

Privatization began everywhere with deregulation, the elimination of restrictions, and with opening the road for establishing private companies. *Grass-roots privatization* was most successful. Entrepreneurial people, those who had some resources or who were able to borrow, established mainly small-scale, family businesses, most often in trade and services. In Hungary, this kind of privatization gained momentum before the collapse of the regime, and roughly one-third of GDP was already produced by small-scale private companies and joint ventures by 1985. Between 1988 and 1993, 87,000 medium-sized firms were privatized, and 663,000 small family firms were established. Poland, where private initiative also gained ground during the reforms of the 1980s, saw 1.8 million small private companies founded during the first four years of transformation. By the summer of 1992 in Czechoslovakia, 1.2 million new businesses, mostly family-run, were established. In Bulgaria, where reprivatization played a decisive role, only 180,000 new businesses were opened in the first three years of transformation. The situation was similar in Romania, where an atmosphere of strict limitations, such as restricting the level of private employment to a maximum of twenty employees, resulted in the foundation of fewer than 150,000 new business enterprises. Newly founded small and medium-sized businesses represented the only progress in Serbian privatization through 2000, when about 60,000 registered enterprises were active in the country (EBRD, 2000: 9).

Small privatization was quick and successful as well. The privatization of dwellings, retail chains, shops, gas stations, restaurants, and branches of nationwide repair service companies was accomplished rapidly. In most of the countries, state-owned apartments were also sold to their occupants. In Hungary and Slovenia, 86% and 88% of the dwellings, respectively, were already privately owned by 1994 (Hegedűs and Tosics, 1998: 166). In Tallinn, 82% of the dwellings were in private hands by 1997, mostly via reprivatization of state-owned apartments to their previous owners (Feldman, 2000: 833). In Poland, 25% of urban dwellings were given over to private ownership in 1988, but by 2002 the figure was nearly 38%.

Altogether, the share of privately owned dwellings increased from 44% to 55% in the country (Van Kempen, Vermeulen, and Baan, 2005: 68).

State-owned retail chains and repair service companies were divided into single units for sale through open bidding. This approach was so successful and fast in Poland that 85 percent of these types of state-owned companies were sold by the end of 1991. In Hungary, the sale of more than 10,000 units was practically complete by the end of 1993. In Czechoslovakia, small privatization began in January 1991, and the sale of 25,000 units was nearly complete by the end of 1993. In the Baltic countries, small privatization began in the fall and winter of 1991. By the spring of 1994, 85 percent of small enterprises were privatized in Estonia. By that time, two-thirds of Latvia's small-scale companies were in private hands. In Romania, where privatization had hardly begun before 1993, 2,000 of the 5,500 small and medium-sized units on the market were sold that year.

Big privatization proved slower and more difficult. In Hungary, the State Property Agency, established before the collapse of the regime in February 1989, transformed state firms into joint-stock companies and began selling them piece by piece. It had a slow start. By the end of 1993, only 14 percent of the big companies had been privatized. The government plan to privatize half the state-owned companies within four to five years failed. In 1993–94, even the banks that had already been privatized were renationalized to consolidate the financial sector. There were not enough domestic resources to buy huge steel mills, chemical factories, banks, or even textile firms. Big companies were mostly bought by foreign investors. Hungary was fortunate because, beginning in the late 1980s, it became the first country in Central and Eastern Europe to attract major foreign investors and multinational companies. In the first half of the 1990s, Hungary received half of the entire foreign capital investment in the region, and big privatization progressed.

Poland also struggled with a lack of domestic capital for big privatization. In spite of its shock therapy approach, the process was extremely slow. By the end of the third year of transformation, a total of twenty-six large state companies had been sold, and only 556 of the 7,000 state-owned companies were privatized. Even by the fifth year of transformation, a mere 13 percent of large industrial firms had found a private owner.

The Czech "big bang" or voucher privatization offered a fast, easy, and fair solution. In November 1990, the government approved a draft law and soon 3,000 state-owned large-scale companies were transformed into joint-stock companies. Each adult citizen received 1,000 points for a nominal fee of $80; this authorized the purchase of thirty shares of state companies on the stock exchange, which opened in 1991. More than

13 million citizens participated in the first round of voucher privatization (with 1,000 companies) in early 1992, and in the second round (with 770 companies) in early 1994. The World Bank celebrated: "almost overnight Czechoslovakia will boast the biggest private sector in Eastern Europe" (World Bank, 1992: 3).

In reality, citizens preferred selling their units for cash: nearly 70 percent of all the vouchers were sold to privatization investment funds. Several hundred such funds were established in 1992, and two-thirds of the vouchers became owned by a single "fund-family." Banks controlled most of the investment funds, and they captured 35% of the first-round vouchers, and 24% of those in the second round. The four biggest banks in the Czech Republic owned 80 percent of total banking assets between 1993 and 1997. However, these banks, which accumulated the bulk of the vouchers, remained state-owned until 1998. The circle was thus completed: state-owned companies remained state-owned. Consequently, the reorganization and restructuring of the state sector did not happen, and the Czech economy declined into crisis in 1997–98. Voucher privatization, while a public relations coup, in practice failed and had to be followed by a real privatization process in the late 1990s.

The Baltic countries followed in the wake of the Central European countries, adopting the proven methods of employee buyouts, voucher privatization, and the sale of single companies. Small privatization went quickly and was mostly accomplished by the mid-1990s, but big privatization went much more slowly than planned. In Estonia, for example, the government planned to privatize the state-owned economy by the end of 1995. Small companies were mostly bought out by employees. Privatization also attracted Scandinavian and Finnish investors, but progress was not faster than in Central Europe. Estonia, using the Hungarian and East German state agency (Treuhandanstalt) pattern, had privatized only 52 of the 500 firms up for sale by 1994.

In Romania, as discussed above, only one-sixth of voucher-privatized companies became majority-private. However, the country began an "experimental" big privatization in 1993, placing thirty-two large companies up for sale. The Balkan countries had an even more difficult time because the bulk of foreign investments were channeled to the Central European countries, and only limited amounts arrived in the Balkans. Uniquely, Slovenia even restricted foreign investments to a maximum of 40 percent foreign ownership of shares.

Big privatization took a long time, and the goal of creating an entirely private-owned economy did not succeed. Although the concept of establishing a mixed economy, on the West European pattern, was rejected in most countries except Romania and Slovakia, in reality, a mixed economy was created. As a result of success in grass-roots and small privatization, and in the first steps toward big privatization, roughly half the economies of the Central European and Baltic countries were already in private hands by the mid-1990s. That figure reached 60% in Hungary and Albania, and 65% in Lithuania. The civil-war-ridden former Yugoslavia made hardly any progress. By the mid-1990s, Slovenia and Croatia had privatized about 40% of their economies, but the other independent republics had barely started down the road to transformation.

During the second half of the decade, big privatization continued. The most important development in the Czech Republic was the accomplishment of bank privatization in the summer of 2001. The telecommunications and gas sectors were also privatized. Estonia completed bank privatization only in 2000, and it privatized its railroads in 2002. Hungary achieved a breakthrough in the mid-1990s by privatizing the power, water, and telecommunications sectors. In 2002, the government accepted a plan to complete privatization in three years, after which only thirty-seven companies would remain in permanent state ownership. Latvia finished bank privatization by 2002, but the energy and transportation sectors remained state-owned. Poland began privatizing the telecommunications sector in November 1998. Bulgaria privatized the first banks in 1997 and its telecommunications company in 2002. Romania privatized the first two state banks only around the turn of the century, but 1,342 companies remained state-owned until 2002. Slovenia privatized the first large commercial bank only in 2002, and in 2003–04 it accepted a new program for privatizing major companies, including telecommunications. By the end of the century, big privatization was accomplished in Estonia, and the privatization of the huge utility, telecommunications, and transportation companies and banks began in 1999. Eesti Telecom, Estonia Gas, Narva Power, Optiva Bank, Rail Estonia, and the local railway company Edelaraudtee were all at least partly privatized between 1999 and 2003 (Jeffries, 2004: 171–73).

Before the eight Central European and Baltic countries joined the European Union, 75% to 80% of each economy was already privatized. This percentage was virtually identical with the proportion of the private sector in the EU-15 countries where, on average, 80% of the economy was in private hands. Slovenia, Romania, and Latvia had a somewhat lower share, 60–65%. The EU candidate countries also made great strides toward privatization: Albania and Bulgaria achieved a 75% private economy, Croatia and Macedonia 60%, and Bosnia-Herzegovina and Serbia around 50–55% (Jeffries, 2004: 166, 208, 245; EBRD, 2002; 2003, 16) (figure 2.1).

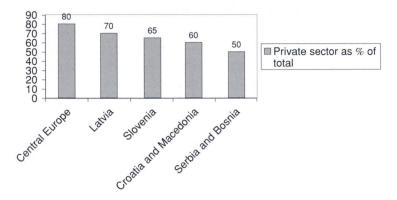

Figure 2.1 The private sector in Central and Eastern Europe, 2004

According to the Heritage Foundation's "economic freedom index," which is based on ten indicators, including trade policy, taxation, monetary policy, the banking system, foreign investment rules, property rights, wage and price controls, the role of the black market, and the government's share in consuming the output of the country, Central Europe and the Baltic countries reached a breakthrough in 2005: on a scale where 1 is the most free economy and 5 is the least free, Estonia reached an index of 1.65, Lithuania 2.18, Latvia 2.31, the Czech Republic 2.36, and Hungary and Slovakia 2.40 and 2.43, respectively. They were on the same footing as Italy, Spain, Portugal, and Japan. A more complex index lists Estonia, Lithuania, the Czech Republic, and Slovakia among the world's forty most free economies in 2007 (Economist, 2005b: 31; 2007: 31).

Policy mistakes and decline

The deregulation, marketization, and privatization process of the transformation of the early 1990s achieved important initial results. Nevertheless, it was peppered with policy errors, which proved overwhelming in the first half of the decade. Some of the most celebrated transforming countries, e.g., Poland and Czechoslovakia, advocated, realized, or at least talked about the fastest possible transformation – so-called shock therapy – not only in stabilization, where it was highly advisable, but also in marketization and privatization. Speed itself acquired a special value. Countries that advertised and introduced shock treatment, and liberalized trade and prices from one day to the next, were extolled by international financial institutions and Western governments. The World Bank "commonly measured the success of privatization programmes by how rapidly programmes were implemented" (Fine, Lapavitsas, and Pincus, 2001: 53). The architects of this policy, Leszek Balcerowicz and Václav Klaus, were loudly applauded by the West, which rewarded Poland – and Poland alone – for the shock therapy by writing off 50% of the country's official debt in April 1991. The American administration reduced Polish debts by 70%, and the remnants were written off in 1993.

Celebrating speed had its own logic. The World Bank, when reporting on the first half decade of transformation in the region, quoted the metaphor of Václav Havel, the Czech president, who announced that "it is impossible to cross a chasm in two leaps" (World Bank, 1996: 9). Leszek Balcerowicz used a different metaphor: "a fire should not be extinguished slowly" (*Rzeczpospolita*, October 9, 1992).

This idea, if not with the same poetic glamor, was repeated constantly. "Why do fast transitions improve the prospects for the development of capitalist democracy?" asked Valerie Bunce in her study for the Joint Economic Committee of the Congress of the United States. Her answer was simple: "Moving more rapidly to capitalism . . . will achieve the results faster" (Bunce, 1994: 60). János Kornai, a leading expert of socialist economy, argued in the same way in December 1992:

The severe decrease of production is a painful side effect of the healthy process of changing the system . . . Its cause is the transition from socialism to capitalism . . . To end the decline one should . . . accomplish even faster the task still remaining. (Kornai, in *Magyar Hirlap* (Budapest), December 24, 1992)

Marie Lavigne, looking back after a decade, was convinced of the "success of shock therapy." She concluded:

The major tenets of the "classical" Washington consensus reemerge unchallenged: "shock therapy" was the right policy. Wherever it has been consistently applied . . . outcomes were positive. (Lavigne, 2000: 480)

Around 2000, most of the countries had indeed recovered from the economic shock of the first years of transformation. However, fast, forced transformation caused severe economic decline. According to Kornai's interpretation, "transformational recession" was an unavoidable consequence of regime change. Kornai listed six main factors of the decline:

Shift from a sellers' to a buyers' market; contraction of investment; a shift in the composition of output; a shift in the composition of foreign trade; disruption of coordination; [and] enforcement of financial discipline. (Kornai, 1993: 2)

True: decline was unavoidable, and the factors Kornai lists were definitely behind it. The previously isolated, non-competitive economies, with low productivity and technological levels, suddenly had to face integration into the world market. Bartlomiej Kaminski expressed this view well: "The full extent of 'misdevelopment' can be observed directly only when central planning is replaced by markets" (1994: 15). When this happened, all of the weaknesses and obsolescence of the socialist economy became, indeed, a bitter daily experience. There is thus much truth in the view "that the widespread economic deterioration and breakdowns that had become epidemic to the region are part of the legacy of communism" (Hardt and Kaufman, 1994: x).

However, these interpretations reflect only a partial truth. The economic decline was not only the consequence of unavoidable factors and a bad legacy, but was also deepened by severe mistakes. One of them was the breakneck speed of shock treatment. John Kenneth Galbraith rejected this idea by stating that "Shock therapy should be applied only in medicine" (*Weltwoche*, October 15, 1992). The movement toward convertibility of currency is one example: it was an important and positive development. As part of the opening of the region, all of the countries committed to convertibility. Nevertheless, it was also mistaken to combine trade liberalization with radical currency revaluation. Convertibility was introduced in Poland and Yugoslavia immediately in 1990, and in Estonia after it gained independence in 1992. Gradual steps – for example, free currency exchange, but with quantitative limitations regulated by quotas – were introduced during the first years of the 1990s. Full convertibility was virtually accomplished by 1995–96 in the entire region.

However, the speed with which convertibility was achieved was far too fast and the devaluation too steep, as the World Bank's Report registered in 1996:

the data suggest that the initial devaluation in Poland and the former Czechoslovakia were four times larger than what would have been necessary to maintain purchasing power parity for Polish and Czech goods . . . the Bulgarian lev fell to one-seventh its purchasing power parity value.[1] (World Bank, 1996: 35)

Estonia followed the same policy. Having introduced the kroon as an independent currency, it was pegged to the German mark, but the established exchange rate seriously undervalued the currency (Nørgaard *et al.*, 1999: 129).

Richard Portes has spoken convincingly about "serious macroeconomic policy errors." Among them, he argued, was the

initial excessive devaluation of the currency . . . a move to convertibility must be accompanied by a sensible exchange rate policy: do not devalue excessively; peg initially: then go to a crawling peg. The opening to trade with the

---

[1] See the explanation of purchasing power parity in chapter 4, p. 121, n. 2.

West – with convertibility, low tariffs, and a few quantitative restrictions – was too abrupt . . . many important industrial branches became vulnerable. (Portes, 1993: 45–46)

Several experts condemned mistaken policy measures in agriculture and industry, and advocated a policy of state assistance, or an industrial policy of modernizing the mostly bankrupt state-owned sector. The conservative journal *The Economist* recommended an "intelligent" alliance of market and state (*The Economist*, September 12, 1992).[2]

Most of the transforming countries in the region, however, followed the opposite path. They had indeed, in their speedy run, written off the state-owned companies and considered them a potential good to sell, and thus a source of state income. They therefore left them alone, instead of reorganizing and modernizing them first and then selling them later. They sought to sell them as soon as possible, nearly regardless of price. Václav Klaus and Marek Dąmbrowski proudly resisted

interventionist pressures . . . the demand for a kind of government investment policy . . . [and] state influence on the branch structure of the economy . . . No industrial policy, no energy policy, no investment strategy. All will come about by itself. (Nove, 1995: 233)

---

[2] Paul Marer, speaking about policy mistakes that might have been avoided, discusses the agricultural dimension of the József Antall government's land privatization policy, which set aside a huge part of Hungary's land to be used for compensation, which consequently remained fallow. Furthermore a huge number of small, uneconomical plots were created based on the interwar populist notion that Hungary "should become the land of small and mid-sized farms whose owners would live in rural simplicity and happiness." Foreigners were forbidden to buy land, which limited investments. Marer also mentioned the policy against collective and state farms, which were considered to be the "undesirable legacy of the old regime," and were thus better dispatched as soon as possible. Other economic mistakes, such as eliminating subsidies and precipitously opening domestic markets led to a severe, though in some measures unavoidable, decline of agriculture. These policy mistakes characterized virtually the entire Central and East European region. Land consolidation took an even longer time in the Baltic countries and in some of the Balkan countries, which strongly contributed to a lack of cultivation and a severe decline of output (Marer, 1999: 169). Domenico Nuti also connected the decline "with the unnecessary consequence of policy failure . . . [most of all] the failure in government management of the state sector" (Nuti, 1993: 2). The economic minister of Saxony, K. Schommer, argued in a similar way in the same year: the state had to support enterprises. He suggested the formation of industrial holdings for non-privatized state-owned companies in former East Germany, and giving assistance to restructure and modernize. Industrial policy is more important for transforming countries than for established market economies (*Frankfurter Allgemeine Zeitung*, March 6, 1993).

Tadeusz Syryjczyk, the minister of industry in the first non-communist government of Poland, similarly stated that, "[t]he best industrial policy is not to have an industrial policy" (quoted in Kowalik, 1992: 4).

Neglecting industrial policy hit the "betrayed" state sector, which produced 50 to 70 percent of domestic output in 1989, hard. The negligence caused severe decline. The famous Gdańsk (formerly Lenin) Shipyard serves as a dramatic example.

Box 2.1 The Gdańsk Shipyard – the most Polish factory

One of the charming jewels in the Hanseatic League chain of cities, Gdańsk (formerly Danzig) had a hard, stormy history. This commercial port became, in succession, part of Prussia, part of Germany, an independent city-state, and then part of Poland. It was the place where World War II began. In 1844 a modern shipyard, the Kaiserliche Werft already existed on the outskirts of the city. By the late nineteenth century, the German shipyards Schichau Werft and, later, Danziger Werft were in operation on the spot. During World War II, both were heavily damaged. After the war, however, the Polish People's Republic built its own model factory, the Lenin Shipyard, on Ostrów Island along the left bank of the Martwa Wisła estuary of the Vistula River. The first freighter ship, the SS *Sołdek*, was launched in November 1947. At its zenith, this huge facility employed 17,000 employees and produced twenty ships per year. In the course of fifty-eight years of operation, nearly one thousand seagoing ships were launched.

The Gdańsk Shipyard gained worldwide fame through its courageous resistance against the state socialist regime: in December 1970, a spontaneous workers' revolt against a major price increase evolved into an uprising against the government. The workers occupied the shipyard and took to the streets. When demonstrations turned violent, 200 shops were destroyed, and public buildings were burned, with at least forty-four people killed and more than a thousand wounded. Ten years later, in the hot summer of 1980, the shipyard became the cradle of a new revolt and the free trade union, Solidarity. Gdańsk made history. The process which led to the collapse of the Berlin Wall, East European state socialism, and the entire Soviet bloc began in this shipyard. Worker heroes and symbols of resistance such as Lech Wałęsa and Andrzej Gwiazda worked here and achieved international fame.

Solidarity finally won its battle in 1989. Polish state socialism collapsed peacefully in the summer of that year after its first, semi-free elections. In 1990, the simple electrician from the shipyard, Lech Wałęsa, became president of Poland.

Nevertheless, this historical victory proved fatal for the Gdańsk Shipyard. In 1990, like many other state-owned factories in Poland, it was transformed into a joint-stock company with 31 percent employee ownership and 61 percent retained by the state. The first Solidarity government introduced a harsh program of "shock treatment," opening the economy from one day to the next and launching privatization. The Gdańsk Shipyard, proud of its political traditions and its connections with Solidarity and President Wałęsa, resisted change. Restructuring of the shipyards in neighboring Gdynia and Szczecin progressed well, but Gdańsk continued to rely on untied subsidies and tax relief. Even though the former Lenin Shipyard had the best prospects of the three to be renewed as a competitive factory, its productivity declined. It took two years to produce a mid-sized container ship in Gdańsk, compared with six months in other yards. Moreover, the management planned to add 6,000 new workers to the existing 17,000 in the early years of transformation.

Market capitalism proved to be a much stronger adversary than the riot police or the army of the Polish People's Republic. The shipyard waited for the government to adjust to the company's requirements. This inertia, in one sense connected to the spectacular political success of the 1980s, led to a total economic failure during the 1990s. The number of employees dropped from 17,000 to 3,000, and annual production declined from twenty ships per year to three. The financial losses became unstoppable, reaching $30 million in 1995 alone, and totaling $100 million by 1996.

Wałęsa himself said the shipyard should become a Solidarity museum. By 1998, bankruptcy officials were preparing to sell and partially close the company. The workers were confident that it would not happen to Gdańsk, and reacted according to the old pattern: they marched on Warsaw to protest, occupied and damaged ministry buildings, and threatened a general strike. In 2005, when the government organized a twenty-fifth anniversary celebration of the historic Gdańsk events of 1980, the workers protested. They produced banners that read "Gdańsk Shipyard, Robbed and Destroyed," and "No Cause for Celebration... Cause for Protest." Andrzej Gwiazda, one of the top workers' leaders of the August days in 1980, added: "it was the working people who brought down the 'workers' republic' – and the workers who were buried in the rubble." One of Solidarity's main spiritual leaders, Father Henryk Jankowski, Wałęsa's confessor, stated at the service held on the anniversary: "The recommendations of Brussels... and Washington... threaten Poland's identity and sovereignty... We are filled with horror when laws are imposed upon us that are thought up by anti-Catholic Masons, Jewish bankers, and hell-born atheistic socialists."

These protests did not help. The workers and managers had to learn that they must adjust to the market (Keat, 2003; *Stocznia Gdańska* webpage, 2005; History News Network, August 14, 2005; *Gazeta Wyborcza*, August 25, 2005; *The Independent* (London), August 29, 2005).

The decline could have been better controlled and restrained by more gradual transformation, the incremental opening of the domestic market and making progress toward convertibility of currency, and a greater state role in guiding the difficult conversion. As Shafiqul Islam argued:

A growth oriented, sector sensitive... gradualist approach has a much better chance at controlling inflation, promoting recovery, and putting the transition economies on a sustainable path toward capitalism than the "creationist model" being tried currently. (Islam and Mandelbaum, 1993: 2110)

Counterfactual analysis to measure the difference between the unavoidable decline and the actual one is hardly possible, but I will return in chapter 5 to certain further aspects of this issue. However, some of the most successful transformations, e.g., the Slovenian and Chinese ones, each following different paths, offer some convincing comparisons. Slovenia, as discussed before, did not rush privatization, but modernized and restructured the state sector, which represented half of the economy until the end of the century, thereby achieving good growth results. China, while opening the door for private and foreign companies, did not begin privatizing the state-owned sector until an efficient private sector was firmly established, and it followed a successful growth-oriented policy. The triumphant Asian modernization model, which passed from Japan to China, via Korea and Taiwan, was characterized by strong state intervention, including selecting and assisting winners. Countries that followed that different road could avoid or at least minimize economic decline.

During the 1990s, East and South East Asia was the only developing region to escape the forced Washington consensus policy. The countries of that region imposed restrictions on imports, often discouraged foreign investments, controlled capital inflow, and owned significant parts of the economy. In Asia, indeed,

governments... were shown to have intervened systematically and strategically to promote manufacturing competitiveness, to enhance technological dynamism and to deepen industrial structure. (Fine, Lapavitsas, and Pincus, 2001: xi, 87)

The World Bank's 1993 report on *The East Asian Miracle* strongly underlined the role of the state in successful modernization. The Bank's 1998 *World Development Report* also stressed the importance of the state in promoting industrialization, including the creation of relevant infrastructure. The new recognition emerged slowly and was still only partially accepted around of the end of the first decade of Central and East European transformation. Some experts, beginning mostly in the mid- to late 1990s, preferred the Asian road and recommended a similar policy for Central and Eastern Europe.

In a January 1998 lecture in Helsinki, Stiglitz argued, as he had before, for state regulations, and consequently for a new post-Washington consensus:

> The state has an important role to play in appropriate regulations, industry policy, social protection and welfare . . . we should not see the state and market as substitutes . . . the government should see itself as a complement to markets, undertaking those actions that make markets fulfill their function better. (Stiglitz, quoted by Fine, Lapavitsas, and Pincus, 2001: 3)

Several economists, however, argue that the Chinese way of transformation was not an option in Central and Eastern Europe. The World Bank, in its 1996 report entitled *From Plan to Market*, argued that China and Vietnam were able "to reform in a partial, phased manner and still grow rapidly," achieving "spectacular growth," but gradualism, the report maintained, was not an option in Central and Eastern Europe:

> This chaotic environment, combining a disintegrating economy with a rapidly weakening government, allowed no scope for gradual reform. For these countries the all-out approach was the only one available. (World Bank, 1996: 11, 19, 21)

Some experts on the Central and East European transformation shared this view.[3]

These arguments, however, neglect some crucial points: chaos, disintegration, and a weak state were not the mere consequence of some kind of

---

[3] Stanislaw Gomulka has stated: "in the countries of central Europe and the former Soviet Union the rapid speed was forced principally by the initial conditions of their deep and all-embracing (economic, institutional and political) crisis" (2000: 73). Barry Eichengreen also rejects the argument that gradual Chinese reform, i.e., "adjusting without serious recession," could have worked in Central and Eastern Europe. In his explanation, it was not an option because: "China's state sector was smaller. Only one-fifth of the labor force was employed by the state, in contrast to upward of 90 percent in Eastern Europe. The Chinese economy was heavily agricultural, which meant that it could be marketized simply by giving the farmers right to their land and deregulating agricultural prices" (Eichengreen, 2007: 317). In László Csaba's argument, the Chinese route was not an alternative for Central and Eastern Europe because it was "driven by a series of factors that are not replicable in other countries." Among them were exceptionally huge foreign direct investment that ranged from $40 to 45 billion per year, "a millennium-long tradition of decentralization," the survival of commercial spirit, and a gigantic transfer of labor from agriculture to industry (Csaba, 2005: 276–93).

"natural disaster," but, at least partly, the consequence of the road chosen. Capital inflow, labor restructuring, and various kinds of market legacies existed in some of the Central European countries as well. Furthermore, gradual reform, which avoided tragic decline, worked not only in China, but also in industrially advanced Slovenia, where the transformational crises and its social pain were by far the mildest in the region:

Slovenia succeeded, in a balanced manner, in all . . . areas simultaneously. Competitive industries and better social indicators did not come at the cost of macroeconomic stability. Dominant neo-corporative institutions, such as legally enforced negotiated agreement–labor relationship, and extended collective agreements have so far been able to deliver the compromises required for a balanced and inclusive agenda. (Bohle and Greskovits, 2007: 17)

Stiglitz maintains that the speed of the transformation was a choice variable, and that choosing a high speed was a major mistake. He has also remarked that "the post-Washington consensus recognizes that privatization was not well planned . . . the advocates of privatization may have overestimated the benefits and underestimated the costs" (Stiglitz, 1999).

Some of the countries chose the wrong path to privatization. Voucher privatization, quite widespread in the region, did not change real ownership and preserved the role of the state, while insider privatization to managers and workers – which took place in most of South Eastern Europe, especially the former Yugoslav republics, where workers' ownership was a legacy of the special Yugoslav system – could not generate investment and restructuring. Privatization to outsiders has been associated with 50 percent more restructuring than privatization to insiders (Papazoglou, 2005: 99). Croat economic experts maintain that

The strategy of privatization has not contributed considerably to restructuring . . . privatization policy . . . should be considered as a cause of stagnation . . . Uncertainty has lead to the collapse of big companies and business systems . . . Privatization by a single move transformed the Croatian economy and society from the big potential winner into the big real loser. (Teodorović *et al.*, 2005: 18, 54, 323)

Some analysts have added that "privatization has been treated as an end itself rather than a means" (Fine, Lapavitsas, and Pincus, 2001: 54).

The speedy opening up of the countries was also a decisive mistake because it happened before the restructuring and modernization of the economy. Central and Eastern Europe, as I argued in chapter 1, declined into an expanded peripheral structural crisis in the mid-1970s, and could not adjust to the new requirements of the world economy. This decline led to a significant slowing down in the late 1970s and during the 1980s,

Table 2.1 Industrial output and animal stock in 1993 as a percentage of 1989

Crude steel[a]	53.7
Sugar beet[b]	45.7
Cotton yarn[a]	38.8
Synthetic fiber[c]	35.0
Number of cattle stock[d]	51.3
Number of poultry stock[d]	51.4
Number of pig stock[d]	58.5
Industrial production[a]	62.7
The average of the above eight sectors	49.6

Source: Based on Mitchell, 1998.

Notes: All averages are unweighted.

a: Bulgarian, Czech, Hungarian, Polish, and Romanian average.

b: Czech, Hungarian, and Romanian average.

c: Czech, Polish, and Romanian average.

d: Bulgarian, Czech, Hungarian, and Yugoslav average.

and caused a collapse after the sudden opening up of the countries in the 1990s. It was at least partly avoidable, had a well-planned state policy of modernization been implemented. In other words, it is a mistake to consider the sharp economic decline of Central and Eastern Europe a mere "transformational crisis." This was only one of the elements: the other was a mistaken policy.

The crisis was also the culmination of the structural crisis which hit the world economy, and which was unsolved in the state socialist countries before the collapse, and only deepened after it. The adopted policy did not take adjusting to this situation into account. Most of the major mistakes were the consequence of the ideologically based, one-sided de-etatization, which fatally weakened state governance when it was badly needed in the difficult time of transformation. The blind belief – also ideologically based – in the automatism of market forces in countries where a full-fledged market was not yet in existence had similarly devastating consequences.

Unavoidable transformational decline, as a consequence of these severe mistakes, became much steeper and sharper, and much more devastating, than necessary. A large part of the economy collapsed: agriculture in the most dramatic and comprehensive fashion, but also several leading sectors of industry. Table 2.1 clearly shows the dramatic 40% to 50% decline in various areas of the economy. The output of several basic industrial and agricultural products, as well as the animal stock, suffered a devastating

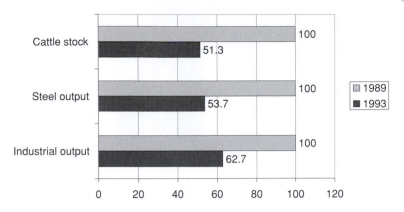

Figure 2.2 Transformational decline in five countries, 1989–1993

decline and were virtually halved during the first years of transformation. Industrial output in five transforming countries dropped nearly 40% until 1993 (figure 2.2). In the very first year of Poland's transformation, industry declined by 23%, but by mid-1992 it was 40% below the 1989 level. In Albania, industrial output dropped in the single year of 1992 by more than 51%, and the next year by another 10%. In 1993, compared to 1990, Albanian industrial production had declined by 77% (Cohen, 1994: 58). In Romania, after the dramatic decline of the early 1990s – in 1992 alone, industry dropped by 22% – output resumed its decline again in the late 1990s (by 6%, 17%, and 9% in 1997, 1998, and 1999, respectively). In Croatia, industrial output dropped by half between 1989 and 1996. In Czechoslovakia and Hungary, industrial production declined by 36% and 40%, respectively, during the first three years of transformation. The Baltic countries, which were part of the huge Soviet economy, experienced the most dramatic decline after having reestablished independence and introducing a free market economy: the industrial output of Estonia dropped by 36%, 19%, and 3%, respectively, during the first three years, 1992, 1993, and 1994. Latvia experienced the same collapse: industrial production declined by 38%, 10%, and 7%, respectively, and Lithuania's industrial output by 1994 hardly surpassed one-third of the 1991 level.

The most dramatic decline was in agriculture: in Hungary, agricultural output declined by 10%, 10%, and 23% in 1990, 1991, and 1992, respectively (figure 2.3). In Bulgaria, agricultural output declined by more than 50% in 1992 and 1993 alone. Latvia's output dropped by 29%, 18%, and 15% in 1992, 1993, and 1994, respectively. In Lithuania, in the same years, the decline was 23%, 6%, and 20% (EBRD, 1996; 2000).

As a consequence, unemployment climbed in Poland and Bulgaria from 0% to 16% between 1989 and 1993, reaching 13% in Hungary and 29% in

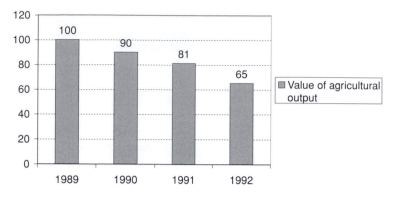

Figure 2.3 Hungarian agricultural decline, 1989–1992

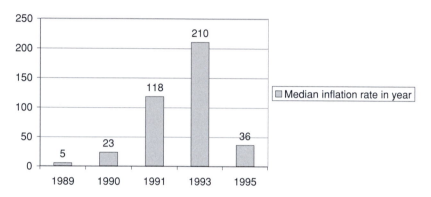

Figure 2.4 Inflation rates in Central and Eastern Europe, 1989–1995

Albania and Macedonia. Just as a high temperature signals sickness in the human body, inflation, in some cases hyperinflation, reflected the ailing economy of the region. The middle value, or median, rate of inflation in Central and Eastern Europe, including the Baltic countries, jumped from 5% in 1989 to 23%, 118%, and 210% annually between 1990 and 1993, respectively, then declining to 85% and 36% in the following two years. Behind these averages, actual inflation rates reached nearly 600% in Poland in 1990 and 200% to 250% in Romania in 1992 and 1993, surpassed 1,000% in Estonia, Lithuania, and Macedonia in 1992, and was more than 1,500% in Croatia in 1993 (EBRD, 2000) (figure 2.4). Economic growth, which slowed during the 1980s, was followed by sharp decline.

During the early 1990s, while income in Western Europe increased slightly and China's income level jumped by nearly 50%, the economic decline in Central and Eastern Europe was dramatic, totaling 20% to 30%, with exceptional 44% to 72% declines in Romania and Yugoslavia. Lithuania's income level dropped by 41%, and the three Baltic countries

Table 2.2 Decline of GDP/capita in transforming countries in the early 1990s

Country	1989	The nadir in the early 1990s	The nadir in % of 1989
Albania	2,482[a]	1,701	69
Bulgaria	6,217	4,767	77
Czechoslovakia (and former Czechoslovakia)	8,729	6,858	79
Hungary	6,787	5,509	81
Poland	5,685	4,739	83
Romania	3,890	1,083	28
Yugoslavia (and former Yugoslavia)	5,917	3,322	56
Central and Eastern Europe	5,902	4,528	77
Former Soviet Union	7,078	3,899	55
Western Europe	15,880	16,538[b]	104
China	1,827	2,653[b]	145
Central and Eastern Europe as % of Western Europe	37	27	

Source: Maddison, 1995a: 150; 2001.
Note: a: 1990.
     b: 1995.

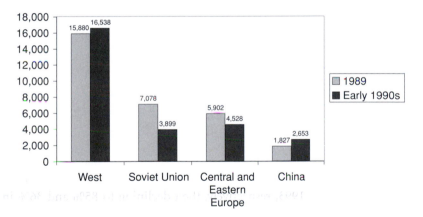

Figure 2.5 GDP/capita, nadir, early 1990s

together experienced a 32% decline of per capita GDP (Economist Intelligence Unit, 1996; 1998) (figure 2.5).

Subregional differences made the decline sharper and more painful in the Balkans. While the lowest level of GDP in 1992 was, on average, 17% below the 1989 level in Central Europe, it dropped by 28% in the Balkans. Furthermore, recovery in Central Europe was roughly accomplished in the late 1990s, while in the Balkans it remained 25% below the 1989 level until

1998. Industrial output in the Balkans dropped to 50% of the 1989 level at its nadir, compared with a 30% drop in Central Europe (Papazoglou, 2005: 10, 14).

Decline was halted, first in Poland in the summer of 1992 and in Estonia the same year, but in general by 1993. Moderate growth began in 1994, averaging 3.7 percent growth among the thirteen countries of the region. Inflation began to decrease, and from 1997, on average, it dropped to an annual single-digit figure. The drama, however, was not yet over. In 1997, rapid inflation returned to Bulgaria and Romania: the former experienced more than 1,000% hyperinflation, the latter a more moderate, but still huge, 154% inflation. Compared to the Central European mean inflation rate of 11% in 1997, South Eastern Europe experienced a resurgence of inflation. The mean reached 250% again. However, that was the last year of triple-digit inflation in the region (EBRD, 2000). Although the decline and social pain were high and would have been at least partly avoidable, the adjustment to the European Union and to the globalized international economy gained momentum in Central and Eastern Europe.

CHAPTER 3

Toward better times: the European Union and its policy of eastward enlargement

By the mid-1990s, Central and East European transformation had gradually consolidated. Institution-building had made progress, macroeconomic stabilization was succeeding, democracy and a market economy were taking root. Most of the countries had achieved economic growth and had begun recovering from the sharp decline of the first years of transformation. Progress, however, was uneven: the Central European countries advanced steadily while the Balkans remained painfully behind. At the end of the twentieth century, Ilya Prizel of Johns Hopkins University noted:

Any traveler who . . . cross[ed] the border between Central Europe and Eastern Europe [the successor states of the Soviet Union and the Balkans] cannot help but be struck by the enormous and ever growing contrast between these two groups of erstwhile communist states . . . [The collapse of communism] in Byzantine Europe did not engender a drive toward social modernization but rather pushed these societies back to the nationalist rhetoric of earlier days. (Prizel, 1999: 1, 9)

The contrast between these two regions was indeed enormous, and the pace of change erratic. Major turmoil gripped most of former Yugoslavia. In 1991, the multinational republic dissolved and a bloody civil war lasted until 1995, damaging several parts of the country, especially Bosnia-Herzegovina and parts of eastern Croatia. The Kosovo crisis came to a head at the end of the 1990s. Serbia launched a destructive war, and the NATO response devastated Serbia. After Kosovo, the war escalated to Macedonia as well. International pressure and peacekeeping forces were able to stabilize the situation. But the dissolution of the former Yugoslavia resumed at the beginning of the twenty-first century, with the emergence of a virtually independent Kosovo and an independent Montenegro.

The status of the political, economic, and security situations was mixed throughout the region after the first transformation years. Some countries saw twelve changes of government in twelve years. Economic decline returned to Romania to the point that in 1997, 1998, and 1999 GDP decreased by 6.1%, 5.4%, and 3.2%, respectively. Severe GDP decline also characterized Bulgaria in 1996 and 1997 (nearly 11% and 7% respectively). The Czech Republic experienced similar GDP decline in three consecutive years between 1997 and 1999. In 1997, hyperinflation (1,082%) returned in Bulgaria, while Romanian inflation reached 154% that year (EBRD, 2001: 59, 61). Albania sank into chaos in 1996–97 with the collapse of pyramid investment schemes and "charity foundations," which had borrowed from the public at up to 300 percent monthly interest, draining virtually the entire domestic savings of the population. General unrest led to a virtual civil war in the country. Order was reestablished with the help of international forces (Muço and Minxhozi, 2003: 197–98).

Box 3.1   The Albanian "pyramid scheme civil war"

The "pyramid scheme" is a fraud. In most countries it is illegal, although since the early twentieth century, when Charles Ponzi introduced it in the United States, it has been used from time to time to attract people who are practically illiterate in financial business. The scheme is simple: it promises profitable investments on short-term contracts, for example, 20% interest for investors on a thirty-day contract, with the promise of 1,000% profit over a short period of time. The entire project and its early success are based on the exponential increase of investors who want to get rich in a few months, and who flock to invest ever greater sums. The fund managers, at the outset, pay the medievally usurious rates of 20 percent a month from the inflow of money from the new investors. The scheme spreads like wildfire.

In late 1996, several Albanian private funds, borrowing from Russia, offered this business to the public. The population of one of the poorest countries of Europe, isolated from it for its entire history, had scant knowledge about financial businesses. They became intoxicated by the possibility of huge profit and, after so much suffering, naively believed that the promised land of market economy had been created. Because the interest was paid out for a while, tens of thousands of people rushed to invest. Most of them immediately reinvested their gains. Several people even sold their homes and livestock to raise cash to invest. The incredible amount of $1.2 billion was ultimately invested in the pyramid funds.

Such schemes naturally must collapse after a while. Since no profitable investment is involved, only money from new investors makes it possible to pay interest. After a certain time there is no more income to pay the return and the pyramid collapses (with a hefty amount stolen by managers of the funds). That happened in Albania on January 24, 1997. Hundreds of thousands of people lost their entire life savings, and sometimes all their assets. Rumors spread that the government was part of the fraud.

The desperate people revolted: 35,000 people flooded Tirana's main square, and the mob clashed with the police and army and burned government buildings in Lushnje. Half a million weapons were looted from army and police arsenals, and a war erupted in the southern part of the country, which soon fell under the control of the rebels. President Sali Berisha promised to repay all the losses by February, and 118 fund managers and officials were arrested. When the protests continued, a state of emergency was declared on March 2, 1997. The uprising became unstoppable, however, fueled by tribal conflicts between south and north, and participation by organized mafias and gangs. The death toll reached 1,500 people. Albania's cities declined into chaos, and 10,000 people escaped to Italy. The Albanian currency lost half of its value, and GDP declined by 8 percent.

In the face of a civil war situation, the United Nations Security Council on April 15 organized "Operation Alba," sending 7,000 mostly Italian troops to restore order. The government and president were removed by the riot, and life in Albania slowly returned to normal (*World News*, January 25, 1997).

One of the most successful transformation countries, Hungary and the Baltic countries suffered a huge budgetary crisis and major slowing down when previous growth rates halved in 2006–08. Transitory halts and corrections were unavoidable during the entire transformation period.

Nevertheless, the worst part of navigating through dangerous whitewater was probably over for most countries. The boat of transformation still had not reached quiet waters everywhere, but recovery and positive results prevailed throughout the region from the mid-1990s on.

The European Union's interest in enlargement and integration

The European Union played an important role in the change for the better in Central and Eastern Europe. What was the interest of the Union and what was its role in the successful transformation of the region?

To be able to answer these questions, one has to recall briefly the beginning of, and some main chapters in, the history of the European Union. The idea of integration of Europe and the foundation of a federal European state emerged after World War II. The bitter lessons of wars, the slaughter of roughly 60 million Europeans, genocide, the elimination of entire minorities, occupations, and suffering generated a spontaneous movement at the end of the war. One of the first intellectual endeavors, the manifesto of two anti-fascist Italian political prisoners, called for the federal reorganization of postwar Europe in 1943. Altiero Spinelli and Ernesto Rossi dreamed about a federal Europe which would manage the economy and a European army, the guarantee against economic nationalism and war (Spinelli and Rossi in Lipgens, 1985).

Cooperation and integration of the European countries were in the air at the end of the war. The Benelux (Belgium, Netherland, and Luxembourg) governments in exile signed an agreement in 1944 to establish an economic union from 1948. The Nordic countries began organizing economic cooperation and founded the Nordic Council. European movements engulfed the continent. The United Europe Movement in Britain, the Catholic and socialist United States of Europe movements in France, the Europa Bund in Germany, and several others led to the foundation of the ten-member Council of Europe in Strasbourg in 1949.

Another decisive factor of integration was provided by the emerging Cold War and the polarization of the world system. The fear of the Soviet Union and the spread of communism mobilized Winston Churchill, and the Truman administration soon afterward, to strengthen Western Europe through integration into a federal state. In his famous Zurich speech in September 1946, Churchill called for the "recreation of Europe," and for the countries of Europe to "build a kind of United States of Europe," with common citizenship. He also suggested an end to retribution, and a French–German partnership as the basis for unification (Churchill, 1943–49). Alan Dulles used similar rhetoric when he suggested the formation of a United States of Europe in 1948. He called the United States of America the only force able to bring the Europeans together in a union, as a "defensive bulwark against communism" (Dulles, [1948] 1993: 111).

President Truman expressed the American goal in March 1947 when he asked Congress to support countries which "are resisting attempted subjugation by armed minorities or by outside pressures." He argued: "the seeds of totalitarian regimes are nurtured by misery and want" (Truman, 1955–56: 106). The Truman Doctrine was followed by the Marshall Plan of 1948, offering $13 billion in aid for European reconstruction and prosperity. One of the prerequisites of the aid was the cooperation of the recipient countries: the Organization for European Economic Co-operation (OEEC) was founded to facilitate this cooperation and to administer the program.

Jean Monnet, the *éminence grise* of European integration, worked out a plan, named after Robert Schuman, the French minister of foreign affairs who launched it, which led to the foundation in 1951 of the European Coal and Steel Community of France, Germany, Italy, and the three Benelux countries. West European integration was underway (Urwin, 1995).

A Dutch proposal in 1953 recommended further development to create a common market in the six countries. Negotiations began in 1955, and the Treaty of Rome was signed in March 1957: the European Economic Community was established. Although the founding fathers of the Community aimed for a federal reorganization of Western Europe, the road toward this goal was via economic integration, the formation of a free trade zone, a customs union, and then a common market. Economic integration gained momentum during the following decades and led to a successfully integrated West European economic system, with a single market, free movement of labor and capital, a common currency, and a central bank: the European Union.

Meanwhile, the Community gradually enlarged. From the original six members, it became a Europe of nine when Britain, Ireland, and Denmark joined in 1974. Beginning in the early to mid-1980s, the Community added new members Greece, Spain, and Portugal. From the late 1980s, a new rush towards Europe was signaled by the application of Turkey (1987), Austria (1989), Cyprus and Malta (1990), Sweden (1991), and Finland, Switzerland, and Norway (1992). Partly because of European refusal, and partly because of rejection in national referendums, only three new countries – Sweden, Austria, and Finland – had joined by 1995 (Dinan, 1994; El-Agraa, 2004).

The European Union had twelve members and was making an impressive run toward further integration when state socialism collapsed in Poland and Hungary, and then throughout Central and Eastern Europe in 1989. The central goal of the former Soviet bloc countries was to join Europe at once. Was it in European interests to accept them? The obstacles were huge. The countries of the region had just emerged from a one-party, non-parliamentary regime, with poor human rights records and weak democratic legacies. Their economies, as discussed in chapter 1, worked as non-market systems, and were nearly entirely state-owned. The countries of the region were debt-ridden and economically bankrupt, their environmental record was tragic, and their infrastructure remained at least half a century behind. The income level of the region, on average, reached only 32 percent of the European Union's average in 1995. If one counts all the twelve candidates who knocked the door of the Union, their combined economic weight was roughly equal to that of the Netherlands. None of them would be a net contributor to the Union's budget. Moreover, they required huge amounts of assistance. Agriculture still represented an important part of their economy. The agricultural population accounted for 22% of the active population in Central and Eastern Europe (35% in Romania, 27% in Poland, and roughly 6% in the Czech Republic and Hungary). Agriculture produced about 9% of the GDP of the region (21% in Romania, 5% in Slovenia).

In addition, with the downfall of communism, including the collapse of the Soviet Union itself, one of the main motivations to integrate Western Europe into a strong and flourishing Union, the Cold War, also disappeared. Within the EU, opponents of further "deepening" integration, most notably Britain's Prime Minister Thatcher, argued for cooperation on a strictly intergovernmental level. Disintegration became a possibility, but just the opposite happened. The Community shifted into full gear to drive toward a higher stage of integration from the late 1980s on.

As Jacques Delors, the visionary president of the Commission of the Community, stated in a speech in Bruges in 1989, there was more reason than ever to deepen integration. His generation of European leaders was still thinking of political unification and federalization, and the indivisibility of European security. Further economic integration could be a "bridge towards political integration," Delors argued:

The Twelve cannot control history but they are now in a position to influence it once again. They did not want Europe to be cut in two at Yalta and made hostage in the Cold War. They did not, nor do they, close the door to other European countries... The present upheavals in Eastern Europe are changing the nature of our problems... All the countries of Europe will benefit from the stimulus and the advantages of a single market... [The Community has to help] the countries of Eastern Europe to modernize their economies. (Delors, [1989] 1998: 59, 66)

European leaders felt moral obligations. The West had left Central and Eastern Europe alone and had remained silent when some of those countries revolted. The "Yalta guilt" complex became a factor of the European reaction. Europe felt it must not "disappoint the trust that these countries have put in us," added German chancellor Helmut Kohl (Baun, 2000: 10).

However, Europe's readiness to consider the future membership of the Central and East European countries was not only or even primarily a moral question. A new incentive, or even imperative, emerged: globalization. In the new world economy, Delors stressed in the same speech, "nations cannot act alone." The reality in the new world system, he argued, was the ... "growing interdependence of our economies [and] the internationalization of the financial world... [which make] full national sovereignty" a fiction. Europe has to consider

worldwide geopolitical and economic trends... [it is] losing its place as the economic and political center of the world... European market and common policies have supported national efforts to adapt to the new world economic order... Europe is once again a force to be reckoned with. (Delors, [1989] 1998: 58, 59, 62)

If globalization required a strong, more integrated Europe, further enlargement offered a huge advantage to the Union. Above all, it would absorb 100 million new, hungry consumers, a rapidly growing market with much greater possibility for exports and strengthening the economy of scale and competitiveness. Europe might become a bigger global actor, with more influence in world trade and in international organizations. Barry Eichengreen compares the situation with the postwar American experience: after World War II, the economic center of the United States shifted to the South, and the country benefited from the South's lower level of unionization, more competitive wage level, more flexible labor market, and liberal land-use policy, which helped "greenfield" investments. "It is fair to ask whether the EU's expansion to the East could have a similar invigorating effect" (Eichengreen, 2007: 406). Indeed, it did, as I will return to in a more detailed discussion of this issue in chapter 4, in connection with the role of foreign direct investment in Central and Eastern Europe.

The question of enlargement toward the East emerged at exactly the same time as the need for major restructuring of the European economy became unavoidable. During the last decades of the twentieth century, three global players represented three-quarters of the world economy. Besides the United States, a strong and rising Asian economy embodied the new challenge for Europe. After Japan and the "small tigers," a third wave elevated China and India into the group of main players.

While the United States traditionally had a Latin American backyard, and the Asian economic center was also surrounded by subordinated and economically integrated countries, Europe, the third player, was not only fragmented into several small and medium-sized countries; it also lacked a network of surrounding economies with cheap labor and resources. The opportunity that opened in 1989 for networking in the immediate neighborhood, for decreasing production costs, and for strengthening competitiveness on the world market offered a great advantage for restructuring the West European economy.

Western Europe could not appropriately respond to the challenge of globalization during the 1970s–80s. Its postwar extensive growth model was exhausted and the introduction of innovation-based intensive growth model was needed. After 1989, Central and Eastern Europe offered a crucial opportunity for Western Europe to stabilize and fortify its position as one of the economic superpowers in the globalized world economy.

This interest, paradoxically enough, merged with the goal of those countries of the European Community, chiefly Britain and Denmark, which opposed further integration and federalization, and which considered a bold enlargement toward the East to be a hindrance to the integration of Europe into a federal reorganization. They advocated enlargement as a brake against further and deeper integration.

In December 1990, negotiations of the twelve member countries began on complete economic and monetary unification in Brussels. The agreement was signed in Maastricht in February 1992 as a new stage in the integration and foundation of the European Union. In principle, the Treaty of the European Union opened the door for non-member countries: "Any European State which respects the principles set out in Article 6 (1) may apply to become a Member of the Union."

At the same time, when the European Council met in Maastricht in December 1991, the Union signed the Europe Agreement with Poland, Hungary, and Czechoslovakia. This agreement was a new version of "association" agreements, signed several times before with Turkey, Greece, Spain, and Portugal. It was suggested by Thatcher as early as November 1989. The next month, the Strasbourg summit decided to work out proposals, and in April 1990 the Dublin meeting of the European Council approved the outlines of the association agreements with the former communist countries. The main elements of the Europe Agreements introduced political dialogue, free trade and freedom of movement, economic, cultural, and financial cooperation, and appropriate institution-building for joint decision-making. It also introduced immediate economic assistance for associated countries.

In May 1992, negotiations on a similar Europe Agreement began with Bulgaria and Romania and, somewhat later, with Slovenia and the Baltic states. They took effect between 1994 and 1996. The agreements envisioned free trade within a decade and export barriers lowered (in an asymmetric way, with earlier reduction by the European Union than by the Eastern countries) within six years, with the exception of the so-called sensitive sectors of textiles, steel, agricultural products, and coal, economic fields where Central and Eastern Europe had some comparative advantages. Until early 1993, 40 percent of the exports of Poland, Hungary, and Czechoslovakia were subject to some form of restraint.

Capital movement and profit repatriations were freed. The associated countries also committed to bringing their laws into line with the Union's legislation. The Union agreed to give technical and economic assistance. Joint parliamentary committees were also established. In the summer of 1994, the Union's Commission clearly declared the goal of the Europe Agreements:

The goal for the period before accession should be the progressive integration of the political and economic systems, as well as the foreign and security policies of the associated countries and the Union ... to create an increasingly unified area. (European Commission, 1994)

The countries that signed the Europe Agreement established institutions to coordinate government actions which were required by the Union. In Poland, the coordinating office was called the Government Plenipotentiary for European Integration and Foreign Assistance. The government approved a "Program of Legal and Economic Adjustment to the Requirements of the Europe Agreement" with a time table. Specialized departments were established at the various ministries to harmonize adoption work. Offices prepared detailed reviews on existing legislation, assessing their compatibility with the relevant Union legislation. Within five years, roughly 1,400 draft legislations were prepared in Poland. The progress toward integration to the Union began (Gower and Redmond, 2000: 50–51).

Even before the collapse of the Berlin Wall, the Union enthusiastically welcomed the Polish and Hungarian events of 1988–89; at its Rhodes and then Madrid summits in December 1988 and June 1989, the Union expressed its readiness to assist the movement to democracy and to support economic reform in the two pioneer countries of transformation. After the Group-7 summit in Paris, the Union's Commission coordinated the aid efforts of the twenty-four OECD countries. The main program of assistance to promote market reforms, "Poland and Hungary Aid for Economic Restructuring" (PHARE), was launched in December 1989, and then reoriented to serve broader economic and political goals in the entire region. In 1990, ECU (European Currency Unit) 300 million was provided for Poland and Hungary, but another 200 million was added for the other transforming countries. The PHARE assistance increased: in 1991 it reached ECU 774 million, and by 1992, 1 billion, and continued to provide roughly €1.5 billion per year for the next few years. From 1992 on, ten transforming countries had already received assistance from the fund. Between 1990 and 1998, PHARE commitments totaled €8.9 billion, but real payments reached only €5.6 billion, 63 percent of commitments.

The Union made a series of bilateral trade agreements with Hungary starting in September 1988. By 1993, similar agreements were signed with all the transforming countries. As a consequence of institutionalized connections, trade between the Central and East European countries and the Union increased dramatically. Between 1989 and 1995, Union exports to the ten transforming countries in the region increased by 131 percent. By the latter year, the Union's net surplus surpassed $9 billion. Between 1992 and 1997, 83 percent of the Union trade surplus originated from the transforming countries. On the other hand, the transforming countries accumulated an ECU 64 billion trade deficit. This was partly the consequence of the Union's continuing protection against those items – textiles, coal, and steel – which the Central and East European countries produced at a comparative advantage and had available for export. Of the Union's 349 anti-dumping proceedings, 38 were filed against Central and Eastern European countries, and 37 percent of those were connected with the iron and steel industry in the 1990s. In 1991, 40 percent of Polish exports to the Union consisted of the products of the "sensitive" sectors (Baun, 2000: 25–37).

The *acquis communautaire* and membership in the Union

Although some basic principles had been stated before, the specific political and economic conditions for joining the Union were first defined by the Copenhagen Council summit in June 1993, which, in a rare gesture, named the countries of Central and Eastern Europe as potential candidates:

Membership requires that the candidate country has achieved stability of institutions guaranteeing democracy, the rule of law, human rights and respect for and protection of minorities, the existence of a functioning market economy as well as the capacity to cope with competitive pressure and market forces within the Union . . . The associate countries in central and eastern Europe that so desire shall become members of the European Union . . . as soon as an associate country is able to assure the obligations of membership by satisfying the economic and political conditions required. (European Commission, 1995)

Although the Europe Agreement was not an official "entrance ticket" to the Union, it played that role for most of the countries. A formal enlargement process had already crystallized in the previous enlargement experience. It had to be initiated by the application of the candidate country to the Council of the Union. It was followed by an analysis by the Commission about the preparedness of the candidate for membership. Sometimes this opinion was prepared over a few months, but sometimes the process took years. If the Commission's *avis* was positive, the Council could decide (which it had to do unanimously) upon the opening of the accession negotiations at an intergovernmental conference.

At its Essen meeting in December 1994, the Council added a new element to the process: it approved a pre-accession strategy and a White Paper, which served as a "road map" for adjusting to the single market's pan-European regulatory regime. It outlined the aspects of the *acquis communautaire*, especially regarding commercial laws and regulations, but also committed to further liberalization of the Union restrictions against the importation of sensitive products from the transforming countries, and increased assistance for them. The *acquis* was a huge body of laws and rules, developed and augmented over the years. When presented to the Central and East European applicants, it comprised thirty-one chapters and 80,000 to 100,000 pages. A huge set of Union laws and regulations had to be implemented and integrated in each country, including market legislation, intellectual property protection, veterinary and plant health inspections, and industrial product testing. The supremacy of the Union norms over existing national ones required new institutional and administrative structures, and sometimes constitutional amendments.

The first phase of the negotiations was a screening process about the potential for adjustment by the candidates. In the second phase, a decision about the terms of the entry was made, and negotiations concluded in a draft treaty of accession. If approved by the European Council, the treaty was ratified and the candidate became a member of the Union. The time between the application and ratification varied between three and nine years.

The countries of the region provided their applications beginning in March 1994. Hungary was the first, followed a month later by Poland. Latvia, Estonia, Lithuania, and Bulgaria applied in the fall and winter of 1995, the Czech Republic and Slovenia in 1996. All the applicants were thoroughly screened: the Commission sent a 200-page questionnaire about legislative achievements and the general progress of the adjustment process in April 1996, with a demanding deadline of July of the same year. Detailed answers were required about the entire process. The Polish answer, for example, came to 2,600 pages; the Bulgarian answer, somewhat later, comprised 5,000 pages.

The Commission issued its opinion on the applications in July 1997, considering Poland, Hungary, the Czech Republic, Estonia, and Slovenia (and Cyprus) ready for negotiations, while Slovakia, Bulgaria, Romania, Latvia, and Lithuania required more preparation. The European Council meeting in Luxembourg decided to begin the accession process in December of that year. The negotiations began with the five best-prepared countries in March 1998:

> There was a considerable outcry from the second group of countries and the Luxembourg Council . . . emphasized that all the applicant countries were to be included in the enlargement process . . . However, in 1999, the . . . Commission suggested that all the applicants should be considered actively for membership and admitted when ready. (Mayes, 2004: 494)

Five more countries thus joined in February 2000, when negotiations opened with Slovakia, Latvia, Lithuania, Bulgaria, and Romania. However, the essence of the negotiations was not true bargaining, but the presentation of a huge list of requirements, the *acquis communautaire*, and the applicants' commitment to fulfilling the Union's requirements.

The officials of the European Union realized that it was not sufficient to harmonize the legal systems, as well as media and telecommunications, monetary, taxation, and competition policies, but that those institutional guarantees were necessary to realize the Union's requirements. Institutional guarantees were crucially important since national administration, as often stated, is an invisible pillar of the Union's laws and regulations. Roughly 80 percent of the Union's budget has shared management by the Commission and the national administration. Only one-sixth of the budget is under the direct control of the Union.

This recognition led to the inclusion of a new element in the accession preparation: the Europeanization of the national administrations. The *acquis* originally did not regulate this sphere, but the new candidates had a rather different administrative legacy that was more politicized, less responsive to its citizens, and less effective than that of previous candidates. The Union required an appropriate administrative capacity to apply the *acquis*. The requirement to "adjust administrative structures" emerged at the Madrid meeting of the European Council in 1995 and, from 1997, the Commission's regular progress reports always analyzed the administrative capacities of the candidates.

A uniform public administrative system did not exist in the European Union. The Copenhagen criteria noted only the need for stable institutions and the rule of law, but a model for implementation also had to be created. A model was completed in 1999, admittedly quite an abstract one, but one based on the Weberian principles of professionalism in civil service without direct political interference, and independence from political bodies. These principles were partly expressed by the more modern New Public Management model, and the candidate countries were pushed to introduce them via civil service legislation.

Before this initiative, some of the transforming countries, such as Hungary, Poland, Latvia, Estonia, and Lithuania, had already passed such legislation. Due to the Union's requirements, all the other candidates passed new laws on the career civil service system between 1997 and 2002. As the consequence of this forced harmonization, as Bojan Bugaric stated,

> while the administrative structures in Central and Eastern Europe look, on the surface, similar to their Western counterparts, they operate very differently... National structures are strongly embedded in a national legal, political, and cultural environment. (Bugaric, 2006: 17–18)

Socially and culturally embedded institutions cannot radically change in a short period of time. Institutional adjustment, as a consequence, reflects "Potemkin harmonization," since the various countries responded only formally to the Union's demand. From the beginning, in contrast to the requirements, Estonia leaned toward the "position model," i.e., a civil service system based on political party affiliation, while Slovakia, Slovenia, Romania, and Bulgaria followed the Union's requirements more closely.

Hungary, Poland, and the Czech Republic had a better position model, which was more responsive and better codified, and they developed a more mixed system. The original civil service laws were amended in Poland (1998), Hungary (2001), and Slovenia (2005) in the direction of a political model. Hungary, for example, in 2001 introduced the institution of 350 "political civil servant" positions, appointed by the prime minister. The Slovene amendment drastically repoliticized the system: originally, top civil servants were selected by a non-partisan committee for a term of five years, but the 2005 change allowed the government to remove all directors-general without cause. Although the Czech draft law was strongly criticized by the Commission and changed, the various countries eventually succeeded in tailoring the system according to their political goals. The administrative systems of the candidate countries were thus somewhat Europeanized, but often represented "formal structures without substance" (Bugaric, 2006: 12, 15–16).

From 1998 onward, the Commission regularly screened the fulfillment of the *acquis* and administration reform, and presented its assessments in annual reports. The reports analyzed political and economic criteria, as well as the compatibility with the *acquis* of the laws, regulations, policies, and administrative and institutional capacities of the candidate countries. These reports sometimes were as long as 120 pages on a single country. Slovakia was rejected at first because the Commission's evaluation was critical of the minority rights situation, the treatment of parliamentary opposition, and the lack of an independent judiciary under the Vladimír Mečiar government.

Recommendations were made regarding the restructuring of the Polish steel industry, Lithuania's energy sector, Latvia's and Estonia's policy toward their Russian minorities, and Romanian and Bulgarian policy on corruption and organized crime. Lithuania and Bulgaria were warned to respect international nuclear safety standards and to close obsolete nuclear power stations. Slovenia and several other countries were criticized for restrictions excluding foreigners from real estate purchases, a practice which violated the single market legislation. All of the countries had to make changes, in some cases constitutional changes, to harmonize with EU law (Baun, 2000: 80, 102, 211).

The role of the European Union can be illustrated by the unique case of the Hungarian Status Law (the law on Hungarians living in neighboring states). It was connected with a political problem, but it clearly reflects the importance and influence of the European Union's regulations in Central and Eastern Europe. In advance of the 2001 Hungarian elections, the populist-nationalist Viktor Orbán government initiated a law which guaranteed special rights for ethnic Hungarians living in Romania, Slovakia, and other neighboring countries. These included various educational rights, work permits, and assistance for ethnic Hungarian organizations in the neighboring countries. The Hungarian parliament overwhelmingly approved the law. Brussels signaled its dissatisfaction, and the Organization for Security and Cooperation in Europe expressed strong critical views. The European Parliament's resolution of September 2001 on Hungary's application for membership required it to change the "special regulations and privileges for foreign citizens of Hungarian origin in compliance with the *acquis communautaire* and with respect to the neighboring countries." After the elections, on December 2002, the letter from the EU commissioner for enlargement, Günther Verheugen, to the new prime minister of Hungary explicitly cited the EU requirement that the law be changed. The new Hungarian government and parliament accepted all the European Union's recommendations, and the 2003 European Commission's Monitoring Report on Hungary's Preparations for Membership concluded that "the modification to the law adopted by Parliament in June 2003 appears to have brought the framework of legislation in line with the acquis" (documents published by Kántor *et al.*, 2004: 581–87). The European Union virtually forced the adoption of the European and international requirements and standards of legislation and practice upon the candidate countries. Irina Bokova's statement in connection with the Bulgarian accession process has a general validity:

The pre-accession strategy directly affects virtually all aspects of life in an applicant country – its industry, agriculture, commercial and financial sectors, consumer practices, the environment, standardization, education and foreign policy. It involves profound changes which sometimes touch the very fabric of society. (Bokova, 2000: 67)

The process of adjusting to the European Union was, indeed, demanding. Several of the candidate countries complained bitterly. Michael Baun collected several outbursts in his detailed description on the accession process. At an early stage of the process, Vladimir Dlouhy, the economics minister of Czechoslovakia, grumbled that, instead of support, "only cold-blooded economic facts are put on the table." Andrzej Olechowski, the chief negotiator of Poland, stated: "we were all disappointed by the format and political climate of the talks. It soon turned into pure trade bargaining by the two sides across the table." Latvia and Lithuania, though far behind Estonia in the process of transformation, were outraged that they were not considered in the first wave together with Estonia. The prime minister of Lithuania, Gediminas Vagnorious, tried to frighten the Union by maintaining that the delay of the country's acceptance "might encourage nationalist forces in Moscow to reassert Russian influence over the Baltic region." He also questioned the objectivity of the European Commission. Latvia expressed similar criticism. The Romanian prime minister demanded the inclusion of his country to the accession negotiations in the first wave as a "symbolic gesture and reward for the difficult reforms that the country [had] made." The Bulgarian government complained that "the accession burden on Bulgaria . . . is far greater than for the previous applicants" (Baun, 2000: 35, 87, 88, 127, 216). In 1998, a hostile Polish reaction blamed the Union for cutting PHARE aid by ECU 34 million, although the reason for the cut was the failure of the Polish government to present acceptable projects in time for funding, and for proposing spending which did not comply with the terms of the agreement:

In perhaps no applicant country has disillusionment with the EU been greater than in Poland, in part the result of numerous disputes with the EU over Polish government policies and preparations for membership since the beginning of the accession process. (ibid.: 215)

Indeed, a survey in October 1999 showed that only 46% of Poles supported Union membership, down from 80% in 1994.

These complaints and disillusionment were baseless, in spite of the unavoidably subordinated position of the candidates, the permanent control and push by the Union, and the ubiquitous red tape. The Commission and the Union were right to force adjustment in such a situation, when the gap between the advanced member countries and the candidates was much wider than before. Without legal and institutional reform and reduction of corruption and crime, the democratic political culture would not develop to enable Central and East European countries to integrate into a well-functioning single market system.

The reaction of the Eastern countries originated from their centuries-old political culture. They firmly believed that they deserved acceptance at once, that they had been betrayed by the West, and that they had the right to demand restitution. As István Bibó maintained in his brilliant postwar analysis of the "misery" of the East European nations, the national elites in their modern history were totally out of step with reality. In their "deformed political character" there was an imbalance between reality and desire. They were accustomed to making unreasonable demands and to formulating policy based on what they wanted, rather than on what could be accomplished, thus disengaging policy from a rationale of cause and effect (Bíbó, [1946] 1986: 226). The reality was simple: if they wanted to join the Union, they had to make adjustments, and it was in their national interest to do so. Besides, the European Union was not an altruistic institution; it looked out for its own interests and did not base its politics on philanthropic or merely moral considerations.

Accomplishing all the prerequisites, however, was indeed a hard burden on the candidate countries. To illustrate the scope of the technical tasks, Estonia had to establish an Estonian Translation and Legislative Support Center in September 1995, which, among other chores, translated the entire Estonian legal code into English and all European Union legislation into Estonian. All the constitutions, property laws, civil and commercial codes, and even ministerial bylaws were translated (Pisnke, 1998: 207). An even more difficult task was to adjust to the legal way of thinking of Europe, as illustrated by a comment about Latvia:

Serious changes are needed in the legal methodology, which civil servants and judges use in applying norms of rights . . . The most important issue is whether Latvia's legal thinking can break out of the isolation . . . and join the legal thinking and practice of the countries of the EU . . . Latvia must undergo a serious and conscientiously promoted "legal revolution" as part of a broad intellectual and educational "revolution." Only then will it have a chance . . . of becoming a modern, law-based country. (Levits, 1998: 195)

Between 1993 and 1995 Estonia changed its property and land registration laws, civil code, apartment ownership act, family law act, succession law, and commercial code. In January 1995, it had to change its discriminatory citizenship law, which was based on a *jus sanguinis* ("blood" or ethnicity) principle and upheld by the 1992 constitution, and instead grant citizenship to everyone who had held citizenship before, regardless of ethnicity, as well as to aliens with five years' permanent residence, knowledge of the Estonian language and constitution, and legitimate income (Ziemele, 1998: 257). The European Union required that the candidates pass through a demanding learning and legislative process. However, since it was also in the Union's interest to enlarge, it combined demands with assistance.

In the summer of 1997, the Commission issued the Agenda 2000 program of preparation for enlargement, which was accepted by the European Council's Berlin meeting in March 1999. The Union announced a plan for adjusting its main policies according to the requirements of the enlargement, including the reform of agricultural assistance (the common agricultural policy, or CAP) and structural and cohesion funds, which assisted backward regions of the Union in catching up with advanced areas. In the proposed budgetary and financial plan for the years 2000–06, the PHARE program was increased, and 70 percent of the funds were channeled into key adjustment sectors. The EU guaranteed so-called pre-accession aid for agricultural transformation of €500 million per year, and structural aid of €1 billion per year. The former served to "cushion" the transformation shock in Central and East European agriculture and assisted with restructuring, while the second served the modernization of the economy.

These amounts were, of course, modest in comparison to the needs. According to convincing calculations, to reach the *acquis* environmental standards alone would require about €100 billion investment in the region over ten years. Upgrading roads and railways to Western standards would involve investment of €50–90 billion over fifteen years (Gower and Redmond, 2000: 21, 83). Nevertheless, EU assistance became substantial and played an important role in the transformation, as discussed below (pp. 98–99, 103).

Not only did the new Union members receive less assistance than previous candidates had done, they had to accept other restrictions as well. The Western countries worried about the high unemployment rate in the candidate countries – in some cases about 20 percent of the labor force around 2000 – and consequently about the danger of mass migration. The negotiated agreements therefore built in certain temporary safeguards to protect the fifteen old members from migration. In other words, the new members could not enjoy free movement of labor for some time. This limitation was projected to end after five years, but it could be extended for two additional years. In those transitory years, the new members would create more jobs and increase living standards domestically to mitigate the push effect of emigration.

Nevertheless, Britain, Ireland, and Sweden opened their doors for workers from the new member countries immediately. Four more old EU members, Spain, Portugal, Greece, and Finland, lifted restrictions on May 1, 2006, while France, Italy, Belgium and Luxembourg softened them (*International Herald Tribune*, May 2, 2006). Economic integration was progressing faster than planned. Nevertheless, labor migration, except in the cases of Poland, Slovakia, Moldova, and Albania, was limited.

The European Union itself had to adjust to the new situation by changing some of its institutions and rules, as well as its policy and budgetary plans. The situation of agriculture, for example, which played an important role in the Union's policy from the beginning, radically changed because of enlargement. The ten candidate countries, which represented nearly 29% of the population of the Union, had more than 56% of its arable land and 23% of its agricultural population, but only about 9% of the value added to the Union's agricultural output. According to the Commission's calculations, the enlargement would increase agricultural assistance (CAP) expenditures by one-third to one-half. Such an increase was not viable.

The Commission recommended further decreasing price supports (for example, by 30%, 15%, and 10%, respectively, for beef, dairy, and cereal support), and a further shift toward income support instead of price support. The new members, whose agricultural price level was roughly 40% to 80% of the Union's level, would not receive direct compensatory payment for years. Agricultural assistance for Poland, the Czech Republic, Hungary, Slovakia, and Slovenia would itself increase the Union's CAP expenditures by 20%, and total budgetary expenditures by nearly 10%. Paying the usual CAP support for Poland would increase agricultural income for the country's rural population by 47%. The introduction of production controls, to guarantee that 10% of arable land remained fallow, played an important role among the reform recommendations (Gower and Redmond, 2000: 89, 92–94). The experience of the first years of Union membership proved that even limited CAP payments doubled the income of the Polish farmers, and increased the income of the Czech agricultural population by 70%, while the Hungarian and Slovak income level increased by 30% in the countryside.

The EU Commission also recommended major reforms in how the structural and cohesion funds, which served the development of backward regions, were used for catching up. According to their calculations, all ten candidate countries qualified for both kinds of assistance, raising the prospect that total tax expenditures would more than double. Of the 268 regions of the European Union, 78 had a GDP level that was less than 75 percent of the EU average, a level which triggered automatic assistance from the funds. Except for Prague and the Central Hungary regions around Budapest, all regions of the transition countries belonged to the "backward" category (Eurostat, 2005b: 41).

Regional disparities are in general quite marked in the transforming countries. This aspect of transformation is largely neglected, but it was very important in Central Europe. In both Poland and Hungary, the central districts that encompass the capital cities are much more developed than the peripheral regions: Poland's Mazowieckie region has a per capita GDP that is 50% higher than the Polish average, and its unemployment is below 14%, whereas in some of Poland's more backward regions unemployment surpasses 25–28%. In the Podlaskie and Podkarpackie regions, income levels are below three-quarters of the national average. In Hungary, the income levels of Budapest are twice the country's average and nearly 90 percent of the EU average. Investments are similarly concentrated in the central regions: in the peripheral regions of Poland, investments are less than one-quarter of the central region's level. Sharp disparities characterize even extremely small countries: in Latvia, the Riga region has twice the per capita GDP of the Latgale region. While in Ventspils the income level was nearly four times the Latvian average, the Kraslava region reached only one-third the national average (Charemza and Strała, 2002: 49).

As a consequence of these regional disparities, it is still difficult to speak about integrated domestic markets in the region. The disparities significantly weakened economic regeneration and competitiveness. Enclaves of a subsistence economy are resistant to market influences in those backward regions. Regional policy, consequently, plays a crucial role in the transformation of these countries.

The importance of Union assistance is clearly expressed by the success of the Operative Program of Regional Development. In Central and Eastern Europe, regional development policy was mostly lacking. Additionally, European integration transforms domestic policy-making structures. In new member countries, transferring important regulatory functions from the national to the European Union level "Europeanizes" public policy. Nevertheless, the transformation countries gradually developed a system of multilevel governance which requires special coordination among three players: the EU, the national government, and regional authorities. This task is not easy for countries with legacies of strongly centralized dictatorial regimes, low levels of social capital, and weak civil societies, phenomena which are characteristic of all of the new member countries. In these new countries, with important differences, corruption and clientelism represent special obstacles (Paraskevopoulos, Getimis, and Rees, 2006).

Nevertheless, regional assistance and policy gradually gained ground in the region. In Hungary, during the first two years of EU membership, 2,300 applications for assistance were filed, nearly 500 were successful, and 50 have been implemented. The eastern Hungarian city, Nyiregyháza, for example, rehabilitated "brownfield" regions, abandoned industrial zones, and former Soviet barracks, using 27% of the grant, while another 49% was spent on educational infrastructure, building and modernizing schools and kindergartens. Investment for tourist infrastructure accounted for 24% of the grant. Of the total amount of 1.15 billion Hungarian forints ($1 = 200 forints), 85% was financed by the European Union and 15% by local authorities (*Népszabadság*, June 23, 2006).

However, regional disparities will still be preserved for a long time. Moreover, in the initial period there may be an increase in these disparities, since backward regions are generally less successful than their more advanced competitors at making bids for Union money, and less able to absorb it effectively if they do succeed. In the first years, most of the regional assistance was indeed channeled into the relatively better-developed regions of the new member countries.

As a consequence, the structural and cohesion assistance available for the old member countries had to decrease. This was partly a function of development in the previously backward Mediterranean countries and Ireland, and partly because absorbing the Central and East European region into the EU decreased the average Union GDP level by 16 percent. As a result, several formerly "backward" regions in old member countries no longer fell into that category, and the proportion of the population in member countries who received development assistance from the Union decreased from 25% to 20%.

According to the Agenda 2000 budgetary plans, the Union's expenditure for these goals reached ECU 275 billion between 2000 and 2006, of which ECU 45 billion went to new members and associates. Nevertheless, the Commission suggested first limiting, and then gradually increasing, the structural assistance to the new members to levels not exceeding 4 percent of each country's GDP. Even under this formula, about one-third of total expenditure from the Union's structural fund in 2006 went to new members (Baun, 2000: 147–50) (table 3.1, figure 3.1). Between 2000 and 2006, EU pre-accession assistance, including PHARE and the pre-accession rural, agricultural, and structural funds, provided nearly €2.7 billion in annual

Table 3.1 Budget commitments of the European Union 2000–2006, in billion €, 1999 prices

Expenditures	2000	2001	2002	2003	2004	2005	2006
Total EU expenditure	91.995	93.385	100.255	102.035	103.085	104.995	107.040
Pre-accession aid	3.120	3.120	3.120	3.120	3.120	3.120	3.120
Post-accession aid	0	0	6.450	9.030	11.620	14.200	16.780
Total for Central and Eastern Europe[a]	3.120	3.120	9.570	12.150	14.740	17.320	19.900
Total for EU-15[a]	78.865	80.205	80.765	80.105	78.455	77.675	77.030
Central and Eastern Europe as % of total	3.4	3.3	9.5	11.9	14.3	16.5	18.6

Source: European Commission, 1999.

Note: a: The difference between the total expenditure and the combined expenditure figures for Central and Eastern Europe and the EU-15 is expenditures on EU administration, reserves, and external policy, which serve both groups.

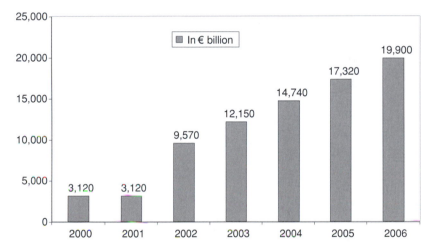

Figure 3.1 The EU's financial assistance to Central and Eastern Europe, 2000–2006

support to the ten candidate countries (European Commission, 1998). The Commission warned the old members:

> The next enlargement . . . will inevitably provoke deterioration in the budgetary positions of all the current member states. This cannot come as a surprise and should not give rise to claims for compensation. (Mayes, 2004: 504)

The original fifteen member countries were thus ready to help pay for the transformation and development of the candidates. They channeled increasing amounts toward that goal, from an initial figure of slightly more than 3%, rising to nearly 19% of the total budget of the Union between

2000 and 2006. It turned out, however, that the new member countries had major difficulties in applying for funds successfully, or using them in time, because of weaknesses in their administration and in their ability to learn the rules.

It is also true that the old member countries expected to profit from trade and outsourcing labor-intensive jobs to the regions with low wages. From the outset, 30 to 40 percent of the structural and cohesion fund assistance returned to the advanced countries of the Union in the form of purchases by the assisted countries. The opening of the Eastern markets ignited an export boom for the West, which doubled or trebled its exports to the area within a decade. Neighboring Austria increased its exports to the region by 3.5 times. The EU became the main trading partner of the transforming countries, and accumulated a huge trade surplus, although this was not uniformly distributed across all countries. Several new member countries – the Czech Republic, Slovakia, Hungary, and Slovenia – had a higher proportion of trade with other member countries than did some of the old members. Conversely and surprisingly, trade between the new member countries, which decreased significantly after 1989, increased by leaps and bounds after 2004. At that stage, there were no losers, only winners, from the enlargement process.

The old member countries were also forced to cope with the highly competitive wage levels of the new members. The workers at two Siemens factories in Germany agreed to work five additional hours per week without extra payment in order to prevent the outsourcing of their jobs to Hungary. French workers at a Bosch factory did the same to prevent outsourcing to the Czech Republic. Austria had to adjust to the more competitive tax system of neighboring Slovakia, which introduced a 19% flat tax rate that forced Austria to lower its tax rate from 34% to 25% (Eichengreen, 2007: 411).

Summing up, I want to call attention to the crucially positive impact of the enlargement policy of the Union on the entire transformation process in the region. As shown before, since the former communist countries sought to join the Union immediately after the regime change, and since the Union made its first steps toward enlargement as early as 1990–91, the pre-enlargement and enlargement process practically guided and commanded the entire transformation. As Stiglitz stated, the European Union demonstrated a sense of responsibility and solidarity

by its assistance to Europe's post-communist countries . . . Europe's unprecedented generosity has paid off: the countries that have joined the EU have outperformed all the others, and not just because of access to Europe's markets.

Even more important was the institutional infrastructure, including the biding commitment to democracy and the vast array of laws and regulations. (Stiglitz, 2007: 2)

One may say that the Union did not merely influence but actually determined the Central European governments' internal policies. This is well illustrated by the fact that, although various political parties rotated in the transforming countries, and while the ruling political forces varied from right-of-center conservatives and nationalists to left-of-center socialists and former communists, the main political trends were nevertheless steady on the basic issues because of the overarching goal of adjusting to the Union's requirements.

If any ultranationalist governments did not follow this line, as in the case of the Vladimír Mečiar government in Slovakia, it was swept away because people did not want to lose the opportunity to join Europe. If governments followed an anti-minority policy, as in Estonia and Latvia, that policy was reined back into line with EU standards. When the populist-conservative József Antall government in Hungary reacted too slowly to the Union's requirements, it was the former reform-communist, socialist Gyula Horn government that realized the radical austerity measures – the so-called Bokros Package – that devaluated the currency by 9%, introduced an 8% import surcharge, reduced real wages by 10%, and heavily cut public expenditures. The government also launched a new privatization campaign, selling strategic public utility companies beginning in the mid-1990s. Sharp political changes characterized Polish politics, but there was little to distinguish the Solidarity and the post-communist governments on the issue of EU accession. In spite of the rhetoric, the pre-accession and accession process smoothed the edges of politics, eliminating the more extreme nationalist tendencies as well as the more traditional socialist political behavior. The ruling political trend was to cleave to the Union's prescriptions and demands.

It is nevertheless paradoxical that the European Union was able to influence Central and East European politics so much more directly before the accession than afterward. In theory, the Union has a weapon in the form of Article 7, namely, the possibility of suspending voting rights when a country violates common principles such as democracy, the rule of law, or the protection of human rights under populist-nationalist governments. In reality this sanction was not used against governments that violated it, such as that of Slovak Jan Slota, who called the minority Hungarians "Mongoloids," and the Polish Kaczynski governments which used the police and investigations as weapons against their "enemies." Similarly, the

Union has less influence to push anti-corruption and anti-crime measures in newly accepted Romania and Bulgaria than before January 2007.

The European Union's impact on the transformation of future candidate countries

The accession process, I should add, also influenced the entire Central and East European region. The influence is evident not only in the countries which were first accepted to begin the process, but also in those countries which had no chance to be included quickly. After the first group of six applicants in 1998, official negotiations began with five more countries in 2000. Although they were far from being prepared, especially in the Balkans, they were clearly influenced by the enlargement process.

This influence was partly the consequence of the demonstration effect: Serbia-Montenegro, Bosnia-Herzegovina, Macedonia, and Albania watched the progress of neighboring countries as they marched toward the European Union. They saw the opportunity and the requirements, and this itself influenced the political and economic trends in these countries. The Union, however, sought to make a direct impact on the region to create lasting peace and security. Stabilization of the area next to its south-eastern borders was a central goal of the Union. To achieve this goal, the transformation and prosperity of that region were required as well.

After the Kosovo war in 1999, the Union decided to give priority to the Western Balkan area, and it announced a special plan to launch a Stability and Accession Process for Southeastern Europe in May 1999. The Brussels summit in April of that year declared the prospect for rapprochement between the region and the Union. As the Commission's report stated in 2002, the

European Union leaders decided that a policy of emergency reconstruction, containment and stabilization was not, in itself, enough to bring lasting peace and stability to the Balkans: only the real prospect of integration into European structures would achieve that. (European Commission, 2002: 4)

The Union applied a gradual process of building institutionalized connections. As a first step, the Stabilization and Association Process was launched and, pending good progress, would be followed by the Stabilization and Association Agreements. Five countries were involved: Macedonia, Croatia, Serbia-Montenegro, Bosnia-Herzegovina, and Albania signed process agreements between 2001 and 2005. By February 2003, trade liberalization agreements were signed, and the region was gradually adjusting to the free trade system of the Union. The Thessaloniki European Union summit in June 2003 announced that "EU accession remained the ultimate aim of the Stabilization and Accession Process for the five participating countries" (EBRD, 2003: 8). In 2004, the Union also announced that these countries might achieve candidate status around 2010 and membership by about 2020.

The integration process in that region has its special difficulties. In addition to their extremely low income level, almost all of these countries have gained independence recently and are in a process of independent nation-building based on ethnic principles. The integration process, on the other hand, requires giving up certain important elements of national sovereignty. Nevertheless, all of the countries of the Western Balkans chose integration, which not only compensated for restricted national sovereignty but also, as the political elites of these countries calculated, better protected their national interests within the European framework.

The Union also realized that the strategy used in Central Europe is not appropriate for the countries of the Western Balkans. Institution-building, legal adjustment, and free trade cannot remedy the towering economic, social, and educational backwardness of those countries. Preparation requires special economic vitalization measures, solutions for the still dominant agricultural sectors of those countries, and assistance for infrastructural improvement. All of these tasks require more substantial financial assistance. Based on that recognition, the Union's budget for 2007–13 offered €11.5 billion for the Western Balkan countries.

The European Union also initiated a development policy by establishing the Community Assistance for Reconstruction, Development and Stabilization (CARDS) Program to help the countries of the region in restructuring and development. The Union offered financial support for the Stability and Accession Process to strengthen regional cooperation and build closer ties to the European Union. This process, however, did not begin in earnest until after the year 2000.

The Integration and Adjustment Process of the Western Balkan countries began immediately. As the European Bank for Reconstruction and Development reported in 2000:

Albania has made progress towards opening negotiations on an EU Stabilization and Accession Agreement . . . Since October 1999, the EU has granted unilateral trade preferences to Albania, including exemptions from duties and abolition of quantitative restrictions for industrial goods . . . About 90 percent of all exports from Albania to the EU are now duty-free. (EBRD, 2000: 126)

Foreign investments in Bosnia-Herzegovina were five times higher in 2004 than at the end of the 1990s. Interest rates halved, and industrial output –

which hit bottom in 1995, with only 5 percent of the pre-civil war level – began increasing from 2001. After hyperinflation of 73,000 percent, the currency, tied to the euro, became stable and inflation was curbed. For the first four years of the century, GDP growth reached about 5 percent annually (Butler, 2005: 76).

The Union signed a Stabilization and Association Agreement with Macedonia in 2001, and the republic graduated to candidate status in 2005. This situation revitalized the Macedonian economy. The clothing industry of Stip, which employed 4,000 workers in 2002, nearly doubled its employment by 2006 through Greek (as well as Turkish and Swiss) investments. The acting chief economist of the European Bank reported in 2005 that "south-eastern Europe saw robust growth and record capital inflows in 2004–5, reflecting an underlying confidence in its future prospects" (EBRD, 2005a: vii). Economic progress became significant. The countries of the Western Balkans reached 6.5% and 4.8% annual economic growth in 2004 and 2005, respectively.

At the beginning of the twenty-first century, some ties between the Union and the Western Balkans strengthened. Croatia's chance to be included in the next stage of the accession process emerged after the death of the extreme nationalist President Franjo Tudjman in December 1999, the democratic elections that followed, and especially in light of its readiness to cooperate with the Hague Tribunal and to extradite war criminals.

Serbia, after the resignation of President Slobodan Milošević, also opened a new chapter of its transformation after 2000: reforms were introduced and the country received a significant amount of investment. As the chief economist quoted above stated, "The progress in Serbia in particular has surprised many observers" (EBRD, 2005a: vii). However, in contrast to Croatia, Serbia's reluctance to cooperate with the Hague Tribunal stymied its prospects of joining the Union. Because it hid – or at least did not find – General Mladić, who was accused of the mass killing in Srebrenica, the door to candidacy was closed for the present. Unlike the Macedonian textile and clothing industry boom, Leskovac, the famous textile and clothing center of Serbia, which employed 11,000 workers in 1990, had fewer than 900 workers in 2006. According to the European Union's evaluation, Serbia lost about $2 billion in investment because of the lack of a Stabilization and Association Agreement (*Economist*, March 24, 2007).

Whenever a country was accepted into the EU and a deadline for joining was set, increased foreign investment immediately followed. Foreign investment almost doubled in the new member countries and reached a record $16.3 billion in 2004, and then nearly $25 billion in 2005. The group of next candidates, Romania, Bulgaria, and Croatia, achieved a record investment level of \$9.2 billion in 2004, and nearly \$12 billion in 2005 (EBRD, 2005a: 35–36). One commentator noted:

The EU has a particularly strong influence over candidate states . . . the prospect of EU accession has influenced virtually every aspect of post-communist change in the candidate countries . . . [there are] EU influences across a range of fields and processes more significant than enjoyed over existing EU members. (Cernat, 2006: 111)

All the deadlines for acceptance are, of course, tentative. Their realization depends on the fulfillment of the Union's requirements. As Olli Rehn, the Union's enlargement commissioner, stated in the European Parliament in June 2005:

the best advice for the candidate countries and potential candidates . . . is that the best way to realize the European perspective is to fulfill the conditions of accession to the letter. (Rehn, 2005: 141)

To do that means a very long road for the Western Balkan countries.

The European Union of twenty-seven countries

The Union's candidate countries from Central and Eastern Europe have meanwhile gradually completed their "homework." The eight Central European countries closed the final chapters of the *acquis* in 2002, fulfilling the Union's requirements, and introduced 50,000 laws and regulations. The negotiations concluded in Copenhagen in 2002. The European Council consequently invited the Czech Republic, Estonia, Hungary, Latvia, Lithuania, Poland, Slovenia, and Slovakia to join the Union on May 1, 2004. These countries, of course, continued reforming, especially in terms of institution-building. Modernization of the financial markets proceeded, and in some countries further privatization and restructuring of certain industrial sectors gained momentum. A modern credit system, including mortgage credit, took root. In Estonia, Latvia, and Hungary, the amount of total credit increased from 20–30% to roughly 60% of GDP between 1999 and 2004.

Several of these countries joined the Union's exchange rate mechanism as the first step toward the introduction of the euro. They made some progress toward the so-called Maastricht criteria for a common currency: national debt no higher than 60% of GDP, fiscal deficit less than 3% of GDP, inflation rate not more than 1.5% higher than the average of the three lowest inflation rates among member countries. These "institutionalized arrangements and detailed criteria on inflation, deficit, public debt, long-term interest rates, and exchange rates" directed Central and East European policy (Dyson, 2007: 3). By 2004, the deficit of the new member countries remained at 2.4% of the GDP, their inflation rate was 4.3%, and their current account deficit had reached 6.6% of GDP. These parameters promised a relatively swift advance toward the euro, which some countries, such as Slovenia, the Czech Republic, Poland, and Hungary, planned to introduce between 2005 and 2007.

Nevertheless, most of these countries struggled with either inflation or current account deficit problems. In 2006, the Latvian current account deficit reached 20% of GDP, which was the highest in the Union. The Bulgarian deficit surpassed 15%, and the Estonian, Lithuanian, and Romanian deficits were all higher than 10% of GDP (*Economist*, March 10, 2007). These and most other candidate countries were not eligible to join the Eurozone.

Several decided to keep their hands free to use a more flexible financial policy and to be able to cope with welfare pressure: "They have domestic economic and social policy and political incentives to lengthen the timetable for [introducing the euro]" (Dyson, 2007: 16). As a consequence, the Czech Republic postponed the introduction of the common EU currency from 2007–08 to 2009–10; Poland favored 2010, but unofficial plans forecast 2012–15; Hungary also shifted the introduction of the euro to 2011–12. In the end, only Slovenia was able to introduce the euro by 2007.

The next wave of enlargement was planned and implemented in January 2007 when Bulgaria and Romania were accepted and joined the EU. These countries were not yet prepared. The European Union had never before accepted countries with such low income levels: Bulgaria's and Romania's GDP per capita reached only $3,500 and $4,500, compared to that of the eight Central European countries that had already joined, which stood at $9,240 in 2004, and to the Union average of more than $29,000. In addition, noted *The Economist*,

they are backward in many other ways. Infrastructure and public services are worse than in the rest of Eastern Europe; corruption is more entrenched, and the political culture more fragile. (*Economist*, January 6, 2007)

Exact deadlines for other countries in the Balkans are not yet decided. The European Union is consistently and rapidly implementing its enlargement policy to adjust to the requirements of the transformed international, globalized economy. The enlargement procedure, on the other hand, became the main guiding force for Central and East European transformation.

CHAPTER 4

Recuperation and growth: the role of foreign direct investment

During the first transformation years of the 1990s, in spite of serious mistakes and avoidable decline, the introduction of a market and private economy progressed well in Central and Eastern Europe. It was strongly assisted by the European Union. As a result of political and economic consolidation and adjustment to the Union's requirements, transformation was essentially accomplished in most of the countries of the region over the decade beginning in the mid-1990s.

In a clear sign of political stability and security, virtually the entire region became part of the Western military alliance system, the North Atlantic Treaty Organization (NATO). As early as 1990, countries of the region were invited to the NATO Parliamentary Assembly as associate members. In the summer of 1997, Poland, Hungary, and the Czech Republic were invited to join NATO, which they did in 1999. Seven other countries from the region – Bulgaria, Estonia, Latvia, Lithuania, Romania, Slovakia, and Slovenia – were invited to join at the November 2002 Prague summit. They joined in 2004. Article 5 of the NATO treaty, the collective security clause, guaranteed security to the members: "The Parties agree that an armed attack against one or more of them in Europe or North America shall be considered an attack against them all." Behind the Western military shield, integration into the West became easier.

The Central European countries began preparing for accession under the guidance of the European Union. They signed the Association Agreement in the mid-1990s, established new legal systems for the economy, introduced convertible currencies, joined the international trade and monetary organizations, reoriented trade with free market economies, and initiated radical sectoral and technological modernization. Ten of the countries joined the European Union in the spring of 2004 and in the beginning of 2007.

The Stability Pact, and the Stabilization and Accession Process which five South East European countries began in the spring of 2001, paved the way for further enlargement of the European Union in the region. Recovery was not fully reached during the first decade and a half in some of the countries, but the vanguard of transformation countries began integrating with the West after signing the Accession Agreements. Domestic economies became part of the large market of the European Union. The new situation opened the gates for international investments. Foreign direct investment became the main vehicle for economic development over the first two decades of transformation.

Capital inflow and foreign direct investment

Big privatization, as discussed before, was based on foreign participation and investment. Consolidation and restructuring of the economy, the introduction of modern technology, and the reorientation of foreign trade would have been almost impossible without a significant capital inflow into Central and Eastern Europe. In the early 1990s, a new Marshall Plan was often suggested. Calculations based on the Marshall Plan experience placed the cost at $10–15 billion annually for Central and Eastern Europe, and another $30 billion for the successor states of the Soviet Union. Economist Jeffrey Sachs, adviser to Poland and other transformation countries, and one of the advocates of such aid, argued:

The amount [of $15 and $30 billion] seems to be large, but let's compare it with the annual budget of NATO, which is now $250 billion (to defend the West) . . . With the military threat ending, the aid would finance itself, since it would make it possible to cut defense expenditure the same amount or even more. (Sachs, 1992: 17)

A new Marshall Plan, however, was not seriously considered by the victors of the Cold War. The Secretariat of the United Nations Economic Commission for Europe maintained that the transformation countries of the region had a limited capital absorptive capacity because of the lack of market-supporting factors and institutions, and thus that a Marshall Plan would not be effective. Instead of a new Marshall Plan, the Secretariat recommended assistance to create more absorptive capacity (Scott, 1999: 129). This decision was questionable because with a substantial aid package indebtedness would have decreased and the backward transportation and telecommunications infrastructure would have benefited.

Nevertheless, the Western countries pledged limited financial aid from the very beginning. Most of the countries of the region each received between $300 and $600 million; two or three countries each received more than $1–1.5 billion in aid per year, which on a per capita basis did not surpass $40 to $100, except in Bosnia, Serbia, Macedonia, and Albania where it reached between $120 and $175 (Economist, 2006b: 44–5).

In November 1989, the month the Berlin Wall collapsed, the European Community's Commission hosted a meeting of the representatives of twenty-four advanced industrial nations and pledged $6.5 billion in economic aid for the two countries that had destroyed state socialism first, Poland and Hungary. Four days later, President Bush signed a bill authorizing nearly $1 billion in aid for Poland and Hungary together. The rush to support transformation culminated in a pledge by the twenty-four most advanced countries to disburse $27 billion over the three years between 1989 and 1991 for economic stabilization and restructuring in the three leading transforming countries, Poland, Hungary, and Czechoslovakia. Moreover, they pledged $62.5 billion over a five-year period for the transformation of the entire Central and East European region (European Union, 1995). In the summer of 1991, the European Commission revealed that only 11 percent of the amount committed was actually sent. In reality, during the first four years of transformation, only $11 billion was disbursed to six countries of the region. If Polish debt reduction is included, the amount reached $19.1 billion (Ners and Buxell, 1995: 34).

According to the opponents of a new Marshall Plan program, the IMF, the World Bank, and most of all private investors would provide the necessary financial resources. Indeed, annual global foreign direct investment (FDI) dramatically increased around the turn of the century: from $60 billion in 1985 to $800 billion by 2000. Only a small segment of total international private investment was channeled into the region, totaling altogether roughly $13 to $15 billion by the end of 1993. FDI represented between 1% (in the Czechoslovak case), and 0.08% (in Romania) of the countries' real GDP. The per capita average assistance amounted to $30 in six countries of the region in 1993, compared to the $5,900 average annual per capita capital inflow to the former East Germany from the former Federal Republic of Germany.

Although Hungary received half of the actual foreign capital inflow to the region, $2.5 billion from the IMF and World Bank, and nearly $7 billion in direct investments, this amount could not even offset the country's repayment burden for its heavy indebtedness. Hungary, without debt restructuring, paid $2.4–3.5 billion annually to its creditors and recorded a net capital outflow from the country until 1993 (Nagy, 1993).

Furthermore, not all of the countries of the region welcomed foreign capital inflow. In the early years of transformation, Solidarity in Poland was strongly against "selling out" the country. As Adam Michnik noted: "Solidarity became a caricature of itself and tried to play in the factories and in the state the role that previously belonged to the Communist party" (Michnik, 2002). Workers' self-management and collective ownership remained the ideal of many during the first years of transformation. In the Polish journal *Kultura*, several articles opposed foreign investments:

The idea that state property . . . would be delivered dirt-cheap into the hands of foreign capital . . . while perhaps effective from the economic point of view, is most assuredly not acceptable from the social point of view. (Romaszewski, 1990: 41)

The most dangerous . . . [risk] involves the sale of enterprises to foreigners . . . [because it] could cause the loss of national property for the benefit of foreign investors. (Polaczek, 1993: 41)

Polish governments launched warfare against Solidarity resistance:

Solidarity leaders were asked . . . to silence the feared mass militancy. Inherited institutions of labour representation as well as local citizen committees that emerged around the changes were dismantled. (Grabowski, 1996: 251)

That was not the case in Romania, and in most of the successor states of Yugoslavia. Slovenia, one of the most successful transformation countries of the region, sought to defend its neocorporatist road and retained strict restrictions on foreign investments until 1997. In certain sectors such as communications, transportation, insurance, mass media, and publishing, entirely foreign-owned companies were not permitted. Company directors and the majority of board members were required to be Slovenian citizens. Approval for transactions was overly bureaucratic and deliberately slow. The situation began changing only after the European Union accession preparations, when a constitutional amendment (Article 68) enabled foreigners to own land, gave equal rights to domestic and foreign investors, and allowed the free transfer of profit and repatriation of capital. All of these measures were prerequisites for signing the European Agreement.

Bureaucratic procedure in the country, however, remained a major barrier to foreign investments in the form of some thirty documents and twenty local and state authorities' permissions required to complete a transaction. When an American company wanted to buy the household appliances manufacturer Rotor, Slovenia's principal daily newspaper *Delo* denounced the transaction in its June 10, 1997, issue as a "hostile takeover," since "the American way of doing business" did not care about workers (Bandelj, 2004: 463–65, 474).

Capital inflow took several forms, such as portfolio inflows, international security issues, international bank lending, and FDI. These forms of capital inflow gained importance from the late 1990s on. Although FDI played the most important role, to which I will return, portfolio investments played the second biggest role in capital inflow to the region. The main forms of it were international bond issues and portfolio equity investment in the region's stock markets. From the mid-1990s, Eurobond issues played an increasing role. The Czech Republic floated its first Eurobond issue in November 1994, Poland joined in April 1996, Latvia and Lithuania in 1997, Estonia in February 1999. In that year, Hungary placed a ten-year Eurobond; in early 2000 Poland issued a €600 million Eurobond, and Slovakia one for €500 million. In 1998 and 1999, overall Eurobond issues by Central European and Baltic countries reached $5–6 billion; this level stabilized after 2000. The main issuing countries were the Czech Republic, Poland, Hungary, and Slovakia. The same countries played leading roles in portfolio equity issues, which reached nearly $5 billion in the late 1990s, and gained further momentum after the turn of the century.

International bank lending, partly long-term, started to play a role in the mid-1990s, mostly for private companies, and reached an average of $5 to $15 billion annually. The main receivers were the Central European countries, but the Balkans also received bank loans (EBRD, 2000: 84–86). The importance of foreign crossborder bank loans is clearly demonstrated by the fact that roughly 40% to 50% of corporate funding in Central and Eastern Europe was covered by it.

A special role was played by the European Bank of Reconstruction and Development, an international institution established on the model of the postwar Bank of Reconstruction and Development or, for short, the World Bank. The European Bank was created with the specific goal of assisting Central and East European transformation.

Box 4.1 The European Bank of Reconstruction and Development

The Soviet bloc was still in existence, but the Cold War had ended and Poland and Hungary were undergoing transformation, when a visionary Frenchman, Jacques Attali, convinced President François Mitterrand that Europe had a responsibility to help transform Central and Eastern Europe on the Western model. The idea was simple. Just as after World War II the victorious countries founded the Bank for Reconstruction and Development, popularly called the World Bank, to assist postwar reconstruction and development, the European Union accepted the idea of establishing a similar bank for Central and Eastern Europe, the European Bank for Reconstruction and Development (EBRD). Mitterrand went to the European Parliament in October 1989 and stated: "the most important event for Europe, perhaps for the world, since the Second World War is what is happening in Eastern Europe . . . What can Europe do? Why not set up a bank for Europe?" In December the European Council endorsed the initiative. By May the agreement was signed, and the EBRD was financed and owned by sixty countries and two intergovernmental institutions. The initial capital in 1991 was $12 billion, which was doubled by 1997. Attali was appointed the first president of the EBRD.

The Bank began operations by assisting the Bank of Poznań in Poland. In the summer of 1991 the first three private-sector projects were launched. The bank financed bank privatizations, road construction, and other modernization projects. More and more countries joined: in the fall of 1991, the three Baltic countries; in December 1992, twelve newly independent states of the former Soviet Union. Fifteen years later the Bank was operating in twenty-seven transforming countries in Europe and Eurasia.

The EBRD became the largest single investor in the region. Although its largest client was Russia, absorbing 20 percent of the entire funding of the Bank between 1991 and 2003, virtually all of the transforming countries were assisted. Its mission is to assist the modernization of state-owned firms, to encourage privatization, and to support new private investment mostly by coinvesting with commercial partners. The Bank's activity is widespread. In 1996, it assisted the modernized reestablishment of the Estonian Hansapank, and it financed a gas distribution project in Macedonia, a power reconstruction system in Bosnia-Herzegovina, a power sector refurbishment in Bulgaria, a road repair project in Romania, and rail transport modernization in Hungary.

Examples of these activities include the Bank providing $40 million for the privatization of the Bulgarian Solvay Soda chemical group in 1997, and another $65 million for a five-year investment program. Besides assisting transformation and economic development, one of the important missions of the Bank is to clean up the highly polluting economies of the region. In Bulgaria, for example, one of Europe's worst lignite-burning, sulfur-polluting power stations at Stara Zagora was modernized by a consortium of the Bank and commercial companies, investing €650 million in 2003 to cut sulfur emissions by 95% by 2007. In Lithuania, the EBRD initiated a transaction which brought the multinational Carlsberg Company into the Lithuanian market: with a 20% stake the Bank established the country's largest beer producer, Utenos. With a 9% stake from the EBRD and the cooperation of major European companies, Slovakia's privatized energy distribution company, Zapodoslovenska Energetika, began transforming the energy system of the country.

In 2001 and 2002, the Bank's investment was $2 billion and $2.4 billion, respectively; in 2003 it reached $3.4 billion. Annual assistance to the eight new member countries of the European Union tops $1 billion. The European Bank disbursed roughly $80 billion between 1991 and 2004 and became a major contributor in transforming, modernizing, and developing Central and Eastern Europe (EBRD website).

Between 1993 and 2002, 26% of capital inflow was loans, and 19% was portfolio investment. Nearly 54% of inflowing capital was used to finance current account deficits, and a further 31% served the creation of internal currency reserves (Teodorović *et al.*, 2005: 84, 86).

The role of capital inflow to Central and Eastern Europe was crucially important, since domestic financial systems remained unable to finance transformation, restructuring, and the growing demand for investment. Foreign financial sources financed fiscal deficits and the private banking and industrial sectors, and accounted for the lion's share of investment in the infrastructure and industry of the region. Capital inflow in all forms reached $15–30 billion annually from the mid-1990s onward. Although it was unevenly distributed, it decisively assisted transformation in the countries of the region. In the Czech Republic, Estonia, and Hungary this contribution reached between 10% to 15% of GDP, while in others the share was about 5%.

On the other hand, the countries of the region accumulated a huge amount of debts, and their annual repayment burden consumed a large part of their export incomes. In 2004, Poland's foreign debt burden surpassed $99 billion, Hungary's reached $63 billion, and the Czech Republic's approached $46 billion. Much smaller and weaker economies, such as the Croatian, Romanian, and Slovak, accumulated $22–32 billion in debts; in Serbia, Bulgaria, and Slovenia it was about $14–15 billion. In the early twenty-first century, the debt burden was higher than the annual GDP in Estonia (by 116%), Croatia (113%), and Latvia (112%), but reached roughly 80% of it in Bulgaria and Hungary. Debt service consumed 44% of Poland's export income, nearly one-third of that income in Croatia and Hungary, one-quarter in Latvia, and between 18% and 22% in Bulgaria, Romania, Slovakia, and Lithuania. Capital outflow was thus quite significant (Economist, 2006b: 42–43).

The largest share of capital inflow comprised FDI, which represented 55 percent of total capital inflow during the transformation period. In

Hungary, it started before the regime collapsed, but it gained momentum throughout the region mostly from the mid-1990s. Direct foreign investment is not only the largest, but also the most important form of capital inflow. It had a decisive impact on the transfer of advanced technology and management, and consequently on the restructuring of the economy, export growth and productivity increase. A few hundred or a thousand multinational companies, virtual international business empires, finance three-quarters of the advanced world's research and development expenditures. As a result they monopolize cutting-edge technology.

Foreign direct investment became the prime mover of structural and technological modernization in the transforming countries. A large part of these investments, however, especially in the early years, originated from small companies and investors. Ninety percent of the more than 13,000 foreign companies in Hungary invested less than $130,000 each in the first years of transformation. The 5,000 foreign companies in Poland accounted for $134,000 in investment per unit at the end of 1991. In the first half of the 1990s, 94 of the 124 Italian investors in Central Europe were small and medium-sized companies with fewer than 500 employees (Mutinelli and Piscitello, 1997). Most of these firms could not play an important role in modernizing the region's economy. This situation, however, soon changed.

During the first decade and a half of transformation, Central Europe and the Baltic countries received roughly $162 billion and the Balkans another $42 billion in FDI. On a per capita basis, it surpassed $2,300 and $830 in these two regions, respectively. In the middle of the first decade of the twenty-first century, FDI inflow reached an average of 2.6% and 4.8% of GDP in Central Europe and the Baltic countries, respectively.

Kosovo, on its way toward independence, remained an exception. FDI to Kosovo reached only 1.2 percent of the GDP even in 2005. It is worthwhile to note that capital inflow to Central and Eastern Europe significantly surpassed FDI inflow to the three Mediterranean countries – Spain, Portugal, and Greece – in the 1980s, the decade of their acceptance by the European Union, when the inflow reached only about 1% to 3% of their GDP.

Behind the average amount, however, huge disparities characterized these investments. The main winners were the Czech Republic, Hungary, and Poland. These three countries received more than $135 billion of the total $204 billion (or, together with the countries of the former Soviet Union, $258 billion) of investment in the entirety of Central and Eastern Europe and the former Soviet bloc. These three countries remained the principal capital importers; by 2004, Poland was still receiving $6.2 billion, the Czech Republic $4.5 billion, and Hungary $4.2 billion. Romania also reached that level of investments ($5.2 billion) in

22%

52%

26%

Czech Republic, Hungary, and Poland

Other Central and East European countries

Soviet successor countries

Figure 4.1 Total foreign direct investment in the former Soviet bloc countries, 1989–2004

that year. Between 1989 and 2005, according to a report by Hungary's Ministry of Economy and Transportation, the country received roughly $60 billion of investment.

From 1997 on, reinvestments by successful foreign-funded companies began playing an important role: in that year, one-quarter of FDI originated from reinvestments, but between 1998 and 2000 this share reached half, and then, between 2001 and 2005, two-thirds of total FDI in Hungary (Hungary, Ministry of Economy and Transportation, 2006; Economist, 2006b: 64) (figure 4.1).

On a per capita basis, the cumulative inflow of FDI, as table 4.1 reflects, was the highest in the Czech Republic, Hungary, and Estonia. Poland, Latvia, Lithuania, Slovenia, and Bulgaria, on the other hand, received only about one-quarter to one-half of the per capita Czech and Hungarian FDI inflow. Albania, Bosnia, and Serbia and Montenegro received only about one-tenth.

Capital inflow in this form remained substantial in the four leading countries. The combined capital stock of FDI in the Czech Republic, Slovenia, Hungary, and Poland increased from less than $82 billion to more than $222 billion between 2000 and 2005 (UNCTAD, 2006). In 2005, they received more than $27.3 billion (UNCTAD, 2005b). The increase in FDI for the first time in the transformation period was even higher in the Balkans: between 2000 and 2005, capital stock rose in value from $15,128 million to $56,562 million, i.e., by 374%, compared to the 270% increase in Central Europe (UNCTAD, 2006).

Foreign companies became dominant in Central European industry. In Hungary, 47% of employment, 82% of investment, 73% of sales, and 89% of industrial exports were made by foreign companies. In Poland these shares were 29%, 63%, 49%, and 59%, respectively. In the Czech Republic, 27% of employment, 53% of investment, 42% of sales, and 61% of exports belonged to foreign companies at the end of the century (*Revue Elargissement*, April 12, 2003).

Table 4.1   Cumulative inflow of FDI

Country	Cumulative FDI inflows 1989–2004, in million US$	Cumulative FDI inflows per capita, 1989–2004, in US$
Czech Republic	41,704	4,045
Estonia	3,846	2,847
Hungary	37,189	3,719
Latvia	3,737	1,612
Lithuania	4,183	1,212
Poland	56,333	1,471
Slovakia	11,263	2,094
Slovenia	3,000	1,507
Total Central Europe and Baltic countries	*161,255*	*2,313*
Albania	1,440	450
Bosnia-Herzegovina	1,493	393
Bulgaria	8,241	1,050
Croatia	9,304	2,106
Macedonia	1,152	576
Romania	16,185	746
Serbia and Montenegro	4,088	491
Total Balkan region	*41,903*	*830*

Source: EBRD, 2005b: 19.

From the late 1990s, some of the Central European countries themselves began investing in the region, in most cases in the promising but lagging Balkan countries. Hungary made the first move: the Hungarian Petroleum and Natural Gas Company (MOL) became the largest Hungarian investor in Romania, Croatia, and Slovakia. In 2000, it acquired one-third of Slovnaft, Slovakia's leading oil refinery, which was the single largest foreign investment in the country at that time. In Slovakia, 600 small and medium-sized enterprises operated with Hungarian capital participation. In 2003, MOL bought 25 percent of INA, the Croatian gas distribution monopoly for $505 million (EBRD, 2000: 206; 2003: 132). Around the turn of the century, Hungarian firms held an interest in more than 3,000 Romanian companies, and Hungary's share of total foreign investment in the country was nearly 4 percent (Réti, 2003: 339–41). Országos Takarékpénztár (OTP), the largest local banking institutions of Hungary, also invested in neighboring countries' banking sectors and acquired an interest in several countries, occupying the seventh place behind West European groups, the main foreign players in the region's banking. Altogether, Hungary increased its foreign investments by nearly six times between 2000 and 2005.

Slovenia became an important investor in the successor states of Yugoslavia. In 2004, when capital inflow to the country represented $524 million, capital outflow matched 95 percent of this amount, so that net inflow was only $26 million. In 1998, FDI from Central European countries for the first time reached $12 billion, 14 percent of the stock of inward FDI. The annual investments by Poland, Hungary, the Czech Republic, and Slovenia in the region reached about $4 billion, while the total stock of their investments surpassed $16 billion in 2005. The four successful Central European countries together increased their investments abroad from $3.8 billion to $19.1 billion, or by five times (UNCTAD, 2006).

Foreign direct investments played the most important role in Central and East European adjustment to the European Union and to globalization. At the same time, it was the most powerful vehicle for the European Union countries to build a huge production network in Central and Eastern Europe and give an appropriate response to the challenge of globalization.

In the globalized world economy three major regional international economic centers emerged: North America, Asia, and Europe. They built up huge international production and supply networks and accounted for three-quarters of the world economy. These regional groupings compete on the world market. When the Berlin Wall collapsed, and in some cases even before that, multinational companies from Asia, the United States, and most of all from Europe turned to the new hunting ground in Central and Eastern Europe. The incorporation of the huge market with its natural and human resources offered several advantages for them. They could increase economies of scale. They could exploit a low-wage and relatively well-educated labor force, and rearrange their production networks with a new kind of division of labor.

In the period around the turn of the century, two processes coincided: the "twin process of transformation in the East and structural adaptation in the West" (Kurz and Wittke, 1998: 64). The North American and Asian regional centers enjoyed organic access to a large and cheap labor force and industrial capacities in their immediate neighborhoods, the Latin American "backyard" of the USA and the populous Asian countries for Japan. The European center lacked this possibility before 1989. Transformation in Eastern Europe opened a window of opportunity for a regional network in a nearby geographical area, in many cases within a distance of 150–500 kilometers. The main investors in Central and Eastern Europe were the member countries of the European Union: in the case of Hungary, they had an 80 percent share of foreign investments, while the

United States had only a 5 percent share (Hungary, Ministry of Economy, 2006).

The main motivation of the multinational companies might be cat-egorized into three major areas, although they often overlap. The first is *market-seeking* investments, which target the new market to buy important raw materials and sell the products or services of the multinational com-pany, without investment into processing or production. Some of the huge multinational companies were seeking to extract and export raw materials, mostly without processing. The danger of this kind of investment is that the extracting industry remains an enclave in the host country without generating any spin-off effect.[1] The investor country or some of the multi-national companies control and extract the host country's resources, and perpetuate the uneven division of labor and distribution of profit. This kind of capital inflow characterized multinational investments in some of the oil-rich former Soviet republics such as Kazakhstan, but was rare in Central and Eastern Europe.

The major European retail chains, the Belgium's Delhaize, Germany's Metro, Tesco of Britain, and Carrefour of France – actually nine of the world top fifteen retail giants – launched shopping malls and supermarkets in the Czech Republic. They built nearly 1,000 hypermarkets and cornered 55 percent of the retail sales in the country by 2002 (Economist Intelligence Unit, 2005: 48). The multinational PepsiCo. opened two bottling plants in Poland with a $60 million investment in 1992, and it announced another $1 billion worth of investment in Central and Eastern Europe over the next three years (*Wall Street Journal*, June 1, 1992). Philip Morris, which bought the Czech Tabak Kutna Hora, a state monopoly, invested in the region to monopolize markets. Philip Morris increased its market share to 75% of the Czech, and 62% of the combined Czech and Slovak, market. The Austrian Julius Meinl food retailer bought up a part of the Hungarian state-owned supermarket chain and started selling its own products in the country. Statoil AS of Norway opened eighty-five service stations in the Baltic countries and others, the Danish supermarket chain, the Moller Group, opened shops in Poland, and IKEA of Sweden opened seven superstores in the region. McDonald's established a dense network throughout the region. The negative effect of their penetration is their hugely increased share in the region's market, or as it is sometimes called, the stealing of markets.

Trading companies, however, sometimes also contracted with local com-panies, or established production factories in the same countries, to secure

---

[1] For more discussion of spin-off effects, see chapter 4, pp. 130, 132, and chapter 5, pp. 159–63.

supplies for its shops on the spot. McDonald's has domestic beef suppliers in the region, and IKEA founded a dozen factories there (*Wall Street Journal*, November 7, 1995).

Market-seeking investments, although serving the monopolization of parts of the domestic markets of the region and repatriating profits, also revolutionized the backward retail trade sectors of these countries and contributed to a substantial increase of services, as part of a belated service revolution. In addition, all of these companies made "crucial contributions to the creation of a modern business technology" in countries which lacked this technology (Dyker, 2004: 159).

Market-seeking investments took on several other forms as well. The Bertelsmann company of Germany bought up *Népszabadság*, the largest daily paper in Hungary, and *Nový Čas*, the leading Slovak newspaper. By 1998, the company owned five magazines in Poland, and gained a stake in Prague's City Radio (*Wall Street Journal*, April 5, 1998). Almost all the major hotel chains built or bought hotels in the region, some of them even before the collapse of the regime. Most of the five-star hotels, serving a booming tourist industry, became foreign-owned in most of the transforming countries during the 1990s.

Several other service possibilities also attracted foreign investments. One of the most important penetrations characterized the telecommunications market. According to various calculations, bringing Central and East European telecommunications up to the Western standard would have required investment of roughly $173 billion by 2000, and an annual 11 percent rate of line growth (Davies *et al.*, 1996). This figure shows the scale of the task. Solving even parts of this problem required foreign participation. One of the first and biggest investments in the area was made by the American–German Ameritech–Deutsche Bundespost consortium, which, at the end of 1993, bought 30.2% of Matáv, the Hungarian state telephone company. In 1995, this share was increased to 67.2%.

Similar investment was channeled into the telecommunications industry in the entire region. In June 1995, five leading telecoms companies participated in the bidding to buy 27% (with the option to increase this share to 34%) of the Czech telecommunications monopoly. The state decided to keep 51% of the shares. The $1 billion deal became one of the biggest transactions in the region (*Wall Street Journal*, June 2, 1995). SPT Telecom, the original Czech public telephone company, was partially privatized in 1995; subsequently the company joined a consortium with Royal Dutch Telecom and Swisscom, gaining a twenty-year monopoly in long-distance and international telephony. A huge part of the Polish telecommunications systems was sold to Ameritech–France Telecom; 35% of the Croatian and

51% of the Slovak telecoms system were sold to Deutsche Telecom. In 1998, Ameritech announced it would invest between $1 billion and $3 billion in Central and Eastern Europe in 1999–2000 (*Wall Street Journal*, March 30, 1998).

The Baltic countries privatized their telecoms systems with leading participation by the Swedish Telia and Finnish Sonera companies, which merged in 2002. The Nordic Company owns 49% of Eesti Telecom of Estonia, 49% of Latvia's Lattelecom, and 60% of Lithuania's Lietuvos Telecomas and 55% of its mobile operator Omnitel (Jeffries, 2004: 171, 211, 246).

Market seeking also strongly characterized financial services. The banking and insurance industries, backward and poor in the region, were almost entirely bought up by Western companies. In Croatia, Privredna Banka Zagreb was sold to Italy's Banca Commerciale, while in the Czech Republic Česká Spořitelna went to the Austrian Erste Bank and Československá Obchodní Banka to KBC of Belgium. At the end of the century, the Czech state controlled only Komečni Banka. Poland's leading insurance company, PZU, was bought by the Eureko group. The Bulgarian Express Bank, Hebros Bank, and Bulbank were sold to Société Générale, the Regent Pacific group, and the consortium led by UniCredito and Allianz, respectively. Erste Bank of Austria bought and merged three Croatian banks. Slovenia resisted privatizing the financial sector, and the first important step was taken only in 2001–02, due to pressure by the European Union: 34 percent of the shares of the largest banking institution of the country, Nova Ljubljanska Banka, were sold to Belgium's KBC.

German, Austrian, and some other West European banks played the leading role in Central and East European banking. While in 1990 foreign banks had a minimal share of 10% in three countries of the region's banking sector, by 2004 80–97% of total assets of local banking were in the hands of foreign banks in Bulgaria (80%), Hungary (83%), the Czech Republic (96%), Slovakia (96%), and Estonia (97%). The only exception was Slovenia, with a foreign share in the country's banking of only 17%. The Central and East European region absorbed 24% of total international banking investments. Only Latin America had a bigger share (58%), while Asia received only 16% (Bethlendi, 2007: 61–62).

Consolidation of the financial market, which began around the mid-1990s, was effected mostly by large foreign investments. This kind of market-seeking foreign penetration secured the bulk of modernizing financial services, recapitalized the weak and crisis-ridden local banks, and supplied the transforming economies with credits and loans. Foreign participation stabilized the local banking sector and made it relatively

independent of local economic troubles. On the other hand, foreign banking institutions earned higher profits and pushed local banks to less profitable and more risky activities. Austrian banks, using 16 percent of their
assets, earned more than one-third of their profits from Central and East
European business activity (Österreichische Nationalbank, 2006).

The second type of investment is *labor-seeking*, or least-cost-approach
investment, which sought to exploit the huge wage differential mostly in
labor-intensive production branches. Such investment involved contracting and subcontracting certain phases of production, frequently in the
assembly phase. At the beginning of the transformation, Central European
wages – counting at exchange rate parity – stood at only 7 percent of the
European Union's wage level. Between 1996 and 2000, average labor costs
in Central Europe and the Baltic countries increased by 8.5%, in Romania
by 70%, and in Bulgaria by 94%. Labor cost per unit continued increasing by 1–2% per year, in the Baltic countries by 6–7%, and in Romania
by 8–12%. The nominal wage increase, however, was mostly eliminated
by inflation. In real terms, using unchanged prices, the labor cost mostly
declined by 1–2 percent (European Commission, 2006: 142–43).

After more than a decade, wages in exchange rate parities increased to
15 percent of the Union's level. The 2001 average Czech-Polish-Hungarian-
Slovak-Slovene monthly wage of €533 was one-quarter – or less – of
French (€2,127), Austrian (€2,205), German (€2,674), and Danish
(€3,047) wages. Romanian and Bulgarian monthly wages, compared to
Central Europe, were even lower, €136 and €100, respectively. At purchasing power parity (PPP),[2] nevertheless, Slovene wages were nearly 60% of
the Austrian level and Polish wages represented 54%, while Slovak wages
stood at about one-quarter of that.

It pays to note that wage level differences varied by industrial branches:
while Hungary's average PPP wage level reached 38 percent of the Austrian
level, in the manufacture of transport equipment and electrical and optical

---

[2] The exchange rate is the price of one country's currency expressed in another country's currency.
For example, in the summer of 2007, €1 = 2.0 Bulgarian leva; €1 = 27.6 Czech koruny; €1 =
254 Hungarian forint. Purchasing power parity compares the values in a different way, based
on the difference of the price levels of the given countries. Less-developed countries generally
have lower prices than advanced ones; consequently, the domestic purchasing power of their
currencies is higher by the percentage attributable to their lower price levels. If the Bulgarian
and Hungarian price level is 50 percent lower than the prices of the Eurozone countries, then
the Bulgarian leva is not €1 = 2 leva, but €1 = 3 leva, and the Hungarian forint is not €1 =
254 forint but €1 = 381 forint. Consequently both the GDP and the wage levels of the Central
and Eastern European countries are significantly higher if we consider purchasing power parity
than official currency exchange rates.

equipment industries, wages were only 19% and 16% of Austrian wage levels (Losoncz, 2003: 14; Palánkai, 2004: 284). The slow rate of decrease in the wage gap will continue for decades. Even in 2004, an autoworker in Slovakia got $5.40 per hour, compared with more than $40 for a similar worker in the German Volkswagen factory. In the Western countries, the average wages and benefits combined for a production worker reached $25–30 per hour in 2005. Reaching that level may take decades in the transforming countries.

While the exchange rate parity calculations, which do not reflect the impact of the lower domestic price level in Central and Eastern Europe, do reflect the labor cost advantage for the foreign companies as well as the export competitiveness of the countries of the region, they cannot express the living standard difference between East and West because of price level differences in the two regions. Lower wages have greater purchasing power because of lower general price levels in less-developed countries. While monthly wages are about 15% of EU wages at exchange rate parity, at purchasing power parity they rise to 30% to 35% of the EU level. An advantage to wage competitiveness in transition countries is that at purchasing power parity, wages are roughly twice as high as at exchange rate parity:

The difference between exchange rate parity and purchasing power parity is an important source of the increase of competitiveness. Because of this difference, employers including companies with foreign participation pay employees' wages and salaries at exchange rate parity, whereas they get access to goods and services at a higher value at purchasing power parity. This reserve of international competitiveness is gradually eroding and [will] finally [disappear] as soon as exchange rate parity approximates purchasing power parity. (Losoncz, 2003: 21)

Outward processing trade[3] was initially mostly concentrated on low-value-added activities. During the 1980s in Hungary, and in the first years of transformation in the entire region, most investments involved either contracting or subcontracting labor-intensive works in textiles, leather, wood, and other so-called light industries. In Poland, clothing and furniture represented less than 7% of exports in 1989, but because of subcontracting this increased to 21% by 1995. In Hungary, the share of these branches in exports increased from 11% to 18% and in Czechoslovakia from 6% to 15% during the first half of the 1990s.

---

[3] Outward processing trade occurs when Western companies subcontract production to low-wage countries. The Western firms keep control of design and sometimes material input within the production process. The subcontractors' deliveries constitute part of the exports of the low-wage countries.

Every second piece of furniture sold in Germany in the mid-1990s was produced by German–Polish factories. Steinhoff's Polish plant employed 4,000 workers. The German clothing industry sought to cut production costs by outward processing trade: 60 percent of their output originated from outside the country in 1995. A large share of the capacity of the Central and East European clothing industry, 70% and 50% in Romania and Hungary, respectively, worked for Western companies. Between 1988 and 1996, outward processing exports from the East to the European Union increased by 24 percent annually. At the beginning, two-thirds of outward processing exports comprised clothing, but footwear and furniture also represented low-skill, labor-intensive sectors (Kurz and Wittke, 1998: 80; Eichengreen and Kohl, 1998: 178).

In 1993, nearly 70 percent of foreign investment targeted labor-intensive industries in the Czech Republic. This share, however, dramatically declined in the following decade. In 2002, investments in labor-intensive sectors represented only 16 percent of total foreign investment (Kippenberg, 2005: 259). In less-developed countries of the region, however, labor-seeking cost-reduction investments remained dominant. In Romania, the textile, clothing, and leather industries, which worked on processing agreements for Western companies in the earlier years, increased their capacities through foreign investment and retained their share of exports even in the early twenty-first century. Romania became part of the production networks of the German, French, and Italian clothing and leather-goods industries (Hunya, 2002).

Low wage levels in the Central and East European countries were combined with a relatively well-trained and educated workforce. Foreign investors, especially in medium-high-tech sectors such as the car industry, prefer this combination and maintain that it is more important than a low wage level by itself. They tend to invest in countries where wages are somewhat higher but the workforce is better qualified. This situation makes it easier for them to impose their technological culture on subsidiaries. The strong base of basic research and talented specialists in important sectors were also combined in Central and Eastern Europe with an outstanding geopolitical situation. Proximity to the advanced countries of Europe – sometimes only 150–500 kilometers distant – fostered labor-intensive sectors of the textile, clothing, leather, furniture, and other industries.

The third type of foreign direct investment is *complementary specialization* investment. Although transferring production of labor-intensive branches from highly developed to less-developed countries does not directly assist technological–structural modernization in the latter (hence the sobriquet "regressive specialization"), complementary specialization opens the door for technological–structural advance. True, the less-developed countries are home to the bottom of the product range at the beginning, but over time a more sophisticated division of labor may emerge through production of key components and advanced products in less-developed countries. In certain cases, the whole value chain and even R&D capacities are planted in the newly integrated countries.

In practice, the three categories of foreign investment mentioned above – market-seeking, labor-cost-decreasing, and complementary specialization investments – are often combined. Market-seeking and outward processing trade often go together, as is illustrated by the Romanian example. The low-labor-cost approach may develop in time to complementary specialization, as in the cases of Slovenia, Hungary, and the Czech Republic. The complementary specialization investments of multinational companies, because of their role in restructuring and technological modernization in the host countries, deserve special attention.

Complementary specialization within the international production network

Targeting complementary specialization in Central and Eastern Europe was an important goal of multinational companies in their effort to restructure and adapt to the globalized world competition. Several of them made "greenfield" investments, i.e., established newly built factories and new, previously non-existent modern sectors of the economy. Others bought existing, often obsolete companies and modernized them, mostly in the Czech Republic, Hungary, Poland, Slovakia, and Estonia.

The first multinational investments were initiated by General Motors in reforming Hungary before the collapse of the regime. The GM greenfield investment in Szentgothard introduced car production to Hungary, although at the beginning it was an assembly factory and most of the parts arrived from other European subsidiaries of GM. Soon, however, 15,000 Opel Astras rolled off the assembly line annually. Major multinationals invested in modern export-oriented car production in Hungary. Japan's Suzuki built its new firm in Esztergom and gradually increased production to 60,000 cars per annum. Volkswagen established an engine factory in Győr and produced the engines for its entire Audi production there.

One of the largest investments in the region was the privatization of Skoda of the Czech Republic (previously Czechoslovakia) by Volkswagen. As a first step in 1991, Volkswagen bought 31 percent of the shares, but according to the agreement Volkswagen planned to invest more than $6 billion to modernize Skoda over seven years. By the early 2000s,

Skoda sold 500,000 cars a year. Volkswagen's Bratislava factory produces 300,000 cars a year and has become the most profitable plant of the company. Besides its new Touareg SUV and Polo small hatchback, VW produces bodies for its Porsche Cayenne SUV in this factory. As noted above, labor costs in Slovakia are much lower than in Germany. The company saves $1.8 billion annually in personnel costs. Slovakia has attracted other carmakers as well. KIA of South Korea built a plant in Žilina; Peugeot of France employed 3,000 workers in its car factory, and created another 6,000 indirect jobs. On a per capita basis, Slovakia became the world's number one car producer with 800,000 cars per year by 2006 (*Automotive News Europe*, May 17, 2004 [Vol. 9, No. 10]).

Box 4.2 Central and Eastern Europe: Volkswagen land

Volkswagen Werke was the child of Hitler's Germany. It bolstered Nazi Germany and its populist propaganda campaign in the 1930s with the attractive concept of a people's car. Volkswagen further served the Nazi war machine in the early 1940s, when slave labor was used for war production. After World War II, the company reemerged as one of the pioneers of the automotive revolution in Europe. It served the rising consumer society and the "people's car" became a symbol of a new age in Europe.

Volkswagen began a company empire during the "golden age" of postwar prosperity, with subsidiaries from Spain to Mexico and Brazil. When state socialism collapsed in Central and Eastern Europe, Volkswagen was among the first multinationals to invest in the region, modernizing obsolete factories and building new ones. It focused on the Czech Republic, Poland, Hungary, and Slovakia, but also penetrated Bosnia-Herzegovina and some successor states of the Soviet Union, such as Ukraine.

Volkswagen closed the single biggest deal in 1991 with the $333 million purchase of 31 percent of Skoda, the most important Czech auto company. The agreement provided for a further increase of Volkswagen's ownership share and an eventual investment of more than $6 billion. A new assembly plant was built in Mlada Boleslav, followed by modernization of the entire Skoda factory. By the early 2000s, Skoda sold 500,000 cars a year.

Skoda represented only the first step. Volkswagen established a new factory in Győr, Hungary, and began producing engines for its luxury Audis. In 2005, an additional plant for chassis production was built in the same place. VW Motor Polska in Polkowice, Poland, was a further step. This factory was enlarged with $90 million in 1999 to produce engine parts and diesel engines. By the early 2000s, production had reached half a million engines per year, with plans on the drawing board to double that capacity. Following the opening in 2002 of its Poznań commercial vehicle and passenger car facility, Volkswagen broke ground five kilometers away for a 31-hectare supplier park, where sixteen international supplier companies established plants, including Viseton, Magnetto, Tennesco, and Kromberg and Schubert. Several other suppliers, among them the German firm Dräxlmaier transferred production from Germany to Poland to make parts for the Volkswagen Passat. The French supplier, Faurecia, opened factories in Poland, some of them only 45 kilometers away from the German border, to equip the VW Golf. In other words, Volkswagen took an entire supplier network to the countries of its new operations. As a consequence, Germany lost roughly 100,000 jobs.

One of Volkswagen's biggest moves, however, was into Slovakia. In its Bratislava plant, VW produces the Touareg premium SUV and the small hatchback Polo. Body production for Porsche's Cayenne SUV was also introduced here. The successful Bratislava factory tripled output within a few years to 300,000 units by 2005. The transfer of the Spanish operations of VW to Slovakia further boosted car production. Volkswagen, with some other multinational carmakers, made Slovakia a "New Detroit." According to the plans, total car production in the Czech Republic and Slovakia will have jumped from 170,000 units in 1990 to 2 million by 2006. In the Central and East European international car industry, which competes with French, Italian, South Korean, Japanese, and American sectors, Volkswagen holds about a one-quarter share of the new production capacity created in the past decade and a half.

The expansion of Volkswagen did not stop in Poland, the Czech Republic, Hungary, and Slovakia. It reached farther north and south. In 2002, Volkswagen placed a Skoda assembly plant in Ukraine which produced 40,000 cars by 2005. Volkswagen entered into a joint venture with the state-owned Bosnian UNIS in 1998 to assemble Octavia Skoda cars in Sarajevo. By 2006, the plant produced about 3,500 cars per year for the Bosnian market.

The Central and East European operations of Volkswagen reduced production costs. The hourly auto worker labor cost in 2004 was $40.80 in the German plants of Volkswagen, higher than in Japan ($35.40) or in the United States ($34.80). Competing on the world market required a dramatic decrease of labor costs, a difficult job in Germany. The Central European empire of Volkswagen helped: although labor productivity in Slovakia, the Czech Republic, or Poland is only half of the German level ($18–$20 value added compared to the $42 in Germany), a Slovak auto worker received

$5.40 per hour, a Czech $6.00, and a Pole $ 7.80; they work nearly 2,000 hours in a year, instead of 1,440 in Germany.

Volkswagen is also developing local markets of 70–80 million people: new registrations in the region are increasing by 6% to 10% annually, with between 1 and 2 million new car owners each year during the early 2000s. These figures are almost doubled if Russia and the other successor states are included. Meanwhile, Volkswagen's operation integrates the transforming countries into the European supply network. VW's output and deliveries represent a huge chunk of modern manufacturing and exports of the transforming countries, thus boosting the transformation process (*Business Eastern Europe*, January 27, 2003 [Vol. 32, No. 5]; *Automotive News Europe*, May 17, 2004 [Vol. 9, No. 10]; *New York Times*, October 26, 2005).

Small wonder that, next to China, the world's fastest-growing automaking center emerged in Central and Eastern Europe, mostly in the Czech and Slovak Republics, Poland, Hungary, and Romania. Since 1995, the leading car-making multinationals have invested $24 billion in the region. In 2006, the Czech and Slovak Republics, instead of their 170,000-unit production in 1990, produced 2 million cars per year. In 2010, these companies are planning to produce 3.8 million cars in the region, equivalent to 20 percent of the West European output, mostly for Western markets.

All the leading companies are present. GM Opel built a factory in Gliwice, Poland. PSA Peugeot-Citroën and Toyota have decided to build a joint-venture factory in Kolin, near Prague, by investing $1.8 billion to produce 300,000 cars a year with 3,000 workers. PSA Peugeot also opened a car factory in Trnava, Slovakia, and produces 300,000 cars; Hyundai invested $1.3 billion in its Žilina, Slovakia, plant, which began producing in 2006. Fiat has made big investments in Poland, and Volvo Bus shifted its Austrian and German production to Wrocław, Poland, to produce 1,000 buses in a year. Further enlargement is already planned with the shift of Volvo's bus production from Scotland and Finland to Poland. Renault bought the Romanian Dacia factory and produced roughly 150,000 cars per year.

In 2000, the ten leading multinationals held an 82% share in Central and East European car production, led by Volkswagen and Fiat with 22% and 10%, respectively. These expanded automotive industries are playing a leading role in economic transformation of these countries. The foreign-owned car industry produces 20% of the industrial output of the

Czech Republic, and Volkswagen is the largest exporter in Slovakia, while its Hungarian engine plant's deliveries represent 7% of total Hungarian exports.

The auto supply industry is also shifting towards the East. Visteon built a plant in Hluk, Czech Republic, where 4,000 workers produce lighting and climate control units. Delphi and Visteon are closing five factories in Western Europe and opening fifteen in the East. One was opened in 2004 in Sibiu, Romania, with a $24 million investment, producing automotive electronics and conducting research in its engineering laboratory (*Business Week Online*, September 5, 2005). Volkswagen built a 31-hectare supplier park within five kilometers of its Poznań factory in Poland and attracted sixteen international suppliers, among them Visteon, Kromberg and Schubert, Magnetto, and Plastal. One of the leading French supplier companies, Faurencia, built seven plants in Poland, and produces instrument panels and door panels for the Volkswagen Golf (*Automotive News Europe*, May 17, 2004 [Vol. 9, No. 10]). Car suppliers in the Czech Republic produce parts valued annually at $2 billion (in Hungary $1.5 billion) and supply more than two dozen carmakers.

As described in box 4.2 the VW–Skoda company became an outstanding practitioner of domestic participation: in 2003, it bought 70 percent of components and 60 percent of materials from Czech-located producers (Steiner, 2003: 93). Central Europe, as a consequence of resettling by suppliers, offers the densest supply network for car factories in Europe (*Business Eastern Europe*, January 27, 2003 [Vol. 32, No. 5]).

The development of other modern *high-tech or medium-high-tech industries*, also gained momentum. High-technology sectors such as pharmaceuticals, medical chemicals, computers, televisions, communications equipment, medical precision and optical instruments, aircraft, etc., and high-tech services, especially in telecommunications and R&D, were either missing or technologically backward in state socialist countries. The same can be said about the medium- to high-tech industries, among others, motor vehicles, locomotives, electrical machinery and equipment, and shipping and transport equipment. After the regime change, foreign investors, important multinational companies, created competitive export sectors in some of the countries of the region, mostly in Hungary, the Czech Republic, and Estonia. This phenomenon resembled the Asian development trend when Japan outsourced labor-intensive production to Thailand and Malaysia, and high value-added sectors to Singapore and later China. The development is also reminiscent of the Irish economic restructuring from multinational investments during the 1970s–1990s.

A landmark first step was taken before the collapse of the regime in Hungary. General Electric bought Egyesült Izzó (Tungsram), at the end of 1989. The Hungarian company had a 5% to 6% market share in Western Europe, and 2–3% share of world light-source markets. Tungsram, the crown jewel of Hungarian industry, however, had not kept abreast of technological advances in the industry. GE invested $600 million by 1995 and restructured the company, upgrading infrastructure and machinery. It cut the workforce by half from 20,000 to less than 10,000, and embarked on a five-year, $30 million retraining program. Production was shifted to high-margin products. It began producing Genura, the world's first and most efficient compact reflector lamps using induction technology. GE closed down several West European plants to concentrate production in Hungary. The company's Nagykanizsa factory became the world largest light-source producer. Its modern and high-quality products were sold worldwide: 10% in Central and Eastern Europe, 15–20% in the United States, 30% in Western Europe, and the rest in the Middle East and Asia.

In a pioneering and promising way, GE rebuilt and modernized the once-famous R&D capacity of Tungsram. Four of GE's eight worldwide R&D programs were located in the company's Nela Park headquarters, but the other four, including all of the former West European R&D facilities, were shifted and consolidated in Budapest with 750 employees (Marer and Mabert, 1996).

Besides GE Tungsram, other high-tech multinationals also penetrated into Hungary. The Dutch firm Philips and Siemens of Germany built production networks for consumer electronics. In 1996, Philips established its monitor factory with 1,000 workers and produced 1 million units per year. The company also founded assembly plants for videocassette recorders and audio equipment. Twelve Philips plants with 5,200 employees produced for export. Nokia of Finland also invested in this field. Nokia's 1995 takeover of Italy's Hantarex's joint venture led to the production of 300,000 monitors per year. Hungary received important investments to produce personal computer systems, hard drives, and monitors. IBM began subcontracting hard-drive head assemblies from 1994. It purchased Videoton, a leading but technologically obsolete domestic company, and invested $110 million, raising the total production capacity to 3 million hard drives per year by 1997. In its Székesfehervár plant, IBM increased production capacity threefold and established its worldwide center for notebook hard disk drive manufacture. The company became one of the best of IBM's ten worldwide plants.

Sony took its first cautious steps in Central Europe by subcontracting in Hungary, Poland, and Slovakia. It then invested $20.4 million in Gödöllő, near Budapest and established its consumer audiovisual production lines. In the first year, 40,000 compact disk players were produced monthly. Later the company moved its video recorder and color television production from France. "This investment," stated the chief executive of Sony's European operations, "points to a coming of age for Central Europe as a manufacturing base" (*Wall Street Journal*, April 5, 1996).

The range of investments was broad. Samsung began in 1989 with a 40 percent stake in Hungary's main radio and television factory, Orion, and then bought the entire company to produce 500,000 color televisions per year. Electrolux privatized Hungary's refrigerator producer, Lehel, in 1991, doubling its output and cutting employment in half by 1997. Four multinational giants, IBM, GM Opel, Philips, and VW Audi, produced nearly one-third of Hungarian exports at the turn of the century.

These foreign companies generated spin-off effects as well: hundreds of small and middle-sized supply companies mushroomed around them. Samsung's color television assembly, for example, was made up of 25 percent locally produced components. Nevertheless, instead of developing into a network of first-tier suppliers,[4] local companies played only a subordinated role in the second- and third-tier supplier chains even a decade and a half after regime change:

Firms from transition countries are simply not capable of achieving the status of first-tier suppliers on their own . . . The key issue of linkages and spillovers outside the area of FDI remains unsolved . . . Even the most advanced transition economies have struggled to generate locally owned supply industries to serve the great international projects. (Dyker, 2004: 12–13)

It was equally important that several other companies besides GE were attracted by the low cost of highly qualified labor, and also established R&D centers in Hungary. Sweden's Electrolux transferred its product development headquarters from Denmark to Hungary in 1996; another Swedish company, Ericsson, started a software support group in Budapest, one of its twenty-five worldwide development centers; and Nokia opened two research centers in the country to develop switching software and applications. Volkswagen's Audi Hungária Motor Kft. established an engine development center in 2001 to develop and produce the new generations of Audi engines. The German supply company KnorrBremse Kft. opened a production facility in Kecskemét, and then added an R&D center at Budapest Technical University, which developed a drive stability control system for heavy commercial vehicles. It resulted in a Hungarian world

---

[4] For more discussion of local supply networks, see chapter 5, pp. 159–63.

patent for rollover prevention (Szalavetz, 2006: 195). The American companies Motorola, Compaq, and Flextronics International also located their R&D divisions in the country. Hungary developed into a supply base for regional electronics sectors and contract manufacturing services (Linden, 1998: 258, 260–63).

Several multinationals, such as ING and General Electric, relocated their service centers, including accounting, customer relations, and call centers, to Hungary as well. Similar developments characterized foreign investment strategies in the Czech Republic. Besides the development of the automotive industry, investment in microelectronics also expanded. Motorola bought a majority in Tesla Sezam in 1997, established integrated circuit production, and also opened a design center. First International Computer of Taiwan built a personal computer assembly plant which produced 10,000 units per month for export from 1998. Japan's Matsushita (Panasonic) established its television tuner and remote control production with a $66 million investment in 1995.

Poland, although primarily a low-value-added producer in the multinational networks, also received investments in more sophisticated branches. Motorola opened a new software development center. Thomson of France bought Polkolor in 1991 and with a $90 million investment was producing 3 million color televisions per year by 1995. South Korea's Daewoo invested in washing machine production in 1995 and produced 100,000 units per year in Poland. Bosch and Siemens also opened washing machine plants in 1995 and produced 25,000 units per year; output reached 200,000 units for export by 1998. Philips expanded its consumer electronics production to Poland and employed 6,000 workers in its plants (Linden, 1998: 257, 262–63). The Swiss multinational Asea Brown Boveri opened thirteen subsidiaries in Poland, which employed 7,000 workers to produce generators and railroad gears (*Wall Street Journal*, April 5, 1996).

Foreign investments in Poland were also concentrated in financial services (22%), trade (18%), and, within the manufacturing sector, food products, tobacco, beverages, wood, paper, and publishing (11%). Foreign investment, nevertheless, played only a secondary role in the country's technological upgrading, and other channels of technology transfer and domestic technological potential proved more important than those from capital inflow (Weresa, 2004: 419, 423–24).

Estonia's widespread privatization program also attracted foreign investors. Between 1993 and 1996, thirty leading companies were sold, mostly to Swedish and Finnish investors. By 1997, 50 percent of Estonian exports were produced by foreign-owned companies. While in the first half of the 1990s 40 percent of investment arrived from abroad, during the late 1990s and in the first years of the new century, Estonia sold off its telecoms system, nationwide gas utility monopoly, half of its oil shale capacity, the entire banking system, and its railroads and local railway passenger-carrier companies. Estonia, more than any other Baltic country, became an integral part of the Nordic production networks (Jeffries, 2004: 170–73, 175).

The spin-off effect of FDI is crucially important for the rise of a modern economy in the transforming countries. In the first years of EU membership, in the middle of the first decade of the twenty-first century, foreign companies supply themselves mostly from their other European factories, and much less from domestic companies in the host countries of Central and Eastern Europe. Foreign owners deliver more than one-third of parts and materials for their Polish and Slovakian subsidiaries from their factories in other countries, although this share is much lower in Hungary, only 18%. The share of imported supplies of the multinational companies reaches nearly 70% in Slovakia, decreasing in Slovenia (58%), Estonia (55%), Poland (52%), and Hungary (50%). The role of domestic suppliers is relatively small: in five countries of the region only 34% of supplies are produced by domestic companies. In Poland this share is 40%, in Slovenia 41%, and in Hungary 45%.

Foreign direct investments generated rapid growth in Central and Eastern Europe, but the process of integrating local firms into the supply chain lagged behind. Only Hungary and the Czech Republic made significant progress in this respect among the new EU member countries. The base of domestic innovation and R&D must also be counted among the weak points of economic modernization in the region. Even in the EU-15, R&D cannot keep abreast of the leading American trend. Since the early 1990s, West European productivity growth slowed down because of "inadequate R&D spending and capital market rigidities." In Central and Eastern Europe, economic growth was "not linked to domestic R&D and technology effects" (Dyker, 2006: 55–56). Moreover, expenditures in that area decreased: in 1989, it reached 1–2.5% of GDP; by 2003, it had declined to 0.5–1.5%. The decline was not restricted to the first, troubled years of transformation. Between 1997 and 2003, average R&D expenditures from GDP decreased by 1.67% annually; only four countries – the Czech Republic, Hungary, Estonia, and Slovenia – had a smaller decrease in these figures.

Industrial innovation depended on purchasing plants and machinery, which consumed half of the innovation expenditures in the region. R&D expenditure is subordinate in Slovakia (15%), Poland (12%), and Romania (10%). In contrast, in the EU-15 machinery purchases account for only

20% of innovation expenditure, while R&D consumes 60% (Dyker, 2006: 138, 146).

FDI in Central and Eastern Europe has played a central role in post-communist economic transformation, creating modern retail networks, banking, and services. It was also the prime mover of economic restructuring, expanding the textile, furniture, and other sectors by subcontracting, and building competitive high-tech and medium-high-tech export industries. Altogether FDI played the most important role in economic growth.

In the first decade and a half of transformation, however, the spin-off effect from foreign investment was limited and the role of domestic research and development contribution even more so. *The beginning of the second stage of modernization, with an emerging domestic innovation base and participation in the production network with a domestic supply contribution, characterized only a few countries of the region.* Central and East European economic transformation in the first decade of the twenty-first century lacks strong domestic roots, and it remains dependent on foreign investment. These weaknesses did not slow down the region's transformation and adjustment to market requirements, but instead created limitations on further stages of transformation to catch up with the advanced West.

The first chapter of transformation and adjustment to the market economy, and integration into the European production network, is thus closed or closing throughout the entire region. With the assistance of the European Union, the accomplishment is significant, although the transforming countries exhibit various degrees of success. Furthermore, even the most successful countries of the region are too dependent on outside factors and suffer setbacks from time to time. The second chapter of transformation – with radical further social and behavioral changes, the emergence of a domestically based, innovation-driven, competitive economy which approaches the West European income level – remains far away even in those countries that have good prospects to achieve it. In others, it may not be achieved at all within the foreseeable future.

CHAPTER 5

Economic restructuring: transforming main sectors, economic recovery, growth, and weaknesses

The most important positive consequences of the economic transformation of Central and Eastern Europe were the modernization of the economy, the progress in technological adjustment, and the improvement of long-neglected infrastructure and services. State socialist economic policy had focused on industrialization and the development of strategic heavy industrial branches. The structural policy applied by the Soviet Union from the late 1920s onward became a mandatory "socialist economic policy" for Central and Eastern Europe after World War II, in a period of technological revolution and of a new orientation in the world economy. Obsolete economic structures dominated by old-fashioned, outdated industries and the neglect of services comprised the legacy of state socialism. Deregulation, marketization, privatization, and the inflow of foreign direct investment marked a turning point, and a crucial restructuring took place in the region.

Restructuring the economy: infrastructure and services, the most dynamic sectors

Building up a modern infrastructure and service sector was one of the most urgent tasks in the transformation, and certainly resulted in one of its most positive economic outcomes. After World War II, a transportation revolution created a new transportation infrastructure in modern economies. Road transportation for both freight and passengers became dominant, requiring extensive construction of roads and fuel and service networks for cars and trucks. The transportation system changed with the development of air transportation as well as with the modernization of the nineteenth-century railroads through electrification, dieselization, and development of new, fast-running trains. Very little happened in these areas before 1989 in Central and Eastern Europe. Christian von Hirschhausen rightly noted:

The infrastructure that had been developed during socialist times turned out to be incompatible with the requirements of emerging market economies in the center of Europe, both in quantitative and in qualitative terms. (Hirschhausen, 2002: 56)

Financial infrastructure, previously non-existent private telecommunications services, and new infrastructural requirements had to be addressed.

The road networks were obsolete and motorways hardly existed in the region until 1990. Hungary had 6.8 kilometers of road per 1,000 square kilometers of land area, compared to 25–30 kilometers in the European Union countries. The limited motorway system stood at roughly one-third of the West European level in 1990. By 2000, with 700 kilometers, the Hungarian motorway saturation reached one-half of the West European level. In Romania, the situation was much worse before 1990. Only 200 kilometers of motorway were in operation in the country, which had a 78,000-km road network. Only 6,000 kilometers of Bulgaria's 37,000-km road network were hard-surfaced road, and hardly more than 300 kilometers was motorway. Poland, a country with an area of roughly 312,000 square kilometers, had only 400 kilometers of motorway even in 2003. In the Czech Republic in that year, 357 kilometers of motorway were in operation, out of a 55,000-km road network. Of the 6,000 kilometers of main roads, 40 percent were in bad shape.

Meanwhile, the car revolution began in the region: car density, only 138 cars per 1,000 people in Poland in 1990, increased to 294 per 1,000 by 2004. The number of cars in the Czech Republic jumped as well: from 2.4 million to 3.8 million between 1990 and 2004, and to 358 cars per 1,000 people. By 2004, twelve of the world's fifty countries with the highest relative car ownership figures (cars per inhabitants) were in Central and Eastern Europe. Slovenia (with 445 cars per 1,000 people) neared the American level, and the Czech Republic and Lithuania (360–370 cars per 1,000) neared the Dutch and Danish level, while Poland, Hungary, Bulgaria, Slovakia, Croatia, and Estonia registered 250–330 cars per 1,000 people, more than in South Korea or Israel. Consequently, almost all of the countries of the region belonged to those fifty countries of the world with the most crowded roads. In 2004, Slovenia and Bulgaria registered roughly 26 cars per kilometer of road. The figure in Croatia was more than 50, and in four other countries it was between 30 and 40 cars per kilometer of road (Economist, 2005b: 69–70; 2006b: 71).

All of these countries initiated major road-building projects. Hungary introduced a seven-year program to construct more than 700 kilometers of new motorways. In Romania, a nearly $7 billion motorway program began in 2004 to build 1,300 kilometers of road, including links between Bucharest and Constanța, Brașov and Borș, and Timișoara and Belgrade. Poland started an extensive road-construction program in 2004. Slovenia built 277 kilometers of motorway and roads between 1994 and 2003, and that year began a ten-year project to build 540 kilometers of motorway, investing roughly $6 billion (Economist Intelligence Unit, 2005).

Central and Eastern Europe did not take part in the communication revolution of the 1970s–1980s and lagged behind the West. By the time the regime collapsed, only 14 percent of the population of Soviet bloc countries had access to a telephone. Telephone line density was only one-third that of OECD countries.

Hungary had 9 main telephone lines per 100 inhabitants, and in total 1 million main lines in 1990. By 2000, the number of fixed lines peaked with 4 million. By 2005 the number had declined to 3.5 million, or 35 lines per 100 people, because of the explosion of mobile telephone use. By 2005, the number of mobile subscribers in Hungary reached 8.7 million, a penetration rate of 87 percent. Mobile phones conquered the Central and East European market in a few years; in Poland, alongside 32 fixed lines per 100 people in 2005, mobile phone subscriptions jumped from 80,000 in 1995 to 24.3 million. In the Czech Republic, the number of fixed lines increased from 15.7 per 100 inhabitants in 1990 to 37.7, but the number of mobile telephones rose from 49,000 in 1995 to 10.2 million by 2005 in a country of 10 million inhabitants. In Slovenia, the number of fixed lines reached 40 per 100 inhabitants by 2003, but everybody had mobile phones by 2004. Romania, one of the most backward in telephony in 1990, already had 58 percent fixed-line household penetration by 2003, and 47 percent mobile phone penetration with 10 million units. Estonia, Latvia, Bulgaria, and Croatia all reached a fixed-line penetration level between 30 and 40 per 100 inhabitants, and 96% and 99% of the population of Estonia and Lithuania, respectively, had mobile phones by 2004. In the less-developed regions, mobile phones predominated: by 2003, there were 18 handsets per 100 inhabitants in Macedonia, 27 per 100 in Bosnia-Herzegovina, and 36 per 100 in Albania (where the number of fixed lines remained the lowest in Europe at 8 per 100 people).

As a consequence of foreign investment in the telecoms systems of the region, most of the Central and East European transformation countries rose in the ranks measuring telephone infrastructure. Between 1990 and 2000, the Czech Republic moved from forty-second to thirtieth place, Slovakia from forty-sixth to thirty-fourth, Estonia from fortieth to twenty-ninth, and Lithuania from forty-ninth to thirty-ninth. Slovenia, Hungary, and Poland improved more modestly, while Yugoslavia's position declined, as did Russia's and Ukraine's. Mobile phone use, because of the previous undeveloped level of the fixed networks, in most cases surpassed the highest Western level by 2005, when five countries from the region ranked among the top thirty countries of the world in terms of mobile phone saturation (Economist Intelligence Unit, 2005; Ehrlich and Szigetvári, 2003: 23; Economist, 2005b: 90–91; 2006b:, 92–93).

The road for *computerization* was also opened. The computer revolution did not reach the region before 1989. A personal computer was a rarity, and mainframe computers were principally used by the military and some of the state and research institutions. Catching up reached a turning point around the turn of the century. Less-developed Romania had 700,000 personal computers in 2001, but this number jumped to 2.1 million in two years; in 2004, the number of computer owners increased by 50% in a single year. This tempo was not unique; countries of the region experienced a 20–30% annual increase in computer and Internet use around the turn of the century. By 2005, half of Estonians and Czechs, more than one-third of Slovenes, and 30% of Slovaks used computers. At that time, 10% of the Albanian, 20% of the Romanian, and 26–28% of the Hungarian and Bulgarian populations used the Internet. In the course of 2005, the number of computers in Poland almost doubled, providing access to 29% of the adult population. In the Czech Republic, the number of Internet users exploded from 263,000 in 1998 to 3.4 million, more than one-third of the population, by 2003, and reached half of the population by 2005. Internet usage in some of the countries of the region already reached the level of the EU-15, or the EU-25 average of 441 per 1,000 inhabitants (Eurostat, 2005a).

The information and communications technology index, which combines all the per capita telephone and computer figures mentioned above, reflects the technological advancement of the region: Estonia surpassed Ireland, Slovenia surpassed Belgium, the Czech Republic reached a higher level than Spain and Italy, and nine Central and Eastern European countries ranked among the top 44 countries of the world (Economist Intelligence Unit, 2005; Economist, 2005b: 60, 91, 93).

In countries of permanent shortage and dull, poorly equipped state-owned retail chains, the *retail trade* began flourishing. Millions of private shops were established even during the first transformation years, and

Table 5.1   The service sector in the Central and East European economy, 2005

Country	Services as % of GDP	Services as % of employment
EU-15	70	66
Czech Republic	61	58
Estonia	67	60
Hungary	69	67
Latvia	71	60
Lithuania	64	56
Poland	66	55
Romania	49	38
Slovakia	67	56
Slovenia	59	54

Source: Economist, 2005b.

a boom in shopping-mall construction followed during the second half of the 1990s. By 2004, 200 hypermarkets were in operation in Poland and modern Western chains controlled 38 percent of the Polish food market. The world's most experienced and largest retailers established their sophisticated networks throughout the region.

Services in general, the most backward sector of state socialist economies, became the fastest-developing branch of the economy in the transformation countries. In 1973, before the economic crisis hit the region, the service branches employed an average 36% of the population. This figure increased through 1989, but approached 50% of employees only in some of the most developed and reform-oriented countries, such as Hungary.

By 2005, as a consequence of a service revolution in the advanced world – when Western Europe already employed about two-thirds of its labor force in services, accounting for roughly 70 percent of the GDP – the service revolution arrived in the region (table 5.1). Service employment in Central and Eastern Europe by that point had reached an average of 56% of the workforce, and the sector accounted for 64% of GDP. In the best-performing countries, the figure reached the EU benchmark of 70% of GDP. The Balkan countries remained behind: the share of services in GDP in Albania was only 50%, in Romania 49%, and in Bulgaria 59%, but the trend of catching up with the West was obvious (figure 5.1).

Nevertheless, services and infrastructure still exhibited major shortcomings. The financial sector, burdened by the legacy of primitive services for the population and manufacturing, remained one of the weakest points

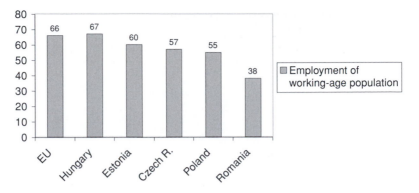

Figure 5.1 Employment in the service sector, 2005

during the 1990s. Undercapitalization, lack of competition, and a habit of serving old clients, mostly large companies, were all aligned against the needs of startup and small enterprises. The Czech Republic had one of the least-developed banking sectors, while Hungary had the best at the end of the century. However, even in Hungary, only 4 percent of bank credits went to small enterprises in 1998 (Dyker, 2004: 154–56).

Bank privatization was delayed in most of the transforming countries but picked up around the turn of the century. In Hungary in 1991, only 15% of bank assets were held by foreign banks; this share was even smaller in several other countries. At the end of 2000, the banking sector in almost all of the countries was predominantly foreign-owned. In Hungary, the Czech Republic, and Poland, respectively, 67%, 55%, and 54% of the banking assets were in foreign hands. The EU accession negotiations stimulated a burst of bank privatization and modernization in the early 2000s. By 2004, the percentage of foreign ownership increased, reaching 87% in Hungary and rising to 59% in Romania, a latecomer in the process. Foreign majority ownership reached 54% in Poland, accounting for 72% of the equity of the banking sector. The financial sector exhibits a high degree of international integration, but also an overwhelming dependence on foreign financial interests (Economist Intelligence Unit, 2005).

Foreign participation triggered a higher degree of bank concentration as well. In the European Union of fifteen countries, the five largest banks controlled 60% of market share. In the Czech Republic this share reached 62%, and in Poland and Hungary more than 50%. In the most advanced transformation countries, "the broad picture shows impressive achievements in the establishment of a modern financial system in a relatively short period of time" (Reininger, Schardax, and Summer, 2003: 346–47, 365–66).

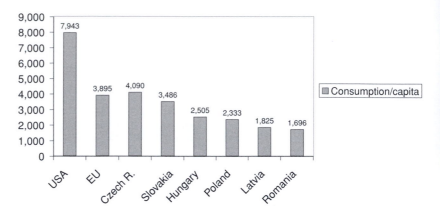

Figure 5.2 Total energy consumption/capita, 2004

The Central and East European banking system, however, remained relatively backward: banking assets compared to GDP reached only one-quarter of the EU-15 level in 2000. While the ratio of non-governmental credit to GDP was 117% in the European Union before the 2004 enlargement, these ratios were only 36.3% and 28.6%, respectively, in the Central European and Baltic countries, and in the Balkans. The highest ratio (an average of 57%) was achieved by Croatia, Latvia, and Hungary, while the lowest (an average of 9%) was found in Albania, Romania, and Serbia (EBRD, 2005a: 41). Although the regulatory and supervisory infrastructure developed steadily, as in many other areas, laws and regulations were not sufficiently enforced. In spite of existing weaknesses, however, a modern, well-capitalized, and more competitive banking system was in the making at the beginning of the new century.

The energy sector also required major renewal and modernization. Energy consumption reached the European Union level in the Czech, Estonian, Slovak, and Slovene cases, but fell short in most of the other countries (figure 5.2, table 5.2). Electricity production in many countries of the region remained reliant on coal. By 2003, more than 95% and 92% of electricity was produced from coal in Poland and Estonia, respectively. In Slovakia and Bulgaria the figures were 58% and 48%, respectively. Nuclear power capacity also played an important role: 82% of Lithuania's electricity was supplied by the Ignalia nuclear power plant, and 40% of Bulgaria's by the six reactors of the Kozlodni nuclear station. Nuclear power played an important role in Slovakia and Hungary as well.

Most of the East European nuclear plants, however, were Soviet types, in several cases Chernobyl-type plants built in the 1970s. The European Union pushed for the closure of these dangerous forms of energy production, but

Table 5.2 Total energy consumption/capita in 2004

Country	Consumption in kg oil equivalent
USA	7,943
EU-15	3,895
World	1,699
Czech Republic	4,090
Estonia	3,342
Hungary	2,505
Latvia	1,825
Lithuania	2,476
Poland	2,333
Romania	1,696
Slovakia	3,448
Slovenia	3,486

Source: Economist, 2005b.

reached agreements on gradual closing only around the turn of the century. Bulgaria agreed in 1999, but the plant will not be entirely closed until 2010. Lithuania postponed the closure of half its nuclear capacity until 2009. Romania modernized and expanded its nuclear capacities: a second unit was added to the Cernavoda nuclear plant by 2005 and a third unit will be in operation by 2010–11 to increase the share of nuclear energy in the power supply from 18–20% to 30%. The modernization of the energy sector of Central and Eastern Europe will require a long period of time.

The science and technology, or research and development, sector also needs revamping. The countries of the region spend a relatively higher amount on R&D, though most served basic (research) and not applied (development) needs; Slovenia, the Czech Republic, and Hungary spent between 1% and 1.5% of GDP; Poland, Slovakia, and Estonia about 0.6% to 0.8%. The transforming countries of Central and Eastern Europe inherited a strong base of basic sciences organized by the research institute networks of the academies of sciences. State socialist organizations of science, however, exhibited some major weaknesses. One of them was the relative backwardness of some of the most modern scientific areas. While achievements in physics, chemistry, and mathematics reached the highest levels, research in biotechnology and artificial intelligence languished. More importantly, the scientific base was characterized by one-sided basic science orientation, to the detriment of applied sciences and innovation. This did not change much during the transformation period. In 2000, development research received only one-sixth of the public funding for basic research in Slovenia:

> Publicly funded research focuses on science citation index and scientific excellence with little, if any, concern for the needs of business [which] has to rely more and more on technology solutions from abroad. (Bučar and Stare, 2006: 248)

Measured by the innovation index, which combines human resource skills, higher education enrollment, market incentives, the interaction between business and scientific sectors, and adoption of new technologies, the Central and East European countries reached only one-half or one-third of the Western level. Only Slovenia belongs to the twenty-five best countries in this respect (Economist, 2005b: 60; 2006b: 62).

This situation was rooted partly in conceptual-organizational constraints, but mostly in financial ones. Research was separated from graduate teaching. During the transformation decades, the old institutional-organizational structure was basically preserved, together with most of its weaknesses. Universities and the research networks of the academies of sciences competed with each other, and defended their vested interests. Combining graduate education with research made very little progress: what was needed was applied research to foster innovation, and this remained relatively weak. In 2006, bitter debates erupted in Hungary about the need for the reform of the Academy of Sciences, whose members and institutes, according to the critics, were living in an ivory tower with safe state financing and high incomes, regardless of useful results. The Academy of Sciences was forced to introduce reform: instead of automatically financing research institutes, applications for financial support were introduced, and reports of research results made mandatory. The science and technology complex in these countries "is still waiting to be restructured, and in extreme cases should be considered a 'liability' rather than an asset" (Dyker, 2004: 151–52).

Nevertheless, human resources in science and technology – measured by people with tertiary education, and employment in professions where this education is required – are quite strong in the region. The EU-15 average in 2002 showed a very high level of human resources: 41.2% of the economically active population belonged to this category. The percentage was even higher in some of the most advanced regions of Central and Eastern Europe, such as the Prague region (55.7%), the Bratislava region (53.0%), and the Central Hungary region (45.4%), as well as the central regions of Bulgaria (47.3%) and Romania (46.3%).

The Lisbon summit of the European Union in 2000 set the goal of R&D expenditures reaching 3% of GDP by 2010. In 2002, the EU-25 area's average was only 1.9%. Of the 268 European Union regions, only 21 reached the 3% level: of the Central and East European regions, only the Prague region is among them (Eurostat, 2005b: 86, 88). In February 2005, the European Commission proposed a new start and issued new guidelines because of these poor results at the midpoint of the program. In 2003, Slovenia, the best in the region, spent 1.5% of its GDP on research and development, and the Czech Republic 1.26%. Spending was much less in other countries: 0.95% in Hungary, 0.83% in Estonia, 0.59% in Poland, 0.58% in Slovakia, and 0.38% in Romania. The enlargement of the Union, alongside other factors, decreased the EU average that in the middle of the decade had been only 1.8%. Stanisław Kubielas noted that in Poland:

A continued downsizing of the country's R&D sector, [the lack of a] science and technology policy, and complete dependence on assimilating foreign innovations led to depleting technology absorption capabilities, structural stagnation and, finally, declining economic growth. (Kubielas, 2006: 201)

In spite of good export performance, even in the new member countries of the European Union, "their own innovative capacities (expressed . . . by the number of international patent applications) remains low" (Kaděřábková, 2006: 145). Furthermore, only Hungary, the Czech Republic, and Slovenia are supporting the integration of domestic enterprises into international networks to take advantage of any spin-off effect from multinational companies (Radosevic, 2006: 48–49).

Other sectors of the infrastructure have developed, but still fall far short of what is needed. In spite of the impressive improvement of the tourism infrastructure and the significant increase in tourists in Prague, Budapest, Riga, Tallinn, and the Dalmatian seashore, capacities remain limited. Hungary, the most successful in this respect, hosts nearly 16 million tourists and saw $16 billion in income from them in 2003, ranking eighth in the world in terms of tourist receipts. In 2004, however, only 12 million tourists arrived and the country declined to the sixteenth place. Poland, on the other hand, rose to fifteenth place with more than 14 million tourists. Croatia in these two years received only 7.4 and 7.9 million tourists, the Czech Republic 5.1 and 6.0 million. Tourism is not ranked among the leading economic sectors of the region, though in Croatia it accounts for about 20 percent of GDP (Economist, 2005b: 75; 2006b: 77). According to some calculations, modernization of infrastructure would require 6 percent of GDP annually between 1995 and 2010. This cannot be achieved because the transformating countries cannot fulfill EU norms and spend less than half of them (Hirschhausen, 2002: 63, 104).

In spite of a troubled legacy and lingering weaknesses, infrastructural development established an appropriate base for further economic development, especially if one considers that Central and Eastern Europe's infrastructure at the time of EU accession was basically equivalent to that of Greece, Portugal, and Spain in the 1980s (Eichengreen, 2007: 406).

Agriculture

Central and Eastern Europe is basically rural. Its history, traditions, and geography make even the Czech Republic, which was the nearest to the West, a mostly rural country. According to the OECD definition, an area is considered to be rural when population density is 100 to 150 inhabitants per square kilometer. Under this definition, 91% of the Czech Republic is rural, as is 63% of the population. The situation in Poland and Hungary is somewhat similar: with 92% and 83% of the area, and 30% and 35% of the population, respectively. The Balkan countries are even more rural than those in Central Europe.

Nevertheless, less than half of the rural land is agricultural. In the EU-15 countries, an average 40% of rural area is used for agriculture; in Central Europe the average is 35% (Ratinger *et al.*, 2006: 2). Agriculture, unlike in most West European countries, is an important factor in the Central and East European economy. One must not forget that almost all of these countries remained agricultural until the middle of the twentieth century, and that agriculture predominates in some of the Balkan countries even today.

Agriculture employed two-thirds to three-quarters of the population in 1910, and still roughly 40% to 60% in 1950. State socialist industrialization efforts led to a decline in agricultural employment to an average 27 percent by 1973. However, in Albania, Romania, and Yugoslavia, agriculture remained the principal occupation. At the same time, West European agriculture employed only 9 percent of the active population. Central and Eastern Europe's agricultural employment was three times higher than that of the West until the collapse of the regime (figure 5.3).

At first glance, it appears that the role of agriculture in Central and Eastern Europe followed the Western pattern after 1989. The decline in agricultural employment was the most striking element of structural change. In the Czech Republic, the average share of employment in agriculture decreased by 71%, from 10% to 4.5% of total employment between 1989 and 2004. In Hungary, the change was even more radical: the

Table 5.3 The role of agriculture in the economy in 2005

Country	Agriculture as % of GDP	Agriculture as % of employment
Eurozone	2.0	4.4
Czech Republic	3.1	4.0
Estonia	4.3	6.0
Hungary	3.3	5.0
Latvia	4.1	14.0
Lithuania	6.2	18.0
Poland	3.4	18.0
Romania	13.1	35.0
Slovakia	3.6	6.0
Slovenia	2.7	8.0

Source: Economist, 2006b.

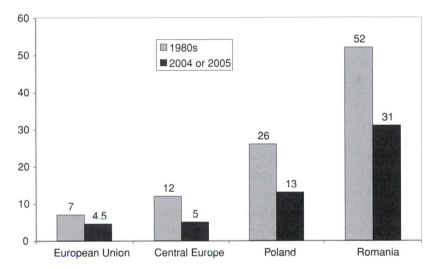

Figure 5.3 Agricultural employment, 1980s and 2004/05

percentage of agricultural workers diminished from 15% to 6% in a decade and a half. The decreased role of agriculture in the production of GDP was also an important element of post-1989 structural modernization. In the decade and a half after regime change, the structure of employment and the role of agriculture in the production of GDP emulated the Western pattern.

In the Czech Republic, Slovakia, Hungary, Estonia, and Slovenia, agriculture accounted for an average 3.4% of GDP and employed roughly 5.8% of the active population in the early 2000s (table 5.3). This approximated the Western average. The agricultural employment level in Poland, Latvia,

Lithuania, and Romania remained higher than 21%, four to five times the Western average; 71% of the Albanian population continued to engage in agriculture (United Nations, 2002; Economist, 2006b).

Although the declining role of agriculture seemed to follow the earlier trend in the West, the driving force behind it was different. In the West, the spread of big agrobusiness, a productivity explosion, and a high level of specialization were accompanied by the transformation of several formerly agricultural functions into independent service activities, performed with high efficiency by specialized companies. Agriculture became linked to food processing. All of these led to a steep decline in agricultural employment along with a steep increase in productivity and output. The even faster pace of growth in other sectors decreased the relative role of agriculture in the economy.

In Central and Eastern Europe, the agricultural labor productivity increase was moderate after 1989. It doubled in the Czech Republic and Hungary, but this proved to be the exception. It declined in several other countries of the region: for example, by 15 percent in Poland. Average regional productivity increased 50 percent, mostly because the labor force decreased. An agricultural laborer in the region produces only 9 percent of the value added by his Western counterpart. Technology input declined because the new small farms could not use the machinery of the former large cooperative enterprises. Specialization remained rare and food processing was seldom combined with agricultural production. Hungary was an exception: agro-food exports increased from $1.7 billion to $2.5 billion between 1989 and 2002, mostly because of the growth in processing capacity. The ratio of Hungarian processed food exports to unprocessed products was 2:1. In most of the cases, however, the declining role of agriculture in employment and output was due to a real slump in the sector. As a consequence, while the new member states increased the European Union's agricultural land by nearly 30%, its agricultural labor by more than half, and its agricultural capacity by one-third, the sector produced roughly 10–15% of the EU's agricultural products and 30–35% of its animal stock.

Agriculture, indeed, became the first victim of transformation. Collective farms were privatized and a large proportion of them dissolved. In some countries, land disputes dragged on throughout the 1990s, which led to uncertainty and blocked agricultural recovery. In Lithuania, only half of the arable land was held by clear title. Foreigners were excluded from buying land until the end of the century. Consequently, the land market was very limited. In Bulgaria, the privatization process approached completion by 2000, the same year land restitution was finally completed, but in Estonia, only 25 percent of the land was privatized by that time. "The privatization of land is the least successful part of the privatization effort," noted one commentator (Jeffries, 2004: 177).

The creation of small private farms in an era of steadily integrating agricultural markets may prove dangerous in the future. Small family farms are less able to react to the changing structural requirements of the market. The traditional grain economy of the region is already obsolete and the land given to grain should be replaced by fruits, vegetables, and industrial crops. However, whether Central and East European family farming will prove flexible enough for this task remains questionable.

The agricultural sector, paradoxically, declined after regime change. Under state socialism the agricultural sector was long neglected and traumatized by brutal collectivization. Nevertheless, the sector was somewhat modernized after collectivization, which, except in Yugoslavia and Poland, was accomplished in the early 1960s. By the 1980s, mechanization of agriculture reached 60 percent of the Western level. The tractors tilling the land in Central and Eastern Europe were mostly heavy-duty, averaging 1,268 horsepower per 1,000 hectares, compared to equipment averaging 2,051 horsepower in the West by 1982–86. Harvesting was also mechanized: four to nine harvesting and threshing combines worked each 1,000 hectares (FAO, 1962; 1990b).

In contrast, the mostly small private farms established in the 1990s were hardly mechanized. While the average total farm assets per hectare of land in the European Union reached €6,000 to €10,000, in Central Europe average farm assets stood at €1,500 to €3,000 at the turn of the century (Davidova *et al.*, 2006: 53). The decrease in the size of farms also went counter to the trend in the West. Big estates were mostly dissolved and privatized after 1989. Farms became fragmented: the average farm size in Poland was only 7 hectares, and half of the 2 million private farms were capable only of subsistence farming, unable to produce for the market. In 1993, 1,058 Lithuanian collective farms were, at a stroke, split up into 413,000 plots with an average size of 3 hectares each. By 1995, the average farm size in the country was 7 hectares. In the Balkan countries, small farms were even more predominant. Only two exceptions are noticeable. In the Czech Republic 5 percent of the largest farms – 95 of them were joint-stock companies and 154 were co-operative farms – cultivated 76 percent of the agricultural land. In Hungary, the average farm size was 80 hectares.

Consequently, Central and East European small private farming was not profitable. In the Czech Republic, 80% of the small private farms were operating at a loss in 2000. In Hungary, taking into consideration land values and unpaid family labor, only 60% of the farms were profitable

(Davidova *et al.*, 2006: 33, 42). Modern, efficient farming, including the use of existing machine inventory, became impossible. Private farming lacked sufficient mechanization and services. Romania had one of the lowest yields in Europe. A livestock recovery program was introduced there only in 2002.

Farm restructuring gained some ground around the turn of the century. The number of commercial companies in the Czech Republic surpassed 2,000, and more than 600 cooperative farms remained in operation, while the number of small private farmers declined to 100,000 by the year 2000. Although the cattle stock declined from 3.4 million to 1.4 million between 1990 and 2003, the country remained 97 percent self-sufficient in agriculture. In Hungary, one-third of the collective farms remained intact, and 60 percent of cultivated land belonged to commercial companies and cooperatives. The more than 5,000 registered farming companies cultivated, on average, 2,500 hectares of land each. Fewer than 900,000 farmers had farms smaller than 10 hectares.

Besides a chaotic transformation, domestic markets had shrunk, and traditional export markets – the Soviet Union and the other bloc countries – also collapsed, since the importer countries were not able to pay. In the early 1990s, one-third of Czech, more than half of Hungarian, and nearly 60% of Polish agricultural exports were reoriented to the European Union. A decade later, however, these shares had declined to 24%, 48%, and 48%, respectively. Competitiveness was the weakness of Central and East European agriculture.

This lack of competitiveness was partly the legacy of a lack of price sensitivity during the state socialist decades, and partly due to the preservation of an obsolete structure of agricultural production. Extensive crop cultivation remained predominant in the region. Hungary, with the best agricultural sector in Central and Eastern Europe, hardly changed the structure of cultivation after the war. In 1938, 62% of the arable land was given over to wheat and corn, and this figure declined only to 58% after World War II. Field crop production, which had represented 83% of the value of crop production in 1938, declined to 72%, while market-garden, orchard, and vineyard production only rose from 12% to 27%. Extensive grain cultivation remained dominant. The situation was even worse in most of the other countries (FAO, 1990b).

The elimination of tariffs and subsidies immediately after 1989–90 also contributed strongly to the lack of competitiveness. The region lost the worldwide subsidy competition: the EU's agricultural subsidies reached 48 percent of the value of production. Although most of the countries of the region reintroduced tariffs and subsidies in later years, the level of subsidy remained far below that of the West. As early as 1991, Poland increased its agricultural tariffs from 10% to 26%. Average subsidies, however, remained much lower than in the West: between 8% and 18% of the value of production in Hungary, the Czech and Slovak Republics, and Poland.

One further factor of weakness was the lack of modern integration of crop and other agricultural production with processing branches. Agricultural exports consisted chiefly of unprocessed products. Without this kind of integration, Central and Eastern Europe could not compete with advanced countries for agricultural markets. Consequently, most of the transition countries became net importers of agricultural products for the first time in their history. This happened in Poland, with its relatively large agricultural sector, by 1993. The agricultural trade deficit, $600 million that year, more than doubled by 1996. Romania, once the breadbasket of Europe and still an agricultural country, became a net food importer as well. While the European Union's food imports from Central and Eastern Europe doubled, the EU's agricultural exports to the region increased by nearly tenfold. Imported food flooded the region. The trade deficit in agricultural products increased in the late 1990s, and continued until the early 2000s. In 2001, only Hungary still had a substantial agricultural export surplus, of roughly $600 million. After joining the European Union, agrarian exports to the EU increased. Poland eventually became a net food exporter again. But food imports, for example in Hungary, increased by 34 percent in the single year of 2004, as a consequence of joining the European Union.

In the first years of transformation, agriculture sharply declined, in some cases by 50 percent. In some countries, this decline continued during most of the 1990s. This was the case in Estonia and Latvia, where after a steady decline by the turn of the century output stabilized at less than half of the 1989 level. Agriculture stagnated in most of the countries during the second half of the 1990s. After the turn of the century, Slovakia's agricultural output surpassed the pre-collapse level by 10%. Albania, an exception, achieved a 30% increase. In most cases, output reached the pre-1989 level only around 2004–05. Gross agricultural output in some of the most developed countries of the region had fallen significantly: in Poland by 13%; in the Czech Republic and Hungary by 30% and 36%, respectively. In the early 2000s, Hungary's agricultural production reached only 60% of the 1989 level (Ratinger *et al.*, 2006: 7, 10). Agriculture thus experienced crisis throughout the entire transformation period.

There was no breaking out of this vicious cycle: because of decline of marketing and output, agricultural inputs also dramatically declined, up to 80 percent during the first years. The use of artificial fertilizer – which surpassed the world average of 88 kg in Albania, Romania, and Bulgaria, and almost reached the most advanced Western level of 300–500 kg in Hungary and Czechoslovakia by the late 1980s – for a period almost disappeared, and remained about 20 percent of the pre-collapse level until the end of the 1990s (FAO, 1990a; 2000). Except in Romania, Albania, and Poland, the agricultural population deserted the sector so that labor input decreased by more than one-third.

Box 5.1 A forgotten country: Moldova

Miroslav Krleža, the outstanding Yugoslav writer, invented a typical East European country, Blitva, in one of his "realistic grotesque" novels. Blitva's history was more than troubled: its borders were always changing, it continuously participated in wars, it was backward and despotic, a country where politics and ideals were built on "mutual rejection." Blitva was late to everything in history, and celebrated the arrival of the Renaissance of the *quattrocento* in the twentieth century. Well, one does not need much fantasy to summon such a "model" country for troubled Central and Eastern Europe: we have a real one, long called Bessarabia, but recently renamed Moldova.

The small country of 34,000 square kilometers and 4.3 million people has a mixed population typical of Central and Eastern Europe. In 1989, nearly 65% of its populace was Moldovan, speaking the Moldovan language, which is a dialect of Romanian. Ukrainians make up 14% of the population, and Russians account for 13%. Nearly 6% are Bulgarian and Gagauz (Turkicized Bulgarians, or Bulgarized Turks, who migrated to the area in the early nineteenth century). In the Transnistrian eastern region of the country, however, Moldovans make up 40% of the population, while Ukrainians and Russians comprise 28% and 25%, respectively. This ethnic mix made the country chaotic and explosive.

Moldova, which became independent in 1991, is one of the most troubled countries of Europe. It belonged to Lithuania and the Hungarian kingdom, was under Ottoman suzerainty after the sixteenth century, was occupied by Russia in 1812, and was turned over to Romania after the Crimean War. It was next regained by Russia at the Congress of Berlin in 1878. The area west of the River Dniestr was reannexed by Romania in 1918 after the Bolshevik Revolution, but this was still not the end of the story. On the Soviet side, a Moldavian Autonomous Soviet Socialist Republic was established in 1924, and the Romanian part was incorporated into it in 1940, when Stalin reoccupied the region. It did not remain that way for long: the next year, Romania, led by General Ion Antonescu in alliance with Hitler, reoccupied Transnistria and launched a bloody Holocaust against the large Jewish community. In August 1944, as a result of the successful offensive of the Red Army, the Soviet Union regained the territory and unified the Moldavian Soviet Socialist Republic. The alphabet was changed to Cyrillic script, and Russian was made an official language. Furthermore, massive Russian and Ukrainian immigration changed the ethnic composition of the region.

During the deep crisis of the late 1980s, as in the Baltic countries, the communist leadership was taken over by locals, who reinvented themselves as nationalists in a popular front. Moldovan was made the official language, and in June 1990 the Moldavian Supreme Soviet voted for a declaration of sovereignty. Independence was gained after the failed anti-Gorbachev coup in August 1991.

The declaration of independence generated strong resistance among the Russian and Ukrainian population. Civil war erupted, and Russian army units arrived. A ceasefire in June 1992 and the formation of a loose tripartite confederation of Moldova, the Transnistrian Russians, and the Turkic Gagauz community could not solve the problems. In 1995, Transnistrian independence was declared. The separatist movements were ultimately consolidated, partly by giving special status to minorities by 1996.

Moldova became a country in a no-man's-land: the Romanian Moldovans look to Romania, but the country signed the Commonwealth of Independent States agreement with most of the successor states of the Soviet Union, even though it did not join the payment and customs union agreement of the CIS. Russia provides all of Moldova's energy. Russia, Ukraine, and Belarus take 60 percent of Moldova's exports, and are the source of two-thirds of its imports.

Economic decline was widespread in Central and Eastern Europe during the first years of transformation, but it proved unparalleled in Moldova: GDP declined in every year except two between 1991 and 2000, by which time it rested at less than one-third of the 1989 level. Livestock was decimated, pig stocks halved. Even so, reagrarization led to an increase in agriculture's share of GDP from 31% to 48%, and agricultural employment occupied roughly half the active population, while industry's share fell to 15 percent. Moldova, with extremely good black soil between the Prut and Dniestr Rivers, remained an agrarian and mostly rural country with a slight majority living outside urban settlements. Inflation climbed to more than 1,200 percent per year in 1992 and 1993. Foreign investors shunned Moldova. While the transformation of the better-situated Baltic countries progressed steadily, Moldova faltered during the 1990s. Between 1991 and 2001, Moldova led the group of worst-performing countries of the world with an annual 8.5 percent decrease in its GDP. While most of the countries of the region showed signs of recovery between the mid-1990s and 2004–05, Moldova's industry declined every year by 2.4 percent between 1994 and 2004. The country, however, regained some dynamism: after 2000, economic growth returned and recovery slowly began. The future, nevertheless, is hardly predictable (Economist Intelligence Unit, 2005; EBRD, various years; Economist, 2006b).

By the time of European Union membership, nevertheless, the agricultural sector had become more or less stabilized. The ten new member countries of the European Union provide 29 percent of the area growing cereals, and they produce 20 percent of the EU-25 total gross harvest. Wheat yields average 34.1 quintals per hectare, nearly 20 percent less than the average yields of the EU-15 countries. The potato yields average 189 quintals per hectare in Poland, compared to 371.4 quintals in the EU-15, but Poland became one of the main producers and delivers more than 23 percent of the EU-15 potato output. The new member countries produce more than 16 percent of the EU-25 sugar beets (Eurostat, 2005b: 25–34).

The most difficult period had passed. Institutional reforms kept pace with accession negotiations from the late 1990s, and European Union subsidies, although limited for a while, resulted in net income to the sector. In 2004, direct EU payments amounted to only 25% of the common agricultural policy (CAP) payment level for old member countries, rising to 35% by 2006, and it will reach the Western CAP payment level by 2013. It was observed that

EU accession leads to increased agricultural incomes... Due to the differentiation of support, however, there will be winners and losers... In general, beef, milk, and oil seeds will gain, while pork and poultry meat production will face difficulties... It has been shown that the Copenhagen Agreement offers good opportunities for the new EU members both in terms of income gains and further improvement of agricultural structures. (Bauer and Möllmann, 2006: 138–39)

The implementation of EU standards promises accelerated adjustment (Csáki, 2005: 14). Real modernization with significant technological input, the integration of crop production and animal husbandry with processing branches, and the establishment of a modern agricultural service sector are, nevertheless, still on the agenda. The process will take a long time to accomplish.

Industrial restructuring

Industrial decline during the first transformation years was devastating, but – using the Schumpeterian term – it was at least partially a creative destruction. The misdirection of industry caused by socialist industrialization policy, and the creation of obsolete, raw material- and energy-intensive "heavy industrial" branches, had to be corrected. The leading sectors of Stalinist and post-Stalinist industrialization, as a consequence, became the victims of transformation. Their collapse cleared the way for modern restructuring. Symbolic expression of this transformation was given in the October 15, 2005, report in the leading Hungarian daily, *Népszabadság*, that the onetime center of the Hungarian coal industry in Nógrád county, which formerly produced up to 40 percent of national output, had been converted into a museum of coal mining (*Népszabadság*, October 15, 2005). Poland, a country of coal, iron, and steel industries, downsized these sectors sharply: steel output dropped from 20 million tons to 8.4 million, hard coal output decreased from 193 million tons to 101 million between the late 1980s and 2004, and production was further cut after that. The coal sector of the Czech Republic employed 186,000 workers in 1990, but only 64,000 by 2003. The downsized sector of heavy industries was also modernized: some branches such as iron and steel attracted Western investments after privatization. Natural and capital endowments were upgraded, increasing the competitive advantage of the sector.

It was mostly positive that deindustrialization resulted in a better sectoral balance more in line with the advanced pattern of the turn of the century. Employment in industry and its contribution to GDP dramatically declined (see table 5.4). Between 1989 and 2004, in Poland, the share of industry in the production of GDP declined from 42% to 33%, in Hungary from 40% to 28%, and in Romania from 57% to 32%. Slovenia experienced a more modest decline from 45% to 38% in the same period of time. The role of industry in the national economy is now more similar to the Western pattern (figure 5.4).

On the downside, most countries of the region, except Slovenia and in some cases Slovakia, have written off important economic sectors and have ignored the possibility they might be modernized. Some less-developed countries of the Balkans, especially Albania and some newly independent successor states of Yugoslavia, experienced a deindustrialization process before successful industrialization. In 1989, 40% of Albanian GDP was produced by mining and industry, but by 2004 this share had dropped to 20%. In Macedonia, the share of industrial contribution to the GDP decreased from 45% to 30% during the first decade and a half of

Table 5.4   Industry's role in the economy in 2004

Country	Industry as % of GDP	Industry as % of employment
USA	18.2	23.0
Eurozone	**27.0**	**31.2**
Bulgaria	30.0	33.0
Czech Republic	38.1	40.0
Estonia	28.9	33.0
Hungary	27.5	34.0
Latvia	23.0	27.0
Lithuania	32.9	28.0
Poland	33.0	29.0
Romania	31.8	30.0
Slovakia	29.7	38.0
Slovenia	38.2	38.0

Source: Economist, 2006b.

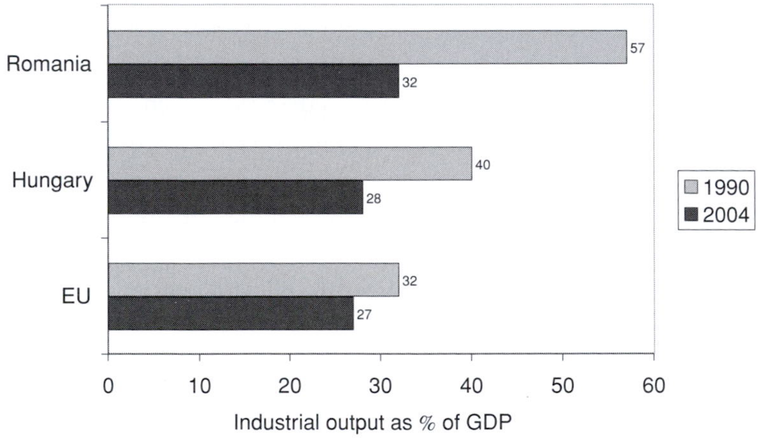

Figure 5.4 Deindustrialization, 1990–2004

transformation. Mining, a leading sector during the Yugoslav period, practically collapsed. The phenomenon in that country was not limited to the first years of a troubled transformation, or even to the civil war period: mining continued to decline by 39% and 66% in 2003 and 2004, respectively.

Unemployment reached a record 38% in Macedonia in 2004. In Kosovo, it remained 43%, but among young people, who represent the largest age group, it was 75%. In Croatia, 36% of the young generation was unemployed although the general unemployment rate according to the

ILO standard remained 15% in 2005. Between 1996 and 2000, employment in the public sector declined by 27% and in the privatized sector by 14%. Unemployment hit a record high among the largest minority of Central and Eastern Europe, the Roma (Economist Intelligence Unit, 2005; Mildner, 2006: 49; Teodorović *et al.*, 2005: 21).

Box 5.2   The largest minority in Central and Eastern Europe: the Roma

The Roma people migrated from northern India to Europe a millennium ago, and today about 8 to 12 million Roma live throughout the world. More than half of them – 6 to 8 million – are in Central and Eastern Europe. Following the disappearance of the Jewish and German minorities during and after World War II, they represent the largest minority group in the region. Reliable numbers are always questionable because of the huge difference between official data and reality. Most of the Roma people, because of discrimination and xenophobia, declare themselves Slovak, Hungarian, or Serb, not Roma, in various censuses. In Slovakia, the official Roma population figure was 83,000 in 2000, while in reality they numbered more than half a million. In Romania, their real number is probably five to six times higher than the official 400,000. Most of the countries of the region have a significant, 400,000- to 800,000-person Roma minority: 11% of the population of Macedonia, 10% of Slovakia, 8% of Bulgaria, 7% of Romania, 6% of Hungary, and 5% of Serbia.

  Although most Roma people adopted the dominant religion of the countries where they lived, they have never assimilated. They have maintained their nomadic practices or lived in Roma ghettos, using their own language, special family structures, marriage habits, traditional skills, and cultural traditions. The various states, from time to time, made efforts to assimilate them. Those attempts have met with failure: both the enlightened absolutist regime of Maria Theresa in the Habsburg Empire and two hundred years later the Czechoslovak communist state in 1958 prohibited the nomadic lifestyle and tried to settle the "new citizens." The communist regimes throughout the region made an effort to settle all of them, offering free housing in prefabricated urban dwellings, and jobs in unskilled construction and industrial works. Most of the children were forcibly enrolled in schools. Even the strict measures of the East European police states were only partially successful.

  Hatred of the "Gypsies" – Cyganie, Cigány, Cigani, Cigan, or Ţigani as they were called in various East European languages – had a long tradition in Europe, on a par with religious anti-Semitism. They were the targets of medieval witch hunts. They were enslaved in the Balkans. Both Emperor Charles VI and Adolf Hitler sought to eliminate them in the early eighteenth and middle of the twentieth centuries, respectively. The majority populations of the region preserved a traditional xenophobic attitude toward alien peoples. The Gypsies were stereotyped as thieves (the German term "Zigainer" probably originated from the expression "ziehende gauner," "traveling thieves"), dirty criminals, beggars, lazy and irresponsible. Recent polls reflect the survival and vitality of these views: 91% of the Bulgarians maintained that Gypsies are born criminals, and 83% think that they are lazy and irresponsible. It is true that the rate of crime is several times higher among the Roma population than the average in these countries. Segregation remained a fact, most dramatically in the Czech town of Usti nad Labem, where in 1999 a wall up to four meters high was put up to isolate the Roma settlement. Around 2000, half of the Roma population in Slovakia remained in Roma ghettos, in 281 segregated settlements without running water or electricity. Roma minority people were often victimized and always discriminated against.

The vast majority of the Roma population lived in deep poverty during the entire modern history of the region. They were losers in the 1989 regime change in Central and Eastern Europe. They lost the security they had gained under oppressive but paternalistic communist rule, which forced their settlement but offered free housing, healthcare, and guaranteed jobs. When job security was lost after 1989, they became the first victims: 85% of the Roma population of the Czech Republic, 75% in Slovakia, and 74% in Hungary became unemployed, and remained so into the early 2000s. The Roma population is disadvantaged in terms of education: 90% of the Roma in Bulgaria do not have elementary education, 50% of the Romanian Roma population are illiterate. Roma children are not welcomed in public schools and sometimes are directed to special schools for retarded children: 75 percent of Roma children in the Czech Republic, and nearly half in Hungary, are in this type of school.

The United Nations Development Programme's first survey on the Roma minority in five Central and East European countries in 2003 revealed that the Roma minority lived in "Third World conditions" in these countries, and the Human Development Index for this group (a combination of per capita GDP, educational level, and life expectancy) is as low as Botswana's. One out of six Roma is starving, four out of ten have no access to running water, and only one out of five is employed. While economic activity among women is nearly 45% in Hungary, among Roma women, it is only 15%. It is not surprising that begging, petty crime, and pickpocketing are practiced by the Roma population in the region.

During the dramatic years of transformation after 1989, public animus against the Roma minority reemerged. The disappointment and misery of the early years generated a wave of violent atrocities against Roma settlements between 1990 and 1993. Skinheads and villagers attacked and even lynched Roma people in the Czech and Slovak Republics, shouting "cikani do plynu" or "Gypsies be gassed." In the spring of 1991, the International Helsinki Federation for Human Rights reported "pogroms against Gypsies in Romania" in twenty-four villages. Roma houses were burned in Bulgaria, and "charred remains of houses burned to the ground" lined the road between Tîrgu Mureş and Cluj in Romania. In Hadareni an entire village participated in burning Roma homes.

Violence remained a constant feature. Amnesty International regularly reported violence against Roma people in the region. After the NATO bombing and the Serb defeat in Kosovo, one of the first actions of the Albanian Kosovo Liberation Army was a widespread and successful ethnic cleansing against the nearly 10 percent Roma minority in the province. Kosovo Albanians declared them loyal to the Serbs and destroyed nearly 15,000 Roma houses. According to some reports, the Roma population of Kosovo dropped from 150,000 before 1999 to 30,000. Roma efforts to emigrate were a hallmark of the entire transformation period in Central and Eastern Europe. Between 1997 and 2005, some 15,000 Roma asked for asylum in the West.

Although the future of the Roma minority remained uncertain in Central and Eastern Europe, there were some positive developments. In some of the countries, Roma people gained minority status, political representation, and cultural organizations. A pan-continental "European Roma Forum" was established. The European Union and eight countries of the region, together with some international institutions announced the "Decade of Roma Inclusion" in 2005. Anti-discriminatory laws were enacted and schools established. Hungary sent the first Roma representative to the European Parliament. The human rights and democratic requirements of the European Union promised a gradual, if slow progress towards inclusion of the Roma in social life (Tanner, 2004; Ringold, 2000; *New York Times*, October 27, 1993; United Nations Information Service, January 21, 2003 [note no. 230]).

Some of the newly established West Balkan countries could not cope with the postwar crisis for long. As a Croat economic expert stated:

The country's economy is still in the stage of prolonged recession...On microeconomic level the degree of instability is increasing...Croatia needs a policy of reindustrialization . . . by creating a new export based manufacturing. (Teodorović *et al.*, 2005: 54)

Deindustrialization destroyed important factors of modernization in that region. This situation exhibits certain similarities with the Greek experience. After joining the European Union, Greece went through a deindustrialization process that happened before appropriate industrialization was accomplished. This peculiar situation might be a central factor underlying Central and Eastern Europe's difficulty in catching up with the Union. The Greek phenomenon was not reproduced in any other relatively backward accession countries after joining the EU.

Despite all these factors, Central and East European industry began recuperating from the mid-1990s. Capital formation, which was high during the state socialist period, but declined during the deep crisis and the first years of transformation, increased from 1993 onward. In Hungary, Poland, and Slovenia, it increased on average annually by 6.3%, 13.5%, and 11.8%. While fixed investments in Slovenia reached 19% of the GDP in 1992, they increased to 26% by 1999. Estonia and Latvia experienced double-digit increases in the second half of the 1990s. The situation was repeated in Bulgaria and Slovakia before the end of the century. Capital accumulation rose rapidly in the Czech Republic and Romania in 1994–95, and then declined between 1997 and 1999. In the first five years of the new century, however, Romanian gross fixed investments grew by 48 percent.

In the late 1990s, the Central and East European countries' innovation expenditures were mostly spent on new machinery. While the EU-15 countries spent only 22% of their innovation expenditures on machinery, Romania spent nearly 90%, Latvia 75%, and Poland, the Czech Republic, and Croatia roughly 50% on such items. Between 1995 and 2001, the machine park (capacity) of the manufacturing industry in the region increased by 151%. The most modern sectors achieved the best results: while the food and textile industries increased their machine park by 70% and 80%, the office machinery and computers; electric machinery; radio and communications equipment; and transport equipment industries increased their machine park by 865%, 532%, 401%, and 360% (Radosevic, 2006: 38; Szalavetz, 2006: 192).

Central and Eastern Europe experienced important structural changes, improved their technological base, and integrated into the European Union's industrial economy. In the first phase of transformation, nevertheless, the industrial sector of the region profited the most from its low wage level. On an exchange rate basis, industrial wages reached only 7% of the Western level in the first transformation years, and then increased to between 15% and 20%. This difference extended a wage advantage for the countries of the region. Croatia was an exception: purchasing parity and exchange rate wages were almost identical, which eliminated any kind of wage advantage for the country.

Outward processing agreements and trade played a leading role in the early years of transformation. Western multinational companies supplied the materials for Central European countries to produce finished and semi-finished products for delivery back to the West. These agreements were most common in low-tech industrial sectors such as textiles, clothing, footwear, and furniture. Hungarian industry began subcontracting production in these branches as early as the 1980s. Poland became a major producer in the consumer goods sector from the early 1990s. Two-thirds of Polish exports to the European Union consisted of products from low human-capital-intensive sectors, with low white-collar workforce participation, but sometimes with high investment and physical capital needs between 1988 and 1996.

By 1996, 75 percent of Central and East European outward processing exports to the European Union originated from such low-tech sectors. Even the middle high-tech sectors, such as electrical machinery production based on subcontracting, played only a minor role, accounting for 14 percent of reimports by the EU. Outward processing trade reached its heights in the first half of the 1990s: in 1993, 17% of Central and East European exports to the European Union were outward processing trade. By 1996, these exports had declined to 13%.

Around 2000, low-tech outward processing was partly shifted to Romania and Bulgaria. In the less-developed countries of the region such as Romania, the role of subcontracting was much higher and maintained a dominant role during the first decade of the twenty-first century as well: roughly one-third of Romanian exports consisted of industrial consumer goods, and Albania's main export remained textiles and clothing products even in 2003–06. Poland preserved its role in producing low-tech products in the European supply network. After a decade and a half of transformation, David Dyker still maintained: "Poland [is] increasingly specializing in low-tech products in international trade, despite the general technological upgrading visible in the Polish domestic economy" (2004: 112).

Outward processing also took a more advanced form: establishing various kinds of assembly works, such as in the car industry, which went hand in hand with building up a supply network in the region, in a spin-off effect. One may differentiate between first-, second-, and third-tier suppliers. The first tier, which collaborates closely with the main firm, produces complex components, such as engines in the car industry. First-tier suppliers must have a technological culture similar to that of the main company they are producing for. As a consequence, they are mostly foreign-owned or joint ventures. Second-tier suppliers, partly local, produce advanced single components for the first-tier suppliers. Firms in the third category supply the second-tier suppliers with simple components. All of these firms are local.

This hierarchy in the supply network opens the window of opportunity for industrial development, as the Asian economic miracle earlier demonstrated. Integration into the supply network becomes one of the main vehicles of technology transfer. In the less-sophisticated cases, management, organization, communications systems, and computerization contribute to modernizing business technology. On a more advanced level, such as in the car industry, the transfer of hard technology triggers spillover effects (Dyker, 2004: 157, 164).

While the less-developed countries remained subcontracting deliverers in the textile, clothing, leather, and furniture industries until 2000–05, the more-developed countries began producing more sophisticated engineering and high-tech products in the European supply chains. In a decade and a half, a visible shift in investment had already taken place, mostly in Central Europe, toward more sophisticated branches of industry, such as engineering, communications technology, and the chemical industry. Here too, the skilled and cheap labor force was a decisive factor. Even less-developed Romania, for example, is a leader in Europe, placing sixth in the world in terms of the number of certified information technology specialists. The Czech Republic, Slovakia, and Hungary have a well-trained workforce, and an outstanding group of engineers, software engineers, and other experts.

In a single decade, the structure of industry dramatically changed and obsolete branches were partly replaced by modern sectors. After a decade and a half of transformation, nearly two-thirds of Hungarian industrial output was produced by the electrical, optical equipment, car, and chemical industries. In the Czech Republic, engineering played an outstanding role: by 2003, 50 percent of exports consisted of machinery and cars. In Slovenia, the car industry and pharmaceutical industry achieved the highest growth rate from the mid-1990s, alongside the traditionally strong and competitive electronics sector.

At the turn of the century, high-tech industries' share in the generation of added value in manufacturing was highest in Ireland (41%), the United States (31%), and Japan (25%); and in the G-7 countries the average was around 20%. In a second group, several West European countries had a share of roughly 15%. Hungary with 24% belongs to the top group, ahead of Canada, Germany, Italy, and Austria. Some countries of the region, such as the Czech Republic and Slovenia, are better placed in medium-high-tech branches. Counting high- and medium-high-tech industries together, Hungary and the Czech Republic – which has the highest share in medium high-tech level (65% together) – reach the G-7's level (67%), behind Ireland (77%) and Germany (70%), while Poland has the lowest percentage (33%) (Piech, 2003: 256–57).

One cannot question the importance of these impressive structural changes. Nevertheless, the real, long-lasting achievements of this restructuring are much less striking if one considers that most of the transformation countries produce mostly parts and components for high-tech products, or perform assembly work. In both cases, a significant part of the job is done by a low-skilled workforce. Roughly 40 percent of the workers in high-tech industries in Central and Eastern Europe have low-skilled occupations. In the top high-tech exporter countries of the region, Hungary and Estonia, the share of low-skilled workforce in high-tech industries is 39% and 59%, respectively, while in the Netherlands it is only 17%. By the same token, the highly skilled workforce is small in the transforming countries, 20 percent lower than in similar industries in the West (Kaděřábková, 2006: 157, 159).

In the high-tech industry in Hungary, IBM's subsidiary contributed to high-tech exports with the production of office, accounting, and computing machinery, but the work performed in Hungary was not knowledge-intensive and was carried out by semi-skilled workers. Attila Havas called these kinds of high-tech production "footloose," meaning not embedded in the domestic production network and without a highly educated and trained labor force. These kinds of industries are ready to move to cheaper production sites, further to the East, or to China. Indeed,

in October 2002 ... IBM relocated a large chunk of its global manufacturing activities in order to cut production costs. As this plant was not integrated into the domestic economy via highly skilled labour, close academia–industry links and/or specialized, indispensable local suppliers the decision was an easy one. (Havas, 2006: 271–72)

High-tech industries, in other words, have yet to sink deep roots in the region, but this is a natural first stage of development that might be followed by domestic research and highly qualified labor input in the next stage of development. The first signs of entering the second stage are already visible in Hungary and in some other countries: more and more foreign companies are establishing research laboratories. The spillover effects resulting from developing roots and domestic networks mark the passage toward a higher development level.

Several less-successful transforming countries, although rid of obsolete "heavy industries," developed mostly consumer-goods industrial branches, especially in the export sectors. Textiles, clothing, leather products, furs, and furniture accounted for more than one-third of Romanian exports in 2003. In Lithuania, food processing proved one of the strongest branches, responsible for nearly one-third of manufactured product sales, employing nearly one-quarter of the labor force, absorbing 36% of industrial investments, and delivering 15% of the country's industrial exports by the second half of the 1990s. Textiles hold a similar position and produce 16% of the country's exports (Van Zon *et al.*, 2000: 66, 69).

Some of the newly independent Balkan countries have continued to base their exports on mining: Kosovo's only export possibility lay in its nickel, magnesium, lead, and zinc resources (Mildner, 2006: 53). Almost all of the countries of the region are becoming integrated with international production networks.

Transforming industries boosted labor productivity. This was partly a consequence of the presence of foreign companies. Increased investment after 1994 renewed the technological base of reorganized industry. Foreign investors, among them several multinational giants, became the pioneers of technology transfer, including "hard" technology. They also transferred knowledge and better management methods, including distribution and marketing practices. They established production and distribution networks, both national and international. Most importantly, they downsized employment in reorganized factories. The Szczecin Shipyard in Poland, for example, dismissed half of its workforce. The same happened when General Electric took over and modernized the Hungarian light bulb factory, Tungsram. As previously noted, the labor force radically decreased in the region's industry.

All these factors contributed to a productivity increase, i.e., an increase in the value of output per worker per hour, from 1994 on. The low productivity level reflected the core weakness of state socialist economy and industry. It had a long tradition in the region, dating back to the slow interwar performance. After World War II, in 1950, labor productivity in the region remained half a century behind that of the West. The gap grew even wider between 1950 and 1973, when Western Europe switched into a higher gear: instead of the roughly 1.7% per annum labor productivity increase during the first half of the century, productivity increased between 1950 and 1973 by about 5% per year and became eight- to ten-fold higher than immediately after the war. This trend continued and, by the 1990s, a West European worker produced an average of $25–$28 value per hour. Between 1980 and 2005, as noted in chapter 1, the West European labor productivity increase, though it slowed somewhat, remained significantly faster – in the case of Britain and France, nearly one-third faster – than the American one.

Central and Eastern Europe experienced stagnating, and in some periods even declining, productivity levels at about $5–$7 per hour until the early to mid-1990s. From that time on, however, productivity increased faster than in the West. This was partly the consequence of a reduced labor force: the number of employees declined by 25% in Hungary, 15% in Slovenia, Slovakia, and the Czech Republic, and 8% in Poland between 1990 and 2001. Average gross industrial output per employed person increased consistently after the sharp decline of the first transformation years, in some years by roughly 5% to 10% per year. Moderate productivity increases characterized other countries as well, although renewed crises between 1997 and 1999 led to a temporary productivity decline in Romania, and four years of productivity decline in Bulgaria between 1996 and 1999 (United Nations, 2004).

Between 1989 and 2002, while European Union countries achieved an annual 1.4% GDP increase per employee, Hungary had nearly a 4% increase, and Slovenia and Poland about 3%. Only Bulgaria (1.1%) and Romania (0.6%) remained behind the West European average rate of productivity increase. In 2002, the level of industrial productivity, i.e., the value of industrial output in an hour, was 254% of the 1989 level in Hungary, 191% in Poland, 167% in Slovenia, nearly 50% higher in the Czech Republic and Romania, and more than one-third higher in Slovakia and Bulgaria (Losoncz, 2003: 7).

Around the turn of the century, South East European productivity thus also improved rapidly. Between 2004 and 2007, while the Eurozone had an average annual productivity increase of 1%, the transforming countries achieved an annual 4% to 5% increase in labor productivity (table 5.5).

The productivity increase in the better-performing Central and East European countries rose two to three times faster than in Western Europe, demonstrating a clear catching-up process. It is mostly characteristic in low-technology sectors, where Western and Eastern technologies are basically the same. In these sectors, the productivity level of the transforming countries may reach the Western level in a few years. In the fish-processing industry, for example, the Polish and Lithuanian productivity level reaches 80% and 30–40% of the Danish level, respectively, and, according to projections, may reach the Danish level in two years. Both full-time and on-the-job training for local workers are important activities of the

Table 5.5 Labor productivity, 1990–2007

Countries	Labor productivity in 2003, 1990 = 100	Productivity increase as % of previous year			
		2004	2005	2006	2007
Bulgaria	161	3.4	3.4	4.3	4.9
Croatia	181	–	–	–	–
Czech Republic	160	4.6	5.0	4.6	4.2
Hungary	275	5.4	3.3	4.4	3.6
Poland	290	–	0.9	2.3	2.7
Romania	177	8.0	3.9	5.3	4.9
Slovakia	147	5.9	3.8	4.8	5.5
Slovenia	185	3.7	3.2	3.7	3.6

Source: Teodorović *et al.*, 2005: 30; European Commission, 2006.
Note: The 2006 and 2007 figures are projections.

multinational companies. This combined with higher wages and better management is the reason that foreign-owned companies in Central and Eastern Europe have double the wage and productivity level of domestically owned companies (Dyker, 2006: 200).

The labor productivity gap between the European Union and Central Europe, measured by GDP per capita, is still huge. In 2002, in the Baltic countries it reached 80%, and in Poland, Hungary, and the Czech Republic 70%; in Slovenia, the best performer in the region, it is 55%. Measuring in terms of purchasing power parity, which is more realistic because it takes into account the different price levels, the gap is smaller on average: 40% in Hungary, Slovakia, and the Czech Republic, about 50% in Poland and Estonia, and only 27% in Slovenia (P. Holmes *et al.*, 2006: 154; Iacovone and Kofoed, 2006: 119).

Industry recuperated in most cases, and output, as a consequence, reached a 50% to 85% higher level than before 1990 (table 5.6).

Restructured foreign trade

As a consequence of structural changes and productivity increases, as well as the strong outward processing positions of Western Europe in the former Soviet bloc area and the penetration of multinational companies, foreign trade was successfully reoriented. Before the collapse of the regime, 40–75 percent of foreign trade was channeled to other Comecon countries. State socialist countries were not successful in Western markets. From the mid-1970s, their average terms of trade, i.e., the relation between export

Table 5.6 Gross industrial output, 2003

Countries	Industrial output in 1990 = 100
Poland	185
Slovenia	185
Croatia	181
Romania	177
Hungary	171
Bulgaria	161
Slovakia	147
Czech Republic	99

Source: Teodorović *et al.*, 2005: 30.

and import prices, declined by 25–30 percent, and resulted in huge trade deficits.

Instead of trying to sell their old export items, which were based mostly on energy- and material-intensive sectors, the transforming countries developed new, salable export goods for Western markets. As we have seen above, the less-developed transforming countries turned toward textiles, clothing, and other low-tech consumer goods. Based on outward processing agreements, they exported the products back to Western countries, which made the production of these items possible with their inputs. From the mid-1990s, the more developed Central European countries, after the first years of similar activities, began exporting medium-high- and high-tech products produced by multinational companies.

In this respect, Hungary and Estonia achieved the best results: 30% of Hungary's and 20% of Estonia's exports consisted of high-tech information and communications technology products in 2000. Their share in 1996 was only 4% and 6%, respectively. This miraculous development put these two countries among the top high-tech exporters. Among 129 countries, Hungary occupied sixteenth and Estonia seventeenth place in terms of high- and medium-high-tech exports, surpassing old leaders such as France, Sweden, Germany, Switzerland, and Hong Kong. In the case of Hungary, nearly 60 percent of the Western exports in 1985 were either primary products or manufactures based on natural resources. Manufactures not based on natural resources were mostly low-tech products. The role of the latter items in Western exports declined from 23% to 15% by 2000. On the other hand, medium-high- and high-technology products, which represented less than 17% of total exports to the West, increased to more than 70% by 2000 (UNCTAD, 2002: 169). This strong specialization

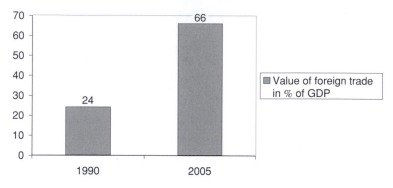

Figure 5.5 Increased role of foreign trade in Central Europe
(four countries), 1990–2005

in high-tech products is not characteristic of other Central and East European countries. The Czech Republic, Poland, and others exported products that were less high-tech, mostly parts and components (Srholec, 2006: 62–63).

Altogether, the role of foreign trade, mostly because of advanced integration into international production networks, dramatically increased. Some countries in the region such as Latvia and the Czech Republic increased foreign trade (in dollar value) by 70% and 80%, respectively, between 1998 and 2003. Bulgaria, a latecomer in the European industrial network, increased the value of its trade by 1,500 times, and the war-ridden successor states of Yugoslavia, such as Croatia, Macedonia, and Serbia, increased their trade by 130, 175, and 4,000 times between 1998 and 2003 (Economist, 2005b: 67).

These previously isolated and self-sufficient countries were transformed into some of the most open countries. In 1990, exports and imports represented 30 and 26% of Hungarian GDP, respectively, only half of the European Union level. By 2005, the figures were 79% and 68% of GDP, respectively, nearing the EU level. Trade reached 69% of GDP in Slovakia, 60% in Estonia, and 56% in the Czech Republic. *The Economist* reported in the summer of 2006 that, among the European countries, "the Czech Republic and Hungary are the most dependent on foreign markets" (figure 5.5). Five countries of the region belonged to the twenty most trade-dependent countries of the world (Economist, 2005b: 34; *Economist*, August 5, 2006).

The reorientation was spectacular. Instead of 40% to 75% of Comecon trade in the region's countries, 60% to 70% of trade was redirected to the West, chiefly to the European Union, and to Germany in particular (figure 5.6). By 2004, Germany bought 24% of the region's exports and

Table 5.7 EU-25's and Germany's role in Central and East European foreign trade in 2004

Country	EU-25's % of export	EU-25's % of imports	Germany's % of export	Germany's % of imports
Czech Republic	83.8	82.5	36.9	32.4
Estonia	74.6	64.7	9.9	11.3
Latvia	75.9	62.9	14.9	16.1
Lithuania	61.3	62.0	10.3	16.5
Hungary	80.7	71.8	30.4	28.6
Poland	79.1	77.6	32.3	24.4
Slovenia	73.3	84.1	23.1	19.3
Slovakia	85.7	82.7	31.1	25.5
Average	76.8	73.5	23.6	21.8

Source: Economist, 2005b; European Commission, 2006: 159, 160.

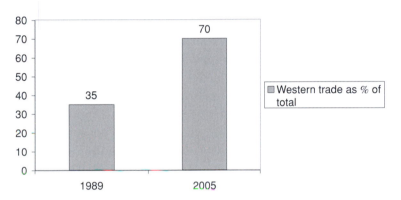

Figure 5.6 Reorientation of Central and Eastern Europe's trade, 1989–2005

sold 22% of the goods imported by Central and Eastern Europe. In most of the countries of the region, Germany had become the number one trade partner and had a higher share in Central and Eastern European trade than was held by the Soviet Union before 1989, while three-quarters of the foreign trade of the Central European and Baltic countries became European Union trade (table 5.7). Central and Eastern Europe became an integral part of the European economic network, strongly rooted into the economy of the European Union. Adjustment to the requirements of globalization both in Western and Central and Eastern Europe gained momentum.

Economic recovery and growth

Recovery followed the free fall of the early 1990s. Poland was the only country in the region where growth resumed by 1992. The next year, the Czech Republic, Slovenia, Albania, and Romania registered positive growth. Croatia reached an average 6.5 percent annual growth after 1995. By 1994, only three countries continued to decline (Estonia, Lithuania, and Macedonia), but Central and Eastern Europe, including the Baltic states and the Balkans, on average reached 3.9 percent GDP growth. From that time onward, economic growth picked up speed (table 5.8).

Central and Eastern Europe as a whole had nearly recovered from the decline by 2002, reaching 97.5 percent of its 1989 level. However, this average is depressed because the Balkan countries, mostly the successor states of war-ridden Yugoslavia, and the Baltic countries, which were previously part of the Soviet Union, remained significantly behind their 1989 economic levels (figure 5.7). After 1995, however, recuperation gained momentum: Croatia increased its GDP by 35%, Macedonia by 14%, and Serbia by 11% by 2003. The former Soviet Union, or the Commonwealth of Independent States, reached only 69% of the pre-collapse level.

Between 1994 and 2006, economic growth, though uneven in the former Soviet bloc countries, was generally relatively fast, especially compared to the slow Western performance. Between 2004 and 2007, the average annual growth in Central Europe, the Baltic countries, and the Balkan countries increased to more than 5 percent per annum. The Baltic countries and some of the Balkan countries, those which lagged behind until the turn of the century, achieved the most rapid development (table 5.9).

In 2005, the Eurozone countries reached an average 2.2% growth rate, and the forecast for 2006 was 2.1%, while the transforming countries on average surpassed 5%, more than twice as high (Economist, 2004: 87–90; European Commission, 2006: 131). Above-average growth rates were recorded in 114 of the 268 EU regions in the first years of the twenty-first century. Of those, thirty-one were in Central and Eastern Europe. Four of the ten most dynamically developing regions were located in the Czech Republic, Hungary, Slovakia, and Romania. Between 1999 and 2002, the Bucharest region achieved a 17 percent higher increase of GDP per capita than the EU-25 average. Except for the Prague and Central Hungary regions, however, all of the other Central and East European regions belonged to those seventy-eight EU regions in which the per capita GDP level remained below 75 percent of the EU-25 average (Eurostat, 2005b: 41–46). Moreover, the most backward region of the European Union was the northeast region of Romania, with a $2,693 per capita GDP,

Table 5.8 GDP growth, percentage change from previous year, 1994–2007

Country	1994	1995	1996	1997	1998	1999	2000	2001	2002	2003	2004	1989 = 100, % in 2004	2005	2006	2007
Central Europe and the Baltic countries	**3.9**	**5.5**	**4.7**	**4.9**	**3.7**	**3.3**	**4.2**	**2.4**	**2.4**	**3.8**	**5.1**	126	**4.2**	**6.1**	**5.7**
Czech R.	2.2	5.9	4.2	−0.7	−1.1	1.2	3.9	2.6	1.5	3.2	4.7	114	6.0	5.3	4.7
Estonia	−1.6	4.5	4.4	11.1	4.4	0.3	7.9	6.5	7.2	6.7	7.8	112	9.8	8.9	7.9
Hungary	2.9	1.5	1.3	4.6	4.9	4.2	5.2	4.3	3.8	3.4	4.6	120	4.1	4.6	4.2
Latvia	2.2	−0.9	3.8	8.3	4.7	3.3	6.9	8.0	6.5	7.2	8.5	90	9.1	8.5	7.6
Lithuania	−9.8	3.3	4.7	7.0	7.3	−1.7	3.9	6.4	6.8	10.5	7.0	89	7.5	6.5	6.2
Poland	5.2	7.0	6.0	6.8	4.8	4.1	4.0	1.0	1.4	3.8	5.3	142	3.2	4.5	4.6
Slovakia	6.2	5.8	6.1	4.6	4.2	1.5	2.0	3.8	4.6	4.5	5.5	121	6.0	6.1	6.5
Slovenia	5.8	4.9	3.6	4.8	3.6	5.6	4.1	2.7	3.5	2.7	4.2	126	3.9	4.3	4.1
Balkan region	**3.8**	**6.4**	**4.2**	**1.1**	**0.6**	**−2.3**	**3.6**	**4.6**	**4.6**	**4.5**	**5.8**	92	**4.7**	**4.9**	**5.0**
Albania	8.3	13.3	9.1	10.2	12.7	10.1	7.3	7.2	3.4	6.0	5.9	131	6.0	–	–
Bosnia and Herzegovina	0.0	20.8	86.0	37.0	15.6	9.6	5.5	4.3	5.3	4.0	5.7	60	5.0	–	–
Bulgaria	1.8	2.9	−9.4	−5.6	4.0	2.3	5.4	4.0	4.8	4.5	5.7	89	5.5	5.4	5.7
Croatia	5.9	6.8	6.0	6.5	2.5	−0.9	2.9	4.4	5.2	4.3	3.8	94	4.3	4.4	4.5
Macedonia	−1.8	−1.2	1.2	1.4	3.4	4.3	4.5	−4.5	0.9	2.8	4.1	80	4.0	4.3	4.7
Romania	3.9	7.1	4.0	−6.1	−4.8	−1.2	1.8	5.3	4.9	5.2	8.4	100	4.1	5.5	5.1
Serbia-Monte negro	2.5	6.1	7.8	10.1	1.9	18.0	5.0	5.5	3.8	2.7	7.2	55	4.0	–	–

Source: EBRD, 2005a: 48; European Commission, 2006: 131, 158.

Note: The 2006 figures are estimates; the 2007 figures are projections.

Table 5.9 GDP growth rates between 1993 and 2003

Countries	Annual % increase in real GDP
Bosnia-Herzegovina	18.5
Albania	6.4
Poland	4.9
Latvia	4.7
Croatia	4.4
Estonia	4.4
Slovakia	4.3
Romania	2.0
Bulgaria	1.3
Macedonia	1.1
Moldova	−3.1
Russia	0.7

Source: Economist, 2005b: 32.

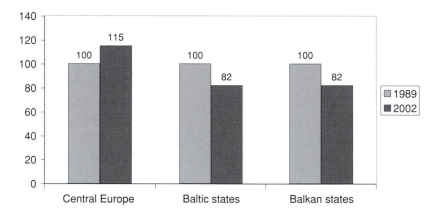

Figure 5.7 GDP/capita, 1989–2002

representing a sharp contrast to Warsaw ($18,600), Budapest ($15,800), and especially the most advanced Belgian Vlaams–Brabant region with a $24,082 per capita GDP (Van Kempen, Vermeulen, and Baan, 2005: 39, 65; Eurostat, 2005b: 52).

The former Yugoslav republics remained far behind. Bosnia-Herzegovina and Macedonia recorded a per capita GDP level similar to that of the most backward northeast Romanian region, and Kosovo's 2005 income level was less than half that of Bosnia (Mildner, 2006: 54). Some analyses maintained that domestic institutional infrastructure is inadequate in the quasi-states of Bosnia-Herzegovina and Kosovo... [where] a culture of aid dependency has already emerged, without... any prospect of self-sustaining development. (Csaba, 2005: 327)

In spite of that, a gradual but unquestionable catching-up process is emerging, though with huge regional disparities.

By comparison, Chinese economic growth, guided by a different privatization and transformation policy which avoided sharp initial economic decline, achieved spectacular, mostly double-digit annual growth rates throughout the decade. China, together with some East Asian countries, reached a labor productivity increase of 8.5% between 1980 and 2005, compared to 1.7% in the United States and 2.1% in the advanced countries overall. The number of people surviving on one dollar per day decreased by half, or 148 million, during the single decade after 1996 (*New York Times*, September 4, 2007). As Rhode and Toniolo stated:

Between 1990 and 2000 the Chinese economy more than doubled its size in real terms, its share in the world economy growing from 7.8 to 12.5 percent... It may be argued that... recent growth performance brought about probably the biggest single improvement in human welfare anywhere, at any time. (2006: 5)

Is the economic transformation accomplished? To answer this question one has to differentiate between a narrow and a broad concept of transformation. In the narrow sense, it basically means adjustment to the European market system, the introduction of market institutions and legal frameworks, integration into the world market and international production network, and the establishment of macroeconomic stability with a balanced budget and low inflation.

According to the European Bank of Reconstruction and Development, the former state socialist countries have a functioning market economy, most of it in private hands. Exports and economic growth increased at a rapid tempo. According to the global competitiveness index, based on 259 criteria including openness, a functioning financial market, quality of infrastructure, business management, and labor market flexibility, Estonia, the Czech Republic, Hungary, Slovakia, and Slovenia belong to the world's fifty most competitive countries. Estonia had a higher position than France, the Czech Republic and Hungary surpassed Spain and Portugal, and Slovakia and Slovenia ranked higher than Italy (Economist, 2005b: 58).

After the Kosovo war a lagging Balkans region also gained ground in transformation. War destruction was severe, about $30 billion of damage in Serbia alone. In addition, disrupted transport routes reduced growth in neighboring countries by 1–5 percent. However, the long-term trend was positive. First of all, lasting peace characterized the Balkans after the troubled 1990s, creating a basic precondition for economic success. In addition, the European Union contributed decisively to stabilizing the Balkan situation and to emerging prosperity in the area:

The international community decided to play a more active role in alleviating the region's economic problems as well as in responding to the urgent need for reconstruction . . . This initiative led to the launching of the Stability Pact for South Eastern Europe . . . The Stability and Association Process . . . imposed certain demanding conditions . . . [and] referred to progress in democratization and economic reform . . . The renewed commitment of SEE to reform and the resulting acceleration have led to significant progress . . . [and an] upturn in the economic performance of the region. (Papazoglou, 2005: 69–70, 119)

Economic growth sped up and reached, on average, 4% to 5% per annum in the Balkans after 2000, faster growth than in Central Europe during those years. Nevertheless, by 2003, the South East European countries still remained far behind and reached only 57% of the Central European per capita GDP (in purchasing power parity), and only 28% of the level of the EU-15 countries. In a narrow sense, Central and Eastern Europe made impressive progress and the Central European subregion basically accomplished the transformation process. The Balkans, though markedly behind, also progressed toward that stage.

However, even that progress is somewhat fragile. Countries in both regions exhibit severe operational weaknesses expressed by huge budgetary deficits and indebtedness, as discussed before. The Czech Republic doubled its public debt from 18.2% to 37.6% of GDP between 2000 and 2003; public debt surpassed 45% of the GDP in Poland by 2005. Croatia's external debt jumped from 60% of GDP in 2000 to 90% by 2004. Ten countries of the region belonged to the thirty-five countries of the world with the largest deficits. Current account deficit in percentage of the GDP is 25–29% in Bosnia-Herzegovina, 13% in Estonia, 13% in Serbia, between 8% and 9% in Hungary, Bulgaria, and Latvia, and around 7% in Croatia, Lithuania, Albania, and Moldova. As an unweighted average, i.e., without considering the different sizes and populations of the countries of the region, the percentage of current account deficit reached nearly 7% in Central Europe and the Baltic countries, and 10% in the Balkans (Economist, 2005b: 36–37; EBRD, 2005a: 54).

Some of these weaknesses, as discussed before, thwarted the original plans of the countries of the region to introduce the common currency, the euro, within a few years after joining the Union. Fulfilling the Maastricht criteria for the euro's introduction was difficult for several well-established Western countries as well. Some of them are unable to meet the criteria even now. Public debt, for example, is more than 10 percent higher than the maximum allowed for the twelve old member countries which already belong to the Eurozone. Instead of 60% of GDP, as required, Belgium's and Italy's debt surpassed 100% in 2005. Although the Czech Republic, Poland, and Lithuania nearly fulfilled the criteria, fluctuating interest rates and rising inflation made introduction of the euro impossible. The inflation rates in Estonia (4.1%), Latvia (6.9%), and Hungary (3.5%) were higher than the required maximum 2.5% in 2005. Hungarian inflation rate even increased and hit 9% in the spring of 2007. The government deficit was twice as high as required in Hungary. Except Slovenia, which joined the Eurozone in 2007, almost none of the other countries are able to follow in its footsteps in the near future and, at the moment, Hungary is the farthest from fulfilling the criteria (Eurostat, various years).

Economic weaknesses

In a broad sense, however, accomplishing transformation is not tantamount to marketization, recuperation from decline, or even restructuring. The complexity of the process includes economic, technological, institutional, educational, social, and cultural elements, which lead more or less to catch-up with the advanced world. In this respect, transformation is incomplete. When I speak about "accomplishing" it, I mean accomplishing the first chapter, or the narrow sense of transformation. The entire or broader concept of transformation is a process that, if successful, may transpire over at least one or two generations, and in some cases even longer than that.

Economic development in that first chapter of transformation in Central and Eastern Europe was highly dependent on foreign investments and multinational companies, and the technology stock and managerial superiority they brought into the region. The domestic base is still weak and requires major further advancement. The domestically based, medium-sized and small companies which play a determining role in West European economic development are not strong in the region. In the European Union, the most flexible small and medium-sized enterprises, employing up to 100 workers, employ about 50% of total employees. In the successful Mediterranean countries, this share reaches 60% to 80%. Italy's economic miracle was heavily based on that domestic strength. The renewal of the Portuguese economy, for its part, was based on a specific government program, Programa Especifico para o Desenvolvimento da Industria Portuguesa, strengthening small and medium-sized domestic companies via financial assistance to replace, at least partially, the dominance of multinational companies, which characterized the first period of transformation (Magone, 2003: 256).

Michael Piore and Charles Sabel, interpreting the economic crisis of the 1970s–'80s, go further and describe a "second industrial divide" from those years onward. In their interpretation, the "first industrial divide," the triumph of mass production over craft production as the dominant industrial organization, emerged in the early nineteenth century. Craft production survived, but played a marginal role through production of luxury goods, experimental products, and specialized equipment:

From the . . . end of the nineteenth century to the present, economic down-turns have periodically enlarged the craft periphery with respect to the mass-production core – but without altering their relationship . . . What is distinctive about the current crisis [in the 1970s] is that the shift toward greater flexibility is provoking technological sophistication . . . In short, craft has challenged mass production as the paradigm. (Piore and Sabel, 1984: 207)

While leading core countries renewed their economies and competitiveness during the last quarter of the twentieth century through multinationalization, certain regions such as the "third Italy" in the center of the country, the Salzburg region in Austria, and Baden-Württemberg in Germany created new, specialty products in precision machine tools, specialty chemicals, ceramic building materials, and industrial instruments. Old industries were renewed by combining craft skill and flexible equipment with the help of computerization and numerically controlled looms, innovations which appeared in the 1970s. According to this interpretation, various regions and entire countries, especially small ones that cannot compete with mass production, might base a new prosperity on the "craft paradigm." Small shops formed into networks offer flexible specialization and decreased dependence on large firms (ibid., 1984: 206–07, 215).

In the transforming Central and East European countries, this kind of flexible specialization has great potential to revitalize domestic economies. In reality, however, no such trend – one leading to the emergence of flourishing old–new industries in several European regions – can be seen. Even in the best cases, such as Poland, Hungary, and Slovenia, only 20% of employees work in small and medium-sized firms. In most other countries of the region, this share is only around 10% of employment. Croatia is an exception, where the role of small-scale enterprises reached 50% of both employment and value added in GDP. This high ratio, nevertheless, is mostly the consequence of the collapse of big companies and the dearth of major new firms (figure 5.8). The lack of a strong domestic base of small and medium-sized companies is a serious weakness of the transforming

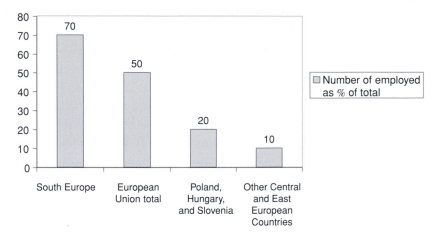

Figure 5.8 The role of small and medium-sized companies (up to 100 workers), 2004

countries (Dyker, 2004: 308–309). It reflects a weakness in the development of *domestic* production networks, as well as a weakness in domestic contacts between manufacturing companies and research institutes and universities.

One of the main shortcomings in transformation economies is the lack or weakness of organized venture capital, a characteristic of the advanced countries in the last decades. Most of the well-known Western success companies, including Amazon, Apple, Fedex, and many others, were financed in an early stage of their development by venture capital investments. Such institutions did not exist before 1989 in Central and Eastern Europe. They emerged, and reached an estimated worth of €7 billion between 1990 and 2004, but fell far short of requirements: in 2003, €29 billion in venture capital investment assisted the rise of startup companies, mostly in high- and medium-high-tech industries, in the European Union. In Central and Eastern Europe, venture capital investment remained only a fraction of the Western investment, €448 million, and assisted fewer than 500 domestic companies. This weakness is a basic obstacle for early-stage companies.

Poland's example characterizes the general situation in the region: in 2001, only €31 million in venture capital was invested and, on per capita basis, the country occupied last place among twenty-one European countries. Early-stage venture capital investment, as a percentage of GDP, reached 0.025% in the EU-15, while in Poland it stood at only 0.007%, Romania 0.003%, Hungary and Slovakia 0.002%, the Czech Republic 0.001% (Petkov Iliev, 2006: 127–29; Gózyński, Jakubiak, and Woodward, 2006: 233).

As a further weakness, a relatively backward banking system was unable to provide sufficient loans to the private sector in Central and Eastern Europe, and especially in the Balkans. In some countries of the region, such as Hungary, impressively, between 1995 and 2005 the value of corporate loans more than quadrupled. Domestic credit provided to the private sector, nevertheless, is only 30% of GDP in Central Europe, and only 5% in Albania, roughly the same in Serbia, 10% in Romania, and 15% in Bosnia-Herzegovina (EBRD, 2004). Bank loans in Germany – to illustrate the difference between the old and new members of the Union – surpassed 86% of GDP in 1980 and reached 121% in 2000. Market capitalization in the United States, by comparison, mostly via the stock exchange, is nearly two-and-a-half times bigger than in Germany (Krénusz, 2007: 55–57).

Successful transformation, furthermore, requires the rise of domestic consumption to create a substantial domestic market, a driving force for economic growth, and a significant change in consumption, savings, and behavior patterns in general. From the turn of the century, consumption gained momentum: in most of the Central European countries the annual increase in personal consumption was roughly 3% to 5%; in the Baltic countries and in some of the Balkan countries it varied between 7% and 8% (European Commission, 2006: 134).

Transformation in the broad sense is in no way over yet and may take another two or more generations. Grzegorz Kołodko was certainly right when he stated that "transition is a generation-long process of change" (2000: 353). Marie Lavigne (2000) added that joining the European Union means closing one chapter of transition, but opening a new transition period, similar to the Spanish and Portuguese post-1986 transformation. Transition from plan to market, i.e., systemic change, has to be followed by transition toward domestically based sustained growth. This latter transition, the development of a domestic innovation base and domestically generated intensive growth, rather than importing existing technology and knowledge via FDI, might characterize the next chapter of development in some countries of the region. This pattern, however, cannot be taken for granted by all of these countries. Nevertheless, the first stage, accomplishing an incomplete transformation, was accomplished.

CHAPTER 6

Transformation and social shock

Longing for Western life and starting to adopt it

Social transformation was part and parcel of regime change, inseparable from political and economic modernization following the Western model. From occupational and income structure to household spending, lifestyle, and behavioral patterns, the entire social fabric loosened into a state of permanent change. Although radical, the post-1989 transformation did not begin from a *tabula rasa*. Instead, existing trends, generated by postwar, state socialist industrialization, were accelerated as well as changed by exogenous factors. The pull effect of the envied and admired West, strengthened by geographical proximity, facilitated the spread of Western influences. It proved overwhelmingly attractive to follow the West's lead down the modernization path first laid out in the nineteenth century.

The "Westernizers" of the region from the early nineteenth century consistently advocated imitative development: Count István Széchenyi of Hungary in 1830 praised Britain as the "core of the world," and recommended adoption of British practices based on the logic that "copying others presents no danger; we can adopt their century-long experiences" (Széchenyi, 1830: 258). A century and a half later, Bronislaw Geremek, one of Solidarity's leaders, made the same argument: Poland had to make the difficult and painful adjustment to Europe to "secure the chances for Poland of getting a place" in the European order (cited in Kowalik, 1994: 122). Nearly ten years later, Aleksander Kwasniewski, President of Poland, repeated in a speech: "Poland needs to bridge the distance separating her from the more advanced countries in Western Europe" (Kwasniewski, 1998: 29). The Polish Committee for European Integration stated in 1997:

The strategic goal of the Polish government and foreign policy of Poland is the country's membership in the European Union. This goal since 1989 . . . exhibits the attempt of the majority of the Polish society to be part of the European structures. (Committee for European Integration, 1997: 68)

These views on the need for imitative development dominated the discourse of all of the countries in Central and Eastern Europe after 1989. The region always sought, from a certain distance behind, to follow the Western development road throughout its history. The state socialist experiment was no exception. Although it was a bitter negation of the West, the essential goal of the dictatorial regime was rapid modernization to reach the Western level to compensate – in the space of ten years – for 50–100 years of lagging behind, as Stalin announced in 1931 (Stalin, 1976: 599).

From the 1970s, Western affluence had a tremendous demonstration effect on the population of Central and Eastern Europe. Polish and Hungarian tourists and Yugoslav guest workers personally experienced the abyss between Western and Eastern standards of living. The famous "kitchen debate" between US and Soviet leaders Richard Nixon and Nikita Khrushchev, and the latter's prediction that the Soviet Union would match and even surpass the American income level, encouraged a consumer mentality in the Soviet bloc. The demonstration effect was strengthened by Western movies and television series, which were screened in Eastern state-owned movie theaters and television channels. By the mid-1980s, even in hard-line, post-1968 Husák's Czechoslovakia, one-quarter of television entertainment programs were imported; 43 percent of the feature films screened in Poland were from the West. In 1986, Hungary purchased 600 Western television programs. "In the early 1980s, there was a qualitative rise in the levels of Western mass communications, which directly and indirectly changed people's perception of life in the West" (Lane, 2006: 147–48).

Easterners were strongly attracted by the sparkling Western life. They longed for Volkswagens and BMWs instead of Trabants and Zhigulis. They were mesmerized by Western pop culture, jeans, and Coca-Cola. The youngsters of the 1960s and '70s in Poland, Hungary, and several other countries became the Beatles generation. Western pop culture penetrated the "Iron Curtain." Nothing was more characteristic than the case of ultra-nationalist, neo-Stalinist Ceaușescu's Romania. With insider experience, Denise Roman recorded: "a real blue jeans mystique traversed the urban . . . youth generations of the mid-1970s, continuing into the 1980s – here considered as the Blue Jeans Generations" (Roman, 2003: 62). Western everyday culture had a penetrating influence on Central and Eastern Europe. Moreover, from a distance, expanded by separation and isolation, Western life was idealized into a "dolce vita" shining beyond the grey everyday Eastern reality. The socialist regimes' anti-Western propaganda campaigns and critique of capitalism became counterproductive; most of the people did not heed the messages and instead nurtured an idealized picture of the West.

In 1989, when the door was opened, imitative development became an official recommendation of the West and government programs in the East. Western institutions and policies were transplanted. Western retail chains and shopping malls set the stage for a new society in the making. Although the region remained several decades behind the West in social structure, lifestyle and behavior, it experienced an agitated rush to catch up and become "Western."

When Easterners made their first steps on the new road they had dreamed of for decades, they also met the first bumps. All of a sudden, people met with negative features of capitalism such as uncertainty, unemployment, and social polarization, which many did not like. I heard remarks such as, "Everything we were told about socialism was wrong but everything we were taught on capitalism was true." The heroic Polish workers who revolted in 1956, 1970, 1976, and 1980, and who finally forced the regime to its knees with their uprisings, strikes, and organization, were, as Michnik noted, "the first who become the victims of the transformation" (1999). Many people lost their jobs and ended up peering into brightened shop windows with empty pockets. The workers of the Gdańsk Shipyard, the cradle of resistance in Poland, declared no reason to celebrate at the anniversary celebration of the collapse of the regime they helped bring down, and they demonstrated against the transformation instead.

The peasantry was still significant in Central and East European societies, especially in Poland and the Balkan countries, where they accounted for one-quarter to one-half of the population. They suffered tremendously during the ruthless collectivization drive in the 1950s. However, those who remained in the countryside slowly adjusted to the new situation. They earned less, but they worked less, got vacation time and health insurance, and sent their children to school and even to university. They did not have to make decisions and produced the basics they needed on a private plot within the collective farm. Most of them, nevertheless, dreamed about independent farming.

Post-1989 decollectivization, as discussed in chapter 5, opened a new horizon, and old dreams about independent farming returned. The new situation required hard work, risk taking, and entrepreneurship, but the region had a hard-working peasant population. Social adjustment, however, proved to be the most difficult in the countryside. Elderly people were often unable to make the transition. A scholar who studied the transformation of the East European countryside on the spot stated: "Family farms have proven difficult to operate when families were without labor, capital, or developed retail possibilities" (Sampson, 1995: 171). A survey of five hundred south Transylvanian villages in 1991 clearly revealed the difficulty of returning to private farming: 39% of the new private owners were pensioners, another 43% were already urban residents, and only 18% were able to cultivate the land (Kideckel, 1995: 49). In a Bulgarian village with 130 inhabitants, 190 members joined a provisional collective farm, several of them from urban settlements:

This group of owners does not foresee developing modern farms in the future, since they do not expect their children . . . to come back to the village . . . They refuse to entertain any kind of large-scale change. (Ivanova, 1995: 233)

The situation was not very different in the Baltic republics. Hundreds of thousands of families applied for restitution of land, and by 1994 13,000 private farms were in operation in Estonia, 58,000 in Latvia, and 130,000 in Lithuania. The number of private farms continued to increase. By 2000, 75,000 farms existed in Estonia with an average size of twenty-two hectares. Nevertheless,

some of the applicants and juridical owners of family farms are unable or unwilling to engage in farming . . . [some] intend to hire or sell their farms. Therefore a large part of the distributed land will remain uncultivated. (Alanen, 1996: 151–52)

Villagers in some places even resisted dissolving the collective farms. In Zalapitsa village, in Bulgaria, peasants occupied the town hall and refused to let the liquidation committee take over the collective farm (Kideckel, 1995: 37). In the fall of 1992, a new Bulgarian collective farm was registered in Zamfirovo village with 546 members. In Romania, when a new law (Law 36) allowed the formation of collective farms, more than 4,000 so-called juridic societies were established with nearly 800,000 members from the old collectives, and 720,000 people created 11,500 kinship collective farms, called 'family societies.' When two agricultural engineers established agricultural enterprises in Feldioara, near Braşov in Romania, most of the peasant landowners gave up their land for a percentage of the income (Kideckel, 1995: 49; Sampson, 1995: 172).

Writing about Bulgaria, Radost Ivanova stated: "Judging by the words and action of the inhabitants of Panaretovo, kinship is a phenomenon on which Bulgarian agriculture will have to rely for [the] indefinite future." In that village, three informal labor associations were established after land privatization: the "members are united mostly on the kinship

principle" (Ivanova, 1995: 231). A great many that had begun private farming practiced primitive cultivation techniques. More than half (53 percent)
of Polish farmers engaged in subsistence farming, and only one-quarter to
one-third of the farms met market criteria. In Latvia

the production of every fifth farm is channeled primarily to the family's own
consumption . . . 70 percent of Latvia's farms are characterized by inefficiency
and marginality. (Alanen, 1996: 154)

Lukewarm stability disappeared, and adjusting to the changes seemed to be
impossible for many. Millions of newly independent farmers could do no
more than supply themselves and lived a rather primitive, almost ancient
life of isolation. A new hidden exodus began. Millions left agricultural activities behind, but – in the environment of sharply rising unemployment –
without leaving the countryside. Most of the newly uprooted people could
not find urban jobs and were unable to rent apartments in cities. Many
of them became unemployed or, to put it better, did not enter the labor
market, but remained hidden from statistics, supported by their families.

Even those who took up private farming had to learn how to adjust
to market requirements, what to produce, and how to sell their products.
Moreover, they had to compete with sophisticated Western companies and
big agrobusiness. Agricultural subsidies, which were mostly eliminated
after 1989, as discussed in previous chapters, constituted only 10% of the
value of agricultural output in Poland before it joined the European Union,
while the Union's subsidies to its farmers reached 35%, and the American
subsidies 21%, of the value of output. The competition became almost
hopeless.

I visited a successful farmer, János Szabó, in Lajosmizse in the heart of the
great Hungarian plain in June 2006. The vigorous sixty-year-old farmer
originated from a well-to-do peasant family. His grandfather and then
father were labeled *kulak*s, or peasant-bourgeois, imprisoned, and beaten
during the collectivization drive in his early childhood. In the 1950s, as
"class enemies," they were not allowed to join a collective farm. After 1956,
however, the situation changed, and Szabó later became successful in the
szak-szövetkezet, a semi-independent farm operation under a collective
umbrella, a specialty of the Hungarian economic reform in that area. After
1989, he regained the old family land and bought more, altogether 1,400
hectares, and installed a mechanized dairy farm with 140 imported Swiss
cows. The entire farm is well equipped, and the work is done by him,
his wife, and four of their sons. The day starts at 3:30 AM and ends at
sunset. He has received a Western offer of €300 million for the entire farm,
but refused it. Enthusiastic and efficient, he proudly runs the "empire" he

created. Nevertheless, he maintained that his days are probably numbered. His only competitive edge is the "free" family labor, but one of his sons has died. Who knows how long he can continue in the face of ruthless international competition? He is deeply disappointed, hates the European Union, and bitterly states: "We have been betrayed and sold out."

The new opportunities, as people realized, came bundled with tremendous challenges, most of all lost security, the imperative for risk taking, and new life strategies. Sweet daydreams about new opportunities became mixed with confusion and disappointment. The combination of the exhilaration of an open horizon combined with despair over the distance required to reach it became a hallmark of the new life.

The social pain of transformation

Systemic transformation and economic decline in the early 1990s shocked Central and East European societies. Entrepreneurial people exploited the situation when the window of opportunity opened widely. As presented in chapter 2, millions of families entered small family business, mostly in services. In Poland, Czechoslovakia, Hungary, and Romania combined, 3.6 million new private businesses were established between 1989 and 1992 (Crane, 1994: 37). Skillful managers and well-trained workers earned higher incomes, in most cases at least twice as high, at mushrooming foreign-owned companies compared to those in domestic private ones. A well-to-do middle class was in the making. In a few years, hundreds of millionaires also emerged in these countries, profiting from privatization. In a single decade, wealth of $20 billion to $40 billion accumulated in the hands of each of a few top entrepreneurs. One-quarter to one-third of the population began to live better than before.

Box 6.1   How to become a billionaire in ten years: two rich men in Hungary

The story of the two richest men in Hungary, each with wealth of about $2.3 billion accumulated over a decade and a half, is rooted, in the most successful market reforms in the Soviet bloc during the 1970s–'80s.

Gábor Várszegi grew up in the shabby 6th district of Budapest and, as a young man, attempted to make a career in rock music. This was not easy in Hungary in the 1960s, when he started out as a bass guitar player and songwriter. In 1965, in a slowly liberalizing Hungary, he founded Gemini, one of the most popular rock bands, which performed successfully until 1979.

Várszegi turned to business, immigrated to the United States in 1980, and made some money there to invest. After four years, he returned to Hungary as an American citizen and established Fotex Kft., a fast film-developing chain. An extraordinary business career began in the reforming, but still "communist" Hungary with its semi-market system. The technology for fast film developing was unknown in Hungary's state-owned companies, and became very profitable. Várszegi owned 49 percent of the company, while American and state-owned Hungarian companies participated.

When state socialism collapsed, Várszegi was already a rich man in Hungarian terms. He transformed the firm into a joint stock company with $1 million in share capital. This was more than doubled by issuing new stocks in the same year, 1990, the starting point of mass privatization in Hungary. Várszegi had enough capital to buy the Glass Company of Ajka. In addition, the Azur Unio and Azurinvest retail interests were amalgamated into his business empire. Várszegi next issued nearly 14 million new stocks, increasing his assets by $44 million. The amount was used to buy other privatized companies, among them the state-owned Ofotert photo chain, the Granvisus contact lens factory, and Balaton furniture factory. In the mid-1990s, Várszegi's wealth reached $100 million. The expansion continued in a new booming business area: shopping mall construction. The Várszegi empire, under the name of L'Optique Carrefour, included twelve shops in the Czech Republic and sixteen in Poland. Twenty years after the foundation of his first private business enterprise in Hungary in 1984, Gábor Várszegi's wealth surpasses $2.3 billion. He has remained the richest man in Hungary over the first decade and a half of transformation.

In the cutthroat competition of the globalized market, however, Várszegi faced competition from stronger multinational players. He was forced to sell the Ofotert chain and to close Keravill, the technical appliances retail chain, because of the competition from Electro World and Media Mart. He also partly closed his Azur department store chain because of competition from the Rossmann Drogerie Markt, and turned more to real estate by 2005.

Sándor Demján, Hungary's second-richest man, was raised in an orphan-age in Etyek, a village near Budapest. He graduated from a trade college in 1965 and began working in a retail trade cooperative in the countryside. The talented young man rose quickly. His real breakthrough came in 1973, when the thirty-year-old Demján became the top founding manager of Skála, a newly established department store in Budapest. He introduced modern, Western commercial practices in Hungary and soon became a celebrated manager and a strong supporter of further market reform in Hungary. By 1986, Hungary had a quasi-market system, and Demján was appointed founding manager of the newly established Credit Bank. When state socialism collapsed in 1989, he was one of the best-known top managers in the country, but, unlike Várszegi, he did not have personal wealth.

Based on his special talent for team building, he was able to bridge this handicap. Former US ambassador Mark Palmer, together with the Hungarian-born Canadian millionaire, Andrew Sarlos, and New York investor Ronald Lauder, provided him $5 million to start. He earned his first million-dollar profit by privatization: Demján bought the Russian Kamaz truck factory, and sold its shares at a price several times higher.

More importantly, Demján, as before, was a most inventive and wide-ranging business visionary. He built the first shopping malls in Hungary. He also established the Central European Development Corporation in 1990–91 to focus on regional development programs. His company, TriGranit, founded in 1996, became a Hungary-based multinational company. It became the biggest investor in Slovakia, rebuilding Bratislava's city center. Demján realized a €1 billion project in Warsaw, and invested €3 billion in Prague, Bucharest, Kraków, and Sofia. In 2005, the newspapers reported his first Polish shopping mall success in Katowice, the first of about a dozen in Poland. With his immense, $2.2 billion wealth, Demján established the Prima Primissima Award for high cultural and scholarly achievements. Some of the new millionaires follow this philanthropic tradition (History News Network, August 14, 2005; *Gazeta Wyborcza*, August 25, 2005; *The Independent* (London), August 29, 2005; Emőd and Szakonyi, 2004).

Box 6.2　The richest Poles: Jan Kulczyk and Zygmund Solorz-Żak

Jan Kulczyk's story might be a key to the secret of business success in transforming Central and Eastern Europe. Kulczyk, who received a law degree from Poznań University, turned to business in 1981, at the very beginning of the Jaruzelski regime's last-ditch attempt at economic reform. His family had been in business for three generations. His father, Henryk, had established three firms after World War II, but all had been nationalized after the communist takeover. Henryk Kulczyk left for Germany in 1956, where he was again so successful that he was able to give a gift of $1 million to his son to start out with. Jan Kulczyk also took over his father's Polish company, Interkulpol, one of the first firms in Poland with foreign capital.

Kulczyk's real chance came with regime change. In 1991, he used his political connections to position his Tradex Company to become the official VW and Audi dealership in the country. Without formal public tender,

Kulczyk soon had sold 3,000 cars to the police. With that base he soon built up a business empire with Kulczyk Holding (1991) and the Euro Agro Centrum (1993) at the center. Kulczyk privatized Poland's largest brewery and controlled 35 percent of the country's beer market. In addition, he has shares in the thirty-nine most prominent, partly state-owned companies of the country in the telecoms, insurance, construction, and petroleum businesses. His specialty became capital operations between foreign investors and state-owned companies.

Building an empire worth $2 billion through privatization deals with foreign partners, as in the case of the Telekomunikacja Polska SA and France Telecom, required the best political connections. In the first years, he had close ties with Solidarity, and later with the Socialist Party. It was a safe way to go: the Bartimpex Company of another multimillionaire, Aleksander Gudzowaty, was known for hiring so many executives with political connections that it was known as the "retirement home for politicians." Being a lone player, on the other hand, was dangerous, as the case of Roman Kluska, the "Polish Bill Gates," showed. A series of tax investigations drove him out of business.

Kulczyk found other security measures as well. While he was the CEO of his holding company, 78 percent of its shares were owned by his wife, Grażyna, who became an Austrian citizen. The other 22 percent belonged to Kulczyk Privatstiftung, the family's Austrian foundation. All these safety arrangements became extremely important in 2003. In July of that year, Jan Kulczyk planned another big business deal: he met in Vienna with Vladimir Alganov, a former KGB agent who had served in Poland before signing on as a businessman with the Russian petroleum giant Lukoil. Kulczyk, referring to his contacts with President Kwasniewski, offered his help to buy the biggest Polish oil company, Gdańsk Refinery. The planned transaction failed, and a scandal ensued. Kulczyk was called before a Sejm (parliament) investigating committee. He refused to appear and, citing health problems, remained in England, where he had previously decamped. His holding company began to sell its shares of various firms to foreign partners, and to invest in the successor states of the Soviet Union.

The pathological connection between business and politics is also well illustrated by the spectacular career of Zygmunt Solorz-Żak, a man from a poor working-class family with vocational training. He began earning money by smuggling goods to and from East Germany. In 1977 he emigrated to the West and became engaged in mafia money laundering. He changed his name and passport several times. He married a German citizen and ran the business under her name in the 1980s, and then established his company, Solpol, in Wrocław. Building up political connections, Solorz-Żak took up importing used cars in 1990 and soon began investing in media. He bought newspapers, founded his Polsat Company and gained a concession for nationwide broadcasting. Solorz-Żak did not hesitate to use illegal methods. He spent more than $17 million to bribe politicians in government circles, and to establish himself as the country's media mogul with assets of $1 billion. Some of these deals came to the surface and led to legal procedures and convictions. The scandal contributed to the collapse of the government (*Wprost*, May 15, 2005; NIE, March 18, 2004; Jasiecki, Wesowski, and Federowicz, 2005).

On the other hand, social security, one of the advantages of state socialism, disappeared. Unemployment decimated the workforce, and people in their late fifties had tremendous difficulties finding jobs. The retirement age, which had been set at age 55 for women and 60 for men in most of the countries, began to rise. The Czech parliament introduced a gradual rise in the retirement age over the course of a decade: for men from 60 years to 62, and for women from 53–57 to 57–61. A gradual increase in the retirement age became a general pattern in the region, and reached a uniform 62 years in Hungary.

Market prices immediately increased, and before governments were forced to cut expenditures, severe inflation eroded welfare subsidies built into the price of basic food products, children's clothing, books, rents, entertainment, and transportation fees. The process was hastened by new regulations that replaced the old ones. In Czechoslovakia, price subsidies were mostly replaced by a flat-rate benefit as early as July 1990. In two years, these subsidies were also partly removed, and then, in 1995, eliminated. The average price level increased by 57% by 1991, while wages rose by only 16%. The purchasing value of the currency declined by 36% in 1991, and reached its nadir in 1994, following a 57% decline. Price increases hit the agricultural population in a classic scissor effect: during the first decade of transformation in Hungary, agricultural prices increased by 510%, but the gap with the industrial price index grew even wider, as it rose by 830% in Hungary (Matějů and Večernik, 1995: 2, 7; Palánkai, 2004: 376).

Macroeconomic stabilization required severe cuts in government expenditures, and the IMF, which assisted stabilization, strictly controlled this process. The stabilization programs were uniform, without country-specific measures. They limited the money supply, which was also connected with credit restraint and the balance of payments. Fiscal deficit reductions, cuts in government expenditures, including subsidies, and public utility price increases were part and parcel of stabilization packages. Currency devaluation also contributed to stabilization by improving balance of payments.

An especially difficult social element of stabilization required restriction of nominal wages to avoid a wage–price spiral. This caused severe problems because in Central and Eastern Europe establishing a market economy required substantial price liberalization through the replacement of artificial fixed prices with rising market prices. The substantial social and political costs of stabilization were not clearly foreseen or, to put it better, were partly miscalculated and partly ignored.

In the summer of 1992, the Polish prime minister, Hanna Suchocka, faced harsh social conflict because of the stabilization process, combined with the opening of the economy. The compulsory deficit reduction from 7.5% of GDP to 5.5%, a condition for IMF assistance, required harsh cuts in government subsidies and expenditures. People had to pay more for medicines, for example, as a result. The population's share in the cost of medicines increased from 18% in 1991 to 46% by 1993. The situation was similar throughout the entire region. As a consequence, medical drug consumption, which was definitely wasteful before 1989, with people often accumulating small pharmacies in their kitchen drawers made up of free or cheap drugs, declined in Hungary in 1991 and 1992 by 22% and 33%, respectively. Many elderly people became unable to buy prescription drugs.

Even without subsidy reductions, welfare institutions eroded in a period of rapid inflation when such expenditures were not inflation-proof. High inflation and an immediate endangerment of welfare institutions decreased pensions, wages, and incomes, which were not indexed. Between 1989 and 1993, real wages decreased by 67% in Lithuania and roughly 50% in Bulgaria and Latvia, but also 38% in Slovenia, 36% in Romania, 29% in Slovakia, and 21% in the Czech Republic. In six out of ten transition countries, the 1989 real wage level was not achieved again until 2001. Moreover, in some countries, the decline continued or the decreased wage level stabilized. In Bulgaria, real wages reached only half of the 1989 level in 2001, in Lithuania and Romania it still remained 44% and 30% behind, and in Slovenia and Slovakia it was around 20% below the 1989 level (Milic-Cerniak, 1995: 28; United Nations, 2004: 167; World Bank, 1996: 70).

Severe cuts in income occurred during the macroeconomic stabilization process in the first years of the 1990s, but austerity measures were also needed from time to time to reestablish lost balance. This happened in 1995 and 2006 in Hungary, in 1997 in Romania and Bulgaria, and at various

Table 6.1 Decline in consumption in ten transition countries, 1989–1994/95

	1989	1994/95	Decline in %
Average calorie consumption/capita, (six countries)	3,077	2,776	10
Average consumption of meat, fish and their products/capita in kg	79	61	23
Average consumption of milk and milk products/capita in kg	263	201	24
Expenditure on food in % of total consumption expenditure (nine countries)	38	43	

Source: UNICEF, 1995: 136–37, 139.

times in several other countries. In the early years of transformation, average monthly income per person in Poland was $89, an amount that did not ensure the fulfillment of basic needs.

Personal consumption also deteriorated. In the Czech Republic, 43% of the population complained about deficiencies in nutrition and 34% perceived a worsened clothing situation. Per capita meat, milk, and sugar consumption in Hungary declined by 23%, 27%, and 33%, respectively, between 1989 and 1996. Over the same period of time, the average consumption of meat and fish declined by 28% in ten transition countries, but in Estonia and Latvia, it dropped by 52% and 40%, respectively. Per capita average milk and milk product consumption also decreased by 28%, but the decline reached 40% in Lithuania and 38% in Bulgaria (Milic-Cerniak, 1995: 7; Matějů and Večernik, 1995: 60; Dalia, 1998: 638; UNICEF, 1995). Consumption in general declined by roughly 10%, but in the Czech republic, Slovakia, and Romania it dropped 18%, 28%, and 30%, respectively (Crane, 1994: 35) (table 6.1).

The so-called Engel Law describes a well-known economic fact: the lower the income, the higher the percentage of expenditure that goes on food and basics. As Western Europe developed in the twentieth century, the share of expenditure on food sharply declined: in 1912, an average Swiss family spent 61% of its income on food and clothing. By the end of the century this figure had dropped to 12%. In 1950, British, German, and French families spent an average of 45% on food. By 1971, the average expenditure on food had declined to 27% in the ten most developed countries of Europe. After 1989, the percentage of expenditure for food increased from 38 to 43% in Central Europe, but in Romania, Lithuania, Latvia, and Bulgaria the figure reached 62%, 60%, 54%, and 49% of family expenses, a level equivalent to that in West European countries before World War I.

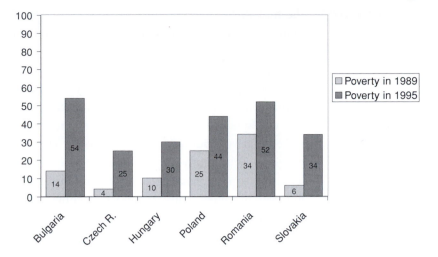

Figure 6.1 Poverty (population with less than 35–45 percent of average wage level), 1989 and 1995

Between 1996 and 2000, in Central and Eastern Europe, except for the Western Balkans, expenditures for private consumption increased by 3.7% per year and, after the turn of the century, the annual increase reached 3–8% per year. Inflation, however, eliminated most of these gains and in real terms consumption mostly stagnated, or increased by around 1% per year. In some years, and in some countries, consumption continued to decline (European Commission, 2006: 134).

Poverty, according to UNICEF, became widespread. There are different ways to measure poverty. The World Bank used a poverty line of purchasing power parity of $4 per day ($120/month) per head. Using this index, in seven Central European countries, poverty increased from 3.3% to 25.5%, and in the three Baltic countries from 1% to 38%. In Lithuania, the decline into poverty was dramatic and reached nearly half of the population. In Estonia and Romania, this percentage was roughly 40 percent. During the first transformation years, 19 million people slipped into poverty in the region.

A totally different definition of poverty is what is called *relative* poverty, which measures the layer of the population that earns less than 35% to 45% of the country's average wage level. Between 1989 and the mid-1990s, people living below the relative poverty line increased in Czechoslovakia from 4% to 25%, in Hungary from 10% to 30%, in Poland from 25% to 44%, in Slovakia from 6% to 34%, in Bulgaria from 14% to 54%, in Romania from 34% to 52%, and in Croatia between 20% to 30% (figure 6.1). In Estonia, Lithuania, and Latvia, poverty had increased by the mid-1990s from 1% to 37%, 30%, and 22%, respectively. Children living in poverty reached 50% to 60% of the child population in the region (Milanovic, 1996: 93–94; UNICEF, 1994: 2).

Using income data is somewhat misleading since income figures are less exact, and do not include secondary incomes from unreported economic activities. The so-called second, illegal, or underground economy was widespread before the collapse of the regime. In Hungary, it is estimated to have produced one-third of GDP. The share of second or illegal economy significantly declined after 1989 because a great part of it was legitimized in the market economy. Unreported illegal economic activity, however, remained significant, reaching roughly 20 percent of the GDP in the second half of the 1990s according to some evaluations. According to the Russian Academy of Sciences, the Russian illegal economy produced more than a quarter of GDP in 1993, and nearly the half of it by 1996 (*Asian Times*, September 3, 1999). A figure of roughly 20 percent seems to be more realistic for Central Europe, rising to one-third and nearly one-half for lagging countries. This is similar to the 20 percent level of the underground economy in some of the Mediterranean countries in the 1980s, and twice as much as the 10 percent average among OECD countries (Palánkai, 2004: 243–44).

Consequently, poverty calculations based on expenditures, instead of incomplete "official" income data, point to a much lower and more realistic poverty level in Central and Eastern Europe: 7%, 10%, 34%, and 48% of the population in Poland, Hungary, Estonia, and Romania, respectively, were living below poverty level in the mid-1990s. This still represents roughly 16 million people in the four countries in 1993–95. The situation was much worse in the war-ridden Western Balkans (Milanovic, 1996: 67–68). The process of increasing poverty, however, was mostly halted by 1992–93. Two-thirds of the UNICEF's twenty key indicators signaled positive change in the previously negative trends, and thus the beginning of a recovery (UNICEF, 1995: v).

In some of the countries, however, a temporary demographic crisis emerged during the first transformation years. UNICEF reported in 1994:

The mortality and health crisis burdening most Eastern European countries since 1989 is without precedent in the peacetime history of Europe in this century. It signals a societal crisis of unexpected proportions. (UNICEF, 1994: v)

In the early 1990s, a spike in the mortality rate affected about 800,000 people, especially men in the 20–59 age group. It reached dramatic proportions in Russia where male life expectancy declined from 70 to 58.6 years, and infant mortality was 4.5 times higher than in the West. Between

1989 and 2005, Russia lost nearly 3 million people. The Baltic countries shared this experience: male life expectancy declined from 65.3 to 60.8 in Latvia, from 65.7 to 61.7 in Estonia, and from 66.9 to 63.5 in Lithuania between 1989 and 1995. Female life expectancy also declined by one to two years. The mortality rate did not return to the pre-crisis level until 2001 (UNICEF, 2003).

Although on a smaller scale, other countries also experienced crisis. In Bulgaria, infant mortality increased from 12.4 deaths per 1,000 live births in the late 1980s to 17.5 per 1,000 during the first transformation years, while the European Union level was 4.6 per 1,000. It took more than a decade to return to the 1989 level in 2003. Male life expectancy also slightly declined from 67.4 years in the late 1980s to 67.1 years by 1994–97; it took a decade to recover, until 2002–03. Between 1988 and 2003, Bulgaria's population declined by 1.2 million people to 7.8 million. In Romania, death rates increased from 10.6 deaths per 1,000 inhabitants to 12.7 per 1,000 between 1990 and 1997. After a few years of decline, death rates increased again to 12.3 by 2003. In Macedonia, life expectancy declined during the 1990s, but recovered by the end of the decade. Albania experienced a different kind of demographic crisis: 1.1 million people, more than one-quarter of the population, emigrated, and the birth rate declined by 43 percent between 1990 and 2001 (Economist Intelligence Unit, 2005).

A major social upheaval gripped the countryside of Central and Eastern Europe: millions of middle-aged and elderly members of cooperative farms had to choose whether to return to the old East European peasant life or keep the collective farm together. Young members of cooperatives often decided to leave and try something else in urban settlements. Meanwhile, hundred of thousands of people migrated in and out of their countries. Tens of thousands of Roma/Gypsies were in permanent movement from Romania, Bulgaria, Slovakia, and Ukraine to all the other countries. Beggars and homeless people, unknown before, flooded the streets of the capitals. In Poland, the number of homeless people was estimated between 150,000 and 300,000 (*Visegrád Yearbook*, 2003: 291).

Box 6.3   Homeless people flood Budapest after 1990

Poverty during the János Kádár regime in Hungary was limited and not visible. A full employment policy and free medical services for every citizen made it hard to drop out of society. Until 1989, state-owned factories maintained workers' hostels with 60,000 beds for those who came from the countryside and did not have a home in the capital city. Unskilled workers from the countryside, who flocked to the capital with its greater job opportunities, were able to rent rooms or beds, or sometimes annexes to existing houses in the suburbs, for an affordable amount of money. People with chronic mental or physical illness were hospitalized, often moving from one institution to another, but were not left on the streets. The police checked the streets and parks, and did not allow anyone to spend the night in public places. Without a job and place to sleep, people were not allowed to stay in Budapest, but were sent back to their villages. State paternalism and police control limited poverty and made it mostly invisible.

At the time of the regime change in 1989, only a single homeless shelter existed in Budapest. Located on Dobozi Street, it had sixteen beds. In 1990, this situation dramatically changed. Most of the workers' hostels were closed down, and several big companies either slashed employment or closed down completely. Unemployment jumped from virtually zero to a double-digit figure. As a social worker put it in an interview, "from one day to the next, 2,000 to 3,000 workers' hostel places were closed in the capital." Within a few years, 6,000 of the original 60,000 beds remained. Temporary workers from the countryside did not return to their villages but waited for work opportunities. The police force, which lost self-confidence under the new democratic rules and political environment, lost control as well. According to the calculations of social workers' organizations, between 10,000 and 15,000 people were thrown onto the streets. Beggars appeared, and homeless people slept on benches and in house entrances. More frighteningly, according to official evaluations, about 300,000 people, roughly 15 percent of the population of Budapest, were at risk of becoming homeless, including those who rented beds or rooms and lived in unused shops and stores. All it would take was the loss of a job for them to become unable to afford basic shelter and be thrown out.

In the first months after the first free elections in March 1990, the first major homeless riot at the South Railway Station shocked the city. On September 15, 1990, the new government appointed a state secretary and opened a "crisis management office" with five staff members to handle the problem of homelessness. In 1993, a new social law was enacted which forced the local city and county authorities to set up a safety net. By 1997, instead of 16 beds in one single homeless shelter, 15 shelters were in operation with 5,000 beds, and 30 transitory shelters and 11 mothers-with-children shelters were opened in Budapest. In addition, 12 public soup kitchens, 9 circulating "tea-serving" trucks, 13 daytime rooms to warm up in, and 7 special ambulatory clinics were opened for homeless people.

It was a major effort, but it was not enough to solve the crisis. Jobless people, including thousands of refugees from Transylvania and the war-ridden

Balkans along with Roma people from the countryside and neighboring countries constituted a permanent "supply" of potentially homeless people. A certain number of marginalized individuals who dropped out of society remained mostly unreachable. Among them were individuals who were mentally ill, disabled, chronic alcoholics, former inmates, and 18-year-olds fresh out of state custody. Some of them – about 5 percent of the homeless people, according to official calculations – rejected even shelters, or any help other than some food and tea. The population of the capital gradually learned to live with this disturbingly visible new phenomenon by throwing some change to beggars, or just trying to look the other way (Iványi, 1997: 10, 32–44, 83).

Social problems were accelerated by refugees arriving from troubled neighboring countries. Transylvanian Hungarians, Croats, and others, including about 35,000 Chinese, arrived in Hungary. Yugoslavs and Albanians went anywhere: first the Serbian "ethnic cleansing" in Bosnia and Kosovo uprooted hundreds of thousands of people, and then, during the second half of the civil war, retaliation pushed Serbs out of Kosovo, Croatia, and Bosnia. Poles ventured to the West in the tens of thousands, and their numbers later reached roughly 2 million. Certain social layers proved to be extremely vulnerable:

The impression of general impoverishment is generated by the fact that the real income of half of the Hungarian society really decreased, while in contrast, the real income of roughly 20 percent of the population increased, and for half of the latter group quite strikingly. These two divergent trends explain the noticeable signs of both impoverishment and enrichment. (Andorka, 1993: 7)

According to a survey on real income changes in Hungary in 1991 and 1992, 9% of households polled suffered significant income loss and 37% a moderate loss, 22% maintained the real value of their income level, 16% achieved a modest gain, and 16% a significant gain (Kolosi and Sík, 1992). Income polarization was a growing trend during the early years of transformation.

The state socialist system was overly egalitarian, but in the new circumstances income disparity suddenly increased. In Poland, after a decade of transformation the highest 20% of the population earns six times more than the lowest 20% (*Visegrád Yearbook*, 2003: 291). People in the lowest and highest deciles represented 4.5% and 20.9% of the population in Hungary, and the ratio between the two deciles was 4.6. In 1994, these figures were 3.4% and 23.8%, and the ratio increased to 7.05. The gap thus increased by nearly two-thirds (Andorka, 1997: 89–90). This trend proved disconcerting in these countries after four decades of relatively egalitarian income distribution and it generated political resistance against reforms.

The 1993–94 income differentiation in real terms, in contrast with the general feeling in the region, was not extreme at all. Comparing the ratio between income levels of the highest and lowest 20 percent of the population, the Polish and Hungarian (3.9), Bulgarian (4.7), Lithuanian (5.2), and Estonian (7.0) level were comparable to the moderate Danish (7.1) and Swedish (4.6) levels, and only roughly half of the US (8.9) and one-third of the Mexican (13.5) and Venezuelan (16.0) ratios. The Czech Republic, where the top 15 percent of entrepreneurial elite gained significantly, but average real wages remained below the pre-collapse level even in 2002, remained the seventh most egalitarian country of the world in terms of income distribution, just behind Sweden and ahead of Finland.

According to the most often used Gini coefficient – an index scale between 0 and 100, when 0 means an absolute equal income for everybody, and 100 expresses that one person gains all the income of the country – the Central and East European countries are ranked in the bottom half of the scale with an average index of 25–28. That was far behind the most polarized Latin American societies, where the Gini coefficient varied between 45 and 63 (World Bank, 1996: 196–97).

During the first half of the 1990s, large segments of the population turned out to be losers as a result of the transformation. In Hungary, 63% belonged to this group, in Poland and Slovakia 55%; in the region overall the figure varied between 30% and 60%. Education and skill played a dominant role in this phenomenon: in Slovakia, nearly 70% of the losers had only elementary education, while 68% of the winners had secondary or/and higher education (Matějů and Večernik, 1995: 73; Bednarik *et al.*, 1995: 17).

The initial troubles of transformation, the growing relative inequality in the previously egalitarian countries, economic decline, and corruption produced "a large number of angry people... [threatening] to create a mass mobilization against the new regime" (Bunce, 1994: 56). The idealist Václav Havel, in an essay from the spring of 1992, "Paradise Lost," painted a gloomy picture on the rising negative phenomena:

Serious and dangerous symptoms... hatred among nationalities, suspicion, racism, even signs of fascism; vicious demagogy... a hunger for power... fanaticism of every imaginable kind; new and unprecedented varieties of robbery, the rise of different mafias; the general lack of tolerance, understanding, taste, moderation, reason... Citizens are becoming more and more clearly disgusted with all these. (Havel, 1992: 6)

Societies in shock

Central and Eastern Europe began marching toward the European Union. The envied market economy was introduced along with its consumer infrastructure. The roadblocks that kept them from being "European" were removed. The societies were no longer "closed" but became "open." Most people in the region, however, found themselves bitter and disappointed. They complained about their governments, about the European Union, about prices and unrealized expectations. Nostalgia for lost security and a more egalitarian society washed over wide swathes of society.

In Poland, after the "negotiated" regime change, "mythologized hopes" prevailed. Three years later these were replaced by deep pessimism and a consensus among three-quarters of the population that the country was going in the wrong direction. In a country where the bulk of the population actively participated in the destruction of state socialism, sociologists concluded, there was "a dramatic decrease in public support for both the capitalist economy and support for democracy" (Adamski, Machonin, and Zapf, 2002: 60, 162, 208, 210).

People had dreamed about free elections for decades, and after decades of staged "elections" they gained the right to choose their own representatives. The first euphoric feelings, nevertheless, were soon replaced by huge disappointment. People spoke about "dirty politics and self-serving corrupt politicians." Poll data from Slovakia between 1993 and 1999 document that a 70% to 80% majority of the population scorned politicians, and about two-thirds of the people maintained that politics was rife with nepotism, careerism, and self-interest (Höchmann, 2001: 281). Small wonder that at the end of the century 55 percent of the Czech population disappointedly believed that lawfulness had declined; three-quarters of them were convinced that social morality had also declined in the country.

At first glance, it looks surprising, but the history of the Mediterranean transformation after the collapse of dictatorial regimes in the 1970s, and of their joining the European Union in the 1980s, clearly shows the need for a long period of time to adjust to the new situation and develop identification with the political system. Italy turned toward democracy immediately after World War II and became one of the founders of the predecessor to the European Union. However, the country had a strong legacy, from at least the middle of the nineteenth century onward, that "democratic regimes were characterized by clientelism, patronage, corruption and manipulation of electoral systems." More than half a century after the reestablishment of democracy, at the beginning of the twenty-first century, a careful analysis concluded:

> The Italian case clearly shows that even if democracy was formally institutionalized, it could be informally hijacked by patrimonial forms of behaviour based on clientelism, patronage, and corruption. (Magone, 2003: 23)

Civil societies in Southern Europe, including Italy, Spain, Portugal, and Greece, which have been members of the European Union for at least two decades, still have difficulties making their voices heard. As a consequence, dissatisfaction with the domestic situation, alienation from institutions, and "democratic cynicism" are strong in the Mediterranean.

One should not be surprised by the strength of dissatisfaction in Central and Eastern Europe where the legacy was gloomier and the immediate past even worse. Societies were characterized by a lack of trust in fellow citizens in general. While in Norway and Sweden two-thirds of the people trusted in others, in Hungary only one-quarter did, while in Poland it was less than one-third. A low level of solidarity and the lack of citizen cooperation weakened social capital and capability (Tomka, 2005: 77).

If political culture was strongly and negatively influenced by the historical legacy of Central and Eastern Europe, more than fifteen years of transformation also had negative effects. Market transformation naturally strengthened new individualism and rising apolitical indifference. The fabric of the society was loosened by "colonization of life by the market" (Magone, 2003: 215). This characterization was first used to describe Mediterranean society, but it proved even more valid for the newly transforming countries. The new "parochial" political culture was ignorant about the system and alienated from political institutions. Positive involvement in political-social processes was rare and the formation of civil society proved difficult. "Associationism," i.e., population participation in various kinds of associations, remained the lowest in Spain, Portugal, and Greece in the European Union in the early twenty-first century. Only about one-quarter of the population is active in this way (ibid.: 228). Central and East European participation, however, did not reach even the Mediterranean level. The impact of membership in the Union will certainly change political attitudes and participation, but, as the Mediterranean example shows, it will take one or two generations.

Disappointment and bitterness, the feeling of being victimized by history again, are part of the culture of complaint in Central and Eastern Europe. Various peoples of the region traditionally identified themselves in similar ways. One common thread could be summed up with "we fought for Europe and were betrayed." Poles quoted their beloved

nineteenth-century romantic poet, Adam Mickiewicz, who called his com-
patriots "the Jesus Christ of nations," crucified for Europe. This view
equally characterized the Hungarians and Serbs. The Baltic peoples felt
abandoned and betrayed by a negligent West during and after World War
II. All of them interpret their history in a similar way: they alone saved
Europe first from the Ottomans, and then from the communist danger,
but they never received just respect or reward. The Central and East European culture of complaint and victimization fueled a bitter, nervous, and
sometimes even hysterical atmosphere.

Another connected and important element of postcommunist "transformation fatigue" was the rise of exaggerated expectations. People and
politicians felt that their own country deserved immediate acceptance by
the European Union. They felt that financial aid to reach the Western
living standard should be forthcoming. They nurtured idealistic views
about the West. They admired the attractive consumerism, ample supply of goods, and high living standards, but overlooked the high prices,
the work ethic, and efficiency that created it. They disbelieved communist propaganda about the negative side of capitalism. Actually, it was
at the time of communist rule in the East when West European capitalism experienced its best prosperity, growth, full employment, and lavish
trappings of the welfare state. Lack of real knowledge and unrealistic expectations were clearly expressed by a poll conducted in 1990–91 in Hungary,
which documented that half of the population believed that the new
democracy would be associated with greater social equality (Spéder *et al.*,
2002: 139).

Slavenka Drakulić wrote about her experiences while traveling throughout Central and Eastern Europe in the mid-1990s. She wrote about Sofia:

capitalism might be here, but ... [there is] no understanding of its principles ... [W]hat a confusing new process capitalism is. Instead of fulfillment
of the promise of an instant welfare society, everyone has to work hard, and
only a few will get rich. And it does not guarantee you a job or security, or
medical care or a pension. The idea of social justice, even if it means no more
than poverty for everyone, is still strongly here, if not politically, then morally.
(Drakulić, 1997: 50)

These factors played a role in transformational disappointment. It would
be a mistake, however, not to realize that the transformation, with all of its
requirements, collided head on with previously dominant values, cultural
habits, and social behavioral patterns. This collision of old internalized
values with new requirements played the central role in the social shock
that staggered the societies of the region.

The population of Central and Eastern Europe had lived under communist rule for two generations by the time the regime collapsed. Whether they liked or hated the regime, whether they were interested in politics and ideology or not, all of the people lived in the same social-institutional system, and were educated in its schools. The society and its institutions were freighted with a set of political and ideological values embedded in the system. Most of the people, although they frequently criticized and even rejected the ideology and values, naturally and often unconsciously adjusted to them.

They grew accustomed to living in security and not taking risks. They earned little, but could make a living. They knew they would have hospital care when they needed it and would receive cheap or free medication. Their children could go to school and even to university for free, and at the age of 55–60, or earlier if necessary, they could retire with a modest but guaranteed pension. Almost everything was guaranteed by the paternalistic state, and hardly anything more was achievable. Opportunity to rise within society was smooth but also restricted to the political hierarchy or through education and training. Risk taking and entrepreneurial attitudes were kept in check and sometimes even punished. Salaries and incomes were low, but overly egalitarian. A highly trained professional earned 15–20% more than the average. University graduates in Poland earned 14% more than the national mean, while those with only elementary education earned only 10% less than average so that the spectrum varied by 24%. Miners, on the other hand, received 36% to 47% more than the average income of the country in the early 1980s (Adamski, Machonin, and Zapf, 2002: 173, 197, 199).

General shortages limited and equalized consumption. Since most of the people suffered from the same lack of opportunity, the same shortage of housing and goods, it was easier to tolerate. (I can recall my personal experience from the 1950s: I had a university position as assistant professor and was married with a child, but did not have an apartment for eight years. All of my friends and colleagues from my generation, however, shared this situation, so it seemed "natural" to me. I wore a winter coat, and virtually every other man had the same coat, as if we had been uniformed. It did not disturb me because it was also "natural.")

Paternalistic state services compensated somewhat for low wages and living standards. One could keep elderly parents in hospital for long periods, and even the required bribe was standardized. A modest but stable life did not require much individual initiative. Nobody could be rich, but the social safety net did not allow the bulk of the population to drop out of the society. Unemployment and homelessness were not dangers to worry

about. People grew used to living in this way. When the situation somewhat improved throughout the region during the 1960s to 1980s, these
basic characteristics of lukewarm egalitarianism at a low but guaranteed
economic standard were preserved. The secure social situation offered by
state socialism had become internalized by the people.

Discussing socialization and social habits in the region, it is certainly
not enough to talk about the experience and habits of two generations
under state socialism. The stereotype attributed to the devastating impact
of state socialism on social habits and patterns in fact had a much longer
history. Central and East European societies and values exhibit centuries-
long legacies. State socialism itself inherited customs and values, which
became amalgamated into social attitudes and value systems under state
socialism. One must not forget that several peoples of the region lived
in communal societies; village communities existed until the early twentieth century in some of the Slavic societies. Three-generation extended
families, with a collectivist way of life, survived in several countries well
into the twentieth century. Collectivist, egalitarian features and the lack
of a market orientation had long penetrated the societies in Central and
Eastern Europe.

An anti-entrepreneurial, anti-capitalist attitude became a kind of
national characteristic. In the Central European noble societies, the Polish
szlachta, the Hungarian *nemes*, and the Romanian *boyar* looked down on
business activities as ungentlemanly. Even the lesser nobility who lost their
landed estates in the nineteenth century could be counted on to grab
secure, if ill-paid, state administrative jobs or to join the officer corps of
the army, before they would stoop to business. Capitalism and business
were considered alien, and were left to non-indigenous elements: Greeks,
Germans, and, in many countries, mostly Jews, who were considered to
be non-indigenous even if they had lived in the countries for generations.
In the Balkan peasant societies where the vast majority of people lived in
subsistence peasant farming households, a capitalist market economy was
virtually unknown (I. Berend, 2003).

As Andrzej Walicki describes the Polish traditions:

The republican and democratic tradition existed in Poland but it was not
grounded in capitalist economy or an individualistic and liberal set of values.
Poland was not transformed by the Protestant work ethic, and its nation-building
elite (first the nobility and later the intelligentsia) did not acquire "bourgeois"
characteristics such as entrepreneurship and thrift. (Walicki, 1991: 32)

Gyula Szekfű, the leading conservative interwar Hungarian historian, similarly spoke about the "anti-commercial and anti-capitalist talents of the

Hungarian race . . . The principle of trading and production for profit dis-
agreed with the Hungarian nature" (1920: 291). He later added:

Bourgeois characteristics were quite far from the mental habit of Hungarians,
nobility and peasantry alike . . . Undoubtedly, the Hungarians may be listed
among those peoples that have the least inclination to develop in a capitalist
direction. (Szekfű, 1922: 81–82)

The Central European gentry's culture penetrated the peasantry and the
entire society and became Polish and Hungarian culture in general. Thrift
was not elegant. Spending more than one earns – the typical gentry attitude – became a model: Gyula Illyés in his sociographical novel of 1930s
Hungary, *Puszták népe* (*People of the Pusta*), described poor peasant families who spent their entire life savings on a lavish wedding party (Illyés,
1935). "Zastaw się a postaw się" – meaning go into debt, but make sure
you impress your guests – was a rule of etiquette for a good host of a lavish
dinner party straight through the 1970s and '80s in Poland.

   Strong elements of premodern society were preserved in the region.
The rural peasant majority and the caste-like hierarchy with restrained
mobility were important elements of it. In Hungary, a strict order of titles
governed how people of different ranks addressed each other into the
middle of the twentieth century. Instead of a uniform "úr" (Mr.), a variety
of addresses were used: "kegyelmes úr" ("merciful sir") and "méltóságos
úr" ("right honorable sir") for various layers of upper-strata gentlemen,
and "nagyságos úr" ("grand sir") at the middle-class level in Hungarian,
while an upper-class gentleman did not use "úr" at all in addressing a lower-
status person. Uses and abuses of titles were common in Poland as well.
Wives of professors or university rectors were called "pani profesorowo"
and "pani rektorowo." It was customary to address somebody as if he
stood one degree higher than his actual rank. "Mr. Docent" (an associate
professor) commonly would be addressed with the full rank of professor
("Panie Profesorze").

   The most characteristic organizational structure of kinship and networking connections remained an integral part of the social fabric in the
region. Modernization brought changes as early as the nineteenth century,
and urban enclaves exhibited Western characteristics, but social modernization trailed economic development. All of these premodern structures
of society were preserved until World War II.

   State socialism destroyed social hierarchy, eliminated the elite and
uprooted millions, and tailored the society according to the requirements of
the industrial age in a painfully short period of time. While the occupational
structure radically changed and the rural peasant society disintegrated,

while urbanization and industrial occupation became dominant, several premodern elements of the society survived and were strengthened. Most significantly, under the cover of a strictly organized, institutionalized dictatorial system, the non-official kinship and networking organization of society became a key element for survival. The traditional paternalistic community and the people's dependence on it became "institutionalized" as state patronage in state socialist society. In some of the Balkan countries, open nepotism and efforts to establish political dynasties also reflected these premodern features. Those behavioral and social customs, which fueled market capitalism, went missing from the historically indoctrinated value systems of the region.

After 1989, the traditional, existing value system was overturned. "Joining Europe," the leading slogan of the time, meant adopting the Western lifestyle, freedom, consumerism, and value system. Risk taking and entrepreneurship became crucially important, and sometimes very profitable. The doors opened widely, but most of the people were frightened of entering an unknown world. Michnik – who spent six years in prison under state socialism and became one of the founders of postcommunist Poland, who asserts that he does not feel any disillusionment since a perfect society does not exist, who celebrates freedom and an open society as the main achievements of regime change – nevertheless acknowledges the shock of the emerging new values:

What emerged after the defeat of communism was the ethos of competition, the ethos of getting wealthy . . . Economic evolution pushed our countries toward . . . heartless market economy. (Michnik, 1999)

Later, in another essay, Michnik added: "a rat race [emerged], and money became the only measure of the value of life's success (2002). Besides painful experiences, the shock to society was largely due to the challenge of adjustment to the new social environment and values. How could you be risk-taking and competitive, how could you create your own security, and how could you compete with your more skillful and well-to-do neighbor? People had to learn how to sell themselves on the labor market as well as what kind of insurance to buy. Most importantly, they had to learn an entirely new life strategy. Instead of working for a company for a lifetime and counting on a fixed pension, it became advisable to change workplaces, permanently looking for new opportunities to save money and provide your own pension. In the old regime, there were only a few paths to success; now several ways opened and required mobility, flexibility, entrepreneurial attitude, and risk taking. All of these new behavioral patterns were difficult to learn. Most of the adult population was unaware of how to behave appropriately in this situation, and became paralyzed and bitter. Like the Jews wandering in the desert towards the land of milk and honey, but longing for the lost low-level security of the slavery in Egypt, a great part of the population of the region looked back to the pre-1989 decades with nostalgia for lost security. Memory was often different from history.

I should like to stress at this point that it would be mistaken to link social shock with economic degradation. The latter hit only certain layers of the society and in many cases only for a few hard years. Social shock was a much more general social phenomenon that characterized a longer period of time in the transforming countries. As Karl Polanyi underlined in his milestone *The Great Transformation* half a century ago:

Social calamity is primarily a cultural not an economic phenomenon that can be measured by income figures ... Not economic exploitation, as often assumed, but the disintegration of the cultural environment of the victim is then the cause of the degradation ... it lies in the lethal injury to the institutions in which his social existence is embodied ... [It] happen[s] to a people in the midst of violent externally introduced, or at least externally produced change ... though their standard of life ... may have been improved. (Polanyi, [1944]1957: 157–59)

Polanyi drew his general conclusion from two different historical experiences: the consequence of the British Industrial Revolution; and the impact of African colonialism, when traditional social institutions were equally "disrupted by the very fact that a market economy [wa]s foisted upon an entirely differently organized community" (ibid.: 159). A somewhat similar situation emerged in turn-of-the-century Central and Eastern Europe.

Social shock, of course, was also directly influenced by frighteningly rising phenomena such as corruption. It was not a new social ill. It penetrated state socialist societies because corruption was the only way to operate a shortage economy. It was natural to "compensate" the butcher in the shop for a good piece of meat, and the surgeon for a hospital bed and better service and care. Corruption and connection oiled the rusty cogwheels of the mechanism of the regime. Most state socialist corruption, however, constituted merely petty deals. The nomenklatura's[1] access to privileges, such as special medical services and easy access to housing and scarce goods, was corrupt, but mostly in a petty way. The transformation, nevertheless, fostered a hotbed of corruption of historical proportions.

Premodern elements of the society were not merely preserved, but strengthened during state socialism; the non-official kinship and networking organizations which flourished under the official institutional system

---

[1] The term is explained in chapter 7, p. 235.

were readymade networks for corrupt privatization. Skillful use of connections, friends and relatives in the right positions, and bribes guaranteed the required inside information to enable a go-getter to be first in line for an unprecedented opportunity. "Postcommunist privatization has become the potentially most corrupt area of transformation" (Adamski, Machonin, and Zapf, 2002: 332). Some Western experts drew gloomy conclusions and made bleak forecasts for the transformation process. David Stark spoke of "path dependence," a trend of transformation in which a previous, inherited socioeconomic environment may determine the emerging new one by reproducing the old structures. He wittily titled one of his forecasts on the sinister future "Privatization in Hungary: From Plan to Market or from Plan to Clan" (Stark, 1990; see also 1992). Broad strata of society shared these views in the early period of transformation in Central and Eastern Europe.

Privatization, indeed, opened the window of opportunity for people with significant amounts of money, or for those who were well connected and did not hesitate to bribe the authorities, to gain easy access to state property and privatize it for themselves. In newly introduced market economies, in most cases without appropriate institutions or legal protection, markets and free competition did not function well at first. Skillful manipulation and corruption could open doors to miraculous opportunities for a handful of people. Corruption became an element of the political and economic system. It reached the highest self-serving echelon of the region's political hierarchy. Prime ministers, deputy prime ministers, and cabinet members were involved in scandals in Poland, Slovakia, and Romania. One observer noted that:

Corruption has become a widespread phenomenon in Slovakia... It is high in public administration, but also... [in] healthcare, the educational system, the juridical system, the police and in politics. (*Visegrád Yearbook*, 2003: 403)

In Croatia, the *Izvješć a Hrvatskog Sabora*, a parliamentary report, concluded that "privatization was associated with criminal acts." The investigation reported that firms were sold at low prices; intentional losses were caused to decrease the value and price of privatized firms; fictional investments were promised but not made after privatization; manipulation was discovered whereby shares were purchased through newly founded financial consulting firms, which made a huge profit from the transactions (Teodorović *et al.*, 2005: 117). In Poland, the "Safe State" program changed the criminal code and introduced the crime of confiscation of property obtained by corruption. "Organized crime and corruption constitute the real plagues for Polish jurisdiction" (*Visegrád Yearbook*, 2003: 298). A small layer of the society got rich from one day to the next, and the brazen public appearance of multimillionaires irritated millions of less lucky citizens. Unscrupulous new elites exploited the opportunity throughout the region.

Absorbing new values and experiencing ugly new phenomena instead of sailing to an imagined paradise contributed to the social shock that the Central and East European societies experienced. Social transformation, including the adoption of a new value system and social behavioral pattern, is a process of several decades. History remains part of the present for a long time. One cannot say that the path is fully determined by the past. However, it is equally wrong to maintain that future is built by people's rational choices. Carrying within them the burden of the past, they make bad decisions based on old practices in a new situation, but sometimes they learn from the mistakes. In the end, both the situation and the people are changing. It takes generations. Based on the economic and political transformation, gradual social adjustment may follow. As long as Central and Eastern Europe gradually catches up and integrates into Europe, social transformation will have room to continue successfully. It will be a key element of appropriate adjustment to a new era and the European Union, and for the subsequent accomplishment of the second chapter of transformation.

CHAPTER 7

Lasting changes in the structure of income, employment, welfare institutions, education, and settlement

Living standards, unemployment, and poverty

Social transformation opened the previously closed societies in hardline countries of the Soviet bloc and abolished state controls and regulations as well as paternalistic patronage in the entire region. The overwhelming atmosphere of freedom filled the air. No sooner was the window of opportunity opened wide to people long dissatisfied with strict limitations than they were hit by the decline of state socialism.

For the majority, however, the negative effects were felt first: erosion and collapse of the social safety net, and the rise of permanent unemployment and poverty. These new phenomena replaced security and egalitarianism and generated social polarization according to the market capitalist pattern.

There were both unavoidable and avoidable dangers on the road of social transformation. There were suggestions that it would be sensible to establish – and there were attempts to do so – an appropriate institutional framework in the form of a social safety net and a corporatist social contract system. It was hoped that these would pave the way for self-restraint and compromise. In turn, necessary reform would follow, and social pain would be mitigated in the process. As one of the experts noted:

In post-war West European history social partnership models have established a long track record that they can successfully manage [the] process of economic and social transformation. It was reasonable, therefore, to expect that especially social corporatism would be [a] popular idea among East European policy makers trying to cope with the transition process. (Heinisch, 1999: 51–52)

Nicholas Crafts also underlined the role of postwar West European "social contracts" which helped "social capability," as Abramowitz called this social factor of economic growth (Crafts, 2006: 33–34).

The Austrian experts of their famous *Sozialpartnerschaft* (social partnership), the trade union and employer organizations Österreichischer Gewerkschaftsbund and Bundeswirtschaftskammer, attempted to "export" social partnership through cooperation with related East European institutions and training courses for public servants of the transforming countries. An early initiative was taken by the Hungarian reform-communist Miklós Németh government in 1988 to form an Országos Érdekegyeztető Tanács (National Council for Economic Reconciliation).

Corporate tripartism, the joint institutions of employees, employers, and state representatives, was enacted in laws in Czechoslovakia in 1990 to establish social partnership organizations. The Rada hospodárské a sociálni dohody, the Council for Economic and Social Agreement, was institutionalized in both the Czech Republic and Slovakia after the separation of the two countries.

In the first years of transformation some initial results held out promise for better social cooperation: agreement on the social security provisions for the Hungarian budget in 1991 and 1992 were achieved, and also some allocation of social expenditures in the Czech and Slovak cases. Nevertheless, both the international environment and the influential international financial institutions worked against such a corporatist arrangement. Unlike the immediate postwar years, social partnership lost importance in the West. The internal situation in Central and Eastern Europe was no better. The weakness of the potential partners, the unwillingness to delegate governmental political power to social partnership institutions, and the lack of enforcement mechanisms blocked the possibility of influencing public policy. All these attempts soon faded, and could not facilitate a smoother social transformation in the region (Heinisch, 1999: 60–67, 74–75, 82).

A belief in market forces as the solution to social problems and the trickle-down potential of a smoothly operating market system, as discussed in detail in chapter 1, became dominant. Characteristically, the Baltic countries, former Soviet republics, introduced the most extreme neoliberal policy:

Low union density, decentralized, uncoordinated wage bargaining and low coverage rates of collective agreements complete the institutional landscape. (Bohle and Greskovits, 2007: 5)

Most of the Central European countries added certain safety measures to their neoliberal policy. Dorothee Bohle and Béla Greskovits called the system "embedded neoliberalism." Elements of corporatism, nevertheless, continued to characterize some of the successor states of Yugoslavia. This was especially true for most of the transformation period in neocorporatist Slovenia:

Slovenia is the only country in the region where negotiation between business and labour, as well as coordination among social welfare, industrial, and macroeconomic policies is fairly well institutionalized. (ibid.)

Even in this country, however, which made some of the best progress in transformation, corporatism was deformed and penetrated by corruption.

Sozialpartnerschaft, nevertheless, generally failed, and this certainly contributed to the difficulties of the first years and the bumpy road of transformation, as discussed in chapter 6. After the dramatic economic decline and skyrocketing unemployment, economies gradually recuperated. It happened by the end of the century in Central Europe, but it took longer in the Balkans. Besides transitory elements in the early 1990s, changes became dominant and characterized the transformed countries' society in a permanent fashion. Unemployment, for example, turned out to be a permanent fixture, in some cases more dramatic than others. Urban unemployment in Poland, for example, increased from virtually zero to 16.4% by 1995; although it then declined to 10% (by 1998), it reached nearly 20% between 2002 and 2004. In former industrial cities, every fourth person was unemployed. In addition, 1 million hidden unemployed, mostly in the countryside, stayed with their families and tried to find some way to make a living without going into the labor market (Van Kempen, Vermeulen, and Baan, 2005: 67). Full employment, a natural basic feature of state socialist welfare system, was replaced by mass unemployment in Central and Eastern Europe where, in some countries, such as Poland, Slovakia, Croatia and Macedonia, double-digit unemployment rates remained dominant until 2007 (table 7.1).

Living standards continued to decline beyond the first few years. Those who could keep or get a job on average also earned less. As one survey concluded in 2004: "Labour was the least well-protected factor of production during the transition" (United Nations, 2004: 167). Per capita real wages in Hungary dropped by 20% between 1989 and 1996, and did not recover significantly until the end of the century; even then, it reached only 85% of the 1989 level. This led to decreased personal consumption, which had declined by 17% by 1996, and the losses were not recouped until the end of the century (when it was 93% of the 1989 level) (Spéder *et al.*, 2002: 85). In the Czech Republic, construction of new housing units fell to less than one-fifth and two-fifths of the 1989 level in the first and then the last years of the 1990s, respectively (Adamski, Machonin, and Zapf, 2002: 40).

Table 7.1   Unemployment (as a percentage of civil labor force), 1995–2007

Countries	1995–2001	2002	2003	2004	2005	2006	2007
Czech R.	6.3	7.3	7.8	8.3	7.9	7.7	7.6
Hungary	8.0	5.8	5.9	6.1	7.2	7.7	7.6
Poland	13.4	19.9	19.6	19.0	17.7	16.2	15.2
Slovenia	6.9	6.3	6.7	6.3	6.3	6.3	6.3
Slovakia	14.8	18.7	17.6	18.2	16.4	15.5	14.8
Central Europe[a]	**9.9**	**11.6**	**11.5**	**11.6**	**11.1**	**10.7**	**10.3**
Estonia	10.7	10.3	10.0	9.7	7.9	7.0	6.3
Latvia	15.7	12.2	10.5	10.4	9.0	8.4	7.9
Lithuania	14.1	13.5	12.4	11.4	8.2	7.1	6.5
Baltic region[a]	**13.5**	**12.0**	**11.0**	**10.5**	**8.4**	**7.5**	**6.9**
Bulgaria	–	18.1	13.7	12.0	9.9	9.0	8.3
Croatia	–	14.7	14.1	13.6	13.2	12.9	12.3
Macedonia	–	31.9	36.7	37.2	36.5	35.6	34.4
Romania	–	7.5	6.8	7.6	7.7	7.8	7.6
Balkan region[a]	**16.3**	**18.1**	**17.8**	**17.6**	**16.8**	**16.3**	**15.7**

Source: European Commission, 2006: 50–115.
Note: a: Unweighted averages.

In the early twenty-first century in Bulgaria and Lithuania, real wages hardly surpassed half of the 1989 level; Slovenia, Slovakia, Romania, and Latvia reached 70% to 80%. In Poland, which was successfully transforming, every fourth household remained below the poverty line (Van Kempen, Vermeulen, and Baan, 2005: 45, 67). In spite of this visibly increasing polarization of the population, average real wages in the most successful countries increased and surpassed the pre-collapse level significantly: in Estonia by 69%, in Poland by 31%, in the Czech Republic and Hungary by 15% and 11%, respectively (United Nations, 2004: 167) (figure 7.1).

The improvement was clearly signaled by the rapid spread of consumer durables. To compare the mid-1980s with the end of the century in Hungary, automatic washing machines were found in 54% of the households, up from 27%, and 89% of households watched color televisions, up from 25%. The proportion of households with video recorders increased from 1% to 43% (Bukodi, 2000).

Nevertheless, not only hardship, but also merely gradual improvement grew less tolerable because one had to face rising wealth at close range. At least one-fifth to one-quarter of the population, on average, earned more than before and became well-to-do, even rich. Instead of the uniform Lada, Wartburg, Polski Fiat, and Trabant cars, suddenly the most fashionable Western luxury cars plied the streets, luxury gated communities grew

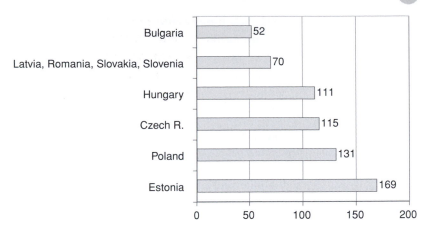

Figure 7.1 Real wages, 2003 (1989 = 100)

in elegant hillsides and suburbs, exotic tourist trips to other continents were advertised and overbooked. The Western lifestyle appeared in the neighborhood.

Income disparity increased during the 1990s from a difference of 4–5 times between the lowest and highest income deciles, to a difference of 8–9 times, and although it did not become extreme in comparison with Europe, that it was strikingly new made the feeling more painful. In Poland, immediately after the regime change, only 55% of the people had the view that higher earnings should be decreased. By 2000, 76% held that belief, and nearly the entire population (93%) shared the view that income inequality had grown too large (Adamski, Machonin, and Zapf, 2002: 165).

Social polarization also led "to growing socio-spatial segregation." Around Prague, a "booming suburban area was mushrooming: the number of completed houses and apartments per 1,000 inhabitants was three times higher than the national average" (Van Kempen, Vermeulen, and Baan, 2005: 18). Life expectancy was the same as in Belgium in the elegant 2nd district in the Buda side of Budapest, with its new luxury, gated communities. In the bankrupt 10th district of Pest with its substandard dwelling units, life expectancy was the same as in Syria, six years shorter than in the 2nd district in the same city (ibid.: 44–46). The situation was similar in the 7th district on the Pest side where the vacant apartments of the old Jewish ghetto were filled by Roma people who migrated from the countryside and often lived in overcrowded, single-room apartments.

The appearance of a new underclass was also connected to rising crime rates. In Hungary the number of reported crimes increased from 329 to 501 per 10,000 people during the 1990s. Registered crime in Lithuanian cities continued to rise: the number of crimes rose from 61,000 in 1995 to 73,000 in 2002. New business owners in some countries were intimidated by the mafia into paying for protection. New millionaires worried about being shot dead while out walking or driving, – as happened in Hungary and especially in Bulgaria. Klaus Jansen reported on the situation in Bulgaria in 2006:

the country's efforts to tackle organized crime were a total mess, and criminal bosses and people traffickers were going unpunished . . . in a country in which [according to the European Union's Commission] there have been 60 to 70 high-profile contract killings in broad daylight in Sofia in recent years. (*Financial Times*, April 26, 2006: 2)

The 2006 Polish elections were won by populists who promised to eliminate hooliganism and corruption. On March 29, 2006, the newspapers reported that new courts were being established, which would work twenty-four hours a day to try criminal cases immediately.

Even the one-fifth to one-quarter of the society who became winners of the transformation were often dissatisfied. Risk takers who established independent businesses found it difficult to succeed. Several took second jobs to get ahead. In the Czech Republic the percentage of people who worked overtime or second jobs doubled between 1984 and 1999 (Adamski, Machonin, and Zapf, 2002: 56). They indeed became more well-to-do: in the Czech Republic at the end of the century, about 45 percent of the people described their situation as improved. They gained new opportunities to enjoy a better life, but also sacrificed leisure time and suffered from pressure and tension. They felt themselves to be part of a race and, even when successful, they saw more successful competitors. Many people felt like losers, not always with reason. Perception and reality did not always match.

People expected miracles and immediate improvement of their situation after the regime change. A significant part of the population, however, remained in poor living conditions, and certain layers declined into permanent poverty: around the turn of the century, between 15% and 20% of the population were living below the absolute threshold of "subsistence needs" in Central Europe, i.e., $4.30/day (in purchasing power parity dollars), even in the successfully transforming Hungary, Estonia, and Poland. This group represented about one-third of the population of Latvia, between 40% and 50% in Romania and Macedonia, and nearly 60% in Albania (figure 7.2). Children were especially endangered by poverty, since even in Estonia nearly half of the families with three or more children lived in poverty at the end of the century (Aidukaite, 2006: 16).

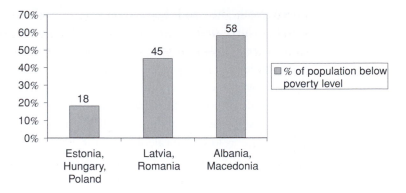

Figure 7.2 Poverty ($4.30/day), 2001

Using the World Bank's absolute poverty line for nontropical countries, i.e., an income level of $2.15 per day, the figures are significantly lower: nearly 7% of the population in Latvia, Romania, and Macedonia and about 12% in Albania lived in extreme poverty. In other countries of the region, the corresponding figure decreased to 1% to 3%.

The percentage of people in relative poverty – people whose per capita expenditure is below half of their country's average – was also significant in some of the transforming countries. Around the turn of the century, it reached 20% of the population in Macedonia, 17% in Poland, and around 13% in Romania, Lithuania, Bulgaria, and Latvia. In other, more successful and more balanced, countries this layer represents 8% to 9% of the population (United Nations, 2004: 170).

In a broad international comparison, however, the Central and East European countries preserved their "European" standard. Even in the nadir of decline in 1992, the so-called Human Suffering Index, a combined index of life expectancy, calorie intake, availability of clean drinking water, immunization of infants, enrollment in secondary education, per capita GDP, inflation rate, civil rights, and the availability of communications technology, placed the twelve Central and East European countries among thirty-four countries with "moderate human suffering," with a score between 25 and 47 on a scale of 0 to 100 (where 100 means "extreme human suffering"). However, they were the only European countries placed in this group.

The United Nations Development Programme, which publishes its Human Development Index based on income level (calculated in purchasing power parity terms), adult literacy, and life expectancy, evaluated 173 countries in its report of 2002. The best results were achieved by Norway, followed by Sweden, Canada, and Belgium. Slovenia was ranked twenty-ninth, the Czech Republic thirty-third, Hungary thirty-fifth, and Slovakia thirty-sixth (*Visegrád Yearbook*, 2003: 390). China's Human Development Index, in contrast, which reached only 32% of the West European level in 1950, rose to 78% of it by 2000, mostly based on advances over the last two decades (Crafts, 2006: 29).

In a scale of 0–100, those countries with a score above 80 have high human development. Between 50 and 79 is considered medium, and below 50 is ranked as low. The calculations for 2005 reflect that all of the West European countries, the United States, Australia, and Canada reached the highest level with a score between 94 and 96; but Central and Eastern Europe chalked up a respectable index too: within the region Slovenia had the highest level, 90, followed by the Czech Republic with a score of 87, Hungary and Poland 86, Estonia and Lithuania 85, Croatia and Latvia 84, Bulgaria 81, and Romania and Macedonia 80 (Economist, 2006b: 30).

Another important index reflecting the living standard of a country is the percentage of household expenditures spent on basics, as mentioned in chapter 6 and quantified by the Engel Law. In 1950, even in the more advanced countries of the region, Czechoslovakia and Hungary, families spent half of their income on food. As a consequence of improved living standards from the 1960s on, the Czech and Hungarian share of household expenditure spent on food decreased to one-third, but still remained around half in several other countries of the region. By 1993, soon after the regime change, more than one-third of total household expenditures went on food and non-alcoholic beverages in eight relatively successful transforming countries. This share was 225 percent of the European Union average.

Some of the countries of the region, such as Lithuania, lagged even farther behind: this expenditure neared half the total. Improvement is clearly signaled by the 2004 figures. The percentage of household expenditures devoted to food in successfully transforming countries declined to less than one-fifth of household spending. In the Czech Republic, Slovenia, and Hungary, it was only about 15–17%, while in Poland, Slovakia, and Latvia this ratio was about 20%, and in Bulgaria, Lithuania, and Romania it stood at 29%, 32%, and 35% of expenditures, respectively. In contrast, spending on recreation and culture, which in the three Baltic countries reached only 2% to 3% of household expenditures in the early 1990s, increased to roughly 7% by 2004. As an average of ten countries of the region, these expenditures reached nearly 8%, roughly three-quarters of the European Union's average by 2004. The pain of the first period of transformation significantly decreased, and even disappeared by the first years of the twenty-first century in some parts of the region (Eurostat, 2005a).

A withering welfare state

One permanently painful phenomenon, which contributed to the public's sense of insecurity, was the erosion and decline of welfare institutions, including pension and healthcare systems. The IMF and World Bank, while assisting macroeconomic stabilization, urged that the Central and East European countries cut welfare expenditures and introduce reforms along laissez-faire principles. These reforms, as in the West, were also forced by towering budget deficits and demographic changes. In the mid-1990s and then again in the early twenty-first century, huge budget deficits pushed the Hungarian government to introduce austerity measures and severe cuts in benefits and state expenditures. Similar problems haunted most of the countries of the region in the period of macroeconomic stabilization, but also at various times later.

More importantly, major demographic changes characterized the entire continent from the later part of the twentieth century. According to the demographic statistics, during the 1960s and 1970s, a European citizen had an average of 47 active and 28 inactive years in his/her lifetime, which was roughly 75 years. Around the turn of the millennium, partly because of a longer period of education and a lifetime longer by about a decade, the average active years decreased to 35 years and the inactive (school and pension time) increased to 50 years. This situation undermined the previous welfare arrangements, most of all those for pensions. The new trends rapidly spread to Central and Eastern Europe.

The population of the region significantly aged during this period. The ratio of people over 65 rose from around 10% in the 1980s to more than 15% by 2004. In Latvia, Bulgaria, Croatia, and Estonia, it reached 22%. Measured by the old age dependency ratio, i.e., the percentage share of the inactive, over-65 population as compared to the active population between the ages of 15 and 64, the trend was more startling: the ratio reached 22–25% in most of the region's countries by 2005. If demographic trends continue, this ratio will reach 28–30% in several countries by 2020, and 40–45% by 2050. Seven countries of the region – Bulgaria, Croatia, Slovenia, Latvia, the Czech Republic, Estonia, and Hungary – in 2005 belonged to the twenty-four countries in the world with the highest median age, 39–40 (Economist, 2006b: 20). This meant that the burden of supporting each elderly person, which was formerly shared by four working people, had to be borne by only two people instead. In Slovakia, already in 2000, for each 100 children there were over 94 retired people. Reforms, indeed, became unavoidable.

The transition toward a market-based pension system is on its way. State socialist, almost flat-rate pension benefits for women at age 55 and men at age 60, based on citizenship rights and a highly egalitarian pay-as-you-go system, are gradually disappearing. The retirement age is gradually but permanently increasing. In many countries it is already universally 62 years and still increasing, though in the first decade of the twenty-first century it still remained lower than in the West.

In place of the socialist pension system, the Western three-pillar system has been introduced throughout the region. It is a combination of three pension schemes: mandatory state-managed; privately managed but compulsory funded; and private, voluntarily paid. Poland and Hungary pioneered this system, followed by Estonia, Latvia, Lithuania, and Slovakia. One-quarter of total contributions were shifted to privately managed but compulsory pension schemes. Countries that had postponed pension reform such as Romania and Bulgaria began to institute it after the economic crisis of 1997. The Czech Republic and Slovenia were, at the beginning, the most resilient in holding out against the pressure for systems recommended by the World Bank, but in the early twenty-first century their pension system hewed closely to the Western pattern. Hungary, on the other hand, as a consequence of competing right-of-center and left-of-center populist parties, returned almost entirely to the old universalist, redistributive system after 1998, so that private pension funds hardly exist. Nevertheless, a new law that will take effect by 2013 goes to the other extreme and eliminates state distribution. The motivation was the huge and increasing deficit in the pension funds, which reached 4 percent of GDP in 2006 (Antal, 2007: 53–54).

Most of the region's countries did not totally eliminate the inherited socialist pension system. Elements of its universalist and corporatist character, influenced by the concept of egalitarianism, social solidarity, and public responsibility are still around. Besides Hungary, Poland (in 1999), Latvia (in 2001), Bulgaria, Croatia, and Macedonia (in 2002), and Slovakia (in 2003) all instituted a mixed pension system with reduced state participation. Estonia and Latvia (in 2001 and 2002, respectively) created a parallel system, in which people may choose between private and state-run systems. Only Kosovo (in 2001) replaced the former state socialist system with an entirely private one. Social assistance in the form of an old age allowance or a "fourth pillar" of the pension system had to be introduced in the later 1990s and was widespread, at least temporarily (Cerami, 2005).

Funding of pension systems, however, decreased substantially. In 2002, only Slovenia had an average monthly pension benefit of more than $740. It was part of a more generous social policy: "Slovenia outpaces all other east-central European states in social expenditure as a proportion of GDP" (Dyson, 2007: 18). The figure in Croatia and Poland was somewhat larger than $200, and in Hungary, Slovakia, Latvia, and Estonia it was around $100. In Bulgaria, Romania, and Albania pension benefits were below the poverty level of $2 per day; and in Moldova benefits declined to less than $1 per day. In most of the countries of the region, pension benefits are under the relative poverty level, i.e., between 30% and 50% of the average wage. In Romania, Macedonia, and Moldova pensions are between 10% and 25% of the average wage. Pension coverage in Albania and Moldova resembles the situation in the Third World in that only 10% to 30% of the population is covered at all. In Romania and Macedonia, half of the population is covered, while in all of the other countries between two-thirds (Latvia, Croatia, and Poland) and three-quarters or more are covered (Orenstein, 2005: 92–95).

Decreased funding and reforms also undermined the relatively generous socialist healthcare schemes in the region:

Under the socialist system, access to health care was not an issue, with universal entitlement to comprehensive and free, but inefficient . . . [and poorly equipped facilities]. Indicators of population health were good by international standards. Tragically, the last decade has seen major reversals in both health and health care. (United Nations, 2004: 170)

Cutting healthcare expenditures was strongly "advised" by international financial institutions, and led to the introduction of various health insurance programs. Sickness benefits dropped in the Czech Republic by 16% and 33% by 1995 and 1999, respectively (Adamski, Machonin, and Zapf, 2002: 42). This went hand in hand with the beginning of the privatization of healthcare services. The process is very slow and gradual. The state basically still covers the deficits, and insurance is provided for roughly 90 percent of the population.

A report in 2006 describes a steeply deteriorating healthcare situation: "Hospitals and other facilities are left to rot for lack of maintenance or shut down altogether . . . Medicines and other substances . . . are no longer affordable." The ILO warned in its 2001 press release: "The economic and social situation in several East European countries has resulted in the near collapse of some health care systems." The People's Security Survey of the ILO reported that most Hungarian families claimed to be unable to afford even basic care. Hungary announced the closing of forty hospitals in the spring of 2006. One in twenty hospitals had to be closed in Poland between 1998 and 2001 (Vaknin, 2006: 1–9). Between 1993 and 2003 the number of hospital beds in Poland decreased from 729 to 645 per 100,000 inhabitants.

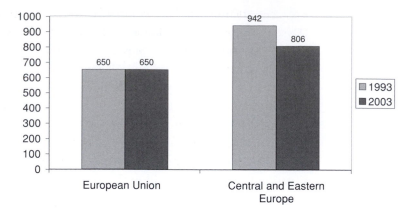

Figure 7.3 Ratio of people to hospital beds, 1993–2003

The trend is the same throughout the region: in the same period, the number of hospital beds decreased from 1,004 to 806 per 100,000 people in Hungary, and nearly halved in Estonia. The average number of hospital beds in eleven countries of the region dropped from 942 to 719 per 100,000 inhabitants in the decade between 1993 and 2003. There is no question that the wasteful use of hospital beds had to be rationalized: expensive hospital beds were often used in the inefficient socialist health regime as nursing home places, and even as homeless shelters. In 1993, the ratio of hospital beds to the population in the region was one-third higher than in European Union countries, and even after the reduction it remained 18 percent higher in 2003. The process is not yet complete (figure 7.3).

Difficulties, however, are mounting. Romania's citizens, after the 1997 health insurance law, have to pay one-third of their health bills. The decline in health, in some of the countries of the region, reached tragic proportions: by the end of the 1990s tuberculosis reemerged. While the Czech Republic and Slovenia experienced 20 cases for every 1,000 inhabitants, Latvia and Lithuania saw 80 cases per 1,000 people, a higher incidence than in the Third World (68.6/1,000). In Romania, the ratio exceeds that of sub-Saharan Africa (World Bank, 2005; Vaknin, 2006: 1–9; Eurostat, 2005a).

The paternalistic state rapidly withered away, and social security payments by the state – in constant prices – fell. Child benefits decreased to less than 43% of the 1989 level by 1995, and less than 33% by 1999. Family allowances decreased from 3.1% of GDP in 1989 to 1.2% and 0.9% by 1998 and 2002 in Hungary.

Romania's infamous orphanage system, with 170,000 children in inhuman circumstances, shocked the world in the early 1990s. The country has accomplished much to improve the situation. Nevertheless, even in the spring of 2006, when the number of children in orphanages declined to 30,000, Mental Disability Rights International, a Washington-based non-governmental institution, reported horrendous scenes in various adult psychiatric hospitals and so-called nutritional recuperation centers, which are equally appalling institutions where "children have simply [been] moved . . . [to be] less visible." In a Braila adult psychiatric hospital the investigators had found forty-six children who "looked like they were from Auschwitz, just skin and bones . . . bedridden teenagers so emaciated that they looked like they were three or four years old" (*New York Times*, May 10, 2006).

Reform and rationalization are needed as well as better health and child services. This double task, however, remained beyond the capabilities of Central and East European countries in the first decade and a half after regime change. Governments are in a difficult situation. Eliminating welfare institutions in democratic countries which have free elections every fourth year is a risky task for governments. Sometimes the opposition mobilized resistance to the introduction of such unpopular steps. The Klaus government in Czechoslovakia did not hesitate to introduce unpopular welfare reforms:

The government's attempt to pass a new law on university education that included introducing tuition fees was blocked by the combined votes of the opposition and some deputies in the government coalition. (Turnovec, 1999: 115)

Klaus also had to postpone the planned privatization of hospitals. The copayment scheme for certain services was rejected by the constitutional court of the country as being inconsistent with the constitution (ibid.). The Hungarian opposition party, FIDESz, reintroduced several state subsidies in 1998 that had been eliminated by its predecessor, the socialist government. The rival parties competed with each other to propose populist measures around the turn of the century, which actually ruined the budget in Hungary. Austerity measures were needed again to reestablish a balanced budget in 2006, which ignited riots and atrocities in the fall of 2006 and the spring of 2007.

A typical example of maintaining, while gradually limiting, social and welfare benefits is the reform of the Hungarian higher educational system. Under state socialism, education at all levels, including universities, was free of charge. In the mid-1990s, the socialist government's minister of finance, Lajos Bokros, announced an end to this system. The government had to withdraw the plan, however. Nevertheless, the number of tuition-free university places in later years was limited to students with the best results, while other candidates were also accepted and enrolled, but had to pay tuition. By 2006, 40 percent of university students paid tuition fees. Further limitation on the number of free places was recommended, and the number of tuition-free places was limited by an additional 10 percent to balance the budget in 2006. From 2007, an adaptation of the Australian system was announced: after graduation students must repay part of their educational costs. The cost of a BA degree is calculated as $10,000, and a Ph.D. is $20,000. The cost of training in law school is 80 percent higher than other degrees and medical school is two-and-a-half times more. The loan does not accrue interest and the annual repayment schedule is capped at 6 percent of a graduate's income. Below a certain income level, repayment is not required. After ten years, 40% to 50% of state expenditures for higher education will be repaid by former students (*Népszabadság*, June 23, 2006).

In the first period of transformation, on the other hand, because of skyrocketing social problems, inflation, unemployment, and a declining birthrate, the Central and East European countries, at least temporarily, had to introduce various kinds of social assistance schemes. These programs were controlled by local authorities and covered the small low-income segment of the population. Families below the poverty threshold were eligible for social assistance benefits in cash or kind (Cerami, 2005). To counter the dramatic decline in the birthrate, Lithuania in 1996 introduced 126 days of paid parental leave. Estonia in 2004 and Latvia in 2005 offered 112 days of leave, paying 60% to 70% of the mother's previous earnings. Latvia and Estonia reintroduced universal child allowances, but the amount is only about 5 percent of the parents' total earnings. These measures also served political interest to disarm the opposition: the Baltic countries "decided to offer ad hoc compensation in the form of relatively generous targeted social protection packages in order to overcome opposition of reforms" (Bohle and Greskovits, 2007: 10).

Generous parental leave and other measures immediately stimulated birthrates in Estonia: in 2004 and then in 2005, 800 and then 1,200 more babies were born than in 2003. Unfortunately, history teaches that this kind of change in trends is short-lived, and that after a few years decline continues (Aidukaite, 2006: 13; *Economist*, May 5, 2006).

The existing, though declining, welfare institutions are still very expensive. Total expenditures on social protection absorb 20% to 25% of GDP in Slovenia, Poland, Hungary, and the Czech Republic, and 13–14% in the Baltic states. This share is near the level of the old Union member countries, and much higher than in Latin America (10%), which has a somewhat similar income level. The redistribution rate of GDP, i.e., the percentage of direct and indirect taxes, and the social security contribution,

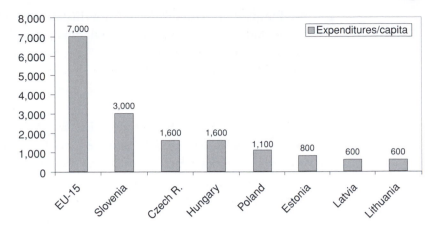

Figure 7.4 Social protection expenditures, 2003 (in €)

is still very high in Central Europe: it surpassed 39% of GDP around the turn of the century. Although this percentage is somewhat lower than in the European Union (more than 43%), it is much higher than in the United States and Japan, 31% and 28%, respectively (Morita, 2000: 4). It represents a heavy burden on the budget and the economy.

Nevertheless, the relative and absolute level of welfare expenditures is far below the average of the EU-15. Total expenditure on social protection in the EU-15 consumes more than 28 percent of the much higher aggregate GDP of the fifteen countries. In 2003, the EU-15 had spent nearly €7,000 on social protection per head, while the most generous Central and East European countries, Slovenia, the Czech Republic, and Hungary, spent roughly €3,000, €1,600, and €1,600, respectively. Poland allocated only €1,100, Estonia €800, and Latvia and Lithuania each €600 expenditures per person (figure 7.4).

Sickness and healthcare benefits, which reached an average €1,900 per person in the EU-15 countries, totaled only €1,300 and €1,000 in Slovenia and the Czech Republic, respectively, €800 in Hungary, €400 in Poland, and around €300 in Latvia and Lithuania (Eurostat, 2005a). One analyst explained the low level of health care benefits as naive "market optimism":

The ideologies and policies that emerged in Central and Eastern European economies in transition have not included the systemic articulation of goals and practices of equity and social justice. Rather they appear to reflect a predomi-nantly naïve market optimism, with expectations that the development of free markets will solve all the societies' problems. (Iatridis, 2000: 33)

The situation, however, is permanently changing and the entire welfare system in Central and Eastern Europe is in a continued transformation. It is only a question of time before the "fourth pillar," comprising the pension system and social assistance in general, disappears. The "harmonization policy" and binding regulations of the European Union, the requirements of the "EU social model," and the pressing economic and budgetary problems of the region create visible conflict and thus a dilemma for further transformation.

What will happen to the Central and East European "premature" welfare state, as János Kornai called the inherited socialist welfare institutions? At first glance, it is not a special question for the region. Hundreds of studies have been published in recent years about the crisis of the West European welfare state. Peter Lindert rightly stated:

This quarter-century has seen a wave of enthusiasm for cutting taxes and transfers [tax-based government spending], privatizing state industries and trimming union power . . . [However] the welfare state is not an endangered species among the industrialized OECD countries. While its growth clearly slackened after 1980, social transfers continue to take a slowly rising share of GDP. (Lindert, 2006: 234)

Indeed, between 1980 and 1998, the twenty-one developed OECD countries increased their social transfers from GDP by an average of 3.8%. Ireland, the Netherlands, and Sweden represented exceptions: their transfers declined by between 1% and 5%. As an average, the Western welfare states devote roughly 20% of GDP to social transfers to assist poor families, to pay unemployment benefits and public pensions, and to finance health expenditures, schooling, and housing subsidies. The most visible cuts were concentrated on the pension systems, a process that was already underway during the period. The same author, Lindert, added:

There is no sign [however] of a global "race to the bottom," either in the 1980s or since 1990. That is nothing [that] even faintly suggests that countries are scrambling to reduce the tax rates implied by their social budget, to compete for mobile factors of production". (ibid.: 261)

In September 2006, the conservative *Economist* stated:

In recent years defenders of the European social model – capitalism tempered by a generous and interventionist welfare state – have taken to praising Scandinavia to the skies. The Nordic region, to go a bit wider, has the world's highest taxes and most generous welfare benefits. And yet Sweden, Finland and Denmark . . . have delivered strong growth and low unemployment, and rank among the world's most competitive economies . . . Their health-care and educational systems are much admired. And, unlike other European countries, most Nordic states run healthy budget and current-account surpluses. (*Economist*, September 9, 2006)

Even if facts demonstrate that Western welfare states, except for their pension systems, are not in a real crisis, the Central and East European countries definitely suffer a peculiar welfare crisis. First of all, they inherited the state socialist legacy of high social spending. That "generosity" was a part of a package of income policy: wages were nearer a Third World level, but were somewhat compensated for by state spending on welfare. During the transformation, wages became market wages and gradually increased. State compensation thus gradually became more problematic, although it was still badly needed.

The other special factor of welfare crisis was the transformational decline. These countries were hit hard and their respective GDPs significantly declined. Several of them still have not recovered. Given their much lower income, the traditionally high state socialist spending became an unbearable burden. Finally, demographic changes became similar on the entire European continent and the rapidly aging population generated the same pension crisis as in the West. Moreover, the state socialist legacy also played a role in this challenge. To make their full employment policy a reality, state socialist countries, as discussed before, introduced the lowest retirement age, 55 and 60 for women and men, respectively. Most of the transition countries were spending a greater share of GDP on pensions than the Western OECD countries. Pension systems thus became an even less bearable burden in the East than in the West.

The economic recovery and post-2000 development somewhat eased the welfare burden in the successfully transforming countries. Cutting welfare expenditures, nevertheless, became unavoidable in Central and Eastern Europe. Some of the countries of the region – Estonia, the Czech Republic, and later Romania and Bulgaria – began trimming welfare expenditures. Some other countries, however – such as Slovenia, Hungary, and Poland – moved in the other direction, or at least kept the previous level of social transfers while incomes declined. Sharp political competition and the race for votes pushed governments and opposition parties alike to promise and even to implement higher social spending. In the long run, however, financial limits are significant. According to a recent evaluation of the European Union, including the new member countries, "if everything remains unchanged by the middle of the century, the public debt of EU Member States will rise from 63 percent in 2005 to 200 percent" (Antal, 2007: 56).

Changing demographic trends

Life strategies and behavioral patterns were strongly influenced by Western models, and were affected by anxiety about the future, which accompanied the transformation. These feelings penetrated the spheres of private life.

During the early years of transformation, as discussed in chapter 6, a demographic crisis emerged in some countries of the region, including a sharp decrease in life expectancy. The most negative demographic phenomena, however, gradually disappeared. Between 1993 and 2005, life expectancy at birth in the twelve countries of the region increased from 65.8 to 69.1 years and reached 90 percent of the EU average. This was mostly the consequence of an impressive reduction in infant mortality, which, as an average in the region, decreased from 13.6 per 1,000 live births in 1993 to 7.8 per 1,000 by 2004. Although this figure was still 86 percent higher than in the old member countries of the European Union, it was depressed by a few lagging countries such as Romania and Bulgaria, where the infant mortality rate remained 16.8 and 11.6 per 1,000 live births, respectively. The most advanced countries of the region, the Czech Republic and Slovenia, had a lower infant mortality rate than the EU average.

Several demographic changes, however, left a permanent negative impact. Within a year after the unification of the two Germanys, the number of births dropped by 40 percent in the former East Germany. The number of marriages also dropped by half. It was sometimes rightly called *nachholende Modernisierung*, catching-up with modern West German customs. Indeed, not only in the German Federal Republic, but in the entire European Union, the number of marriages declined in the decade between 1993 and 2004 from 5.33 per 1,000 people to 4.70 per 1,000, or by 12 percent. Meanwhile half of the marriages ended in divorce (2.14 per 1,000 people), and births outside marriage, somewhat more than every fifth child in 1993, increased to nearly one-third of newborn children by 2004. Over the same period, the mean age at first marriage in the EU reached 30.5 for men and 28.2 for women.

Besides copying Western life strategies, people in the transforming countries were also shocked by newly experienced insecurity. To quote Drakulić's description of the atmosphere in the Czech Republic:

what people today miss the most is the security they have lost with the fall of communism . . . As a result, you don't invest, build or save in the name of the future. You just grab what there is today, because it might not be there tomorrow. So future is still not-existent in practical terms; it is . . . not yet to be trusted. (1997: 67)

These feelings were also mixed into the Central and East European *Zeitgeist* and had a role in undermining families, delaying marriage, and strengthening birth control. In the decade after regime change, the average age of

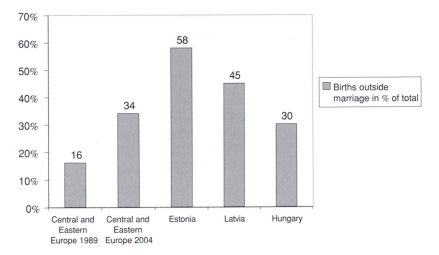

Figure 7.5 Births outside marriage, 2004

males marrying in twelve countries of the region rose from 24.4 to 27.9 years, and for females from 22.2 to 25.2 years. Meanwhile, the entire institution of family was traumatized. The number of marriages declined by 13 percent in a decade to 4.83 per 1,000 people. The lowest marriage rate in Europe was registered in Slovenia, with 3.3 marriages per 1,000 people in 2003. Another sign of the crisis of the family was the skyrocketing divorce rate. The divorce rate in Europe was also the highest in some of the transforming countries: the Czech Republic and Lithuania led the European statistics with 3.2 divorces per 1,000 people, followed by Estonia with 3.1 divorces.

Births outside marriage surpassed the Western level: these accounted for only 5% of births in Hungary before the collapse of the regime, but increased to 30% over fifteen years. This rate more than doubled in the region as a whole, and reached 34% of total births by 2004. The highest rate of birth outside marriage was found in Estonia, at 58%; Latvia was next with 45% of births taking place outside marriage (Eurostat, 2005a; Maddison 1995a; 2001) (figure 7.5).

During this period, the natural population increase, i.e., birthrates minus deathrates, decreased. The natural population increase in the Czech Republic decreased from 7.7 per 1,000 people in 1970 to 0.1 per 1,000 by 1992, and to −20 per 1,000 by the end of the decade. At the other end of the region, in Bosnia-Herzegovina, the ratio fell from 15.4 per 1,000 in 1990 to 9.3 per 1,000 by 2003, a 40 percent decline.

The decline in the fertility rate was, of course, not a new phenomenon. Inaccurate statements maintain that "bad demographics are a communist

Table 7.2 Fertility rate: children per woman

Year	Bulgaria	Hungary	Poland
1900	7.0	5.0[a]	6.2
1950	2.9[b]	2.5[c]	3.8
1989	1.9	1.8	2.1

Source: Based on Rallu and Blum, 1991.
Note: a: 1901–05.
    b: 1946.
    c: 1936–40.

era fluke" (*Economist*, May 5, 2006). In reality, the fertility decline has a long history which characterized the entire twentieth century. The population growth of the region exhibited a kind of fluctuation in the long run: between 1820 and 1870, the annual rate of population growth reached 0.7%. Between 1870 and 1913 it increased to 1.1% per year. During the decades between 1913 and 1950, it dropped back to 0.4%, but between 1950 and 1973 it again reached 1.0% per year. In the period between 1973 and 1992, it dropped again to 0.4% per year.

In spite of its fluctuating character, the overwhelming trend of reduced fertility in the twentieth century is clear. It may be illustrated by three countries of the region (table 7.2). In 1958, Hungary became the first country in Europe where the fertility rate declined below reproduction level. In the early 1960s, the Hungarian birthrate was the lowest in the world. Between 1967 and 1973, generous child care allowances and other benefits were introduced, which boosted the fertility rate above the reproduction level again, but this reverse trend was short-lived and decline resumed afterwards (figure 7.6). The average rate of growth of the Central and East European population was 13.5% between 1950 and 1960, 10.9% between 1960 and 1970, 8.3% in the next decade, and 4.2% during the 1980s. The average fertility rate in twelve countries of Central and Eastern Europe declined below replacement level, to only 1.6 children per family in 1993, and it further sharply declined, by more than 20 percent, to 1.27 by 2004. In some of the countries, such as the Czech Republic and Lithuania, the decline was roughly 28%, in Poland and Slovakia it was about 35%. The average fertility rate in the region in 1993 was still nearly 9 percent higher than in the fifteen countries of the European Union; by 2004 it had dropped to 84 percent of the EU-15 average. In the period from 2000 to 2005, eleven Central and East European countries numbered among the world's twenty-five countries with the lowest fertility rate, with 1.2–1.3 children per woman. The transforming countries surpassed the Western level in most of the

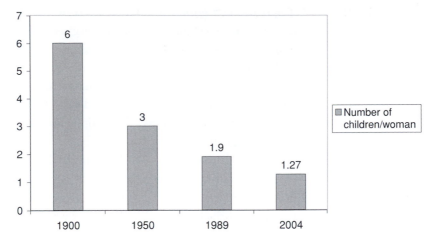

Figure 7.6 Decline in fertility, 1900–2004 (1900 and 1950 = three countries; 1989 and 2004 = eleven countries)

negative demographic trends in an extremely short period of time. This dramatic change, while seemingly imitates the Western trend, is hardly explainable without the impact of social shock. It is also true, however, that Europe's demographic characteristics are growing more uniform:

[In] a general downward trend in the fertility level . . . differences . . . between countries have declined . . . [It] can be explained by the concept of the "second demographic transition," assuming a common pattern of cultural change across Europe. (Eurostat, 2005b: 21)

Population decline and a fertility rate below the reproduction level (which is 2.1 children per family) became common, and the family as an institution was essentially undermined across the entire continent. For Central and Eastern Europe, the trend was accelerating at a dangerously fast rate:

Poor countries have high birth rates. As they get richer, family size drops. That is a handy rule of thumb, but one that post-communist Europe is disproving . . . Ex-communist countries risk growing old before they become rich. (*Economist*, May 5, 2006)

Although the turn-of-the-century demographic changes in the region are not unique and equally characterize the entire European continent, it may have a more devastating impact on Central and Eastern Europe than on the advanced West. It may undermine further successful transformation. It may eliminate a decisive wage advantage that may help attract future foreign investments and create competitive benefits. The rapidly aging population may further sap the fragile welfare institutions, thus endangering social stabilization and providing greater room for populism.

Right and Left populism flooded the region in the first dramatic years after regime change but soon became marginalized. It is not accidental that populism returned with accelerated strength in 2006–07. In Poland and Slovakia, populist governments were formed, and in Hungary the strong populist opposition mobilized violent mass demonstrations and riots. The popularity of populist parties and leaders is fueled by endangered and trimmed welfare institutions, corruption, and other weaknesses of the transforming regimes.

Countries of the region with historically developed and traditionally strong nationalism and xenophobia might not be able to handle a massive inflow of immigrant labor, if it is needed, which is a difficult problem even for well-established democracies. In other words, the same demographic trends may cause more severe problems in transforming Central and Eastern Europe than in the Western member countries of the European Union.

Educational changes

Demographic and economic changes were accompanied by educational transformation. The importance of education has long been recognized. From the nineteenth century, the permanent spread of elementary, secondary, and tertiary education characterized the advanced world. After World War II, however, education gained a new and increasing importance. Breathtaking technological developments and an unprecedented rise of modern health systems, welfare institutions, and mass tourism formed a development trend often called the "service revolution." Millions of white-collar workers and experts came into demand, and literacy and basic education were no longer sufficient qualifications for a good job. The importance of secondary and higher education became broadly recognized. Economists discovered the "residual" factor in economic development and tried to measure the impact of education on economic growth. Several studies analyzed the demand for scientists, engineers, technicians, and various highly trained experts. The OEEC organized a special conference in The Hague in 1959 on "Techniques for Forecasting Future Requirements of Scientific and Technical Personnel."

Europe was shocked to learn after the war that it had fallen behind in higher education: in the developed half of Europe, only 5% to 7% of the college generation enrolled in higher education, while this percentage was more than 30% in the United States and Canada in the 1950s. Educational expenditures acquired the status of crucial investment for economic growth, and the advanced countries of Europe increased their "human investment" in education by 15% per year in the postwar quarter of a century. Expenditure on education rose from 2–3% of GDP in 1950–54 to 5–6% of GDP by 1970.

Postwar industrialization and social modernization, as well as Cold War military and economic competition, inspired the state socialist countries to come to grips with their educational backwardness, which was quite marked before the war. One of the most impressive changes between 1950 and 1989 was the establishment, from a near zero level, of a well-developed kindergarten and comprehensive preschool system in the entire region, which absorbed more than 90 percent of the children between the ages of three and five. Basic general school education was expanded to 8 to 10 years. Roughly 80% to 90% of 14- to 18-year-olds attended school, compared with 5–10% in the prewar era. A similar educational revolution characterized higher education. The percentage of 18- to 24-year-olds enrolled rose to about 10–15%, up from 1–2% before the war.

In spite of the significant expansion at all levels, the entire educational system, however, suffered from the burden of obsolete educational structures. Secondary education retained its largely practical, vocational orientation. In Czechoslovakia, one of the most developed countries of the Soviet bloc in 1990, more than 60% of the relevant age group was enrolled in secondary vocational schools, and a further 20% in technical schools, while less than 20% enrolled in a general education curriculum along the German gymnasium model. In Poland,

vocational schools, which offer a very limited education and qualifications, were dominant among upper-secondary schools . . . Although favourable changes . . . occurred in the last ten years they are still insufficient. (Radosevic, 2006: 166)

This structure of secondary-level schooling was typical of the entire region and there was little radical change. An international survey on functional illiteracy in 2000 found that, in well-developed Slovenia, only one-quarter of the adult population achieved the level of grade three or higher in reading, though this is the minimum level for successfully entering a knowledge-based society. Another sign: 40 percent of the unemployed in the country had less than secondary education (Bučar and Stare, 2006: 242).

The transformation of the school system is still an issue to be addressed. Further reforms are coming: Poland, for example, introduced a new general educational structure in the 1999–2000 school year. Instead of eight years of primary education and four years of secondary education, either in a general-education or vocational school, a six-year primary school was introduced, followed by a general-education three-year gymnasium for everybody. After the two stages, a three-year lyceum followed. The options are general, specialized, technical (four years), and two or three years of vocational training. University entrance examinations were replaced by an external final examination, the *matura*, at the end of high school, which serves as a qualifying exam for higher education (Radosevic, 2006: 165–66). Slovenia is also transforming its educational system by introducing nine years of primary education and changing the training provided in high school.

A vocational orientation characterized state socialist higher education as well. In most *Hochschule*-type institutions, an overspecialized practical curriculum transferred practical knowledge without a strong theoretical base. Some students learned practical skills, to work in agricultural state farms or cooperatives; others studied foreign trade technical skills and the required foreign languages in order to work for trade companies; specialized schools taught medium-level managerial knowledge for construction work; and some other institutions were specialized for teaching accounting skills and practical knowledge for the hotel and restaurant business. This kind of education was rigid and soon became obsolete. Real modern business schools did not exist. Half of the students in higher education studied in specialized *Hochschule*-type institutions, and half of the total student body took evening courses and participated in part-time (distance) training while holding full-time jobs. At schools of economics and engineering, students specialized in one of thirty to fifty fields and received specialized diplomas. General education lost ground to overspecialized, strongly practical, and strictly vocational training which did not provide a good foundation for further education, retraining, and flexibility (I. Berend, 1978).

The entire educational system, which was built up after World War II, served the goal of industrialization and reflected its requirements. *The Economist* accurately described the educational needs of industrialization:

Manufacturing required a pyramid: lots of unskilled manual workers, some skilled ones, plus a few highly educated managers. The schools . . . meet this old demand – with early selection of students into academic and vocational streams, elite academic colleges and good vocational training. (*Economist*, March 25, 2006)

Central and East European education was stuck in an industrial mindset and had not adapted to the postindustrial world. The imperative to restructure the entire educational system was debated for years in some of the countries. What happened during the first decade and a half after the regime change was, however, very controversial.

In the Czech Republic, the basically rigid vocational character of secondary education did not change. Among twenty-five OECD countries,

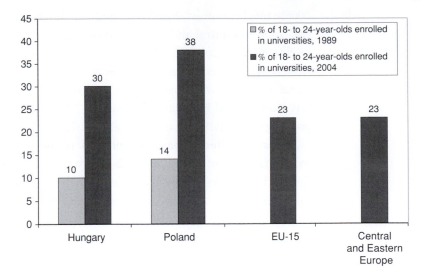

Figure 7.7 Enrollment in universities, 2004

the country had the lowest rate of general secondary schooling. Slovakia had a similar educational structure, leading to a situation in 2000 whereby nearly 35 percent of the registered unemployed were graduates of vocational secondary schools (*Visegrád Yearbook*, 2003: 93, 390).

Certain areas that previously had reached a standard higher than in the West, such as preschooling, declined. The excellent and inexpensive kindergarten and preschool systems run by the state, communities, and companies mostly collapsed and have only been very partially replaced by expensive private institutions for a segment of the 3- to 5-year-old population. This happened at a time when Western Europe was expanding preschool education.

At the other end of the spectrum, however, roughly fifty new universities were established in the region during the 1990s and, more importantly, enrollment in higher education roughly doubled, so that it reached the West European level of 20–25% of the college generation. In some countries the results were even more impressive: in Slovenia, university enrollment dramatically increased and reached 68% of the population between the ages of nineteen and twenty-three by 2005. Latvia and Lithuania have 72% and Estonia 66% enrollment in tertiary education as a percentage of the relevant age group. In Hungary, university enrollment among students aged eighteen to twenty-two increased from 10% to 30% between 1990 and 2005. In Poland this share reached 38% (figure 7.7). In the Bucharest region the percentage of college-age students who are actually enrolled in college is nearly 37% (*Visegrád Yearbook*, 2003: 94, 192, 302; Eurostat,

2005b: 136; Economist, 2006b: 78). By 2005, the gross entry ratio to tertiary education in Central and Eastern Europe reached or neared the Western level (UNESCO, 2006: 117).

Nevertheless, expanded higher education lacked the requisite additional resources. In Slovenia, the explosion of higher education was not accompanied by enlarged resources: "the number of students [was] growing much faster than the resources (financial resources as well as in terms of professor/student ratio and in terms of available physical space)" (Bučar and Stare, 2006: 242–43). While the universities of the area opened their doors widely and doubled or tripled their enrollment, their infrastructure and teaching staff remained the same. In Hungary, where enrollment tripled, "the real value of budget support per student fell to 40 percent during the first decade of transformation" (Hrubos, 1999: 4). Central and Eastern Europe's expenditure on education reached between 2.6% (Albania) and 6% (Slovenia) of GDP, a proportion reached in the West more than a third of a century before. Moreover, the region's GDP was less than half that of the West.

In several fields the level of education, especially higher education, declined (UNESCO, 2006: 121). As anecdotal evidence: the Budapest University of Economics doubled its enrollment without constructing additional buildings or hiring teaching staff. As a consequence, freshmen lecture classes by the end of the 1990s enrolled 1,000 students, who sat in two auditoriums while the lecture was delivered in one of them and broadcast to the second. Seminars were held with sixty students. Teaching faculty often took on several jobs to supplement their income. It was not exceptional to have two full-time jobs at two universities. Hungary only recently banned having *more* than two fulltime jobs at universities.

The structure of higher education changed according to a new fashion: dozens of new, mostly private, and often low-quality business schools were established. In Poland, the fashionable "Economics Academies" attracted more students than technical universities in 2002, and only 20 percent fewer students than all other universities combined (*Visegrád Yearbook*, 2003: 301).

A breakthrough toward postindustrial educational requirements did not materialize. The strongly specialized and overwhelmingly vocational character of secondary education remained characteristic in most of the countries: at the turn of the century, 79% of the students enrolled in upper secondary education in the Czech Republic were trained in vocational schools, 75% in Slovakia, 74% in Croatia, 69% in Slovenia, and 64% in Romania. Very few of the transforming countries significantly reduced their share of specialized vocational training: Estonia (29%), Lithuania

(26%), and most notably Hungary (13%) went the furthest. In 2005, thirteen countries of the region registered, on average, nearly half of the upper secondary-level students in vocational training, while in the West this share dropped to less than one-third (UNESCO, 2006: 96, 104).

The marketization of education is spreading, partly through the pluralization of the school system and the establishment of private schools, and partly by the introduction of tuition for higher education. The first step was the limitation of the number of "free places," while allowing further enrollment for students who were ready to pay tuition. A second step made tuition general but as a state loan, repayable after graduation from the income the former students earned.

The transformation of the Central and East European educational systems has been influenced by the European Union's harmonization projects, which were included under the terms of the EU Treaty. The Leonardo da Vinci vocational training program, the Comenius high-school program, and the Erasmus university program initiated the gradual homogenization and "Europeanization" of the school system. These include the teaching of three European languages in high schools, and the so-called Bologna Process of creating a common higher educational structure in the member countries with credit transfer among European universities.

An additional problem is the lack of flexibility in, and the backwardness of, lifelong training to retrain the adult population:

There is ... little retraining of adults over 18 years of age ... Adult participation in training is 5 percent at the most in Poland, less than 2 percent in Bulgaria and in some places nonexistent, while in Western Europe it is 11 percent. With economies becoming more complex, without lifelong learning, productivity will not increase in these countries. (*International Herald Tribune*, August 30, 2007)

Structural changes in society

This section does not offer a methodological sociological approach to transforming societies. The main goal here is the presentation of the social impact of the tectonic forces which transformed these countries politically and economically and consequently changed the entire social fabric and attitude of the societies. The shift also generated increased mobility, dramatically restructured the occupational pattern, led to the rise of new elite, and rendered certain layers of society déclassé. I discuss these social changes in a comparative historical method. The most important conclusion of this approach is that Central and Eastern Europe went through a belated but rapid social modernization by following postwar Western trends. This approach employs certain categories such as class, or

Bourdieu's social sectors and fields, and his useful concept that social, cultural, and economic capital is convertible.

In certain respects, social transformation represented not only an acceleration of postwar trends during the socialist regimes, but also a turn toward Western social patterns. Central and Eastern Europe slowly followed in the footsteps of the West during the state socialist industrialization drive. The decrease in the rural, peasant population is a marked example. The forced collectivization drive of the 1950s had already reduced the agricultural population. The shift of a noteworthy layer of the population from agriculture to construction and industry led to a belated repetition of nineteenth-century Western occupational-social changes.

The "disappearance" of the peasantry has been a social trend in the West since the British Industrial Revolution. That transformation, however, did not take root in Central and Eastern Europe until the middle of the twentieth century. As a consequence of rapidly industrializing state socialism, this trend became the hallmark of social restructuring.

A similar, but less dramatic social phenomenon, *viz.*, an increase in white-collar workers, intellectuals, and professionals, and a more educated middle class, also characterized state socialism from the late 1960s and early 1970s on. This trend also mirrored the Western development trend, though with a half-century delay. Nevertheless, the gap between the modern Western and semimodernized Eastern social structure remained huge during the state socialist era.

Regime change in 1989 marked a turning point which provided new impetus for social modernization. Based on the economic transformation, which was discussed in previous chapters, it accelerated the catching-up process toward Western-type social structures and characteristics. This was true of demographic changes and of occupational shifts, including the sudden new mass exodus of the agricultural population. In a strikingly short period of time, the Central and East European demographic trends and social structure approached the more advanced Western pattern. Besides the "disappearance" of the peasantry, the steady increase in the number and percentage share of blue-collar workers not only stopped, but reversed; for the first time in a century, their numbers decreased. On the other hand, the dynamically developing service sector absorbed the greatest part of the workforce.

In a new phenomenon, a class of business owners or capitalists was also formed, as well as a new underclass, a permanently unemployed layer, which lost its bearings in the workplace. A new top and bottom layer of society were in the making during the first decade and a half of transformation. Here, Bourdieu's categories are helpful for understanding this complex phenomenon.

Economic transformation was accompanied by a discernible change in the occupation of the population. A relatively high percentage of the population dropped out of the workforce. As an average, the employment rate in Central and Eastern Europe in 2005 was only 56%, well below the EU-15 level. The 2003–05 employment rates for males in Denmark, the Netherlands, Sweden, and Britain was 70%. Britain and the Netherlands had the highest female employment rate, 65%. The EU-15 average male employment rate was 67%.

The employment rate in 2003 was high in only 88 of 254 EU regions. Conversely, employment fell below 60 percent in 77 EU regions, among them all the Polish, one Czech, three out of four Slovak, and four out of seven Hungarian regions. The female employment rate in 2003 was rather low in Central and Eastern Europe: it fell below 50% in most of the Polish, Hungarian, Bulgarian, and Romanian regions and stood at 57–59% in the Baltic republics.

The Central and East European employment rate thus fell short of the European Union's Lisbon target of 70% male and 60% female employment (World Bank, 2005; Eurostat, 2005b: 62–65). On the other hand, the decline of the old agricultural and industrial sectors, the exodus from reprivatized agriculture, and the mushrooming of family businesses in the service sector shifted millions of people from one occupational field to another.

At the zenith of postwar state socialist economic development, agriculture still employed a significant number of people, while most workers were employed in industry, mining, and construction. This was in sharp contrast to the situation in the European Union: the Western countries employed only a small proportion of the population in agriculture, and services had become the main employer. By 2000, the occupational structure of the twelve Central and East European countries became more similar to that of the West because of the decline of agricultural and the rise of service employment. The five most advanced countries of the region, the Czech Republic, Slovakia, Estonia, Hungary, and Slovenia, employed hardly more than 7 percent in agriculture. In some of the most successfully transforming countries, such as Hungary and Estonia, the service sector already employed about two-thirds of the population. This occupational structure dynamically moved toward the Western pattern (figure 7.8, table 7.3).

It is also interesting to compare Central and Eastern Europe to the Mediterranean countries, which began catching up with the West during the last third of the century: in 1973 they had an occupational structure very similar to that of Central and Eastern Europe, with 28% of the labor

Table 7.3 Occupational structure as a percentage of economically active
population

Year	1975	1975	2000	2000	2005	2005
Sector	*EU-15*	*Central and Eastern Europe*	*EU-15*	*Central and Eastern Europe*	*Eurozone-12*	*Central and Eastern Europe*[a]
Agriculture	12	33	4	15	4	11
Industry	42	36	21	33	31	33
Services	46	31	75	52	65	65

Source: Eurostat, various years.

Note: a: Bulgaria, Czech Republic, Estonia, Hungary, Latvia, Lithuania, Poland, Romania, Slovakia, Slovenia.

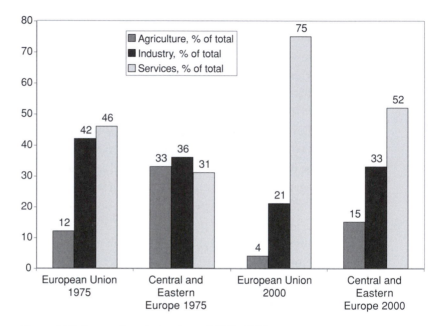

Figure 7.8 Occupational structure, 1975–2000

force working in agriculture, 35% in industry and construction, and 37% in services. By 2000, however, the Mediterranean countries approached the most advanced West. Agricultural employment had declined to less than 10%, industry and construction to 31%, and services neared 60%. This structure shows that, by 2000–05, the most successful transforming countries of Central and Eastern Europe had reached the Mediterranean or less-developed European Union level with respect to occupational structures. At the turn of the century, only two countries in the region preserved a backward preindustrial or early industrial occupational structure: in Albania, 71% of the population worked in agriculture, and in Romania more than 65% were engaged in agriculture, industry, and construction. Some other countries, such as Macedonia, Poland, and Lithuania, also remained behind, with 20% still engaged in agriculture, and service employment remaining somewhat low, around 50% (United Nations, 2002). Taken as a whole, a modern occupational structure was in the making.

Social mobility was high in the 1950s and '60s. It slowed down in the next two decades, and was revitalized in Central and Eastern Europe after 1989. In Poland, the number of people who changed careers doubled in the first years of transformation. This figure stood at 10–20% of the workforce between 1983 and 1988 and reached 20% between 1988 and 1994. On the other hand,

comparison of mobility patterns suggests that the collapse of communism did not reshape the map of intergenerational movements in significant way . . . the deep systemic changes did not weaken the mechanisms of the intergenerational transmission of social status. (Adamski, Machonin, and Zapf, 2002: 178, 185)

In 1987, 40% of men in Poland gained different socio-occupational training than did their fathers; at the end of the 1990s, that figure was still 38%. Before the collapse of the regime, 61% of the sons of managers and the intelligentsia remained in the same category, or in other white-collar positions. A decade later this percentage had declined somewhat to 58%, but a further 19% became entrepreneurs and owners.

One of the most emotionally discussed and analyzed trends of social transformation in the region was the change in the elite. This question attracted wide interest, and several empirical and analytical studies discussed the phenomenon. In the early years of transformation, several academic prophecies forecast the rise of "political capitalism" or the transformation of the old nomenklatura[1] into a new capitalist class, exchanging its political capital for physical capital. Elemér Hankiss and Jadwiga Staniszkis forecast the formation of bourgeoisie in Central and Eastern Europe in this way in 1990 and 1991 (Hankiss, 1990; Staniszkis, 1991). A more recent version of the transfiguration of the old communist nomenklatura elite into new nationalist political elite, "a new rationalization and legitimization of the old, but threatened power," is still around. According to this theory, one can see "continuity between communist-nomenklatura and nomenklatura-nationalist eras" (Dyker, 2004: 26).

---

[1] The nomenklatura comprised those in senior political, economic, cultural, and military positions in state socialist countries. Appointment to such elite positions required various levels of Communist Party approval. This system guaranteed party control of leadership selection. The number varied country by country and in different periods, but generally contained several thousand positions.

Can we see this kind of continuity between the old and new elite? What happened in reality with the Central and East European elite? For a better understanding, one has to look back to postwar elite changes that happened two or three times after 1945. Regime changes triggered the elimination of the old, and the rise of a new, or at least partly new, elite. At certain times, the old elite was punished, their top layer even physically eliminated, as after World War II. Alongside the regime change, emigration also decimated the old elite: that happened in 1945 and 1947–48 in the entire region, in 1956 in Poland and Hungary, and in 1968 in Czechoslovakia and Poland. Tens and even hundreds of thousands of people left these countries, among them highly educated people who belonged to particular layers of the regime's intellectual elite.

The new elite, however, emerged quickly. Although often radical, the change never created an entirely new elite. It was not a *tabula rasa* situation. The old elite in many areas could not be totally replaced. Experts in the economic, academic, and administrative worlds, who were not strongly involved politically, and even in the army and jurisdictional fields, remained in place. If not the former leaders themselves, often their deputies became part of the newly emerging elite. This was equally true after World War II in formerly fascist countries in the West, and in Sovietized Central and Eastern Europe.

In the latter region, especially after 1989 when several new independent small states were established, it was impossible to create new managerial, academic, legal, administrative, and other types of elite from one day to the next. Of sixteen independent (or quasi-independent) states, five – Montenegro, Estonia, Latvia, Kosovo, and Slovenia – were mini-states of 2 million inhabitants at most. Another six countries were small, with about 3–5 million inhabitants, and only two – Poland and Romania – had more than 20 million citizens. In small countries, only a small segment of the population had business, legal, administrative, or academic training and experience. There was always room for younger, relatively new members of the old elite, mostly from the second and third tiers, to fill empty positions. A radical changing of the guard characterized only the political elite.

In the former Soviet bloc, only the former German Democratic Republic experienced a radical and general elite change. After unification a wholesale replacement of the nomenklatura, mostly with West German appointees, transformed not only the political, but also the business, academic, and administrative elites. Nothing similar happened elsewhere. This model was not applicable in the other former Soviet bloc countries, where no "older brothers" of the West German type existed.

Former émigrés were not able to play an important role in the formation of the new elite either. First of all, half a century had passed since their departure, making continuity impossible. Additionally, people expressed hostility against returned emigrants who were not on the ground in difficult times and did not share the destiny of the population. Only a very few émigrés returned and became part of the political and business elite. In some of the countries, people elected former émigré prime ministers and presidents, and even welcomed returning members of old dynasties. That was, however, the exception and not the rule.

Box 7.1 Kings knock at Balkan doors

All the Balkan monarchies were eliminated after World War II. The Hohenzollern-Siegmaringen King Mihai of Romania, the Saxe-Coburg-Gotha Tsar Simeon II of Bulgaria, King Peter II of the domestic Karadjordje dynasty in Serbia-Yugoslavia, and the Albanian King Zog were all deposed, and exiled for half a century. Some of them died. King Simeon II and the son of Peter II, crown prince Alexander of Serbia, however, have returned to live in the old Royal Residence of Vrana and the Royal Palace of Belgrade, respectively.

After the collapse of communism, the surviving former kings or their heirs tried to regain their lost thrones. King Zog's son, Leka, an arms merchant in South Africa, visited Albania in 1997 to test the waters. He received a chilly welcome. Gunfire opened on his convoy in one of the cities he visited. King Mihai was forced to leave Romania in December 1947, and for a while the government did not even allow him to visit Romania. In April 2000, as a guest of the Patriarch, he was able to celebrate Easter in the country, but a political role was not open to him.

Crown Prince Alexander Karadjordje is the son of the last king of Yugoslavia, Peter II, who emigrated to England after the Nazi occupation of his country. Alexander was born in a suite in Claridge's Hotel, London (which was declared to be Yugoslav territory by Winston Churchill), in 1945. The family lived in England and the United States, where his father died in 1970. Alexander was trained to be king. He learned several languages, enrolled in military academies in the United States and Britain, and rose to the rank of captain in the British army. In 1972, Alexander married the first cousin of King Juan Carlos of Spain, who was himself Alexander's third cousin, and he became a businessman.

After the collapse of communism, Alexander visited the country he had never seen before. He traveled to Montenegro, Kosovo, and Bosnia in 1991,

1992, 1995, and 1999. Alexander was well received, and when Slobodan Milošević lost the 2000 elections, he moved back to Belgrade. His role model was King Juan Carlos, his relative, who had helped democratize post-Franco Spain. The new government returned a few royal palaces to the family, and in July 2001 he moved in. Certain political forces such as the Serbian Renewal Movement of Vuk Drasković took an interest in the restoration of a constitutional kingdom.

Alexander began his political activity by mobilizing and trying to unite the anti-Milošević opposition, which was represented by seventeen parties. He conducted high-profile conferences with this goal in Budapest and Athens in 1999 and 2000, saying "my contribution, as I see it, will be to unite people from across the spectrum – to help to resolve the differences that divide them." He became a nonpartisan symbol of nationhood.

Simeon II, or as he started to call himself, Simeon Borisov Sakskoburggotski, was born in the Bulgarian royal palace in 1937. In 1943, at the age of six, after the strange and sudden death of his father, Tsar Boris (after a dinner with Hitler), he became the tsar under a regency. He was deposed in 1946 and left the country with his Italian mother from the House of Savoy. In 1951, Francisco Franco granted them asylum. He was also trained to be king. He received military training in the United States, but then became a businessman, as chairman of the Spanish subsidiary of the French electronic giant Thomson.

During the first transformation years, Simeon was not allowed to visit Bulgaria, but in 1996, when he received permission, thousands demonstrated for the restoration of the monarchy. He moved back to Bulgaria with his family and established his own party, the National Movement Simeon II, in 2001. He considered a run for the presidency that year, but was denied because of the constitutional requirement of at least five years' residency. However, he did move into the palace where he was born. In the June elections of 2001, his party gained nearly 43 percent of the votes and half the seats in parliament, and formed a coalition government. For the first time in history, a former tsar became a democratically elected prime minister who took an oath to the republican constitution. His political success, which was based on the people's disappointment with partisan politics, nevertheless turned out to be short-lived. In the June 2005 elections, his party received only 20 percent of the votes and was replaced by a socialist government.

Exiled Balkan kings and their heirs are still waiting for the appropriate time to make a comeback. (Malic, 2001)

After 1989, there was no significant emigration of the former elite to decimate the top layer of society. The old elite was not severely punished either; retribution against its members was rare. Only a few countries, such as Romania, Bulgaria, and Albania, punished the old leading elites, but even in these cases it was not in large numbers. The Ceauşescu couple was executed, their son imprisoned, and a few members of the Politburo got fifteen- to twenty-year prison sentences in Romania. In Bulgaria, three former prime ministers were imprisoned and purges were conducted in the civil service and universities. In Albania, the widow of the former dictator Enver Hoxha, his successor, Ramiz Alia, and a dozen party secretaries, Politburo members, and other party officials were tried and sentenced. After the 1995 lustration law, two dozen former functionaries were tried.

In most of the countries, however, the former elite were not punished. Tadeusz Mazowiecki, the first freely elected Polish prime minister, and Michnik, the prestigious former dissident and then editor-in-chief of Poland's leading daily newspaper, explicitly warned against retribution and witch hunts to avoid polarizing the country and paralyzing the state apparatus. Altogether eight army officers, who ordered shots to be fired against the demonstrators in Gdańsk in 1970, and the killer of a dissident priest were arrested in Poland. Václav Havel argued for "collective guilt" in Czechoslovakia, where the 1991 lustration act ordered the screening of certain categories of people. Former members of the state security apparatus were disqualified from working in state agencies, and 10 percent of judges eventually had to leave the service. In Hungary, neither judges nor prosecutors were reviewed, and no disqualifications took place.

Stephen Holmes maintained in 1994:

By quarantining a few, the majority of citizens would metaphorically cleanse themselves ... it happened to a limited extent in the Czech Republic, [but] it occurred virtually nowhere else ... Public appetite for purges ... proved vanishingly small ... The dreaded witch hunt ... completely failed to materialize ... Decommunization has now almost everywhere guttered to a quiet end. (S. Holmes, 1994: 33–34)

Indeed, Todor Zhivkov, the Bulgarian communist dictator, was sentenced to seven years in prison, but never served them for health reasons. In Romania, the last two officials imprisoned for their responsibility for the December 1989 massacre were released in December 1993. Was it the consequence of public skepticism about the politicization of morality, or the recognition "that the most pressing need in these societies was social reconciliation, not collective self-laceration" (ibid.: 33–35)?

The process of facing the past, however, is not yet over. The new Romanian government appointed a committee to evaluate the communist past and responsibilities in 2006. The Kaczinski government in Poland also opened the files of the secret police to unveil people who reported on others. Reports on people who reported to the secret police continued to be published in journals in Hungary. Pope Benedict XVI touched on this subject during his 2006 spring visit to Poland when he said:

We must guard against the arrogant claim of setting ourselves up to judge earlier generations, who lived in different times and different circumstances . . . Humble sincerity is needed in order not to deny the sins of the past. (*New York Times*, May 26, 2006)

Samuel Huntington correctly observed that: "prosecution of the old elite did not occur where reformist elements within the former regime had initiated or negotiated the transition" (1991: 211). As Wictor Osiatinski maintained:

the desire to close the books or the crimes of the past, the resistance to the retributive phase of the revolution – with its predictable violence, injustice, and destructiveness – [is] one of the most important successes of the post-communist transformation. (Borneman, 1997: 163; see also 6–9, 146–52)

This policy definitely helped promote social consolidation and relatively smooth sociopolitical change. This atmosphere also allowed the advancement of mostly young, second- and third-tier cadres to leading positions in the reform-communist parties. They were often new recruits of the former communist elite, often from the countryside, not visible to the public when the system change took place. They often became leaders of postcommunist, now socialist parties, and became members of parliament and socialist governments.

In reality, nevertheless, the bulk of the old communist nomenklatura was unable to preserve power, and the old political elite mostly disappeared. The assumption that the old nomenklatura reinvented itself as new nationalist political elite is based on a few examples: the ones often cited include the Serbian Milošević and the Romanian Ion Iliescu. Even those who posit this assumed continuity, and the "about-face" from communism to nationalism, also agree that the reform-communist party of Poland, which won the 1993 elections, as well as the reform-communist party of Hungary which formed the government in 1994, and then twice again in the early twenty-first century, did not exhibit nomenklatura-nationalist characteristics, and that Poland, Hungary, and the Czech Republic "do not fit the pattern" (Dyker, 2004: 37–38). It is more useful to acknowledge that the assumed pattern does not exist. As the authors of a study on postcommunist Hungary stated: "Only a narrow circle of political leaders had the chance to preserve their advantageous position" (Spéder *et al.*, 2002: 106).

Box 7.2 Communists reinventing themselves as nationalists? The case of Slovakia

Discussions of the rise of the postcommunist elite often pivot on the stereotype of the turncoat former communist careerists who have reinvented themselves as nationalists in order to keep power. There is no doubt that this often happened. Even more often, however, it is an oversimplification. Gil Eyal's excellent sociological analysis of the origins of the Slovak postcommunist elite, which will be the basis of the discussion below, presents a much more complex picture of that case.

Several members of professional, technocratic, managerial, and humanist intellectual elite, among them several historians active during the communist regime, became important leaders in the new Slovak political elite after regime change. They filled most of the economic portfolios, and became prime ministers, ministers, deputy ministers, and influential members of the parliament. A great many of them were communists before the Prague Spring and expelled from the party afterwards, and several were rehabilitated relatively quickly. Many remained untouched by the purges, and almost all had medium-level positions in the hardliner Húsak regime. Very few became dissidents or internal exiles. They never left the public sphere, but remained part of the regime, well connected both inside and outside the party. As reform-minded communists they believed in renewal through reform and the importance of their expert work within the system. Several who worked as prognosticators in economic institutes, managers in various major companies, or professors and researchers in universities and academy institutes, even under communism, were genuine Slovak nationalists who turned to internal reform "for the welfare, security, and identity of the national community," i.e., the special interest of Slovakia. Managers such as Peter Baco, who served as the chairman of the United Farmers Cooperative under the communist regime, became minister of agriculture after 1989. Ján Ducký (deputy minister of industry before, and minister of industry after, 1989) and Vladimir Lexa (deputy minister of industry before, and deputy prime minister after, 1989) were both party members until 1989, and they advocated special Slovak economic interests before the regime change and were appointed to postcommunist governments to pursue them. They were part of a typical phenomenon: well-positioned communist technocrats with good education, skills, and connections, but who were not deposed because they were mostly deputies. They accomplished the "revolution of the deputies," and easily became members of the new elite.

Several of this group, former communist historians and humanist intellectuals who formed the Slovak National Party after 1989 and joined the governments as ministers of culture (Dušan Slobodník), ministers of education (Matús Kucera), and even as deputy prime minister (Marián Andel), were "Marxist" champions of establishing a new national myth before 1989. They wrote about the Great Moravian Empire, "the first Slovak state," which existed centuries before the Hungarian occupation and forcibly incorporated the Czechs. The Hungarian conquerors inherited the Slovak agricultural and commercial achievements, and Slovak history was not lost, but became an autonomous part of the Hungarian history. This group of communist historians and archeologists were not "unscrupulous and cynical individuals, who first adopted communism . . . and now have simply decided to play the nationalist card in order to facilitate their survival in power." They were nationalists during the communist regime and cultivated their nationalist agenda using Marxist phraseology. An interesting example is the case of Slobodník, who was equally involved in the wartime Slovak fascist regime and both the communist and postcommunist regimes, but who remained a Slovak nationalist throughout. Eyal described in detail a huge mural in the Hall of the Knights in Bratislava Castle, "Od Veľkej Moravy po dnešok," which depicts the unity of Slovak history from Great Moravia up until today, created by F. Gajdoš in 1984. This mural summarizes the nationalist myth, as the above-mentioned nationalist historians were able to interpret it under communism. After regime change, they continued the nationalist program by simply dropping the communist rhetoric.

Nationalists in Hungary such as Imre Pozsgay and Mátyás Szűrös, who promoted reforms to separate Hungary from the Soviet Union during the communist regime, easily accommodated themselves to the postcommunist nationalist Right. Nationalist Yugoslav communists who believed they served the national agenda by siding with Tito easily evolved into ardent Serbian nationalists when confronted with Croat and Bosnian nationalism. Romanian "national communists" of the Ceauşescu era made a smooth transition to becoming "national democrats." Slovak and Croat nationalists turned to Hitler and introduced fascist regimes to realize their national program in the 1930s and 1940s. Nationalism was also packed into communism before 1989, but the nationalist agenda was unpacked again after 1989 (Eyal, 2003: 93–134; Verdery, 1991).

Fortunately, a broad sociological investigation – "Social Stratification in Eastern Europe After 1989" – was initiated in 1993–94 by Professor Iván Szelényi of the University of California Los Angeles, and conducted by a huge group of scholars in six transforming countries in Central Europe, the Balkans, and Russia. In each of these countries, about 5,000 people were surveyed in personal interviews (Eyal, Szelényi, and Townsley, 1998: 199). The results of this investigation offer exact knowledge about the elite change. In 1993, only 3% of the Czech, somewhat more than 6% of the Hungarian, and 9% of the Polish former nomenklatura members had higher political offices in 1993. The bulk of the former political elite became déclassé; one-quarter to one-third of them retired, the majority of them via early retirement. The percentage of Communist Party members in the early retired (under the age of 60) nomenklatura elite was roughly 90% in the three countries. Another 6% to 13% of the former nomenklatura became workers.

A relatively large number of the economic elite kept their previous managerial jobs, or returned to their original occupation and became managers: in the Czech Republic 42% of the former nomenklatura people were parts of the new managerial elite, but 13% of them had earlier held low-level managerial posts. In Poland, 31% of the former economic elite remained managers, but 9% had already been in low-level managerial positions; in Hungary the figure was 27%, with nearly half having been in lower-managerial posts. Another 12–20% of the former nomenklatura elite became professionals, mostly returning to their original skills.

The transformation of the nomenklatura elite into a new capitalist class, using their political power to privatize state-owned companies for themselves, was relatively marginal in the social transformation of Central and Eastern Europe, in contrast to various claims. In 1993, in the Czech Republic, Hungary, and Poland, less than 6% of the former nomenklatura elite became entrepreneurs. Not even the former economic elite emerged into the rank and file of new bourgeoisie: hardly more than 5% of them became entrepreneurs. As the investigation proved:

findings directly refute arguments . . . that it was the political fraction of the former communist elite who were best placed to take advantage of post-communist market reforms; rather we find that members of the economic nomenklatura were much bigger beneficiaries. (Eyal, Szelényi, and Townsley, 1998: 121)

Former managers, some of them excellent and experienced, proved indispensable and remained in the economic elite. The academic elite changed very little. Continuity, in this respect, was thus strong:

the new elite has few genuine newcomers. Entrepreneurs forming the elite of economic life, well-to-do technocrats and freelancing intellectuals had usually been members of the elite under state socialism, even if they may not have enjoyed exactly the same social status. (Enyedi, 1992: 11)

The same commentator later added:

The major beneficiary of the transformation was the late communist technocracy and the managerial elite [while] the majority of the former communist top political nomenklatura lost its position. (Enyedi, 1998: 27)

It should be added that the old–new managerial elite was able to establish itself in the new order because of its members' skills and knowledge. It almost never happened that members of the former political elite, state, or party apparatchiks transformed their position into leading managerial posts: the above-cited investigation proved that "about 1–2 percent of the managers of larger firms in Central Europe in 1993 were party or state functionaries in 1988" (Eyal, Szelényi, and Townsley, 1998: 166).

The concepts of "political capitalism" and "nomenklatura nationalism," i.e., the transformation and survival of the old political elite into nationalist political and/or capitalist elite, were not realistic assumptions except in a very few, random cases. The transformation did not lead to the reproduction of the old power structure, and capitalism was not built "with the ruins of socialism," but "on the ruins" of it (Stark, 1992; Eyal, Szelényi, and Townsley, 1998: 38). If political capital was rarely transferable after 1989, economic, managerial, and cultural capital, knowledge, and skill definitely played an important role in the formation of the new elite. In small countries this kind of continuity was inevitable and unavoidable.

Several new layers emerged into the elite as well. Newcomers in the elite were recruited from highly qualified and mobile, risk-taking people, who easily became self-made men. Experts and innovators in the new high-tech sectors also moved up fast as did former small entrepreneurs who accumulated money during state socialism, especially in reforming countries such as Poland, Hungary, and Slovenia. Former workers, who had participated in the so-called second economy before 1989, also accumulated expertise and some capital, which helped them to rise into the new entrepreneurial elite. Various kinds of people who had money became part of the privatization process. Some of them made millions and even billions of dollars in a few years.

The complexity of new elite formation is best expressed by the reemergence of the descendants of prewar elite groups:

many of those who are now arriving at the top are coming from families, which owned a significant amount of (real or symbolic) capital before the war. Their

ranks were swelled by large segments of the technocratic elites of late state socialism, or by the entrepreneurs of the newly emerging black economy . . . who felt
increasingly frustrated with the limited opportunities for economic competition
and gain. Thus, all the above (often overlapping) groups – the heirs of the prewar
elite, the new technocrats, and the new entrepreneurs – were ready to accept a
new system of values and a new ideology. (Ferge, 1997: 107)

Former dissidents found their place in newly formed political parties and
soon gained power. Most of them, nevertheless, could not adjust to the new
political realities. Being in opposition required different characteristics and
skills than being in power. Many disappeared from the political arena and
continued as journalists, writers, and professors.

The bulk of the new elite, however, emerged from the grey crowd of
employees: millions opened various kinds of independent family businesses. In Poland, in the early twenty-first century, 44% of the 3.5 million
small business owners came from blue-collar families and another 20%
from farming families (*Visegrád Yearbook*, 2003: 285). Lawyers and medical
doctors entered into private legal or medical practice. Jobs and activities
that had not even existed under state socialism offered good opportunities:
employment as real estate agents, tax and business consultants, and stock
brokers promised high incomes and attracted entrepreneurial people. A
new middle class was in the making.

One of the most important factions of the old elite, the intelligentsia,
dropped into an entirely new environment. Central and East European
intelligentsia traditionally held prestigious positions in the society.
Writers, poets, university professors, journalists, and top actors and
actresses belonged to the highest echelon of the society. To be an intellectual did not only mean to practice a profession, but – above all – to
be a *public* intellectual. The legacy of prophet intellectuals, inherited from
the age of early nineteenth-century romantic nationalism, was preserved
during state socialism.

A sector of the public intellectuals served the communist regimes, but
played a role of opposition from within, especially in reform-oriented
countries, criticizing and attacking the shortcomings, mistakes, poorly
operating institutions, and bad habits of the regime, believing in its
reformability, and sometimes working to correct it. Several others dis-
tanced themselves from the regime, remained independent, became dissidents, and belonged to the opposition. In the latter case, though they
were sometimes imprisoned or punished by the authorities, they became
famous both at home and abroad. All of the public intellectuals enjoyed a
special status and respect.

In the new capitalist society, the status of intellectuals dramatically changed: they lost their social importance and prophetic role. Michnik clearly expressed the changed requirements:

In the epoch of dictatorship, an intellectual was the one who spoke in the name of the gagged nation. Today the nation is not gagged anymore and therefore an intellectual is no longer its guide. (Michnik, 2002)

They were, of course, free to say what they wanted to, and their situation was not threatened by political power, but the paucity of public interest was disappointing for them. The old governments, even the dictatorial ones, had worried about such people and responded to every action and publication harshly. The new authorities did not care or react. Public intellectuals, nevertheless, continued writing and publishing their bitter critiques and prophecies, but their publications failed to attract public interest. The echoes of their passionate discussion of issues in newspapers, private gatherings, and clubs began to fade.

The formation of the new elite in Russia and some of the Balkan countries such as Romania and Bulgaria was significantly different and exhibited, at least partially, the phenomena of "political capitalism." Corrupt privatization opened the window of opportunity for ascending into the new economic and entrepreneurial elite. In Russia, for example, instead of the 1–2% in Central Europe, 10% of the top managers in 1993 formerly held state or party jobs in 1988.

Settlement structure: unchanged urbanization level, but changing cities

Radical occupational changes, including a sharp decline in agrarian workers and the rise of the service sector, made surprisingly little impact on settlement structure and the urbanization process. Central and Eastern Europe went through a process of rapid urbanization during the state socialist decades. Between 1950 and 1990 the region belatedly followed the nineteenth-century Western trend. The share of urban population increased from 32% to 61% in Poland. The Czech Republic, with the most developed urban network, reached the Western level of more than 70% of the population being urban. Two-thirds of the population of Lithuania and Bulgaria lived in cities, and the percentage of city dwellers in most of the other countries of the region reached 50–60%. Only Albania (37%) and Bosnia-Herzegovina (34%) remained sparsely urbanized.

The cities, including the historical, cultural, and political centers, became industrialized, polluted, and run-down. New industrial "socialist"

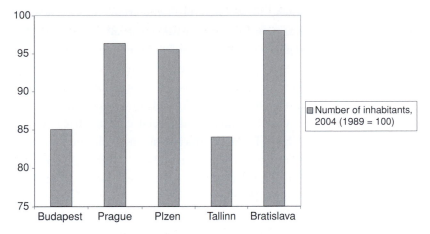

Figure 7.9 Deurbanization: number of urban inhabitants, 1989–2004

cities were also built. Buildings missing their plaster coatings and covered with soot were a common sight. Most of the new buildings were boring, standardized, low-quality prefabricated houses that made the suburbs uniform across the region. Infrastructure was insufficient everywhere.

After 1989, during the transformation period, urbanization either stagnated or, in most cases, declined somewhat. In Hungary, very typically, outmigration from cities to villages became characteristic, especially in the first years of transformation. While the country's population declined by 1.1%, urban population decreased by 2.5%. Budapest had 2.02 million inhabitants in 1990, but only 1.72 million by 2003. Similar trends emerged in the Czech Republic, where the entire population declined by 0.7%, but the populations of Prague and Plzen fell by 3.7% and 4.5%, respectively. Tallinn, also a capital city, decreased in population by 16% between 1989 and 2003, and the same decline was experienced by Latvia's big cities. Bratislava became the capital city of newly formed independent Slovakia, but its population decreased by 2%. The decline of the urban population was thus faster than that of the countries as a whole (Van Kempen, Vermeulen, and Baan, 2005: 82, 134, 159, 193) (figure 7.9).

This phenomenon was generated by various socioeconomic changes. One of them was the crisis and collapse of the former "socialist cities," postwar industrial centers, and the fortresses of socialist heavy industries. Black mining cities of Poland such as Żory, Głogów, Lubin, and Tichy, the copper-mining town of Polkowice, new centers of the Polish chemical industry Kedzierzyn and Police, and the Hungarian equivalents, the mining towns of Tatabánya and Komló, the greenfield investment iron and steel center Sztálinváros (later renamed Dunaujváros), the other metallurgical town, Ózd, and the Hungarian heavy chemical industrial centers, Kazincbarcika and Tiszaujváros: all suffered spectacular decline after the regime change. The "Polish Manchester," Łodź, one of the first nineteenth-century industrial cities in the region, experienced a "demetropolization." Even Budapest's industrial population dropped from 347,000 to 128,000 during the first transformation years.

On the other hand, social changes triggered rapid suburbanization. Prague, Budapest, Bucharest, and Sofia equally experienced this trend (Van Kempen, Vermeulen, and Baan, 2005: 21, 40, 65). While the population of Budapest declined by 4.4%, the population of the forty-four settlements comprising the Budapest agglomeration increased by 4% during the first half of the 1990s. The same trend was reproduced in thirty-two metropolitan areas in Hungary: their population dropped by 2.9%, but the number of inhabitants in their suburbs increased by 2.3% (Ladányi and Szelényi, 1998: 68–69).

Although the rate of urbanization remained virtually unchanged, urban settlements were transformed. Suburbanization was only one of the elements of change. The meaning of "suburbs" altered as well. During the entire twentieth century suburbs in Central and Eastern Europe meant a mixture of industrial zones, working-class residential "dormitory" towns, with commuting residents who worked in suburban industry or the city's other industrial zones, and rural, semi-village areas, where the residents kept pigs and goats and grew vegetables for the family. During the transformation period, the deindustrialization and deagrarization of most of the suburbs was accompanied by the Western type of middle-class suburban developments in certain areas.

A second characteristic following Western patterns was the rise of service cities, which were replacing socialist industrial cities. Comparing the transformation of Prague, Budapest, and Warsaw, Luděk Sỳkora describes a belated deindustrialization and "transformation towards the postindustrial model" from the late 1980s on (Sỳkora, 1998: 111). This modern transformation, however, was temporarily accompanied by the decline of the urban landscape: "postindustrial" for a while meant a great number of abandoned factory buildings, and mounting garbage in residential areas.

Reconstruction of urban areas, however, also began. From the mid-1990s, intensive, high-standard housing development began in Bratislava's Staré Mesto center. In 1992, a large-scale rehabilitation program began in Middle Ferencváros, one of Budapest's worst slum areas. Obsolete, comfortless small buildings were torn down and a thousand new dwelling units were built. Another thousand were completely renovated (Kovács, 2006: 57). Some old factory buildings were remodeled and rebuilt as shopping centers following the Canary model of San Francisco. In Marcali, a small trans-Danubian township in Hungary, a 1.6-hectare "brownfield" site, an abandoned former engineering factory exactly in the center of the city, was cleaned up and replaced with a park surrounded by cultural and commercial buildings (*Népszabadság*, June 23, 2006).

The capital cities became the centers of banking, multinational companies, and various service branches. Prague's historic downtown area lost nearly one-quarter of its population between 1991 and 2004 because the "originally strong residential function has been turning into . . . predominantly administrative and business functions" (Burcin and Kučera, 2006: 178–79). In the mid-1990s, more than two-thirds of Poland's banking equity capital was concentrated in Warsaw. One-third of the registered firms in Prague were international companies. Half of the foreign-owned companies of Hungary were located in Budapest. Austrian, German, French, Finnish, and Swedish developers erected modern, Western-type office buildings throughout the region. In Prague, 70 percent of the new and modernized office space was jammed into the city center. Several former tenement buildings in the central regions were remodeled into offices. By the middle of the decade, about three-quarters of all floor space in the historical core of Prague was in nonresidential use, driving out residential functions (Sỳkora, 1998: 124).

The rise of the service city is clearly characterized by the rapid transformation of employment structure in Budapest: in the first half-decade after the regime change, industrial and construction employment declined from 48% to 36%, while employment in telecommunications, finance, real estate, and other service sectors increased from 59% to 68% (Budapest Statisztikai Évkönyv, 1992; 1996). Following the Western model, the city centers developed into business areas. Expanding commercial sectors, offices, banks, branches of multinational chains such as Benetton, Chanel, Pizza Hut, McDonald's, and Burger King, and new shopping malls transformed the old, residential center regions.

Tourism became a primary business. Tallinn, Prague, Budapest, and Kraków attracted millions of visitors every year. It is hardly possible to go in to the St. Vitus Cathedral in Prague or the Matthias Church in Budapest, or to admire the Wawel in Kraków, because they are always packed with tourists. The historical centers became tourist regions with hundreds of new hotels and thousands of new restaurants, coffee, and gift shops. Kraków's oldest historical center, the depressed and degraded Kazimierz – which, without renovations and repair, became the underclass crime district after World War II and was gradually depopulated, with hardly more than one-third of the low-quality apartments being inhabited –

experienced a "profound change" from the early 1990s: parts of the area have "transformed into a new lively center of leisure, tourism, and cultural life." The number of cafés and restaurants increased from 39 to 133 in the decade between 1994 and 2004. Run-down tenement houses were remodeled into hotels. "As the commercialization of the quarter progresses, the inhabitants are more visibly pushed out" (Murzyn, 2006: 88–93).

In Budapest new luxury hotels and restaurants contributed to the change in the character of the old city center: in addition to the older first-class hotels along the Danube and the new Kempinski and Meridien Hotels, the landmark turn-of-the-century Gresham and New York buildings were renovated as luxury hotels and restaurants and contributed to the character change of the old center. Some of the inhabitants of these old neighborhoods are migrating to the suburbs.

In the outskirts of big cities, extensive shopping mall construction is leading another characteristic change. In the case of Warsaw, the huge Panorama shopping mall, the Ikea superstore, and the Janki Retail Center occupy more than 50,000 square meters with the usual well-known multinational retailers, 15 kilometers from the center (Sỳkora, 1998: 131). The transformation of the suburbs, partly by malls and superstores, and partly by gentrification, is creating a new urban world in Central and Eastern Europe.

Box 7.3 Changing the skyline: a new type of urban architecture

From the early nineteenth century, modern capital cities were built in Central and Eastern Europe. Western architecture became the model for elegant, sometimes even provocatively large public buildings. Neoclassical national museums and libraries, neo-renaissance national theaters and opera houses, and neo-gothic churches and parliament buildings were erected. They embodied the national spirit and national goal of joining the ranks of advanced European nations.

Regime change after 1989 inspired an unprecedented wave of construction in the declining main cities of the region. The new spirit of the age and the leading philosophy of transformation are well represented by the new buildings. Under the banner of free market capitalism, the free movement of people, and the free inflow of foreign investment, the dominant, newly emblematic type of "public" buildings of the age are luxurious shopping malls, elegant hotels, and modern office buildings.

Almost all of them were private initiatives, with an important contribution from the municipalities, which, as a consequence of postcommunist decentralization, gained more independence. Unfortunately, in the first decade, revitalized construction work in the neglected urban centers was rather spontaneous. Urban planning, after decades of failed central planning, was discredited. The blind faith in market forces and automatism led to a somewhat chaotic building boom. For years, even the capital cities lacked approved long-term master plans regulating building and development activities and zoning. The old master plans from the 1970s had become obsolete, and revised new ones were not approved before the 1990s: in Prague (1999), in Bratislava (1993 and 2000), in Budapest (1997, but implemented only in 1999). In Warsaw, a master plan was not approved until 2003. "Urban planning," stated Merje Feldman of Tallinn, "has been taking place without a master plan throughout the 1990s" (2000: 833).

Uncertainty over ownership was another obstacle. A long privatization process exacerbated this problem. For example, in Tallinn, only 82 percent of houses were privatized by 1997. Democratization went hand in hand with decentralization and created several independent communities within the big cities. Warsaw consisted of seventeen independent communities guaranteed by the new constitution. The Act of Municipalities and the Act on Local Self-Government in Czechoslovakia and Hungary, respectively, created fifty-seven autonomous local districts in Prague, seventeen in Bratislava, and twenty-three in Budapest. These units became the basic level of urban planning. This situation led to fragmented and unplanned building activities.

These factors notwithstanding, privatization of land and property – together with the rise of private property, the development of industry, and increasing foreign investments – led to a construction boom in several cities. In the Slovak capital, Bratislava, the Eurovea, a new riverfront development adjacent to the historic city emerged with the Galleria Eurovea shopping mall, 112,000 square meters of office space, and a series of restaurants and cafes. The five-floor 77,000m^2 Yosaria Plaza Center, another shopping mall in the city, has 300 shops, 14 restaurants, a hypermarket, a fitness center, a skating rink, and a swimming pool.

Warsaw's skyline was radically transformed by several new high-rise buildings. During the 1990s and early 2000s, several dominant new buildings were constructed: the Blue Tower (twenty-nine floors), the FIM Tower (twenty-six floors), the Millennium Plaza (twenty-eight floors), the Eurocentrum (twenty-two floors), the Warsaw Financial Center (thirty-two floors), the Warsaw Trade Tower (forty-three floors), the Intercontinental Hotel (forty-three floors), and the 60,000m^2 Promenada Shopping Center. In the first decade of transformation, a total of 1,196,200 square meters of modern office space and 400,000 square meters of retail space were added. In central Budapest, the architectural environment was changed by vast shopping malls such as the West End City Center (using this English name), the Asia Center, and the Mammuth Centers I and II, among others, with new luxury hotels and dozens of modern office buildings.

Belgrade and Tirana followed in the early twenty-first century. The first Serbian skyscraper, a forty-story hotel building, signaled for the local media the beginning of the rise of a "little Manhattan" on the Sava River. The Belgradska Arena with 20,000 seats was designed to be "Europe's largest" stadium to express the new national pride in Belgrade. Danish, Belgian, and Dutch projects transformed the central Scanderbeu Square in Tirana. Twelve high-rises, a new opera house, a new national bank, and a new national museum building are planned for the early 2000s.

New capital cities such as Vilnius and, from the early 2000s, Sarajevo became huge "construction sites." Dozens of modern high-rises transformed Vilnius: the Panorama Mall with two fifteen-floor towers, the Vilnius Gate, the Helios and Kareivin Towers (twenty-five and sixteen floors, respectively), and several residential 16- and 23-floor high-rises. In Estonia, with 70% to 90% of foreign direct investment channeled into the capital, the amount of office and service space increased by one-third in 1997 alone. A half-billion-dollar renovation project was begun on a 21-hectare waterfront complex for industrial and military use within five minute's walking distance from the medieval center. According to plans from June 1997, a luxury district will be built, consisting of 42% office space, 20% retail and service space, 14% residential space, and 10% space for entertainment and sports facilities.

A feverish construction boom of practical but also symbolic landmark buildings characterized cities other than national capitals as well: in Kraków a witty combination of modern glass and steel with some old red-brick structures form the new Galeria Kazimierz, with cinemas, shops, and even shoeshine stands along American lines. Both the twelve-story Aupark shopping and entertainment center, on a three-hectare tract in Košice, Slovakia, with a two-level underground garage and glassed-in promenade, and Klaipeda's (Lithuania) collection of twenty- to thirty-story office and residential buildings, signal a new national pride. Throughout these countries, new residential districts are being created. The emerging new business and political elite moved to villas in newly built gated "residential parks."

Although the new business orientation is openly represented by a large number of new privately constructed buildings, national pride in Hungary also required the construction of a new National Theater and next to it a new National Concert Hall at the Pest side of the shore of the Danube in Budapest. Riga, using an architectural Latvian metaphor, constructed a "glass mountain" of a National Library; Zagreb a Museum of Modern Art; and Warsaw a Museum of Contemporary Art and a Museum of the Warsaw Uprising.

Although several of the Central and East European cities – among others, Prague, Kraków, Budapest, Riga, Tallinn, Sarajevo, and Dubrovnik – are genuine world cultural heritage cities, the "Europeanization" of the urban settlements is in the making, and will require decades of reconstruction and renovation (Keivani, Parsa, and McGreal, 2002; Nedović-Budić, 2001; Feldman, 2000).

This urban development is linked to rapidly advancing European integration. In the previously deserted border regions, where entry was once forbidden to all nonresidents, flourishing new zones of international cooperation emerged. European Union grants encouraged connections between neighboring countries, especially along the former "iron curtain." Foreign direct investment coming from old EU member countries also favored nearby regions. Establishing factories just over the border in the former Soviet bloc countries became a popular investment strategy. The Vienna-Bratislava-Győr triangle represents one of the best examples. These big cities in the border areas of Austria, Slovakia, and Hungary lie close to each other. Vienna and Bratislava, two capital cities, are located only thirty miles apart. The border area of the three countries has 4 million inhabitants and employs 1.7 million people, nearly two-thirds of them in the service sector. Infrastructures are connected and intensive commuting and lively daily contacts have been established.

The European Union's PHARE program included a multiyear project in the second half of the 1990s to support crossborder undertakings in Estonia, Latvia, Lithuania, and Poland with old EU member countries, such as Finland, Denmark, Sweden, and Germany. This program initiated extensive development programs in the Baltic countries. The Pomerania Euroregion was established in 1995, with twenty-seven Polish communities around Szczecin and eight German counties in Mecklenburg-Vorpommeran. The border regions of Germany, the Czech Republic, and Poland formed the Nissa Euroregion, while the Viadrina region incorporates twenty-one Polish communities from Gorzów county and four German counties around Frankfurt an der Oder. Poznań, Wrocław, Kraków, and Lublin, located along the second belt of the Polish border region, have begun to play an important role in German–Polish economic cooperation. Most of the twenty-one Polish border regions, including the maritime boundary, "are growth areas . . . and have a potential to become nuclei of planned core areas" (Potrykowski, 1998: 234, 239, 250). Cooperation is also lively in the Czech–German and Polish–German border regions with subsidiaries, and first- and second-tier suppliers for multinational car companies, newly established on the Czech and Polish sides of the border. New binational or multinational European regions are in the making, which will further transform the urban landscape of Central and Eastern Europe (Rechnitzer and Döményová, 1998: 255, 263).

Social and urban transformations are organic parts of European Union-led globalization and the integration of Central and Eastern Europe into the European production network.

CHAPTER 8

Epilogue: the future of catching up in the European "melting pot"

Backwardness was perpetuated in the Central and East European region during the entire modern period. After a series of failed attempts to modernize, the average per capita income level in the region remained about half that of the West. That was the case in 1870, and with some fluctuation, it hardly changed for a century. During the 1970s–'80s, it declined to 40 percent of the Western level, and by the mid-1990s to less than one-third of it.

This failure was especially painful since other European laggards on the Mediterranean and Northern peripheries had broken out from backwardness: it happened to the Northern countries before the middle of the twentieth century. Sweden, Denmark, Norway, and Finland, on average, reached 65% of the West European per capita GDP in 1870, but had surpassed the West by 3% in 1950. Finland's per capita GDP was hardly more than half that of the Western level in 1870 and 81 percent of it in 1950, but it surpassed the Western average at the end of the century.

The Mediterranean countries and Ireland accomplished a successful catching-up process after World War II, and in particular after 1973. In 1950, the average per capita income level of Spain, Portugal, and Greece stood at only 39% of the West European level, less than that of Central and Eastern Europe. By 1973, however, Southern European per capita income slightly surpassed that of Central and Eastern Europe's, at 49% of the Western level. Moreover, between 1973 and 1992, average income in the Southern peripheries increased by 38% while it declined in Central and Eastern Europe by 19%. Income in the three Mediterranean countries gradually neared the West European level, from only 41% of it in 1950 to nearly two-thirds by 1973, and roughly three-quarters by the end of the century. Ireland reached only 57% of the West European level in 1973, but it surpassed the Western average at the end of the century.

Table 8.1 Central and Eastern Europe's (nine countries) GDP/capita as a percentage of Western Europe (twenty-three countries) and the overseas West (four countries)

Year	% of Western Europe	% of overseas West
1820	59	64
1870	51	45
1913	46	32
1950	51	28
1973	47	36
1989	40	32

Source: Maddison, 1995a: 228.

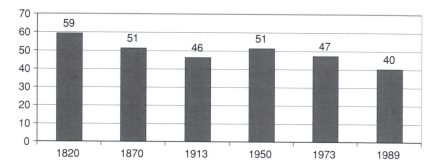

Figure 8.1 Central and Eastern Europe's economic backwardness in historical perspective, 1820–1989: Central and Eastern Europe's (nine countries) GDP/capita as % of Western Europe (twenty-three countries)

Central and Eastern Europe, on the other hand, was unable to break out from its distinctive backwardness and remained the only backward periphery of the continent (figure 8.1, table 8.1). The countries, seeking a miracle model for modernization – economic nationalism in the interwar decades, a centrally planned economy after World War II – failed again and again. Their postwar drive for industrialization and modernization became a detour from periphery to periphery. The countries of Central and Eastern Europe ultimately shared the same destiny, following the same path yet again, and became more similar than ever before.

At the time they joined the EU in 2004, the average income in the eight most advanced countries of Central and Eastern Europe was only 45 percent that of the fifteen countries already in the Union. The West European countries sounded somewhat utopian when they first spoke about new EU members catching up. Looking back to the final third of the century, this possibility now seems somewhat more realistic. In a generation, Ireland,

Spain, and Portugal, from an analogous backward position, caught up in a spectacular fashion to become equal or almost equal members of the club of the advanced world. If one speaks about catching up, it always means a process stretching over one or two generations. In other words: the Central and East European countries, in the best case, may reach or approach the European Union's average income level of 2005 around 2025–30. To accomplish this miracle, these countries must achieve roughly two to three times' higher economic growth than the old member countries of the Union.

It is a statistical commonplace that the rate of growth depends heavily on the level of the base year or period. At a lower income level, it is easier to reach a higher growth rate. That was the basis of Nobel laureate Robert Solow's statement that the wider the development gap, the faster the catch-up rate. The Harvard economic historian Alexander Gerschenkron spoke about the "advantage of backwardness": the possibility of adopting technology, management – the entire pool of knowledge – from advanced countries and reaching faster growth. These proclamations are basically true regarding a certain level of backwardness, but not when backwardness has eliminated the social capability to absorb modern technology and knowledge. Most of the Central and East European countries are above that threshold. In theory, catching up is possible.

A country with an annual 7–8% economic growth can double its income level in a single decade. China achieved this result between 1993 and 2006 with an annual 8–9% growth rate. Some of the Central and East European countries also reached very high growth rates in certain periods: Bosnia saw 18.5% annual growth from an exceptionally low level around the turn of the century. Albania had a 10.3% annual growth rate between 1993 and 1996, and 6.4% in the decade 1993–2003. Poland reached 6.4%, Slovakia 6.2%, and Estonia 5.6% growth between 1994 and 1997; Latvia, Estonia, and Lithuania had 13%, 11%, and 8% growth in 2005. Such performance, however, is rare over a longer period of time.

The possibility of reaching the Western level strongly depends on future capital inflow to the region. The European Union and its assistance play an important additional role. On December 17, 2005, the Union approved its budget for the seven-year period of 2007–13. As proved by the experience of previous decades, the total amount, although a relatively small $1,036 billion (€862 billion) compared to the roughly $4.8 (€4) trillion of total aggregate national budgets of the member countries, plays a huge role in assisting the less-developed member countries. Nearly 36 percent of the budget, about $337 billion, finances the Union's cohesion fund to subsidize the less-developed countries and regions. The new member countries will receive $120 billion (or €100 billion): Poland will receive €56 billion, the Czech Republic €23 billion, and Hungary €22 billion. The budget also distributes another $60 billion among the Union's so-called partner countries in the Balkans region.

In addition, the controversial agricultural budget, 43 percent of the total, also assists the weak agricultural sector of the Central and East European economies. Britain argued that it would have been much better to cut agricultural subsidies sharply, because they guarantee commodity prices that are one-third higher than on the world market for the small fraction of the EU population engaged in farming. Moreover, 80 percent of farm support is given to the richest 20 percent of farmers (which is to say agrobusinesses). Unfair as this is, not to mention harmful for the world market and Third World countries, Central and Eastern Europe is profiting from it. In most cases, the European Union's budget is the only source for agricultural financing in the region. Already between 2004 and 2006, the farmers of the new member countries saw subsidies averaging €250 per hectare, even though they received only 25% of the common agricultural policy payments that are paid to farmers in the old member countries. This amount is gradually increasing and in the second half of the new budget period, it will reach parity with the old member countries. In the case of the Czech Republic, for example, agricultural subsidies will amount to $4.32 billion in direct payments and $3 billion in subsidies; altogether the agricultural assistance is roughly $1.2 billion/year during the seven-year period.

Altogether, Central and Eastern Europe will receive more from the European Union during the 2007–13 budget period than from a Marshall Plan aid package, which was rejected after 1989 by the West. This aid will definitely help the new countries to achieve a growth rate higher than the EU average, thus contributing to the catching-up process with the West.

The process of convergence is strongly influenced by the present and future growth of the "old" European Union. Catching up is extremely difficult if the target country or countries are running fast. In such a situation, as the Queen of Hearts said to Alice in Wonderland, one has to run as fast as possible to stay in place and twice as fast to get ahead. What is the possible rate of growth for the former European Union of fifteen countries? It is impossible to make a solid forecast. Between 1950 and 1973, Western Europe reached its fastest-ever economic growth rate of 4.08% per year. Between 1973 and 1998, however, the average annual growth of the region declined to 1.78%. Between 1993 and 2003, the Eurozone experienced 2.1% annual growth. In 2005, the rate was only

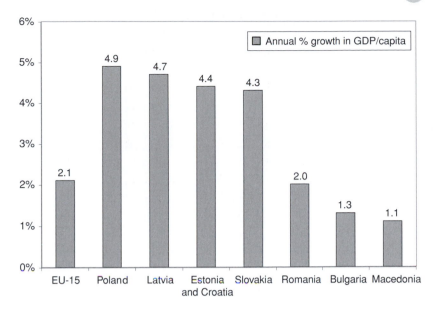

Figure 8.2 Annual growth rates, 1993–2003

1.6%. Catching up with Western Europe would be hopeless if the region regained its postwar quarter of century speed of around 4% per annum. If it continues, at the slower 2% annual growth rate, however, reaching a two- or two-and-half-times faster rate in Central and Eastern Europe is possible. As noted before, in this latter case, the process would require a generation to succeed.

The first years of the twenty-first century have already offered a solid comparison between the old and new (and candidate) countries of the Union. After the sharp decline of the early 1990s was halted, recovery was relatively fast in Central and Eastern Europe. Between 1993 and 2003, Poland reached an annual 4.9% growth rate, Latvia 4.7%, Croatia and Estonia 4.4%, and Slovakia 4.3%, more than twice that in the West. On the other hand, Moldova had only 3.1%, Romania 2.0%, Bulgaria 1.3%, and Macedonia 1.1% growth (figure 8.2). Between 2001 and 2005, the average annual growth of the ten countries that joined the Union in 2004 and 2007 was 4.3%. Here too, there were major differences: the Czech growth rate was 2.6%; Poland's 2.8%; Hungary's 3.1%; Latvia's 6.5%; and Lithuania's 6.2%. In 2005, the Czech Republic, Hungary, and Poland reached 4.9%, 4.5%, and 3.7% growth, respectively. Industrial output increased in the same period, averaging 5.4%. In 2005, Poland had 8.5% industrial growth, while Hungary and the Czech Republic reached 7.7% and 7.2%, respectively (figure 8.3).

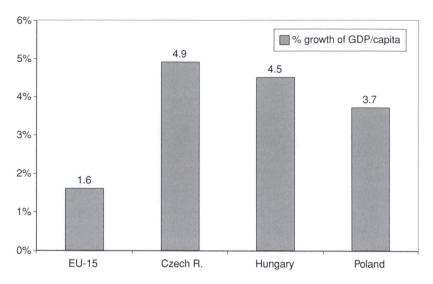

Figure 8.3 Comparative economic growth, 2005

During the first half-decade of the twenty-first century, productivity increases in manufacturing (GDP/hour) increased by 38% in the eight new member countries, in some of them even by 50%. The rate of increase was 2.5 times faster in the transition countries than in Germany, France, and Austria. Increasing productivity still may be combined with relatively low wages in Central and Eastern Europe for quite a while; together the two trends form the main attraction for foreign investors as well as the engine of growth.

Convergence in wages has also begun: between 1995 and 2005, unit labor cost in Hungary increased by 65%. Between 1999 and 2005 alone, it increased by 40%. In the same period labor costs increased even faster in Estonia, the Czech Republic (by 50%), and Romania (by 80%) (Viszt, 2007: 83). In 2004, the average wage of the eight new Central European member countries of the EU stood at 26% of the EU-15's average. According to the UNCTAD forecast, by 2020 the eight transition countries' average will reach 39% of the "old" Union members' average (UNCTAD, 2005a). A more optimistic forecast suggests that, "at this rate, living standards will catch up with the European average within a generation" (*Economist*, July 22, 2006). On the other hand, certain forecasts underline the possibility of faster wage increases because of a rapidly declining population and labor force (*International Herald Tribune*, August 30, 2007).

Based on the comparative performance of the EU's old and new member and candidate countries in the early 1990s and early 2000s, one may risk the forecast that the old EU-15 countries may continue to see relatively slower growth of around 2–3% per year, while the ten or fifteen new members and potential candidates from the region may reach 4–6% annual growth. If this performance is realized, the catching up of Central and Eastern Europe is possible in one or two generations' time. According to one forecast in 2000, Hungary, Slovakia, Poland, and Estonia need thirty to thirty-five years to catch up with the European Union average. The same progress might be achieved in Latvia, Bulgaria, and Romania in forty to forty-three years. Lithuania, however, will need seventy years, and at the other end of the region, Slovenia will require only eight years to catch up (Simai, 2006: 9).

The catching up with the West has actually begun. Hungary's example is a significant index: the country's income level was somewhat less than 50% of the old Union member countries' in 2000, but reached 62% of it by 2005. If the trend continues, by 2015 the country's level will approach 75% of the fifteen old Union member countries. Between 1995 and 2005, catching up characterized all of the Central European countries. Based on Eurostat's figures, Poland's per capita purchasing power parity GDP increased from 41% to 48% of the EU-15 average; Slovakia's from 44% to 54%; Slovenia's from 68% to 79%; and the Czech Republic's from 70% to 73%.

It is important to note, however, that *average* Central and East European growth and a *general* catching-up process are mere abstractions which do not exist in reality. The performances of the countries of the region are already markedly different, and the differentiation will continue in the coming decades. Successful catching up with the old EU countries cannot be taken for granted. Economic success or failure will be decided mostly at home. It depends on political stability or imbalance, good or mistaken domestic economic policy, geopolitical advantages or disadvantages, international influence, and the ability to adjust to the impact of globalization. The future and uncertain process of globalization itself may play an important role. As P. Rhode and G. Toniolo maintain:

Globalization remains an ongoing process, with a long road ahead . . . This road may yet be blocked by any backlash against globalization if policy makers overlook the social impact of the changes in income distribution that accompany freer trade. (Rhode and Toniolo, 2006: 18)

Some of the countries, mostly in the Balkans, were disadvantaged by globalization because of unfortunate circumstances. Nonindustrialized countries may pay a high price for free trade since their deindustrialization began before industrialization had occurred, or at least finished. That was the case in Greece after it joined the Union in 1981. Small wonder that Greece

Table 8.2   GDP/capita in PPP ECU

Region	1990	1995	2005	2015[a]
Central Europe[b]	7,903	8,978	13,875	20,539
Balkans[c]	4,961	4,919	6,617	9,795
EU-15	14,609	17,699	22,153	27,005
Central Europe as % of EU	54	51	63	76
Balkans as % of EU	34	28	30	36

Source: Based on Teodorović *et al.*, 2005: 326.
Note: ECUs in current PPP and constant PPP from 2000.
a: Forecast.
b: Czech Republic, Hungary, Poland, Slovakia, Slovenia.
c: Bulgaria, Croatia, Macedonia, Romania.

was the only one among the member countries that joined the Union in the 1980s that did not succeed in catching up. The country was unable to achieve the higher-than-average growth rates reached by other member countries and, unlike Ireland, Spain, and Portugal, suffered a relative decline.

The extreme further Balkanization of the Balkans, the creation of ten small independent countries (including the virtually independent Kosovo) by 2008, instead of the four countries in 1989, might also create obstacles for them, if they are unable to break out of isolation and too backward to take advantage of possible cooperation.

Overly optimistic forecasts hold out the possibility of double-digit annual growth because of market-friendly institutions and policies and the huge inflow of capital from rich countries. Nicholas Crafts' calculation is more modest: in the long run, according to him, Central and Eastern Europe may reach annual growth of nearly 4% (while the Czech Republic, Slovakia, Estonia, and Hungary may have a yearly growth between 4% and 5%) (Crafts, 2006: 40).

Based on the assumption that the European Union will reach 2%, and the Central and Eastern European countries 4%, annual GDP growth, and that the population will not increase, the level of GDP per capita in purchasing power parity may reach an average of three-quarters of the EU level in the most successful Central European countries of the region, while others still remain just above one-third of its level by 2015 (table 8.2).

Grzegorz Kołodko has a more detailed forecast and speaks about the possibility of at least four different scenarios for patterns of development in Central and Eastern Europe. A vanguard group may reach four times' faster growth than the old European Union countries, around 7.5% per year. Very few countries could achieve that. However, a second group, including the bulk of the countries of the region, might eliminate relative backwardness with an annual growth rate twice that of the West, or 4% to 6%, at least for a while. Even if their growth rate slows to 3% in the second decade, in the span of one generation they might double their average income, and in half a century could reach a level five times higher than in 2000. Kołodko speaks about a third group, certainly only a minority of the countries of the region, which reach the same speed of growth as the West of between 2% and 3% and are thus unable to catch up, but do not lag further behind either. Finally, some countries may form a fourth group, which decline further relative to the West, unable to reach even 2% annual growth.

Kołodko also calls attention to the fact that the task of reaching the Western income level of 2000 requires extremely different efforts from the various countries, which have great variations in their income level. The per capita average income of Western Europe was between $25,000 and $30,000 at the beginning of the twenty-first century. To reach that income level, Slovenia must double its current income, the Czech Republic and Estonia must triple theirs, and Slovakia, Hungary, and Croatia need a 3.5 times' increase. Poland needs a fourfold increase, Bulgaria and Latvia nearly eightfold, and Romania and Macedonia nearly tenfold (Kołodko, 2001). Of course, one cannot exclude the possibility of the fastest possible growth in these countries, but the timespan required to double the income level, or increase it by ten times, makes prediction about other relevant factors no longer meaningful.

Most of the forecasts are based on anticipated growth rates, which are mere extensions of recent growth trends. That may have little to do with future reality. During the transition period between 1989 and 2007, economic growth was based on the recovery from disruptions generated by the deep crisis and the collapse of state socialism and the steep decline that followed. A kind of reconstructive growth, which is genuinely faster than growth that occurs after the countries' potential has been reached, influenced economic performance during the entire 1990s and, in the Balkan and Baltic regions, even into the first decade of the twenty-first century. In the past transformation period, underemployed rural labor and superfluous (overemployed) industrial labor were rationalized, and the economies and employment restructured. This also contributed to economic growth. The most important growth factors, nevertheless, were the inflow of foreign capital, advanced technology, and managerial skill. This was somewhat similar to growth performance in post-World War II Western Europe: rapid growth and convergence were mostly based on the existing and imported stock of technological knowledge and high level of investment.

The available factors for extensive economic development that existed in the first period of transformation, however, were exhausted in Western Europe after a quarter of a century, and will be exhausted in Central and Eastern Europe as well. The first signs that foreign direct capital investment was shifting further to the East appeared already in the early twenty-first century. In the coming decades, a radical shift toward an intensive, innovation-based development model will be needed to perpetuate rapid economic growth in Central and Eastern Europe. A functional local innovation base of research and development, improved education and training, well-functioning institutions and improved social capital based on trust, cooperation, and political stability must underlie this trend. The countries of the region have to cope with the immense danger of Right and Left populism and competition for buying votes by reckless spending. Wages must not increase faster than productivity. Irresponsible policy is present almost everywhere in the region. *The Economist* painted a frightening picture of the dramatically negligent policy of several governments in the summer of 2007:

Latvia accumulated a current-account deficit, which reached 21 percent of GDP, that reflects soaring consumption and household debt, financed mainly by foreign-owned banks ... Poland and Romania, in particular, have proved alarmingly ready to make expensive spending pledges for political reasons ... The lesson that other countries take from Hungary's financial shenanigans is that it is possible to spend like crazy to win an election and then sober up afterwards ... Almost everywhere, public spending is higher than it should be for middle-income developing economies. (*Economist*, July 7, 2007)

True, between 1996 and 2006, Hungarian growth was higher than the average EU growth rate but, from the last quarter of 2006 and during 2007, its growth remained behind the EU average; that is, the catching-up process, at least temporarily, stopped. Continuous rapid growth performance also requires speeding up spinoff effects, absorbing imported technology faster and spreading it wider and more thoroughly, and integrating local industry and services into the multinational supplier chain.

Radical further reforms and changes are needed, but until 2006–07, few countries of the region exhibited signs of changes in this direction. Slovenia, the Czech Republic, and – and until its 2006–07 economic troubles – Hungary made the most of what progress there was toward a new growth model. However, the 2007 ranking of member states by the London-based Center for European Reform clearly reflected a mixed picture: while the Czech Republic, Estonia, and Latvia had improved their positions somewhat from 2005 to 2006, Hungary had declined from fifteenth to nineteenth place, and Slovakia and Poland had also lost some ground. The report mentioned that Hungary was long a pioneer of reforms among the candidate countries, but this trend stopped in 2006 (*Figyelő*, March 22, 2007).

One may not anticipate rapid change. In spite of the spectacular catching-up process in Ireland, a certain dualism characterizes even this most successful and rapidly developing newer EU country. Its growth was driven by foreign investments, but local companies remained still far behind and linkages between the foreign subsidiaries and local companies are not yet satisfactory. This is even more true in Spain, and in spite of the significant progress of Portugal and Greece they are still, even at the beginning of the twenty-first century, a generation after joining the European Union,

dependent on international foreign direct investments and have a low level of research and development spending... [Their] industrial sector is dominated by low-cost labor intensive industries. (Magone, 2003: 13)

There is a long way to go.

Instead of catching up with the EU-15, a dual economy may emerge in several new member countries of the European Union. This is even more likely in the candidate countries of the Balkan region. In such a scenario, the level of development would improve after joining, but would remain stuck behind the Western level. Multinational companies would constitute the advanced sector of the economy, while an adequate national innovation system would not develop and local companies would remain in a backward situation. In this case, multinationals may form isolated enclaves in the national economy, while the host countries remain on the periphery of Europe, with an institutionalized division of labor separating advanced countries from laggards. In other words, some countries of the region could remain behind and profit less from globalization with a resource-driven specialization and/or as providers of cheap labor in low-tech sectors for advanced partners. A much lower living standard than in the core would result. Instead of calculating the years and decades of catching up, one has to consider markedly different outcomes of the ongoing transformation, which would result from the failure to catch up in some countries or in subregions of Central and Eastern Europe. Different models and development levels may emerge in the region in the coming decades.

The first chapter of transformation – adjustment to the market economy and integration into the European production network – is thus closed or closing in the entire region. With the assistance of the European Union, the accomplishment is significant, although the transforming countries exhibit various degrees of success. Furthermore, even the most successful countries of the region are too dependent on outside factors and are fragile and suffer setbacks from time to time. The second chapter of transformation – characterized by further radical social and behavioral changes, the emergence of a domestically based, innovation-driven, competitive economy, and nearing and reaching the West European income level – is either far away in some countries that have a good chance to achieve it, or may not happen at all in others in the foreseeable future.

Bibliography

Abramowitz, Moses, 1971. "Resource and Output Trends in the United States Since 1870," in Nathan Rosenberg (ed.), *The Economics of Technological Change*, Harmondsworth: Penguin Books.

Adamski, Władisław, Pavel Machonin, and Wolfgang Zapf (eds.), 2002. *Structural Change and Modernization in Post-Socialist Societies*, Hamburg: Reinhold Krämer.

Aidukaite, Jolanta, 2006. "Reforming Family Policy in the Baltic States: The Views of the Elites," *Communist and Post-Communist Studies*, Vol. 39, No. 1.

Alanen, Ilkka, 1996. "The Privatization of Agriculture and the Family Farm Ideology in the Baltic States," in Raimo Blom, Harri Melin, and Jouko Nikula (eds.), *Between Plan and Market: Social Change in the Baltic States and Russia*, De Gruyter: Berlin.

Andorka, Rudolf, 1997. "The Development of Poverty During the Transformation in Hungary," in Ivan T. Berend (ed.), *Long-Term Structural Changes in Transforming Central and Eastern Europe*, Munich: Sudosteuropa Gesellschaft.

1993. "Növekvő társadalmi különbségek," *Napi Gazdaság*, Budapest, December 4.

Antal, László, 2007. "Pension Reform: Its Present and Future," *Development and Finance*, No. 3.

Bandelj, Nina, 2004. "Negotiating Global, Regional and National Forces: Foreign Investment in Slovenia," *East European Politics and Societies*, Vol. 18, No. 3.

Bauer, Kai, and Tanja Möllmann, 2006. "Effects of EU Agricultural Policies on the New Member States: Simulation Analysis," in Sophia Davidova, Kai Bauer, and Michael Cuddy (eds.), *Integrated Development of Agriculture and Rural Areas in Central European Countries*, Lanham: Rowman and Littlefield.

BIBLIOGRAPHY

Baun, Michael J., 2000. *A Wider Europe: The Process and Politics of European Enlargement*, Lanham: Rowman and Littlefield.

Bednarik, Rastislav, Zdena Danekova, Jana Filipova, Silvia Rzbarova, and Silvia Valna, 1995. "Social Cost of Transition: National Report, Slovak Republic," in *Social Cost of Economic Transformation in Central Europe*, Vienna: Institut für die Wissenschaften vom Menschen.

Berend, Ivan T., 2008. "Globalization and Its Impact on Core–Periphery Relations," in Peter Reill (ed.), forthcoming.

2005. "What Is Central and Eastern Europe?," *European Journal of Social Theory*, Vol. 8, No. 4, November.

2003. *History Derailed: Central and Eastern Europe in the Long Nineteenth Century*, Berkeley: University of California Press.

1998. *Decades of Crisis: Central and Eastern Europe Before World War II*, Berkeley: University of California Press.

1996. *Central and Eastern Europe, 1944–1993: Detour from the Periphery to the Periphery*, Cambridge: Cambridge University Press.

1990. *The Hungarian Economic Reform 1953–1988*, Cambridge: Cambridge University Press.

(ed.), 1989. *A Gazdasági reformbizottság programjavaslata 1990–1992*, Budapest: Közgazdasági Kiadó.

1979. *A szocialista gazdaság története Magyarországon*, 1945–1973, Budapest: Kossuth Kiadó.

1978. *Öt előadás gazdaságról és oktatásról*, Budapest: Magvető Kiadó.

Berend, Nora, (ed.) 2007. *Christianization and the Rise of Christian Monarchy: Scandinavia, Central Europe and Rus' c. 900–c. 1200*, Cambridge: Cambridge University Press.

2001. *At the Gate of Christendom*, Cambridge: Cambridge University Press.

Bernini Carri, Carlo, 1995. "Source of Output Growth and Agricultural Performance in EU Countries 1960–1980," *European Review of Agricultural Economics*, Vol. 22, No. 2.

Berthelot, Yves, 1997. "Lessons from Countries in Transition," in Emmerij, 1997.

Bethlendi, András, 2007. "Foreign Direct Investment in the Banking Sector," *Development and Finance*, No. 1.

Bibó, István, [1946] 1986. "A kelet-európai kisállamok nyomorúsága," in *Bibó István Válogatott tanulmányok, 1945–1949*, Vol. II, Budapest: MagvetőKiadó.

Boffey, Philip M., William J. Broad, Leslie H. Gelb, Charles Mohr, and Holcomb B. Noble, 1988. *Claiming the Heavens: The New York Times Complete Guide to the Star Wars Debate*, New York: Times Books.

Bohle, Dorothee, and Béla Greskovits, 2007. "Neoliberalism, Embedded Neoliberalism and Neocorporatism: Towards Transnational Capitalism in Central and Eastern Europe," *West European Politics*, online, May 1.

Bokova, Irina, 2000. "Integrating Southeastern Europe into the European Mainstream," *South East Europe Review for Labour and Social Affairs*, No. 3–4.

Boltho, Andrea, 1982. *The European Economy: Growth and Crisis*, Oxford: Oxford University Press.

Borneman, John, 1997. *Settling Accounts: Violence, Justice, and Accountability in Postsocialist Europe*, Princeton: Princeton University Press.

Brenner, Robert, 1998. "Uneven Development and the Long Downturn: Advanced Capitalist Economies from Boom to Stagnation, 1950–1988," *New Left Review*, Special Issue, May–June.

Bučar, Maja, and Metka Stare, 2006. "From Quantity to Quality: Critical Assessment of Slovenia's Potential for Knowledge-Based Growth," in Piech and Radocevic, 2006.

Buček, Ján, 2006. "Post-Socialist Urban Development, Planning and Participation – the Case Study of Bratislava City Centre," in Enyedi and Kovács, 2006.

Budapest Statisztikai Évkönyv, 1996. Budapest: Központi Statisztikai Hivatal. 1992. Budapest: Központi Statisztikai Hivatal.

Bugaric, Bojan, 2006. "The Europeanization of National Administration in Central and Eastern Europe: Creating Formal Structures Without Substance?" in Wojciech Sadurski, Jacques Ziller, and Karolina Zurek (eds.), *Apres Enlargement: Legal and Political Responses in Central and Eastern Europe*, Florence: Robert Schuman Center.

Bukodi, Erzsébet, 2001. *A háztartások gazdálkodási magatartásának néhany eleme*, Budapest: Központi Statisztikai Hivatal.

Bunce, Valerie, 1994. "Sequencing of Political and Economic Reforms," in *East-Central European Economies in Transition*, 1994.

Burcin, Boris, and Tomáš Kučera, 2006. "Socio-Demographic Consequences of the Renewal of Prague's Historical Centre," in Enyedi and Kovács, 2006.

Bush Library website, public papers, 1991. G.H.W. Bush Presidential Library and Museum, Bushlibrary.tamu.edu/research/public_papers.php, "Address Before a Joint Session of the Congress on the Cessation of the Persian Gulf Conflict," 1991–03–06.

Butler, Lawrence, 2005. "Peace Implementation in Bosnia and Herzegovina: Challenges and Results," *Südosteuropa Mitteilungen*, No. 4–5.

Caron, François, 1979. *An Economic History of Modern France*, New York: Columbia University Press.

Carter, F. W., and Ewelina Kantowicz, 2002. "Poland," in Carter and Turnock, 2002.

Carter, F. W., and David Turnock (eds.), 2002. *Environmental Problems of Eastern and Central Europe*, London: Routledge.

Cerami, Alfio, 2005. "Social Policy in Central and Eastern Europe: The Emergence of a New European Model of Solidarity," third annual ESPAnet Conference, September 2–24, University of Fribourg, Switzerland.

Cernat, Lucian, 2006. *Europeanization, Varieties of Capitalism and Economic Performance in Central and Eastern Europe*, Houndmills: Palgrave Macmillan.

Charemza, Wojciech W., and Krystyna Strzała (eds.), 2002. *East European Transition and EU Enlargement: A Quantitative Approach*, Heidelberg: Physica Verlag.

Charles, David, and Jeremy Howells, 1992. *Technology Transfer in Europe: Public and Private Networks*. London: Belhaven Press.

Churchill, Winston, 1943–49. *His Complete Speeches, 1897–1963*, Vol. VII, Chelsea House.

Clark, Ian, 2001. *The Post-Cold War Order: The Spoils of Peace*, Oxford: Oxford University Press.

Clauge, Christopher and Gordon C. Rausser (eds.), 1992. *The Emergence of Market Economies in Eastern Europe*, Oxford: Blackwell.

Cohen, Robert, 1994. "Economic Transformation in Albania," in *East-Central European Economies in Transition*, 1994.

Committee for European Integration (Poland), 1997. *National Strategy for Integration*, Warsaw: Committee for European Integration.

Crafts, Nicholas, 2006. "The World Economy in the 1990s," in Paul W. Rhode and Gianni Toniolo (eds.), *The Global Economy in the 1990s: A Long-Run Perspective*, Cambridge: Cambridge University Press.

Crane, Keith, 1994. "The Costs and Benefits of Transition," in *East-Central European Economies in Transition*, 1994.

Csaba, László, 2005. *The New Political Economy of Emerging Europe*, Budapest: Akadémiai Kiadó.

Csáki, Csaba, 2005. "Agriculture in Central and Eastern Europe – Status and Progress of Reforms," *Development and Finance: Quarterly Hungarian Economic Review*, No. 2.

Dalia, László, 1998. "Demján Sándor," in Kurtán Sándor, Péter Sándor, and László Vass (eds.), *Magyarország évtized könyve: a rendszerváltás (1988–1998)*, Budapest: Demokrácia Kutatások Alapítvány.

Davidova, Sophia, Matthew Gorton, Tomas Ratinger, Katarzyna Zawalinska, and Belen Iraioz, 2006. "Variations in Farm Performance: Evidence from the New Member States and EU-15 Member States," in Sophia Davidova, Kai Bauer, and Michael Cuddy (eds.), *Integrated Development of Agriculture and Rural Areas in Central European Countries*, Lanham: Rowman and Littlefield.

Davies, Gareth, Steve Carter, Stuart McIntosh, and Dan Stefanescu, 1996. "Technology and Policy Options for the Telecommunications Sectors," *Telecommunications Policy*, Vol. 20, No. 2.

Delors, Jacques, [1989] 1998. "Address by Mr. Jacques Delors, Bruges, 17 October 1989," in Brent F. Nelsen and Alexander Stubb (eds.), *The European Union: Readings on the Theory and Practice of European Integration*, Boulder: Lynne Rienner.

Deraniyagala, Sonali, 2001. "From Washington Consensus to Post-Washington: Does It Matter for Industrial Policy?" in Fine, Lapavitsas, and Pincus, 2001.

Dinan, Desmond, 1994. *Ever Closer Union?* Boulder: Lynne Rienner.

Dingsdale, Alan, Imre Nagy, Gyorgy Perczel, and David Turnock, 2002. "Hungary," in Carter and Turnock, 2002.

Drakulić, Slavenka, 1997. *Café Europa: Life After Communism*, New York: W. W. Norton.

Duchene, François, and Geoffrey Shepherd (eds.), 1987. *Managing Industrial Change in Western Europe*, London: Pinter.

Dulles, Allen, [1948] 1993. *The Marshall Plan*, Houndmills: Palgrave Macmillan.

Dyker, David, A., (ed.), 2006. *Closing the EU East–West Productivity Gap: Foreign Direct Investment, Competitiveness and Public Policy*, London: Imperial College Press.

    2004. *Catching Up and Falling Behind: Post-Communist Transformation in Historical Perspective*, London: Imperial College Press.

Dyson, Kenneth, 2007. "Euro Area Entry in Central and Eastern Europe. Pardoxical Europeanisation and Clusteral Convergence," *West European Politics*, online, May 1.

Earle, John S., and Álmos Telegdy, 2002. "Privatization Methods and Productivity Effects in Romanian Industrial Enterprises," *Journal of Comparative Economics*, Vol. 30, No. 4.

East-Central European Economies in Transition: Study Papers Submitted to the Joint Economic Committee, Congress of the United States, 1994. Washington, DC: US Government Printing Office.

EBRD (European Bank of Reconstruction and Development), 2005a. *Transition Report 2005: Business in Transition*, London: European Bank for Reconstruction and Development.

2005b. *Transition Report Update 2005*, London: European Bank for Reconstruction and Development.

2004. *Transition Report 2004: Infrastructure*, London: European Bank for Reconstruction and Development.

2003. *Transition Report 2003: Integration and Regional Cooperation*, London: European Bank for Reconstruction and Development.

2002. *Transition Report 2002: Agriculture and Rural Transition*. London: European Bank for Reconstruction and Development.

2001. *Transition Report 2001: Energy in Transition*, London: European Bank for Reconstruction and Development.

2000. *Transition Report 2000: Employment, Skills and Transition*, London: European Bank for Reconstruction and Development.

1996. *Transition Report 1996: Building an Infrastructure for Transition and Promoting Savings*, London: European Bank for Reconstruction and Development.

Economist, 2007. *World in Figures 2008*, London: Profile Books.

2006a. *Pocket World in Figures 2007*, London: Profile Books.

2006b. *World in Figures 2007*, London: Profile Books.

2005a. *Pocket World in Figures 2006*, London: Profile Books.

2005b. *World in Figures 2006*, London: Profile Books.

2004. *The World in 2005*, London: Economist.

Economist Intelligence Unit, 2005. *Country Reports*.

1998. *Economist Intelligence Unit, Quarterly Country Reports on Estonia, Latvia and Lithuania*, 1st quarter.

1996. *Economist Intelligence Unit, Quarterly Country Reports on Estonia, Latvia and Lithuania*, 4th quarter.

Ehrlich, Éva, 1993. *Shift in the Size Structure of Manufacturing Establishments and Enterprises: An International Comparison*, Budapest: Institute of World Economics, Working Papers.

Ehrlich, Éva, and Gábor Révész, 1991. *Összeomlás és rendszerváltás Kelet-Közép Európában*, Budapest: Institute of World Economics.

Ehrlich, Éva, and Tamás Szigetvári, 2003. *Az infrastruktúrák nemzetközi össze-hasonlítása: 1990–2000*, Budapest: MTA Világgazdasági Kutatóintézet.

Eichengreen, Barry, 2007. *The European Economy Since 1945: Coordinated Capitalism and Beyond*, Princeton: Princeton University Press.

[1994] 1996. "Institutions and Economic Growth. Europe After World War II," in Nicholas Crafts and Gianni Toniolo (eds.), *Economic Growth in Europe Since 1945*, Cambridge: Cambridge University Press.

Eichengreen, Barry, and Richard Kohl, 1998. "The External Sector, the State, and Development in Eastern Europe," in John Zysman and Andrew

Schwartz (eds.), *Enlarging Europe. The Industrial Foundation of a New Political Reality*, Berkeley: University of California.

El-Agraa, Ali M., 2004. *The European Union: Economics and Politics*, Harlow: Prentice Hall.

Emmerij, Louis (ed.), 1997. *Economic and Social Development into the Twenty-First Century*, Washington, DC: Inter-American Development Bank.

Emőd, Pál, and Péter Szakonyi, 2004. *A száz leggazdagabb magyar 2004-ben*, Budapest: Magyar Hírlap Időszaki Kiadványa.

Enyedi, György, 1998. *Social Change and Urban Restructuring in Central Europe*, Budapest: Akadémiai Kiadó.

1992. "Urbanization in East Central Europe: Social Process and Societal Responses in State Socialist System," *Urban Studies*, No. 29.

Enyedi, György, and Zoltán Kovács (eds.), 2006. *Social Changes and Social Sustainability in Historical Urban Centres: The Case of Central Europe*, Pécs: Centre for Regional Studies, Hungarian Academy of Sciences.

European Commission, 2006. *European Economy*, Brussels: European Commission, Directorate-General for Economic and Financial Affairs, No. 2.

2002. *The Stabilization and Accession Process for South East Europe, First Annual Report*, Brussels: European Commission.

1999. "Special Berlin Council 24–25 March, Conclusion of the Presidency," *Bulletin of the European Union*, No. 3.

1998. *Communication to the Council and to the European Parliament on the Establishment of a New Financial Perspective for the Period 2000–2006*, Luxembourg: Office for Official Publications.

1995. *The European Councils, 1993: Conclusions of the Presidency 1992–1994, European Council in Copenhagen 21–23 June 1993*, Brussels: European Commission.

1994. *The Europe Agreements and Beyond: A Strategy to Prepare the Countries of Central and Eastern Europe for Accession*, Brussels: European Commission.

Eurostat, 2005a. *Eurostat Yearbook: A Statistical Eye on Europe, 2005*, Luxembourg: European Commission (online).

2005b. *Regions: Statistical Yearbook 2005*, Luxembourg: EU Office of Publications.

1998–99. *Eurostat Yearbook: A Statistical Eye on Europe, 1998–99*, Luxembourg: European Commission.

1994. *Basic Statistics of the Community 1994*, Brussels: Statistical Office of the European Communities.

1977. *Basic Statistics of the Community 1977*, Brussels: Statistical Office of the European Communities.

1971–80. *Eurostat Yearbook: A Statistical Eye on Europe, 1971–80*, Luxembourg: European Commission.

European Union, 1995. *Coordinated Economic Assistance, Brussels, June 13, 1991*: *G-24 Scoreboard of Assistance Commitments to the CEEC 1990–1994*, Brussels: European Union, February 8.

Eyal, Gil, 2003. *The Origins of Postcommunist Elites: From Prague Spring to the Breakup of Czechoslovakia*, Minneapolis: University of Minnesota Press.

Eyal, Gil, Iván Szelényi, and Eleanor Townsley, 1998. *Making Capitalism Without Capitalists: Class Formation and Elite Struggles in Post-Communist Central Europe*, London: Verso.

FAO (United Nations Food and Agriculture Organization), 2000. *Fertilizer Yearbook, 1990, 2000*, Rome: Food and Agriculture Organization.

1990a. *Fertilizer Yearbook, 1990*, Rome: Food and Agriculture Organization.

1990b. *Productivity Yearbook, 1990*, Rome: Food and Agriculture Organization.

1962. *Productivity Yearbook, 1962*, Rome: Food and Agriculture Organization.

Feldman, Merje, 2000. "Urban Waterfront Regeneration and Local Governance in Tallinn," *Europe–Asia Studies*, Vol. 52, No. 5.

Ferge, Zsuzsa, 1997. "Is the World Falling Apart? A View from the East of Europe," in Ivan T. Berend (ed.), *Long-Term Structural Changes in Transforming Central and Eastern Europe*, Munich: Südosteuropa-Gesellschaft.

Fine, Ben, Costas Lapavitsas, and Jonathan Pincus (eds.), 2001. *Development Policy in the Twenty-First Century: Beyond the Post-Washington Consensus*, London: Routledge.

Fischer, Wolfram, 1987. "Bergbau, Industrie und Handwerk," in H. Aubin and W. Zorn (eds.), *Handbuch der deutschen Wirtschafts- und Sozialgeschichte*, vols. I–II, Stuttgart: Klett.

Fischer, Wolfram, Jan A. van Houtte, and Herman Kellenbenz, 1987. *Handbuch der Europäische Wirtschafts- und Sozialgeschichte vom Ersten Weltkrieg bis zur Gegenwart*, vol. VI, Stuttgart: Franz Stein Verlag.

Flemming, John, 1997. "Lessons from Countries in Transition," in Emmerij, 1997.

Friedman, Milton, 1978. *The Tax Limitation, Inflation, and the Role of Government*, Dallas: Fisher Institute.

1969. *The Optimum Quantity of Money and Other Essays*, Chicago: Aldine Publishing Co.

1963. *Inflation: Causes and Consequences*, New York: Asia Publishing House.

1959. *The Program for Monetary Stability*, New York: Fordham University Press.

Garton Ash, Timothy, 1989. "Refolution: The Springtime of Two Nations," *New York Review of Books*, June 15.

Gomulka, Stanislaw, 2000. "Macroeconomic Policies and Achievements in Transition Economies, 1989–1999," in United Nations, *Economic Survey of Europe*, New York: United Nations.

Gower, Jackie, and John Redmond (eds.), 2000. *Enlarging the European Union: The Way Forward*, Aldershot: Ashgate.

Gózyński, Michał, Małgorzata Jakubiak, and Richard Woodward, 2006. "Key Challenges to the Development of the Knowledge-Based Economy in Poland," in Piech and Radocevic, 2006.

Grabbe, Heather, 2006. *The EU's Transformative Power: Europeanization Through Conditionality in Central and Eastern Europe*, Houndmills: Palgrave Macmillan.

Grabowski, Tomek, 1996. "The Party That Never Was: The Rise and Fall of the Solidarity Citizens' Committees in Poland," *East European Politics and Societies*, No. 10.

Hankiss, Elemér, 1990. *East European Alternatives*, Oxford: Clarendon Press.

Hardt, John P., and Richard F. Kaufman, 1994. "Introduction," in *East-Central European Economies in Transition*, 1994.

Havas, Attila, 2006. "Knowledge-Intensive Activities Versus High-Tech Sectors: Learning Options and Traps for Central European Policy-Makers," in Piech and Radocevic, 2006.

Havel, Václav, 1992. "Paradise Lost," *New York Review of Books*, April 9.

Hayek, Friedrich, 1960. *The Constitution of Liberty*, Chicago: University of Chicago Press.

1944. *The Road to Serfdom*, London: Routledge.

Hegedűs, Jozsef, and Ivan Tosics, 1998. "Towards New Models of Housing System," in Gyorgy Enyedi (ed.), *Social Change and Urban Restructuring in Central Europe*, Budapest: Akademiai Kiadó.

Heinisch, Reinhard, 1999. "The State of Corporatism in Central and Eastern Europe in Transition," in Irwin Collier, Herwig Roggemann, Oliver Scholz, and Horst Tomann (eds.), *Welfare States in Transition*, Houndmills: Macmillan Press.

Hertzman, Clyde, and Shona Kelly, 1996. *East–West Life Expectancy Gap in Europe: Environmental and Non-Environmental Determinants*, Dordrecht: Kluwer Academic.

Hirschhausen, Christian von, 2002. *Modernizing Infrastructure in Transformation Economies*, Cheltenham: Edward Elgar.

Höchmann, Hans-Herman (ed.), 2001. *Kultur als Bestimmungsfaktor der Transformation im Osten Europas*, Bremen: Edition Temmen.

Hoffman, George W., 1990. *Europe in the 1990s: A Geographic Analysis.* Sixth edn., New York: John Wiley & Sons.

Holmes, Peter, Javier Lopez-Gonzales, Johannes Stefan, and Cordula Stolberg, 2006. "Can EU Policy Intervention Help Productivity Catch-Up?," in David Dyker (ed.), *Closing the EU East–West Productivity Gap, Foreign Direct Investment, Competitiveness and Public Policy*, London: Imperial College Press.

Holmes, Stephen, 1994. "The End of Decommunization," *East European Constitutional Review*, Vol. 3, No. 3–4.

Hrubos, Ildikó, 1999. "Transformation of the Hungarian Higher Educational System in the 1990s," in *Discussion Series*, Vol. 1, No. 2. Budapest: Civic Educational Project.

Hungary Ministry of Economy and Transportation, 2006. *Report of the Ministry of Economy and Transportation*, Budapest: Ministry of Economy and Transportation, July 12.

Huntington, Samuel P., 1991. *The Third Wave: Democratization in the Late Twentieth Century*, Norman, OK: University of Oklahoma Press.

Hunya, Gábor, 2002. "Restructuring Through FDI in Romanian Manufacturing," *Economic Systems*, Vol. 26, No. 4.

Iacovone, Leonardo, and Niels Kofoed, 2006. "Checking the Results of the Case Study Interviews – An Essay in Triangulation," in David Dyker (ed.), *Closing the EU East–West Productivity Gap, Foreign Direct Investment, Competitiveness and Public Policy*, London: Imperial College Press.

Iatridis, Demetrius S. (ed.), 2000. *Social Justice and the Welfare State in Central and Eastern Europe*, Westport, CT: Praeger.

Illyés, Gyula, 1935. *Puszták népe*, Budapest: Nyugat Kiadó.

Islam, Shafiqul, and Michael Mandelbaum (eds.), 1993. *Making Markets: Economic Transformation in Eastern Europe and the Post-Soviet States*, New York: Council on Foreign Relations Press.

Ivanova, Radost, 1995. "Social Change as Reflected in the Lives of Bulgarian Villagers," in Kideckel, 1995.

Iványi, Gábor, 1997. *Hajléktalanok*, Budapest: Sík Kiadó.

Jánossy, Ferenc, 1971. *The End of the Economic Miracle: Appearance and Reality in Economic Development*, White Plains, NY: International Arts and Sciences Publisher.

Japan Ministry of Trade, 1992. *Japan's Postwar Experience: Its Meaning and Implication for the Economic Transformation of the Former Soviet Republics*, Tokyo: Research Institute of the Ministry of International Trade and Industry.

Jasiecki, Krzysztof, Wodzimierz Wesowski, and Micha Federowicz, 2005. "The Polish Business Elite," in Helmut Steiner, and Pál Tamás (eds.), *The Business Elites of East Central Europe*, Berlin: Trafo Verlag.

Jeffries, Ian, 2004. *The Countries of the Former Soviet Union at the Turn of the Twenty-First Century*, London: Routledge.

Jochimsen, Reimut, 1999. "The Role of the IMF in the Transformation Process and the Integration of the Former Socialist Countries into the World Market System," in Harriet Matejka and Mihály Simai (eds.), *Aspects of Transition* (World Development Studies 13), Helsinki: WIDER, United Nations University.

Kádár, Béla, 2007. "Gazdasági fejlődésünk mérlege, 1990–2006," in *Ezredforduló: stratégiai tanulmányok a Magyar Tudományos Akadémián*, Budapest: MTA Társadalomkutató Központ.

Kadeřábková, Anna, 2006. "Skills for Knowledge-Based Economy in Central Europe," in Piech and Radocevic, 2006.

Kaminski, Bartlomiej, 1994. "The Legacy of Communism," in *East-Central European Economies in Transition*, 1994.

Kántor, Zoltán, Balázs Majtényi, Osamu Ieda, Balázs Vizi, and Iván Halász (eds.), 2004. "The Hungarian Status Law: Nation Building and/or Minority Protection," *Slavic Eurasian Studies*, No. 4.

Keat, Preston, 2003. "Fallen Heroes: Explaining the Failure of the Gdansk Shipyard and the Successful Early Reform Strategies in Szczecin and Gdynia," *Communist and Post-Communist Studies*, Vol. 36, No. 2.

Keivani, Remin, Ali Parsa, and Stanley McGreal, 2002. "Institutions and Urban Change in a Globalizing World," *Cities*, Vol. 19, No. 3, June.

Kideckel, David A. (ed.), 1995. *East European Communities: The Struggle for Balance in Turbulent Times*, Boulder: Westview.

King, Charles, 2000. "Post-Postcommunism. Transition, Comparison, and the End of Eastern Europe," *World Politics*, Vol. 53, No. 1.

Kippenberg, Eva, 2005. "Sectoral Linkages of Foreign Direct Investment Firms to the Czech Economy," *Research in International Business and Finance*, Vol. 19, No. 2.

Kiss, Károly, 1993. *Western Prescriptions for Eastern Transition: A Comparative Analysis of the Different Economic Schools and Issues*, Budapest: Institute for World Economics.

Klein, Lawrence, 1997. "Success and Failures of Development Experience Since the 1980s," in Emmerij, 1997.

Kołodko, Grzegorz W., 2001. *Globalizacja a perspektywy rozwoju krajow posocjalistycznych toruń*, Warsaw: Wydawnictwo Dom Organizatora.

2000. *From Shock to Therapy: The Political Economy of Post-Socialist Transformation*. Helsinki: United Nations University.

Kolosi, Tamás, and Endre Sík, 1992. "Munkaerőpiac és jövedelmek," in György Tóth and Endre Sík, *Jelentés a Magyar Háztartás Panel I hullámának eredményeiről*, Budapest: TARKI.

Koncz, Katalin, 2006. *Nők a politikai hatalomban*, Budapest: Magyar Női Karrierfejlesztési Szövetség.

Kondratiev, Nikolai, [1922] 1984. *The Long Wave Cycle*, New York: Richardson & Snyder.

Kornai, János, 1993. "Anti-Depression Cure for Ailing Postcommunist Economies," *Transition: The Newsletter About Reforming Economies* (World Bank), Vol. 4, No. 1, February.

1992. *The Socialist System. The Political Economy of Communism*, Princeton: Princeton University Press.

1989. *Indulatos röpirat a gazdasági átmenet ügyében*, Budapest: HVG Kiadó.

Kovács, Zoltán, 2006. "Social and Economic Transformation of Historical Districts in Budapest," in Enyedi and Kovács, 2006.

Kowalik, Tadeusz, 1994. "The 'Big Bang' as a Political and Historical Phenomenon. A Case Study on Poland," in Ivan T. Berend (ed.), *Transition to a Market Economy at the End of the Twentieth Century*, Munich: Südosteuropa-Gesellschaft.

1992. "Creating Economic Foundation for Democracy," conference paper, presented at UCLA.

Kozminski, Andrzej K., 1997. "Restitution of Private Property: Re-Privatization in Central and Eastern Europe," *Communist and Post-Communist Studies*, Vol. 30, No. 1.

Kregel, Jan, Egon Matzner, and Gernot Grabher, 1992. *The Market Shock: An Agenda for the Economic and Social Reconstruction of Central and Eastern Europe*, Vienna: Austrian Academy of Sciences.

Krénusz, Ágota, 2007. "Determinants of Capital Structure," *Development and Finance*, No. 2.

Kubielas, Stanisław, 2006. "Key Challenges to the Development of the Knowledge-Based Economy in Poland," in Piech and Radocevic, 2006.

Kurz, Constanze, and Volker Wittke, 1998. "Using Industrial Capacities as a Way of Integrating Central and Eastern European Economies," in John Zysman and Andrew Schwartz (eds.), *Enlarging Europe: The Industrial Foundation of a New Political Reality*, Berkeley: University of California Press.

Kwasniewski, Aleksander, 1998. "Poland's Foreign Policy in a Changing Europe," in Thanos M. Veremis and Dimitrios Triantaphyllou (eds.), *The Southeast European Yearbook, 1997–1998*, Athens: Hellenic Foundation.

Ladányi, János, and Iván Szelényi, 1998. "Class, Ethnicity and Urban Restructuring in Postcommunist Hungary," in Enyedi, 1998.

Lane, David, 2006. "From State Socialism to Capitalism: The Role of Class and the World System," *Communist and Post-Communist Studies*, Vol. 39, No. 2, June.

Lavigne, Marie, 2000. "Ten Years of Transition: A Review Article," *Communist and Post-Communist Studies*, Vol. 33, No. 4.

Lenin, Vladimir I., 1974. *Selected Works in One Volume*, New York: International.

Levits, Egils, 1998. "Harmonization of the Legal Systems of Latvia and the European Union Community" in Tālavs Jundzis (ed.), *The Baltic States at Historical Crossroads*, Riga: Academy of Sciences, Latvia.

Linden, Greg, 1998. "Building Production Networks in Central Europe: The Case of the Electronics Industry," in John Zysman and Andrew Schwartz (eds.), *Enlarging Europe: The Industrial Foundation of a New Political Reality*, Berkeley: University of California Press.

Lindert, Peter H., 2006. "What Is Happening to the Welfare State?," in Paul W. Rhode and Gianni Toniolo (eds.), *The Global Economy in the 1990s: A Long-Run Perspective*, Cambridge: Cambridge University Press.

Lipgens, Walter (ed.), 1985. *Documents on the History of the European Integration*, Vol. I, Berlin: Walter de Gruyter.

Losoncz, Miklós C., 2003. *Hungary's Competitiveness in International Comparison and Its Driving Forces*, Budapest: Economic Research Co. (paper)

Maddison, Angus, 2001. *The World Economy: A Millennial Perspective*, Paris: OECD.

    1995a. *Monitoring the World Economy 1820–1992*, Paris: OECD.

    1995b. *Explaining the Economic Performance of Nations*. Aldershot: Edward Elgar.

    1989. *The World Economy in the Twentieth Century*, Paris: OECD.

    1985. *Two Crises: Latin America and Asia 1929–1938 and 1973–1983*, Paris: OECD.

Magone, José M., 2003. *The Politics of Southern Europe: Integration into the European Union*, Westport: Praeger.

Malic, Nebojsa, "The Return of Kings," *Balkan Express*, June 21, 2001 (www.antiwar.com/malic/m02101.html).

Marer, Paul, 1999. "Economic Transformation, 1990–1998," in Aurel Braun and Zoltan Barany (eds.), *Dilemmas of Transformation: The Hungarian Experience*, Lanham: Rowman & Littlefield.

Marer, Paul, and Vincent Mabert, 1996. "GE Acquires and Restructures Tungsram: The First Six Years (1990–1995)," in OECD, *Performance of Privatized Enterprises: Corporate Governance, Restructuring, Profitability*, Paris: OECD.

Mastanduno, Michael, 1992. *Economic Containment: CoCom and the Politics of East–West Trade*, Ithaca: Cornell University Press.

Matějů, Petr, and Jiři Večerník, 1995. "Social Cost of Transition: National Report, Czech Republic," in *Social Cost of Economic Transformation in Central Europe*, Vienna: Institut für die Wissenschaften vom Menschen.

Mayes, David, 2004. "Enlargement," in El-Agraa, 2004.

McDaniel, Douglas E., 1993. *United States Technology Export Control: An Assessment*, Westport, CT: Praeger.

Michnik, Adam, 2002. "Confessions of a Converted Dissident," Essay for the Erasmus Prize 2001. Alexandria Biblioteka online (www.alexandria-press.com/online/online20_adam_michnik_confessions.htm), posted on January 31.

    1999. "The Return to History," *Central Europe Review*, Vol. 1, No. 17, www.ce-review.org/99/17/michnik17_speech.html.

Milanovic, Branco, 1996. *Income, Inequality and Poverty During the Transition*, Washington, DC: World Bank.

Mildner, Kirk, 2006. "Die Volkswirtschaft des Kosovo am Vorabend der Statusverhandlungen," *Südosteuropa Mitteilungen*, Vol. 46, No. 2.

Milic-Cerniak, Róża, 1995. "Social Cost of Transition: National Report, Poland," in *Social Cost of Economic Transformation in Central Europe*, Vienna: Institut für die Wissenschaften vom Menschen.

Mitchell, Brian R., 1998. *International Historical Statistics: Europe 1750–1993*, 4th edn., London: Macmillan.

Morita, Tsuneo, 2000. *Facts and Lessons of Ten Years of System Transformation in Central European Countries*, Namura Research Institute, Kitakyushu: International Center for the Study of East Asian Development.

Muço, Marta, and Luljeta Minxhozi, 2003. "Albania: An Overview Ten Years After," in Domenico Nuti and Milica Uvalic (eds.), *Post-Communist Transition to a Market Economy: Lessons and Challenges*, Ravenna: Longo Editore.

Mueller, Bernard, 1965. *A Statistical Handbook of the North Atlantic Area*, New York: Twentieth-Century Fund.

Mueller, John, 1992. "Quiet Cataclysm: Some Afterthoughts on World War III," in Michael J. Hogan (ed.), *The End of the Cold War*, Cambridge: Cambridge University Press.

Murell, Peter, and Yijiang Wang, 1993. "When Privatization Should Be Delayed: The Effect of the Communist Legacies on Organizational and Institutional Reforms," Working Paper No. 93–1, Washington, DC: University of Maryland, Department of Economics.

Murzyn, Monica A., 2006. "Winners and Losers in the Game: The Social Dimension of Urban Regeneration in the Kazimierz Quarter of Krakow," in Enyedi and Kovács, 2006.

Mutinelli, Marco, and Lucia Piscitello, 1997. "Differences in the Strategic Orientation of Italian MNEs in Central and Eastern Europe: The Influence of Firm-Specific Factors," *International Business Review*, Vol. 6, No. 2.

Nagy, Pongrác, 1993. "Van-e forráskiáramlás Magyarorszagról?," *Napi Gazdaság*, Budapest, July 9.

Naray, Peter, 1999. "The Uruguay Round and the WTO," in Harriet Matejka and Mihály Simai (eds.), *Aspects of Transition* (World Development Studies 13), Helsinki: WIDER, United Nations University.

Nedović-Budić, Zorica, 2001. "Adjustment of Planning Practice to the New Eastern and Central European Context," *Journal of American Planning Association*, Vol. 67, No. 1, Winter.

Ners, Krzysztof J., and Ingrid Buxell, 1995. *Assistance to Transition Survey 1995*, Warsaw: PECAT.

Nørgaard, Ole, Lars Johannsen, Mette Skak, and René Hauge Sørensen, 1999. *The Baltic States After Independence*, 2nd edn., Cheltenham: Edward Elgar.

Nove, Alec, 1995. "Economics of Transition: Some Gaps and Illusions," in Beverly Crawford (ed.), *Markets, States, and Democracy*, Boulder: Westview Press.

1992. *An Economic History of the USSR 1917–1991*, Harmondsworth: Penguin Books.

1977. *The Soviet Economic System*, London: Allen & Unwin.

1966. *The Soviet Economy*, New York: Praeger.

Nuti, Domenico M., 1993. "How to Contain Economic Inertia in the Transitional Economies?," *Transition: The Newsletter About Reforming Economies* (World Bank), Vol. 3, No. 11, December–January.

OECD (Organization for Economic Cooperation and Development), 1987. *Structural Adjustment and Economic Performance*, Paris: OECD.

1974. *Economic Outlook No. 15*, Paris: OECD.

Orenstein, Mitchell A., 2005. "The New Pension Reforms: Lessons for Post-Soviet Republics," in Michael Cain, Nida Gelazis, and Tomasz Inglot (eds.), *Fighting Poverty and Reforming Social Security: What Can Post-Soviet States Learn from the New Democracies of Central Europe?* Washington, DC: Woodrow Wilson International Center for Scholars.

Österreichische Nationalbank, 2006. June Report. Vienna: ÖN.

Palánkai, Tibor, 2004. *Economics of Enlarging European Union*, Budapest: Akadémiai Kiadó.

Papazoglou, Christos, 2005. *The Economies of South Eastern Europe: Performance and Challenges*, Houndmills: Palgrave Macmillan.

Paraskevopoulos, Christos, Panagoitis Getimis, and Nicholas Rees (eds.), 2006. *Adapting to EU Multi-Level Governance: Regional and Environmental Policies in Cohesion and CEE Countries*, Aldershot: Ashgate.

Pavlínek, Péter, 2002. "Czech Republic," in Carter and Turnock, 2002.

Pestoff, Victor A. 1995. "Reforming Social Services in Central and Eastern Europe: Meso-Level Institutional Changes and Shifts in the Welfare Mix," in Kideckel, 1995.

Petkov Iliev, Ilian, 2006. "Barriers to Venture Capital Investment in Innovative Small and Medium Enterprises in Central and Eastern Europe: Causes and Policy Implications," in Piech and Radocevic, 2006.

Piech, Krzysztof (ed.), 2003. *Economic Policy and Growth of Central and East European Countries*, London: School of Slavonic and East European Studies.

Piech, Krzysztof, and Slavo Radocevic (eds.), 2006. *The Knowledge-Based Economy in Central and Eastern Europe: Countries and Industries in a Process of Change*, Houndmills: Palgrave Macmillan.

Piore, Michael J., and Charles F. Sabel, 1984. *The Second Industrial Divide: Possibilities for Prosperity*, New York: Basic Books.

Pisnke, Heiki, 1998. "The Process of Bringing Estonia's Legal System into Conformity with the European Union's Acquis Communautaire," in Tālavs Jundzis (ed.), *The Baltic States at Historical Crossroads*, Riga: Academy of Sciences, Latvia.

Polaczek, Stanislaw, 1993. "Polityka pieniezna panstwa w latach 1989–1992," *Kultura*, No. 5.

Polanyi, Karl, [1944] 1957. *The Great Transformation: The Political and Economic Origins of Our Time*, Beacon Hills: Beacon Press.

Portes, Richard, 1993. "From Central Planning to a Market Economy," in Islam and Mandelbaum, 1993.

Potrykowski, Marek, 1998. "Border Regions and Trans-Border Co-operation: The Case of Poland," in Enyedi, 1998.

Prizel, Ilya, 1999. "The First Decade After the Collapse of Communism: Why Did Some Nations Succeed in Their Political and Economic Transformation While Others Failed," *SAIS Review*, Vol. 19, No. 2.

Radosevic, Slavo, 2006. "The Knowledge-Based Economy in Central and Eastern Europe," in Piech and Radocevic, 2006.

Rallu, Jean-Louis, and Alain Blum (eds.), 1991. *European Population*, Vol. I, Paris: Éditions John Libbey Eurotext.

Ranke, Leopold von, [1824] 1909. *History of the Latin and Teutonic Nations (1494 to 1514)*, London: George Bell.

Ratinger, Tomas, Tibor Ferenczi, Jerzy Wilkin, and Helga Bright, 2006. "The Central European Countries: Heritage and Challenges," in Sophia Davidova, Kai Bauer, and Michael Cuddy (eds.), *Integrated Development of Agriculture and Rural Areas in Central European Countries*, Lanham: Rowman and Littlefield.

Reagan, Ronald, 1983. "Address to the Nation on the Strategic Defense Initiative," in P. Edward Haley and Jack Merritt (eds.), *Strategic Defense Initiative: Folly or Future?*, Boulder: Westview Press.

Rechnitzer, J., and M. Döményová, 1998. "Vienna, Bratislava, Győr – a Potential Euroregion," in Enyedi, 1998.

Rehn, Olli, 2005. "The Plan 'C' for Enlargement – Speech at the European Parliament Foreign Affairs Committee, June 21," *Südosteuropa Mitteilungen*, No. 4–5.

Reininger, Thomas, Franz Schardax, and Martin Summer, 2003. "Financial System Transition in Central Europe: The First Decade," in Gertrude Tumpel-Gugerell and Peter Mooslechner (eds.), *Economic Convergence and Divergence in Europe*, Cheltenham: Edward Elgar.

Réti, Tamás, 2003. "Hungary's Trade and Capital Export Relation with the CEFTA Countries," in M. Uvalic and D. M. Nuti (eds.), *Post-Communist Transition to a Market Economy: Lessons and Challenges*, Bologna: Longo Editore.

Rhode, Paul W., and Gianni Toniolo (eds.), 2006. *The Global Economy in the 1990s: A Long-Run Perspective*, Cambridge: Cambridge University Press.

Ringold, Dena, 2000. *Roma and the Transition in Central and Eastern Europe: Trends and Challenges*, Washington, DC: World Bank.

Roman, Denise, 2003. *Fragmented Identities: Popular Culture, Sex, and Everyday Life in Postcommunist Romania*, Lanham: Lexington Books.

Romaszewski, Zbigniew, 1990. "Trudne drogi demokracji," *Kultura*, No. 9.

Sachs, Jeffrey D., 1992. "Honnan jöhetnek a százmilliárdok: észrevételek Berend T. Iván tanulmányához," *Népszabadság*, Budapest, January 11.

Sampson, Steven, 1995. "All Is Possible, Nothing Is Certain: The Horizons of Transition in a Romanian Village," in Kideckel, 1995.

Schumpeter, Joseph, 1976. *Capitalism, Socialism and Democracy*, London: Allen & Unwin.

1928, "The Instability of Capitalism" in Nathan Rosenberg (ed.), *The Economics of Technological Change*, Harmondsworth: Penguin.

Scott, Norman, 1999. "The Response of the United Nations to the Challenge of Economic Transition," in Harriet Matejka and Mihály Simai (eds.), *Aspects of Transition* (World Development Studies 13), Helsinki: WIDER, United Nations University.

Semler, Dwight, 1994. "Focus: The Politics of Central Banking," *East European Constitutional Review*, Vol. 3, No. 3–4.

Simai, Mihály, 2006. "The World Economy and Europe at the Beginning of the Twenty-First Century," *Development and Finance*, No. 1.

Singh, Inderjit, 1991. "China and Central and Eastern Europe: Is There a Professional Schizophrenia on Socialist Reform?," *Research Paper Series*, No. CH 9, Washington, DC: World Bank.

Solow, Robert, 1966. "The Capacity to Assimilate an Advanced Technology," in Nathan Rosenberg (ed.), *The Economics of Technological Change*, Harmondsworth: Penguin.

Spéder, Zsolt, Zsuzsanna Elekes, István Harcsa, and Péter Robert, 2002. "Hungary," in Adamski, Machonin, and Zapf, 2002.

Srholec, Martin, 2006. "Global Production Systems and Technology Catching Up: Thinking Twice About High-tech Industries in Emerging Countries," in Piech and Radocevic, 2006.

Stalin, J. V., 1976. *Problems of Leninism*, Peking: Foreign Language Publisher.

Staniszkis, Jadwiga, 1991. "Political Capitalism in Poland," *East European Politics and Societies*, Vol. 5, No. 1.

Stark, David, 1992. "Path Dependence and Privatization Strategies in East Central Europe," *East European Politics and Societies*, Vol. 6, No. 1.

1990. "Privatization in Hungary: From Plan to Market or from Plan to Clan," *East European Politics and Societies*, Vol. 4, No. 3.

Steiner, Michael, 2003. "Restructuring Industrial Areas: Lessons in Support of Regional Convergence in an Enlarging Europe," in Gertrude Tumpel-Gugerell and Peter Mooslechner (eds.), *Economic Convergence and Divergence in Europe*, Cheltenham: Edward Elgar.

Steward, Frances, 1997. "On John Williamson and the Washington Consensus," in Emmerij, 1997.

Stiglitz, Joseph E., 2007. "The EU's Global Mission," in *Project-Syndicate* (www.project-syndicate.org/commentary/stiglitz85), April 22.

1999. *Wither Reform? Ten Years of Transition*, keynote address at World Bank Annual Conference on Development Economics, Washington, DC, July 30.

1998. "More Instruments and Broader Goals: Moving Toward the Post-Washington Consensus," WIDER annual lecture, Helsinki, January 7.

Strak, Antal, 2007. "Nemzetgazdaságunk a rendszerváltás után," *Historia*, Vol. 29, No. 3.

S`ykora, Luděk, 1998. "Commercial Property Development in Budapest, Prague and Warsaw," in Enyedi, 1998.

Szalavetz, Andrea, 2006. "From Industrial Capitalism to Intellectual Capitalism: The Bumpy Road to a Knowledge-Based Economy of Hungary," in Piech and Radocevic, 2006.

Széchenyi, István, 1830. *Hitel*, Pest: Petrózai Trattner.

Szekfű, Gyula, 1922. *A Magyar bortermelő lelki alkata*, Budapest: Minerva Társaság.

1920. *Három nemzedék: egy hanyatló kor története*, Budapest: Egyetemi Nyomda.

Szűcs, Jenő, 1983. *Vázlat Európa három történeti régiójáról*, Budapest: Magvető.

Tanner, Arno (ed.), 2004. *The Forgotten Minorities of Eastern Europe*, Helsinki: East–West Books.

Teodorović, Ivan, Željko Lovrinčević, Davor Mikulić, Mustafa Nušinović, and Stjepan Zdunić (eds.), 2005. *The Croatian Economic Development. Transition Towards the Market Economy*, Zagreb: Institute of Economics.

Tomka, Béla, 2005. "The Politics of Institutionalized Volatility: Lessons from East Central European Welfare Reforms," in Michael Cain, Nida Gelazis, and Tomasz Inglot (eds.), *Fighting Poverty and Reforming Social Security: What Can Post-Soviet States Learn from the New Democracies of Central Europe?* Washington, DC: Woodrow Wilson International Center for Scholars.

Truman, Harry S., 1955–56. *Memoirs*, Garden City, NY: Doubleday.

Turnock, David, 2002. "Romania," in Carter and Turnock, 2002.

Turnovec, František, 1999. "Political Economy of Social Welfare Reform: The Parliamentary Election of 1996 in the Czech Republic," in Irwin Collier, Herwig Roggemann, Oliver Scholz, and Horst Tomann (eds.), *Welfare States in Transition*, Houndmills: Macmillan Press.

UNCTAD, 2006. *World Investment Report*. New York: United Nations Conference on Trade and Development.

2005a. *Handbook of Statistics* (online).

2005b. *World Investment Report*. New York: United Nations Conference on Trade and Development.

2002. *World Investment Report: Transnational Corporations and Export Competitiveness.* New York: United Nations Conference on Trade and Development.

UNESCO, 2006. *UNESCO Statistical Yearbook,* Paris: UNESCO.

UNICEF, 2003. *Social Monitor 2003.* Florence: Innocenti Research Centre.

1995. *Economies in Transition Studies, Regional Monitoring Report,* No. 3.

1994. *Central and Eastern Europe in Transition. Public Policy and Social Conditions: Crisis in Mortality, Health and Nutrition.* Regional Monitoring Report, No. 2, August 2.

United Nations, 2004. *Economic Survey of Europe,* No. 1, Geneva: United Nations.

2002. *Yearbook of Labour Statistics, 2002,* Geneva: United Nations.

1990. *Statistical Yearbook 1990,* New York: United Nations.

1975. *Yearbook of Labour Statistics, 1945–1989,* Geneva: United Nations.

Urwin, Derek, 1995. *The Community of Europe: A History of European Integration Since 1945,* London: Longman.

Vaknin, Sam, 2006. "The Dying Breed: Healthcare in Eastern Europe," samvak.tripod.com/pp143.html.

Van der Wee, Herman, 1986. *Prosperity and Upheaval: The World Economy 1945–1980,* Berkeley: University of California Press.

Van Kempen, Ronald, Marcel Vermeulen, and Ad Baan, 2005. *Urban Issues and Urban Policies in the New EU Countries,* Aldershot: Ashgate.

Van Zon, Hans, Brian Dillon, Jerzy Hausner, and Dorota Kwiecińska, 2000. *Central European Industry in the Information Age,* Aldershot: Ashgate.

Verdery, Katherine, 1991. *National Ideology Under Socialism. Identity and Cultural Politics in Ceauşescu's Romania,* Berkeley: University of California Press.

The Visegrad Yearbook, 2003, 2003. edited by Adam Kégler, Budapest: Central European Student Partnership Organization.

Viszt, Erzsébet, 2007. "Review of GKI's Competitiveness Yearbook 2006," *Development and Finance,* No. 2.

Walicki, Andrzej, 1991. *Trzy patriotyzmy,* Warsaw: Res Publica.

Weresa, Marzenna Anna, 2004. "Can Foreign Investment Help Poland Catch Up with the EU?," *Communist and Post-Communist Studies,* Vol. 37, No. 3.

Williamson, John, 2000. "What Should the World Bank Think About the Washington Consensus?" *World Bank Research Observer,* Vol. 15, No. 2.

1997. "The Washington Consensus Revisited," in Emmerij, 1997.

World Bank, 2005. *World Bank Report, 2005.* Washington, DC: World Bank, October 12.

1998. *World Development Report: Knowledge for Development,* Washington, DC: World Bank, September 30.

1996. *From Plan to Market: World Development Report 1996,* Washington, DC: World Bank.

1993. *The East Asian Miracle: Economic Growth and Public Policy.* Washington, DC: World Bank, September 30.

1992. *Transition: The News Letter About Reforming Countries.* Washington, DC: World Bank.

Yudanov, Andrei Y., 1997. "USSR: Large Enterprise in the USSR – The Functional Disorder," in Alfred Chandler, Franco Amatori, and Takashi Hikino (eds.), *Big Business and the Wealth of Nations,* Cambridge: Cambridge University Press.

Ziemele, Ineta, 1998. "The Role of State Continuity and Human Rights in Matters of Nationality of the Baltic States," in Tālavs Jundzis (ed.), *The Baltic States at Historical Crossroads,* Riga: Academy of Sciences, Latvia.

Index